RESTATEMENT OF THE LAW THIRD

THE AMERICAN LAW INSTITUTE

RESTATEMENT OF THE LAW

TORTS

Products Liability

As Adopted and Promulgated

BY

THE AMERICAN LAW INSTITUTE

AT WASHINGTON, D.C.

May 20, 1997

§§ 1 – End

Tables and Index

ST. PAUL, MN
AMERICAN LAW INSTITUTE PUBLISHERS
1998

Library of Congress Cataloging-in-Publication Data

Restatement of the law, torts—products liability : as adopted and promulgated by the American Law Institute at Washington, D.C., May 20, 1997, tables and index.
p. cm.
ISBN 0-314-23194-3 (hc.)
1. Products liability—United States. I. American Law Institute.
II. Title: Restatement of the law third
KF1296.R467 1998
346.7303'8—dc21 98-20875
CIP

ISBN 0-314-23194-3

The American Law Institute

** As of March 15, 1998*

COUNCIL

The Executive Office
THE AMERICAN LAW INSTITUTE
4025 Chestnut Street
Philadelphia, Pennsylvania 19104–3099

* *Director Emeritus*

REPORTERS

*JAMES A. HENDERSON, JR., Cornell Law School, Ithaca, New York

*AARON D. TWERSKI, Brooklyn Law School, Brooklyn, New York

ADVISERS

KENNETH S. ABRAHAM, University of Virginia School of Law, Charlottesville, Virginia

SHEILA L. BIRNBAUM, New York, New York

ROGER C. CRAMTON, Cornell Law School, Ithaca, New York

OSCAR S. GRAY, University of Maryland School of Law, Baltimore, Maryland

MICHAEL D. GREEN, University of Iowa College of Law, Iowa City, Iowa

ROBERT L. HABUSH, Milwaukee, Wisconsin

ROBERT E. KEETON, United States District Court for the District of Massachusetts, Boston, Massachusetts

CAROLYN DINEEN KING, United States Court of Appeals for the Fifth Circuit, Houston, Texas

HANS A. LINDE, Salem, Oregon; Senior Judge, Oregon Supreme Court

JOHN W. MARTIN, JR., Dearborn, Michigan

VINCENT L. MCKUSICK, Portland, Maine; Retired Chief Justice, Supreme Judicial Court of Maine

ROBERT L. RABIN, Stanford Law School, Stanford, California

PAUL D. RHEINGOLD, New York, New York

GARY T. SCHWARTZ, University of California at Los Angeles School of Law, Los Angeles, California

VICTOR E. SCHWARTZ, Washington, District of Columbia

MARSHALL S. SHAPO, Northwestern University School of Law, Chicago, Illinois

MICHAEL TRAYNOR, San Francisco, California

BILL WAGNER, Tampa, Florida

PAUL C. WEILER, Harvard University Law School, Cambridge, Massachusetts

EDITORIAL ADVISER

DAVID G. OWEN, University of South Carolina School of Law, Columbia, South Carolina [from 1996]

EX OFFICIO

ROSWELL B. PERKINS, New York, New York
Chair of the Council, The American Law Institute

CHARLES ALAN WRIGHT, Austin, Texas
President, The American Law Institute

GEOFFREY C. HAZARD, JR., Philadelphia, Pennsylvania
Director, The American Law Institute

---

* Professors Henderson and Twerski were jointly designated American Law Institute R. Ammi Cutter Reporters as of 1997.

MEMBERS CONSULTATIVE GROUP

(as of April 14, 1997)

ROGER I. ABRAMS, Newark, New Jersey

FREDERICK RANDOLPH ANDERSON, JR., Washington, D.C.

JENNIFER H. ARLEN, Los Angeles, California

ROBERT E. AUSTIN, JR., Leesburg, Florida

MARK L. AUSTRIAN, Washington, D.C.

JOSEPH R. BANKOFF, Atlanta, Georgia

PETER V. BAUGHER, Chicago, Illinois

WALTER HULL BECKHAM, JR., Miami, Florida

FORTUNATO P. BENAVIDES, United States Court of Appeals for the Fifth Circuit, Austin, Texas

MARGARET A. BERGER, Brooklyn, New York

RICHARD LYLE BERKMAN, Philadelphia, Pennsylvania

ANDREW T. BERRY, Newark, New Jersey

ROBERT DALE BICKEL, St. Petersburg, Florida

LAWRENCE BILDER, New Jersey Superior Court, Appellate Division, Jersey City, New Jersey

ANTHONY J. BOCCHINO, Philadelphia, Pennsylvania

EUGENE M. BOGEN, Mississippi Circuit Court, Greenville, Mississippi

GARY LEE BOLAND, Baton Rouge, Louisiana

LOUIS F. BONACORSI, St. Louis, Missouri

RICHARD A. BOOTH, Baltimore, Maryland

AMELIA H. BOSS, Philadelphia, Pennsylvania

PHILLIP D. BOSTWICK, Washington, D.C.

HILDY BOWBEER, Minneapolis, Minnesota

AUBREY R. BOWLES III, Richmond, Virginia

MYRON J. BROMBERG, Morristown, New Jersey

BRITAIN H. BRYANT, St. Croix, U.S. Virgin Islands

JOHN P. BURTON, Santa Fe, New Mexico

ELIZABETH J. CABRASER, San Francisco, California

SAMMY CACCIATORE, Melbourne, Florida

STEPHEN CALKINS, Washington, D.C.

ELENA A. CAPPELLA, Philadelphia, Pennsylvania

JIM R. CARRIGAN, United States District Court for the District of Colorado, Denver, Colorado

GEORGE J. CASPAR III, Avon, Connecticut

JORDAN B. CHERRICK, St. Louis, Missouri

STEPHEN YEE CHOW, Boston, Massachusetts

NEIL B. COHEN, BROOKLYN, New York

JAMES H. COLEMAN, Jr., New Jersey Superior Court, Appellate Division, Springfield, New Jersey

CALVIN J. COLLIER, Northfield, Illinois

WAYNE DALE COLLINS, New York, New York

ROXANNE B. CONLIN, Des Moines, Iowa

DENNIS R. CONNOLLY, New York, New York

THE RT. HON. THE LORD COOKE OF THORNDON, Wellington, New Zealand

GEORGE W. COOMBE, JR., San Francisco, California

MEMBERS CONSULTATIVE GROUP

ALFRED W. CORTESE, JR., Washington, D.C.

JAMES DONALD COWAN, JR., Greensboro, North Carolina

LOUIS A. CRACO, New York, New York

ROBERT A. CREAMER, Chicago, Illinois

MARGARET ELLEN CURRAN, Providence, Rhode Island

FRANK J. DAILY, Milwaukee, Wisconsin

CHRISTOPHER SCOTT D'ANGELO, Philadelphia, Pennsylvania

JOHN B. DAVIDSON, Chicago, Illinois

KEITH L. DAVIDSON, Chicago, Illinois

FREDERICK BENJAMIN DAVIS, Memphis, Tennessee

JOHN LESTER DIAMOND, San Francisco, California

CHARLTON DIETZ, St. Paul, Minnesota

ANTHONY M. DILEO, New Orleans, Louisiana

JOHN M. DINSE, Burlington, Vermont

ANTHONY E. DIRESTA, Atlanta, Georgia

DAN B. DOBBS, Tucson, Arizona

MITCHELL F. DOLIN, Washington, D.C.

WILLIAM V. DORSANEO III, Dallas, Texas

WILLIAM A. DREIER, New Jersey Superior Court, Appellate Division, Springfield, New Jersey

ROCHELLE C. DREYFUSS, New York, New York

W. WAYNE DRINKWATER, JR., Jackson, Mississippi

JOHN P. DRISCOLL, JR., Boston, Massachusetts

ALBERT W. DRIVER, JR., Mountainside, New Jersey

KEVIN PATRICK DUFFY, Springfield, New Jersey

DIANE DURGIN, Atlanta, Georgia

WARREN W. EGINTON, United States District Court for the District of Connecticut, Bridgeport, Connecticut

GREGORY A. EIESLAND, Rapid City, South Dakota

DORSEY E. ELLIS, JR., St. Louis, Missouri

CHARLES M. ELSON, St. Petersburg, Florida

DONALD J. FARAGE, Philadelphia, Pennsylvania

JEFFREY M. FELDMAN, Anchorage, Alaska

DAVID A. FISCHER, Columbia, Missouri

JOHN G. FLEMING, Berkeley, California

PETER FLYNN, Chicago, Illinois

GEORGE CLEMON FREEMAN, JR., Richmond, Virginia

WILLIAM FREIVOGEL, Chicago, Illinois

LEWIS R. FRIEDMAN, New York State Supreme Court, New York, New York

HALEY J. FROMHOLZ, Superior Court of California, Pomona, California

WILLIAM C. FRYE, Tampa, Florida

KOICHIRO FUJIKURA, Tokyo, Japan

JOSE A. FUSTE, United States District Court for the District of Puerto Rico, San Juan, Puerto Rico

BRUCE E. GAGNON, Anchorage, Alaska

MARSHA GARRISON, Brooklyn, New York

VINCENT F. GARRITY, JR., Philadelphia, Pennsylvania

WILLIAM L. GARWOOD, United States Court of Appeals for the Fifth Circuit, Austin, Texas

MEMBERS CONSULTATIVE GROUP

JANINE P. GESKE, Wisconsin Supreme Court, Madison, Wisconsin

JAMES D. GHIARDI, Milwaukee, Wisconsin

A. SPENCER GILBERT III, Jackson, Mississippi

MARGARET GILHOOLEY, Newark, New Jersey

R. NICHOLAS GIMBEL, Philadelphia, Pennsylvania

JOSEPH GOLDBERG, Albuquerque, New Mexico

MURRAY C. GOLDMAN, Pennsylvania Court of Common Pleas, Philadelphia, Pennsylvania

JEROME C. HAFTER, Greenville, Mississippi

RALPH L. HALPERN, Buffalo, New York

CHARLES HANSEN, St. Louis, Missouri

EUGENE M. HARING, Newark, New Jersey

ROBERT E. HARRINGTON, New Orleans, Louisiana

PHILIP LEE HARRIS, Chicago, Illinois

RICHARD E.V. HARRIS, San Francisco, California

HARRIS L HARTZ, New Mexico Court of Appeals, Albuquerque, New Mexico

CHARLES A. HARVEY, JR., Portland, Maine

PATRICK J. HEAD, Chicago, Illinois

ROGER C. HENDERSON, Tucson, Arizona

ERIC B. HENSON, Philadelphia, Pennsylvania

DAVID F. HERR, Minneapolis, Minnesota

GREGORY ALAN HICKS, Seattle, Washington

RICHARD DEC. HINDS, Washington, D.C.

ERIC M. HOLMES, Lexington, Kentucky

DOUGLAS G. HOUSER, Portland, Oregon

EDWIN E. HUDDLESON III, Washington, D.C.

RICHARD W. HULBERT, New York, New York

DAVID W. ICHEL, New York, New York

EDWIN J. JACOB, New York, New York

LAURENCE M. JOHNSON, Boston, Massachusetts

VINCENT R. JOHNSON, San Antonio, Texas

PAUL F. JONES, Buffalo, New York

MICHAEL ALEXANDER KAHN, San Francisco, California

PETER J. KALIS, Pittsburgh, Pennsylvania

SIDNEY K. KANAZAWA, Los Angeles, California

JOSEPH A. KATARINCIC, Pittsburgh, Pennsylvania

JOHN E. KEEFE, New Jersey Superior Court, Appellate Division, New Brunswick, New Jersey

CORNELIA G. KENNEDY, United States Court of Appeals for the Sixth Circuit, Detroit, Michigan

ROBERT W. KENT, Chester, New Jersey

CATHERINE KESSEDJIAN, Paris, France

GLADYS KESSLER, Superior Court of the District of Columbia, Washington, D.C.

EDWIN A. KILBURN, Secaucus, New Jersey

MARK R. KILLENBECK, Fayetteville, Arkansas

MICHAEL PATRICK KING, Superior Court of New Jersey, Appellate Division, Westmont, New Jersey

MEMBERS CONSULTATIVE GROUP

DAVID G. KLABER, Pittsburgh, Pennsylvania

MARC S. KLEIN, Newark, New Jersey

HOWARD C. KLEMME, Boulder, Colorado

ANDREW D. KOBLENZ, Washington, D.C.

MARTIN A. KOTLER, Wilmington, Delaware

LARRY KRAMER, New York, New York

NOEL ANKETELL KRAMER, Superior Court of the District of Columbia, Washington, D.C.

SHELDON KRANTZ, Washington, D.C.

WILLIAM P. KRATZKE, Memphis, Tennessee

EDWARD LABATON, New York, New York

EDWARD V. LAHEY, JR., Purchase, New York

LOUISE A. LAMOTHE, Los Angeles, California

HOWARD I. LANGER, Philadelphia, Pennsylvania

RICHARD W. LANGERMAN, Phoenix, Arizona

HOWARD A. LATIN, Newark, New Jersey

PAUL A. LEBEL, Williamsburg, Virginia

ROBERT O. LESHER, Tucson, Arizona

JOHN LEUBSDORF, New York, New York

WILLIAM G. LEVI, Kansas City, Missouri

CHARLES L. LEVIN, Michigan Supreme Court, Detroit, Michigan

VICTOR B. LEVIT, San Francisco, California

JOSEPH W. LITTLE, Gainesville, Florida

DAVID A. LOGAN, Winston-Salem, North Carolina

THAD G. LONG, Birmingham, Alabama

JEAN C. LOVE, Iowa City, Iowa

MITCHELL A. LOWENTHAL, New York, New York

ROBERT E. LUTZ II, Los Angeles, California

M. STUART MADDEN, White Plains, New York

MARK S. MANDELL, Providence, Rhode Island

EDWARD FRANCIS MANNINO, Philadelphia, Pennsylvania

BASIL S. MARKESINIS, London, England

PRENTICE H. MARSHALL, Ponce Inlet, Florida

JOANNE MARTIN, Chicago, Illinois

ARVIN MASKIN, New York, New York

DAVID C. MASON, Missouri Circuit Court, St. Louis, Missouri

KIRK MARTIN MCALPIN, Savannah, Georgia

JAMES T. MCCARTT, Houston, Texas

FRANK MCCLELLAN, Philadelphia, Pennsylvania

JOHN L. MCGOLDRICK, New York, New York

POWELL MCHENRY, Cincinnati, Ohio

JAMES F. MCHUGH III, Massachusetts Superior Court, Lincoln, Massachusetts

KENNETH JAMES MCINTYRE, Detroit, Michigan

DOUGLAS MCKAY, JR., Columbia, South Carolina

M. MARGARET MCKEOWN, Seattle, Washington

MARY A. MCLAUGHLIN, Philadelphia, Pennsylvania

A. DOUGLAS MELAMED, Washington, D.C.

RICHARD S. MILLER, Honolulu, Hawaii

J. W. MONTGOMERY III, Pittsburgh, Pennsylvania

MEMBERS CONSULTATIVE GROUP

STEVE MORRIS, Las Vegas, Nevada
LUTHER T. MUNFORD, Jackson, Mississippi
BARRY J. NACE, Washington, D.C.
RICHARD L. NEUMEIER, Boston, Massachusetts
GEORGE M. NEWCOMBE, New York, New York
THOMAS R. NEWMAN, New York, New York
RICHARD E. NOLAN, New York, New York
VIRGINIA NOLAN, San Diego, California
JOHN KRANZ NOTZ, JR., Chicago, Illinois
JEFFREY O'CONNELL, Charlottesville, Virginia
MICHAEL D. O'KEEFE, St. Louis, Missouri
MARIAN P. OPALA, Supreme Court of Oklahoma, Oklahoma City, Oklahoma
JOSEPH J. ORTEGO, Uniondale, New York
GEORGE W. OVERTON, Chicago, Illinois
DAVID G. OWEN, Columbia, South Carolina
PRISCILLA R. OWEN, Texas Supreme Court, Austin, Texas
JACK BYRON OWENS, Modesto, California
JERRY RICHARD PALMER, Topeka, Kansas
ROBERT L. PARKS, Miami, Florida
ROBERT W. PASS, Tallahassee, Florida
RICHARD N. PEARSON, Gainesville, Florida
HARVEY S. PERLMAN, Lincoln, Nebraska
COURTLAND H. PETERSON, Boulder, Colorado
CARTER G. PHILLIPS, Washington, D.C.
JERRY J. PHILLIPS, Knoxville, Tennessee
THOMAS R. PHILLIPS, Chief Justice, Texas Supreme Court, Austin, Texas
STEVEN R. PLOTKIN, Louisiana Court of Appeal, Fourth Circuit, New Orleans, Louisiana
GEORGE R. POEHNER, Dallas, Texas
PAUL M. POHL, Pittsburgh, Pennsylvania
WILLIAM CHARLES POWERS, JR., Austin, Texas
FREDERICK A. PROVORNY, Washington, D.C.
MICHAEL CHARLES PRYLES, Melbourne, Australia
ROBERT G. PUGH, JR., Shreveport, Louisiana
THOMAS A. QUINTRELL, Cleveland, Ohio
ROBERT D. RACHLIN, Burlington, Vermont
BERNARD D. REAMS, JR., Jamaica, New York
JOHN M. REED, Boston, Massachusetts
DOUG RENDLEMAN, Lexington, Virginia
RICHARD L. REVESZ, New York, New York
HUGH E. REYNOLDS, JR., Indianapolis, Indiana
WILLIAM L. REYNOLDS, Baltimore, Maryland
PATRICK W. RICHARDSON, Huntsville, Alabama
CLIFFORD A. RIEDERS, Williamsport, Pennsylvania
DAVID W. ROBERTSON, Austin, Texas
JAMES L. ROBERTSON, Jackson, Mississippi
JAMES K. ROBINSON, Detroit, Michigan
WM. T. ROBINSON III, Covington, Kentucky

MEMBERS CONSULTATIVE GROUP

ANTHONY Z. ROISMAN, Lyme, New Hampshire

LEE H. ROSENTHAL, United States District Court for the Southern District of Texas, Houston, Texas

KENNETH ROSS, Minneapolis, Minnesota

GITA F. ROTHSCHILD, Newark, New Jersey

THOMAS D. ROWE, JR., Durham, North Carolina

TIMOTHY C. RUSSELL, Washington, D.C.

MICHAEL L. RUSTAD, South Burlington, Vermont

L. F. SAMS, JR., Tupelo, Mississippi

PETER M. SAPAROFF, Boston, Massachusetts

GARY L. SASSO, St. Petersburg, Florida

SOL SCHREIBER, New York, New York

ROBERT A. SCHUETZE, Boulder, Colorado

WILLIAM SCHWARTZ, New York, New York

ANTHONY J. SCIRICA, United States Court of Appeals for the Third Circuit, Philadelphia, Pennsylvania

KARL E. SEIB, JR., New York, New York

CARL M. SELINGER, Morgantown, West Virginia

MARC M. SELTZER, Los Angeles, California

GEORGE W. SHADOAN, Rockville, Maryland

E. DONALD SHAPIRO, New York, New York

DONALD R. SHULTZ, Rapid City, South Dakota

CATHY R. SILAK, Idaho Supreme Court, Boise, Idaho

RICHARD A. SILVER, Stamford, Connecticut

RONALD SIMON, Washington, D.C.

BEVERLY MCQUEARY SMITH, Huntington, New York

R. GORDON SMITH, Richmond, Virginia

STEVEN R. SMITH, San Diego, California

CHRISTINA A. SNYDER, Los Angeles, California

CARL A. SOLANO, Philadelphia, Pennsylvania

JOAN E. STEINMAN, Chicago, Illinois

JEFFREY W. STEMPEL, Tallahassee, Florida

EDWIN H. STERN, New Jersey Superior Court, Morristown, New Jersey

LARRY S. STEWART, Miami, Florida

DONALD I STRAUBER, New York, New York

GUY MILLER STRUVE, New York, New York

JOHN T. SUBAK, Philadelphia, Pennsylvania

Patrick James Sullivan, San Diego, California

RICHARD L. SUTTON, Wilmington, Delaware

LES SWANSON, Jr., Portland, Oregon

LEE C. SWARTZ, Harrisburg, Pennsylvania

STANLEY L. TEMKO, Washington, D.C.

WILLIAM H. THEIS, Chicago, Illinois

GERALD F. TIETZ, Philadelphia, Pennsylvania

CARL W. TOBIAS, Missoula, Montana

WILLIAM A. TRINE, Boulder, Colorado

BOWEN H. TUCKER, Chicago, Illinois

H. WOODRUFF TURNER, Pittsburgh, Pennsylvania

MEMBERS CONSULTATIVE GROUP

Debra A. Valentine, Washington, D.C.

John Franklin Vargo, Indianapolis, Indiana

Charles J. Walsh, Newark, New Jersey

Ronald Frederick Waterman, Helena, Montana

Priscilla Peterson Weaver, Chicago, Illinois

Robert C. Weber, Cleveland, Ohio

Louise Weinberg, Austin, Texas

Robert N. Weiner, Washington, D.C.

David H. Weinstein, Philadelphia, Pennsylvania

Michael Wells, Athens, Georgia

Stephen J. Werber, Cleveland, Ohio

Jerry Wertheim, Santa Fe, New Mexico

Ronald P. Wertheim, Superior Court of the District of Columbia, Washington, D.C.

Malcolm E. Wheeler, Denver, Colorado

Stephanie M. Wildman, San Francisco, California

Stephen F. Williams, United States Court of Appeals for the District of Columbia Circuit, Washington, D.C.

James W. Wilson, Austin, Texas

Samuel Brown Witt, III, Arlington, Virginia

Nicholas J. Wittner, Torrance, California

Jerome T. Wolf, Kansas City, Missouri

Margaret Smith Woodruff, Philadelphia, Pennsylvania

Richard W. Wright, Chicago, Illinois

Mark G. Yudof, Austin, Texas

Michael J. Zimmer, Newark, New Jersey

Guy A. Zoghby, Pittsburgh, Pennsylvania

Harvey L. Zuckman, Washington, D.C.

FOREWORD

Restatement of the Law Third, Torts: Products Liability is the first product of the Institute's long-term undertaking to revise and update the Restatement Second of Torts. The Restatement Second was conceived as a single project, with the brilliant and indefatigable William L. Prosser serving as the sole Reporter. It was eventually completed, after Dean Prosser's resignation, under the reportership of another great torts scholar, John W. Wade. Such a comprehensive engagement with the law of torts is no longer feasible. The subject has become too broad and too intricate to be encompassed in a single project, even one as prolonged as Restatement Second, or by a single directing intelligence, even one as powerful as Bill Prosser's or John Wade's. Moreover, as everyone knows who is familiar with the Products Liability project, many subjects in tort law have become very controversial. Attending to strongly conflicting views and seeking to work out rational and responsible resolution among such views entail additional complexity and require more time and energy. Hence, we have had to undertake Restatement Third in segments.

The Institute is committed to further projects in Restatement Third of Torts. A project on Apportionment of Liability (joint and several liability, etc.) is nearing completion. A project addressing General Principles of Tort Law has been commenced. We contemplate several more torts projects in the coming years. I have little doubt that most of these subjects will be controversial in one degree or another, although that on Apportionment has, happily, been relatively pacific. This quietude may result from the fact that the subject of Apportionment is strongly shaped by statute (shifting primary controversy to the legislatures) and perhaps also because the subject's complexities defy the simplistic epithets with which controversy is typically conducted. The subject of Products Liability is of course "political" in that it involves issues of distributive justice and has attracted the attention of vocal and aggressive partisans in legislative forums and election campaigns. Nevertheless, the Institute cannot withdraw from important legal subject matter simply because it entails controversial issues.

More important, in my judgment the controversy attending the drafting of Products Liability has in general been conducted according to the best standards of professional and academic tradition. The Reporters, Professors James A. Henderson, Jr., and Aaron D. Twerski, had views of the subject when they began. What experienced legal scholars could not have views about a subject in which their minds had been engaged for years? Nevertheless, the Reporters listened to criticism and, in my assessment, gave heed to it. The critics, from various viewpoints, expressed their views in specific legal terms, generally supported by the best legal analysis that could be mustered. The Members Consultative Group provided a valuable forum for concentrated focus on viewpoints other than those being expressed by the Advisers and the Council and at our Annual Meetings. A limited number of relevant legal "interest groups" were given audience and made very competent suggestions.

The resultant text of course "goes beyond the law" as the law otherwise would stand. A Restatement that was simply a photograph would not be worth the effort that goes into an Institute product. Moreover, a photograph of the law in this field would have been a blurred image of confusion. No one can seriously argue that the law of products liability in any jurisdiction has evolved in a straight line from § 402A of the Restatement Second. Professor Max Radin once famously analogized development of common-law rules to the twisting and sometimes misdirected course of a runaway calf. See Max Radin, *The Trail of the Calf*, 32 Cornell Law Quarterly 137 (1946). The law of products liability certainly was such. This Restatement puts this body of law much straighter.

We express our appreciation to those who think that the present formulations are about right. We also express our respect for those who think they are not quite right. The life of the law consists of experience, as Justice Holmes said, as well as logic. The life of the Institute's process gives expression to varieties of experience. The work of the Institute proceeds by discussion, not *diktat*. The participants in the discussions in this project, as in our other projects, include practitioners of various viewpoints, academics of even more various viewpoints, and judges. It is the judges who hold highest responsibility for giving the law coherence and sound substance, and whose contributions we therefore especially appreciate.

We acknowledge our debt to the Reporters for their thoughtfulness and diligence and to the Advisers for their counsel and their sustained commitment to the enterprise. We note with particular pleasure that the Institute's Executive Committee has designated Professors Henderson and Twerski as joint holders of the R. Ammi Cutter Reporter's Chair, an honor reserved for Institute Reporters whose service is regarded as especially outstanding.

GEOFFREY C. HAZARD, JR.
DIRECTOR
THE AMERICAN LAW INSTITUTE

January 12, 1998

REPORTERS' PREFACE

Over the five-year period in which this Restatement underwent numerous iterations and drafts the Reporters were fortunate to have the wise counsel of our knowledgeable and dedicated Advisers, who saw and commented on every draft. We also benefited from the input of literally hundreds of members of the Institute and interested observers who wrote to us suggesting changes to enhance the work. Many of these submissions were lengthy and well researched. They were invaluable to us in refining and polishing the various drafts. We are indebted to all who expended effort to improve this Restatement and the law of products liability. We would be remiss if we did not single out for special appreciation Professor David G. Owen of the University of South Carolina School of Law, who served as Editorial Adviser in the final year of this project. His contribution has been invaluable.

Finally, as Reporters we can say that the experience of serving on this project and learning from bench, bar, and academia has been most gratifying. We come away from our labors with the deepest respect for The American Law Institute and for the fairness and openness with which it conducts its deliberations. We are proud to have shared some moments in the history of this important American institution.

JAMES A. HENDERSON, JR.
AARON D. TWERSKI

January 8, 1998

*

SUMMARY OF CONTENTS

*

TABLE OF CONTENTS

CHAPTER 1

LIABILITY OF COMMERCIAL PRODUCT SELLERS BASED ON PRODUCT DEFECTS AT TIME OF SALE

TOPIC 1. LIABILITY RULES APPLICABLE TO PRODUCTS GENERALLY

Section | Page

CHAPTER 2

LIABILITY OF COMMERCIAL PRODUCT SELLERS NOT BASED ON PRODUCT DEFECTS AT TIME OF SALE

CHAPTER 3

LIABILITY OF SUCCESSORS AND APPARENT MANUFACTURERS

TABLE OF CONTENTS

CHAPTER 4

PROVISIONS OF GENERAL APPLICABILITY

TOPIC 1. CAUSATION

TABLE OF CONTENTS

*

Cite thus:

Restatement Third,
Torts: Products Liability § ______

*

RESTATEMENT OF THE LAW THIRD

THE AMERICAN LAW INSTITUTE

RESTATEMENT OF THE LAW
TORTS

PRODUCTS LIABILITY

*

INTRODUCTION

This Restatement deals with the liability of commercial product sellers and distributors for harm caused by their products. To understand its place in the law, products liability must be examined in historical context. In 1964 The American Law Institute adopted § 402A as part of the Restatement Second of Torts. Section 402A was entitled "Special Liability of Seller of Product for Physical Harm to User or Consumer." It marked the first recognition by the Institute of privity-free strict liability for sellers of defective products. The major thrust of § 402A was to eliminate privity so that a user or consumer, without having to establish negligence, could bring an action against a manufacturer, as well as against any other member of a distributive chain that had sold a product containing a manufacturing defect. Section 402A had little to say about liability for design defects or for products sold with inadequate warnings. In the early 1960s these areas of litigation were in their infancy.

In restating the law of products liability more than a quarter of a century later, the Institute had before it thousands of judicial decisions that had fine-tuned the law of products liability in a manner hardly imaginable when Restatement Second was written. Issues that had not occurred to those members involved in drafting Restatement Second had become points of serious contention and debate in the courts. What should be the governing standard for design and warning liability? Is there a cause of action for defective prescription drug design? What rule should govern when a plaintiff establishes that enhanced harm was suffered as a result of a defect in a defendant's product, beyond that which would have resulted from other causes, but the plaintiff cannot quantify the amount of the enhancement?

On almost every page of Restatement Third, Torts: Products Liability, the Institute has had to respond to questions that were not part of the landscape 35 years ago. This Restatement is, therefore, an almost total overhaul of Restatement Second as it concerns the liability of commercial sellers of products.

Several sections of the Restatement Second of Torts address the liability of suppliers of products ("chattels") known to be dangerous for intended uses (§ 388), unlikely to be made safe for use (§ 389), or supplied to users known to be incompetent (§ 390). Although these rules apply to commercial product suppliers (see §§ 391–393), they also apply to noncommercial suppliers and thus extend beyond the scope of this Restatement. To the extent that these rules reflect the basic principle that an actor is subject to liability for harm caused by the actor's negligence, however, they do not necessarily conflict with this Restatement (see § 2, Comment *n*). Consistent with Comment *n*, claims based on product defect must meet the requisites set forth in Chapter 1 of this Restatement. As long as these requisites are met, doctrinal tort categories such as negligence or strict liability may be utilized in bringing the claim.

This Restatement is divided into four Chapters. Chapter 1 sets forth the rules that govern the liability of commercial product sellers based on product defects at the time of sale. The Chapter is divided into two Topics. Topic 1 contains the liability rules applicable to products generally. Topic 2 encompasses the liability rules applicable to special products or product markets (component parts, drugs, food products, and used products).

Section 2(b) generated considerable controversy. It calls for proof of a reasonable alternative design in order to sustain an action for defective design. As § 2, Comment *b*, makes clear, however, § 2(b) is not the only method for establishing defective design. Section 3 allows a plaintiff to draw an inference of defect in circumstances in which common experience teaches that an inference of defect may be warranted under the specific facts, including the failure of the product to perform its manifestly intended function. A plaintiff proceeding under § 3 need not establish a reasonable alternative design. Furthermore, § 2, Comment *e*, leaves open the possibility that, even absent an alternative design, courts may find that some products are not reasonably safe because they present an extremely high degree of danger and provide negligible social utility. Finally, under § 4, when a product design violates an applicable governmental safety standard, it is defective without regard to the availability of a reasonable alternative.

In short, Topic 1 contains four sections. It must be read as a whole. Overzealous advocates may seek to focus the attention of courts on § 2(b) alone. Users of this Restatement are cautioned against such a fragmented reading.

CHAPTER 1

LIABILITY OF COMMERCIAL PRODUCT SELLERS BASED ON PRODUCT DEFECTS AT TIME OF SALE

TOPIC 1. LIABILITY RULES APPLICABLE TO PRODUCTS GENERALLY

TOPIC 2. LIABILITY RULES APPLICABLE TO SPECIAL PRODUCTS OR PRODUCT MARKETS

TOPIC 1. LIABILITY RULES APPLICABLE TO PRODUCTS GENERALLY

§ 1. Liability of Commercial Seller or Distributor for Harm Caused by Defective Products

One engaged in the business of selling or otherwise distributing products who sells or distributes a defective product is subject to liability for harm to persons or property caused by the defect.

Comment:

a. History. This Section states a general rule of tort liability applicable to commercial sellers and other distributors of products generally. Rules of liability applicable to special products such as prescription drugs and used products are set forth in separate Sections in Topic 2 of this Chapter.

The liability established in this Section draws on both warranty law and tort law. Historically, the focus of products liability law was on manufacturing defects. A manufacturing defect is a physical departure from a product's intended design. See § 2(a). Typically, manufacturing defects occur in only a small percentage of units in a product line. Courts early began imposing liability without fault on product sellers for harm caused by such defects, holding a seller liable for harm caused by manufacturing defects even though all possible care had been exercised by the seller in the preparation and distribution of the product. In doing so, courts relied on the concept of warranty, in connection with which fault has never been a prerequisite to liability.

The imposition of liability for manufacturing defects has a long history in the common law. As early as 1266, criminal statutes imposed liability upon victualers, vintners, brewers, butchers, cooks, and other persons who supplied contaminated food and drink. In the late 1800s, courts in many states began imposing negligence and strict warranty liability on commercial sellers of defective goods. In the early 1960s, American courts began to recognize that a commercial seller of any product having a manufacturing defect should be liable in tort for harm caused by the defect regardless of the plaintiff's ability to maintain a traditional negligence or warranty action. Liability attached even if the manufacturer's quality control in producing the defective product was reasonable. A plaintiff was not required to be in direct privity with the defendant seller to bring an action. Strict liability in tort for defectively manufactured products merges the concept of implied warranty, in which negligence is not required, with the tort concept of negligence, in which contractual privity is not required. See § 2(a).

Questions of design defects and defects based on inadequate instructions or warnings arise when the specific product unit conforms to the intended design but the intended design itself, or its sale without adequate instructions or warnings, renders the product not reasonably safe. If these forms of defect are found to exist, then every unit in the same product line is potentially defective. See § 2, Comments *d*, *f*, and *i*. Imposition of liability for design defects and for defects based on inadequate instructions or warnings was relatively infrequent until the late 1960s and early 1970s. A number of restrictive rules made recovery for such defects, especially design defects, difficult to obtain. As these rules eroded, courts sought to impose liability without fault for design defects and defects due to inadequate instructions or warnings under the general principles of § 402A of the Restatement, Second, of Torts. However, it soon became evident that

§ 402A, created to deal with liability for manufacturing defects, could not appropriately be applied to cases of design defects or defects based on inadequate instructions or warnings. A product unit that fails to meet the manufacturer's design specifications thereby fails to perform its intended function and is, almost by definition, defective. However, when the product unit meets the manufacturer's own design specifications, it is necessary to go outside those specifications to determine whether the product is defective.

Sections 2(b) and 2(c) recognize that the rule developed for manufacturing defects is inappropriate for the resolution of claims of defective design and defects based on inadequate instructions or warnings. These latter categories of cases require determinations that the product could have reasonably been made safer by a better design or instruction or warning. Sections 2(b) and 2(c) rely on a reasonableness test traditionally used in determining whether an actor has been negligent. See Restatement, Second, Torts §§ 291–293. Nevertheless, many courts insist on speaking of liability based on the standards described in §§ 2(b) and 2(c) as being "strict."

Several factors help to explain this rhetorical preference. First, in many design defect cases, if the product causes injury while being put to a reasonably foreseeable use, the seller is held to have known of the risks that foreseeably attend such use. See § 2, Comment *m*. Second, some courts have sought to limit the defense of comparative fault in certain products liability contexts. In furtherance of this objective, they have avoided characterizing the liability test as based in negligence, thereby limiting the effect of comparative or contributory fault. See § 17, Comment *d*. Third, some courts are concerned that a negligence standard might be too forgiving of a small manufacturer who might be excused for its ignorance of risk or for failing to take adequate precautions to avoid risk. Negligence, which focuses on the conduct of the defendant-manufacturer, might allow a finding that a defendant with meager resources was not negligent because it was too burdensome for such a defendant to discover risks or to design or warn against them. The concept of strict liability, which focuses on the product rather than the conduct of the manufacturer, may help make the point that a defendant is held to the expert standard of knowledge available to the relevant manufacturing community at the time the product was manufactured. Finally, the liability of nonmanufacturing sellers in the distributive chain is strict. It is no defense that they acted reasonably and did not discover a defect in the product, be it from manufacturing, design, or failure to warn. See Comment *e*.

Thus, "strict products liability" is a term of art that reflects the judgment that products liability is a discrete area of tort law which borrows from both negligence and warranty. It is not fully congruent with classical tort or contract law. Rather than perpetuating confusion spawned by existing doctrinal categories, §§ 1 and 2 define the liability for each form of defect in terms directly addressing the various kinds of defects. As long as these functional criteria are met, courts may utilize the terminology of negligence, strict liability, or the implied warranty of merchantability, or simply define liability in the terms set forth in the black letter. See § 2, Comment *n*.

b. Sale or other distribution. The rule stated in this Section applies not only to sales transactions but also to other forms of commercial product distribution that are the functional equivalent of product sales. See § 20.

c. One engaged in the business of selling or otherwise distributing. The rule stated in this Section applies only to manufacturers and other commercial sellers and distributors who are engaged in the business of selling or otherwise distributing the type of product that harmed the plaintiff. The rule does not apply to a noncommercial seller or distributor of such products. Thus, it does not apply to one who sells foodstuffs to a neighbor, nor does it apply to the private owner of an automobile who sells it to another.

It is not necessary that a commercial seller or distributor be engaged exclusively or even primarily in selling or otherwise distributing the type of product that injured the plaintiff, so long as the sale of the product is other than occasional or casual. Thus, the rule applies to a motion-picture theater's routine sales of popcorn or ice cream, either for consumption on the premises or in packages to be taken home. Similarly, a service station that does mechanical repair work on cars may also sell tires and automobile equipment as part of its regular business. Such sales are subject to the rule in this Section. However, the rule does not cover occasional sales (frequently referred to as "casual sales") outside the regular course of the seller's business. Thus, an occasional sale of surplus equipment by a business does not fall within the ambit of this rule. Whether a defendant is a commercial seller or distributor within the meaning of this Section is usually a question of law to be determined by the court.

d. Harm to persons or property. The rule stated in this Section applies only to harm to persons or property, commonly referred to as personal injury and property damage. For rules governing economic loss, see § 21.

e. Nonmanufacturing sellers or other distributors of products. The rule stated in this Section provides that all commercial sellers and distributors of products, including nonmanufacturing sellers and distributors such as wholesalers and retailers, are subject to liability for selling products that are defective. Liability attaches even when such nonmanufacturing sellers or distributors do not themselves render the products defective and regardless of whether they are in a position to prevent defects from occurring. See § 2, Comment *o*. Legislation has been enacted in many jurisdictions that, to some extent, immunizes nonmanufacturing sellers or distributors from strict liability. The legislation is premised on the belief that bringing nonmanufacturing sellers or distributors into products liability litigation generates wasteful legal costs. Although liability in most cases is ultimately passed on to the manufacturer who is responsible for creating the product defect, nonmanufacturing sellers or distributors must devote resources to protect their interests. In most situations, therefore, immunizing nonmanufacturers from strict liability saves those resources without jeopardizing the plaintiff's interests. To assure plaintiffs access to a responsible and solvent product seller or distributor, the statutes generally provide that the nonmanufacturing seller or distributor is immunized from strict liability only if: (1) the manufacturer is subject to the jurisdiction of the court of plaintiff's domicile; and (2) the manufacturer is not, nor is likely to become, insolvent.

In connection with these statutes, two problems may need to be resolved to assure fairness to plaintiffs. First, as currently structured, the statutes typically impose upon the plaintiff the risk of insolvency of the manufacturer between the time an action is brought and the time a judgment can be enforced. If a nonmanufacturing seller or distributor is dismissed from an action at the outset when it appears that the manufacturer will be able to pay a judgment, and the manufacturer subsequently becomes insolvent and is unable to pay the judgment, the plaintiff may be left to suffer the loss uncompensated. One possible solution could be to toll the statute of limitations against nonmanufacturers so that they may be brought in if necessary. Second, a nonmanufacturing seller or distributor occasionally will be responsible for the introduction of a defect in a product even though it exercised reasonable care in handling or supervising the product in its control. In such instances, liability for a § 2(a) defect should be imposed on the nonmanufacturing seller or distributor. See § 2, Illustration 2.

REPORTERS' NOTE

Comment a. History.

1. Abundant authority recognizes the division of product defects into manufacturing defects, design defects, and defects based on inadequate instructions or warnings. See, e.g., Caterpillar Tractor Co. v. Beck, 593 P.2d 871, 881–82 (Alaska 1979) (Accord, Shanks v. Upjohn Co., 835 P.2d 1189, 1194 (Alaska 1992)); Dart v. Wiebe Mfg., Inc., 709 P.2d 876, 878–79 (Ariz.1985) (en banc); Barker v. Lull Eng'g Co., 573 P.2d 443, 454 (Cal.1978) (recognizing that different

liability standards apply depending on which type of defect is involved); Cassisi v. Maytag Co., 396 So.2d 1140, 1145 (Fla.Dist.Ct.App.1981); Hunt v. Harley–Davidson Motor Co., 248 S.E.2d 15, 15–17 (Ga.Ct.App. 1978) (drawing distinction between duty of manufacturer to design and warn and cases in which products contain latent manufacturing defects); Toner v. Lederle Labs., 732 P.2d 297, 316 (Idaho 1987) (Bakes, J., concurring) ("The definition of 'in a defective condition unreasonably dangerous to the user or consumer' also takes on somewhat different meanings depending on the context of the products liability cause of action, i.e. whether the cause of action is premised on an alleged defect in the product's design, or in the product's manufacture [in faulty execution of the design], or in the product's warning concerning its known dangers."); Hoffman v. E.W. Bliss Co., 448 N.E.2d 277, 281 (Ind.1983); Ulrich v. Kasco Abrasives Co., 532 S.W.2d 197, 200 (Ky.1976) (Accord, Nichols v. Union Underwear Co., 602 S.W.2d 429, 433 (Ky.1980)); Cosse v. Allen–Bradley Co., 601 So.2d 1349, 1351 (La. 1992) (See also La. Rev. Stat. Ann. §§ 9:2800.55–57 (West 1988) (establishing different liability tests for manufacturing defects, design defects, and failure to warn)); Phipps v. General Motors Corp., 363 A.2d 955, 959 (Md.1976) (See also Ziegler v. Kawasaki Heavy Indus., Ltd., 539 A.2d 701, 703 (Md.Ct.Spec.App. 1988)); Back v. Wickes Corp., 378 N.E.2d 964, 970 (Mass.1978); Prentis v. Yale Mfg. Co., 365 N.W.2d 176, 182 (Mich.1984); Bilotta v. Kelley Co., 346 N.W.2d 616, 621–22 (Minn.1984) (holding that strict liability test, which is appropriate for manufacturing defects, is not appropriate for design defects); Miss. Code Ann. § 11–1–63 (1993) (establishing different liability tests for manufacturing, design, and failure to warn defects); Nesselrode v. Executive Beechcraft, Inc., 707 S.W.2d 371, 375–77 (Mo.1986); Rix v. General Motors Corp., 723 P.2d 195, 200 (Mont.1986); Thibault v. Sears, Roebuck & Co., 395 A.2d 843, 846–47 (N.H.1978); O'Brien v. Muskin Corp., 463 A.2d 298, 304 (N.J.1983) (Accord, Jurado v. Western Gear Works, 619 A.2d 1312, 1317 (N.J. 1993); Cepeda v. Cumberland Eng'g Co., 386 A.2d 816, 824–25 (N.J.1978). See also N.J. Stat. Ann. §§ 2A:58C–2, 3 (West 1987) (establishing different defenses based on whether product was defective in manufacture, design, or warning); Voss v. Black & Decker Mfg. Co., 450 N.E.2d 204, 207 (N.Y. 1983) (See also Denny v. Ford Motor Co., 662 N.E.2d 730, 735 n. 3 (N.Y. 1995)); State Farm Fire & Casualty Co. v. Chrysler Corp., 523 N.E.2d 489, 494 (Ohio 1988) (See also Ohio Rev. Code Ann. §§ 2307.74–76 (Anderson 1991) (establishing different liability tests for manufacturing defects, design defects, and failure to warn)); Phillips v. Kimwood Mach. Co., 525 P.2d 1033, 1035–38 (Or.1974) (See also Or. Rev. Stat. § 30.900 (1991); Glover v. BIC Corp., 987 F.2d 1410, 1414 (9th Cir.1993) (amended and superseded on other grounds 6 F.3d 1318 (9th Cir.1993))(applying Oregon law)); Turner v. General Motors Corp., 584 S.W.2d 844, 847–48 (Tex.1979) (adopting a risk-utility test for conscious design defect and specifically rejecting consumer expectations for conscious design choice cases—presumably allowing consumer expectations as a test for manufacturing defect) (See also Tex. Civ. Prac. & Rem. Code Ann. § 82.005 (West 1993) (sets standards for proving a design defect which do not govern a manufacturing defect)); Peterson v. Safway Steel Scaffolds Co., 400 N.W.2d 909, 912 (S.D.1987); Baughn v. Honda Motor Co., Ltd., 727 P.2d 655, 661 (Wash.1986) (See also Wash. Rev. Code Ann. § 7.72.030 (West 1992) (establishing different standards for manufacturing, design, and failure to warn defects)); Morningstar v. Black & Decker Mfg. Co., 253 S.E.2d 666, 682 (W.Va.1979).

Support among the treatise writers for a functional definition of defect, differentiating among manufacturing, design, and failure to warn defects, is equally strong. Most casebook authors and treatise writers organize their discussions concerning defect around these functional categories. See, e.g., Fischer and Powers, Products Liability: Cases and Materials Ch. 2C (1988); Franklin and Rabin, Tort Law and Alternatives 492–541 (6th ed. 1996); Henderson and Twerski, Products Liability: Problems and Process Parts I and II (3d ed. 1997); Madden, Products Liability: Chs. 8, 9, 10 (2d ed. 1988); Noel and Phillips, Products Liability: Cases and Materials Chs. 5–7 (1976); Owen, Montgomery and Keeton, Cases and Materials on Products Liability and Safety Ch. 7 (3d ed. 1996); Phillips, Terry, Maraist, McClellan, Tort Law: Cases, Materials, Problems 717–30 (1991); Keeton, Dobbs, Keeton and Owen, Prosser and Keeton, On the Law of Torts § 99 (5th ed. 1984 & Supp. 1988); Shapo, The Law of Products Liability Chs. 9, 19 (2d ed. 1990). See also Model Uniform Products Liability Act § 104 (1979).

Law review commentary similarly recognizes the distinction as necessary to a coherent discussion of the bases of liability. See, e.g., Birnbaum, Unmasking the Test for Design Defect: from Negligence [to Warranty] to Strict Liability to Negligence, 33 Vand. L. Rev. 593, 599–600 (1980); DeWolf and Allen, Liability for Manufacturers in Washington: When Is Strict Liability Appropriate?, 27 Gonz. L. Rev. 217, 235–39 (1991/1992); Dobbels, Missouri Products Liability Law Revisited: A Look at Missouri Strict Products Liability Law Before and After the Tort Reform Act, 53 Mo. L. Rev. 227 (1988); Kenney, Products Liability in Massachusetts Enters the 1990's, 75 Mass. L. Rev. 70 (1990); Miller, Design Defect Litigation in Iowa: The Myths of Strict Liability, 40 Drake L. Rev. 465, 471 (1991); Mowery, Comment, Torts—A Survey of the Law of Strict Products Liability in New Mexico, 11 N.M. L. Rev. 359, 383–387 (1981); Moylan, Comment, In Pursuit of the Appropriate Standard of Liability for Defective Product Designs, 42 Me. L. Rev. 453, 454–55 (1990); Note, Minnesota Replaces the Restatement Standard with a Negligence Standard, 11 Wm. Mitchell L. Rev. 891, 892–96 (1985); Owen, The Moral Foundations of Product Liability Law: Toward First Principles, 68 Notre Dame L. Rev. 427, 437, 466–67 (1993); Powers, A Modest Proposal to Abandon Strict Products Liability, 1991 U. Ill. L. Rev. 639 (1991); Sales, Product Liability Law in Texas, 23 Hous. L. Rev. 1, 15–97 (1986); G. Schwartz, Foreword: Understanding Products Liability, 67 Cal. L. Rev. 435, 460–81 (1979); Wade, On the Nature of Strict Tort Liability for Products, 44 Miss. L.J. 825, 830–38 (1973).

2. Several courts have indicated that strict liability holds the seller to the expert standard of knowledge available to the relevant manufacturing community at the time the product was manufactured. See, e.g., Anderson v. Owens–Corning Fiberglas Corp., 810 P.2d 549 (Cal.1991);

Woodill v. Parke Davis & Co., 402 N.E.2d 194 (Ill.1980); Owens–Illinois, Inc. v. Zenobia, 601 A.2d 633 (Md. 1992).

Comment c. One engaged in the business of selling or otherwise distributing.

1. American courts universally hold that only sellers who are in the business of selling products are strictly liable. Thus, noncommercial sellers of products are liable only if shown to have been negligent. See, e.g., Smith v. Stewart, 667 P.2d 358 (Kan.1983) (implied warranty of merchantability does not apply to noncommercial sale of boat by private owner, a dentist); Elley v. Stephens, 760 P.2d 768 (Nev.1988) (private, noncommercial owners of prefabricated house built on a lot were not strictly liable for harm caused by latent defect, even assuming house was a product).

2. The commercial seller must be in the business not only of selling products, but selling products of the type that harmed the plaintiff. See, e.g., Jones v. South Eastern Pennsylvania Trans. Auth., 1993 WL 410222 (E.D.Pa.1993); Counts v. MK–Ferguson Co., 680 F.Supp. 1343 (E.D.Mo. 1988), aff'd, 862 F.2d 1338 (8th Cir. 1988) (no strict liability for isolated sale of crop storage facility); Johnson v. Supro Corp., 498 So.2d 528 (Fla. Dist.Ct.App.1986) (no strict liability against commercial seller of ribbon blender because seller not in business of selling such products); Ridenhour v. Colson Caster Corp., 687 S.W.2d 938 (Mo.Ct.App.1985); Santiago v. E.W. Bliss Division, 492 A.2d 1089 (N.J.Super.Ct.App.Div.1985) (isolated sale of discarded 23–year-old punch press; no strict liability). See also Galindo v. Precision Am. Corp., 754 F.2d 1212 (5th Cir.), reh'g denied, 762 F.2d 1004 (1985) (summary judgment for defendant reversed; casualness of the sale was for the jury to determine).

When products are given away as part of the promotion of defendant's business enterprise, the requirement that the defendant must be in the business of selling that type of product is often relaxed. See § 20, Comment *b*.

Comment e. Nonmanufacturing sellers or other distributors of products.

1. Comment *f* of § 402A states that any seller in the chain of distribution (manufacturer, wholesaler, retailer) is liable for the sale of a defective product that was a cause of the plaintiff's injury. Support for the rule is widespread. See Vandermark v. Ford Motor Co., 391 P.2d 168, 171–72 (Cal.1964) (en banc); Cottom v. McGuire Funeral Service, Inc., 262 A.2d 807, 809 (D.C.1970); Smith v. Fiat–Roosevelt Motors, Inc., 556 F.2d 728 (5th Cir.1977) (applying Florida law) (importer-distributor subject to strict liability for uncrashworthy car); Visnoski v. J.C. Penney Co., 477 So.2d 29 (Fla.Dist.Ct.App.1985); Mobley v. South Florida Beverage Corp., 500 So.2d 292, 293 (Fla.Dist.Ct.App. 1986), reh'g denied, 509 So.2d 1117 (Fla.1987); Lawrence v. Brandell Prods., Inc., 619 So.2d 427 (Fla.Dist. Ct.App.1993); Curry v. Sile Distrib., 727 F.Supp. 1052 (N.D.Miss.1990) (The court held that the leading case holding to the contrary, Sam Shainberg Co. of Jackson v. Barlow, 258 So.2d 242 (Miss.1972), although not explicitly overruled, is no longer the rule in Mississippi. In Coca Cola Bottling Co. v. Reeves, 486 So.2d 374, 379 (Miss.1986), the Mississippi Court held that *Shainberg* was "anomalous if not irrational."); Keener v. Dayton Elec. Mfg. Co., 445 S.W.2d 362 (Mo.

1969) (retailer liable for defective design); Mead v. Warner Pruyn Div., Finch Pruyn Sales, Inc., 394 N.Y.S.2d 483 (N.Y.App.Div.1977); Giuffrida v. Panasonic Indus. Co., 607 N.Y.S.2d 72 (1994); Moss v. Polyco, Inc., 522 P.2d 622, 626–27 (Okla.1974); Berkebile v. Brantly Helicopter Corp., 337 A.2d 893, 898 n. 3 (Pa.1975) (seller liable for failure to warn); McKisson v. Sales Affiliates, Inc., 416 S.W.2d 787, 790 n. 3 (Tex.1967) (distributor liable for failure to warn); Oser v. Wal–Mart Stores, Inc., 951 F.Supp. 115 (S.D.Tex.1996) (retail seller subject to liability for defective shopping bag that tore causing injury to plaintiff); Zamora v. Mobil Corp., 704 P.2d 584 (Wash.1985); Dippel v. Sciano, 155 N.W.2d 55 (Wis.1967).

See also Fischer and Powers, Products Liability—Cases and Materials 588 (1988) ("The overwhelming majority of courts have followed the position taken in *Vandermark* and Comment *f* by applying strict tort liability to retailers."); Madden, Products Liability § 3.16 (2d ed. 1988) ("Decisions in most jurisdictions have held that the doctrine of strict tort liability may be applied against the ordinary retailer in products liability cases."); Cavico, The Strict Tort Liability of Retailers, Wholesalers, and Distributors of Defective Products, 12 Nova L. Rev. 213, 218 (1987) ("A great majority of states have followed the *Vandermark* principle.").

The legislative response to the common-law rule has been varied. A few states bar a strict liability action against nonmanufacturer sellers. See, e.g., Ga. Code Ann. § 51–11.1 (Supp. 1996); Neb. Rev. Stat. § 25–21,181 (1989); S.D. Codified Laws Ann. § 20–9–9 (1987). A host of statutes bar an action for strict liability depending on whether jurisdiction may be obtained against the manufacturer and whether the manufacturer is able to satisfy a judgment. See, e.g., Del. Code Ann. tit. 18 § 7001 (1989); Idaho Code § 6–1407 (1990); 735 Ill. Comp. Stat. Ann. 5/2–621(a)-(c) (1993 & Supp. 1996); Iowa Code § 613.18 (1996); Kan. Stat. Ann. § 60–3306 (1983 Supp. 1993); Ky. Rev. Stat. Ann. § 411.340 (Michie 1992); Md. Code Ann., Cts & Jud. Proc. § 5–311 (1982); Minn. Stat. Ann. § 544.41 (West 1988); Mo. Rev. Stat. § 537.762 (1988); N.C. Gen. Stat. § 99B–2 (1989); N.D. Cent. Code § 28–01.1–06.1 (1991); Ohio Rev. Code Ann. § 2307.78 (Anderson 1991); Tenn. Code Ann. § 29–28–106 (Supp. 1992); Wash. Rev. Code Ann. § 7.72.040 (West 1991).

2. One of the implications of these statutes is that, on occasion, a plaintiff will not be able to establish negligence against the retailer or strict liability against the manufacturer and thus may be left with no remedy. See, e.g., Saieva v. Budget Rent–A–Car of Rockford, 591 N.E.2d 507 (Ill.App.Ct. 1992) (The lessor of a van was exempt from strict liability under an Illinois statute which allows such an exemption when a nonmanufacturer who is sued for strict liability identifies the product manufacturer. The lessor was granted summary judgment on the plaintiff's claim of negligence because there was no proof that the lessor was negligent in failing to discover a defect in the brakes of the leased van. Ford, the manufacturer of the van, also was granted summary judgment because plaintiff was unable to establish that the van was defective when it left the hands of Ford.).

§ 2. Categories of Product Defect

A product is defective when, at the time of sale or distribution, it contains a manufacturing defect, is defective in design, or is defective because of inadequate instructions or warnings. A product:

(a) contains a manufacturing defect when the product departs from its intended design even though all possible care was exercised in the preparation and marketing of the product;

(b) is defective in design when the foreseeable risks of harm posed by the product could have been reduced or avoided by the adoption of a reasonable alternative design by the seller or other distributor, or a predecessor in the commercial chain of distribution, and the omission of the alternative design renders the product not reasonably safe;

(c) is defective because of inadequate instructions or warnings when the foreseeable risks of harm posed by the product could have been reduced or avoided by the provision of reasonable instructions or warnings by the seller or other distributor, or a predecessor in the commercial chain of distribution, and the omission of the instructions or warnings renders the product not reasonably safe.

Comment:

a. Rationale. The rules set forth in this Section establish separate standards of liability for manufacturing defects, design defects, and defects based on inadequate instructions or warnings. They are generally applicable to most products. Standards of liability applicable to special product categories such as prescription drugs and used products are set forth in separate sections in Topic 2 of this Chapter.

The rule for manufacturing defects stated in Subsection (a) imposes liability whether or not the manufacturer's quality control efforts satisfy standards of reasonableness. Strict liability without fault in this context is generally believed to foster several objectives. On the premise that tort law serves the instrumental function of creating safety incentives, imposing strict liability on manufacturers for harm caused by manufacturing defects encourages greater investment in product safety than does a regime of fault-based liability under which, as a practical matter, sellers may escape their appropriate share of responsibility. Some courts and commentators also have said that strict liability discourages the consumption of defective products by causing the purchase price of products to reflect, more than would a rule of negligence, the costs of defects. And by eliminating the issue of manufacturer fault from plaintiff's case, strict liability reduces the transaction costs involved in litigating that issue.

Several important fairness concerns are also believed to support manufacturers' liability for manufacturing defects even if the plaintiff is unable to show that the manufacturer's quality control fails to meet risk-utility norms. In many cases manufacturing defects are in fact caused by manufacturer negligence but plaintiffs have difficulty proving it. Strict liability therefore performs a function similar to the concept of res ipsa loquitur, allowing deserving plaintiffs to succeed notwithstanding what would otherwise be difficult or insuperable problems of proof. Products that malfunction due to manufacturing defects disappoint reasonable expectations of product performance. Because manufacturers invest in quality control at consciously chosen levels, their knowledge that a predictable number of flawed products will enter the marketplace entails an element of deliberation about the amount of injury that will result from their activity. Finally, many believe that consumers who benefit from products without suffering harm should share, through increases in the prices charged for those products, the burden of unavoidable injury costs that result from manufacturing defects.

An often-cited rationale for holding wholesalers and retailers strictly liable for harm caused by manufacturing defects is that, as between them and innocent victims who suffer harm because of defective products, the product sellers as business entities are in a better position than are individual users and consumers to insure against such losses. In most instances, wholesalers and retailers will be able to pass liability costs up the chain of product distribution to the manufacturer. When joining the manufacturer in the tort action presents the plaintiff with procedural difficulties, local retailers can pay damages to the victims and then seek indemnity from manufacturers. Finally, holding retailers and wholesalers strictly liable creates incentives for them to deal only with reputable, financially responsible manufacturers and distributors, thereby helping to protect the interests of users and consumers. For considerations relevant to reducing nonmanufacturers' liability, see § 1, Comment *e*.

In contrast to manufacturing defects, design defects and defects based on inadequate instructions or warnings are predicated on a different concept of responsibility. In the first place, such defects cannot be determined by reference to the manufacturer's own design or marketing standards because those standards are the very ones that plaintiffs attack as unreasonable. Some sort of independent assessment of advantages and disadvantages, to which some attach the label "risk-utility balancing," is necessary. Products are not generically defective merely because they are dangerous. Many product-related accident costs can be eliminated only by excessively sacrificing product features that make products useful and desirable. Thus, the various trade-offs need to be considered in determining whether accident costs are more fairly and efficiently borne by accident victims, on the one hand, or, on the other hand, by consumers generally through the mechanism of higher product prices attributable to liability costs imposed by courts on product sellers.

Subsections (b) and (c), which impose liability for products that are defectively designed or sold without adequate warnings or instructions and are thus not reasonably safe, achieve the same general objectives as does liability predicated on negligence. The emphasis is on creating incentives for manufacturers to achieve optimal levels of safety in designing and marketing products. Society does not benefit from products that are excessively safe—for example, automobiles designed with maximum speeds of 20 miles per hour—any more than it benefits from products that are too risky. Society benefits most when the right, or optimal, amount of product safety is achieved. From a fairness perspective, requiring individual users and consumers to bear appropriate responsibility for proper product use prevents careless users and consumers from being subsidized by more careful users and consumers, when the former are paid damages out of funds to which the latter are forced to contribute through higher product prices.

In general, the rationale for imposing strict liability on manufacturers for harm caused by manufacturing defects does not apply in the context of imposing liability for defective design and defects based on inadequate instruction or warning. Consumer expectations as to proper product design or warning are typically more difficult to discern than in the case of a manufacturing defect. Moreover, the element of deliberation in setting appropriate levels of design safety is not directly analogous to the setting of levels of quality control by the manufacturer. When a manufacturer sets its quality control at a certain level, it is aware that a given number of products may leave the assembly line in a defective condition and cause injury to innocent victims who can generally do nothing to avoid injury. The implications of deliberately drawing lines with respect to product design safety are different. A reasonably designed product still carries with it elements of risk that must be protected against by the user or consumer since some risks cannot be designed out of the product at reasonable cost.

Most courts agree that, for the liability system to be fair and efficient, the balancing of risks and benefits in judging product design and marketing must be done in light of the knowledge of risks and risk-avoidance techniques reasonably attainable at the time of distribution. To hold a manufacturer liable for a risk that was not foreseeable when the product was marketed might foster increased manufacturer investment in safety. But such investment by definition would be a matter of guesswork. Furthermore, manufacturers may persuasively ask to be judged by a normative behavior standard to which it is reasonably possible for manufacturers to conform. For these reasons, Subsections (b) and (c) speak of products being defective only when risks are reasonably foreseeable.

b. The nonexclusiveness of the definitions of defect in this Section. When a plaintiff seeks recovery under the general rule of liability in § 1, in most instances the plaintiff must establish a prima facie case of product defect by satisfying the requirements of § 2. Section 2 is not, however, the exclusive means by which the plaintiff may establish liability in a products case based on the general rule in § 1. Some courts, for example, while recognizing that in most cases involving defective design the plaintiff must prove the availability of a reasonable alternative design, also observe that such proof is not necessary in every case involving design defects. Sections 3 and 4 and Comment *e* to § 2 provide approaches to the establishment of defective design other than that provided in § 2(b).

Section 3 provides that when circumstantial evidence supports the conclusion that a defect was a contributing cause of the harm and that the defect existed at the time of sale, it is unnecessary to identify the specific nature of the defect and meet the requisites of § 2. Section 3 frees the plaintiff from the strictures of § 2 in circumstances in which common experience teaches that an inference of defect may be warranted under the specific facts, including the failure of the product to perform its manifestly intended function. When the defect established under § 3 may involve product design, some courts recognize consumer expectations as an adequate test for defect, in apparent conflict with the reasonable alternative design requirement in § 2(b). But when the claims involve a product's failure to perform its manifestly intended function and the other requisites of § 3 are met, the apparent conflict disappears.

Section 4, dealing with violations of statutory and regulatory norms, also provides an alternate method of establishing defect. A plaintiff is not required to establish the standard for design or warning under § 2, but merely to identify a government-imposed standard.

Comment *e* provides a further qualification of the rule in § 2(b). This Restatement recognizes the possibility that product sellers may be subject to liability even absent a reasonable alternative design when the product design is manifestly unreasonable. When § 2(b) is read in conjunction with these other provisions that allow for other avenues for determining defective design, it reflects the substantial body of case law suggesting that reasonable alternative design is the predominant, yet not exclusive, method for establishing defective design.

c. Manufacturing defects. As stated in Subsection (a), a manufacturing defect is a departure from a product unit's design specifications. More distinctly than any other type of defect, manufacturing defects disappoint consumer expectations. Common examples of manufacturing defects are products that are physically flawed, damaged, or incorrectly assembled. In actions against the manufacturer, under prevailing rules concerning allocation of burdens of proof the plaintiff ordinarily bears the burden of establishing that such a defect existed in the product when it left the hands of the manufacturer.

Occasionally a defect may arise after manufacture, for example, during shipment or while in storage. Since the product, as sold to the consumer, has a defect that is a departure from the product unit's design specifications, a commercial seller or distributor down the chain of distribution is liable as if the product were defectively manufactured. As long as the plaintiff establishes that the product was defective when it left the hands of a given seller in the distributive chain, liability will attach to that seller. Such defects are referred to in this Restatement as "manufacturing defects" even when they occur after manufacture. When the manufacturer delegates some aspect of manufacture, such as final assembly or inspection, to a subsequent seller, the manufacturer may be subject to liability under rules of vicarious liability for a defect that was introduced into the product after it left the hands of the manufacturer. Although Subsection (a) calls for liability without fault, a plaintiff may seek to recover based upon allegations and proof of negligent manufacture. See Comment *n*. For the rule governing food products that contain impurities or foreign matter, see § 7. For the rule governing commercial used-product sellers' liability for harm caused by manufacturing defects, see § 8.

Illustrations:

1. Jack purchased a bottle of champagne from the BBB Liquor Mart. The champagne was bottled by AAA Inc., utilizing bottles manufactured by CCC Glass Co. While Jack was opening the bottle it suddenly exploded, causing disfiguring cuts to his face. The trier of fact determines that, originating with CCC, the bottle contained a manufacturing defect and that the defect caused the bottle to explode. AAA, BBB, and CCC are subject to liability even though they exercised reasonable care in the prepa-

ration and distribution of the defective bottle of AAA Champagne. The weakness in the glass structure in the bottle that caused Jack's harm was a departure from the product's intended design, subjecting each of the sellers in the distributive chain to strict liability for selling a defective product.

2. The same facts as Illustration 1, except that the trier of fact determines that the manufacturing defect in the bottle resulted from customer abuse of the bottle while it was on display at the BBB Liquor Mart prior to sale to Jack. BBB is subject to liability for selling a defective bottle of champagne to Jack even though it exercised reasonable care in its marketing of the champagne. Neither CCC nor AAA is subject to liability if the trier of fact determines that the bottle was not defective when it left CCC's or AAA's control.

d. Design defects: general considerations. Whereas a manufacturing defect consists of a product unit's failure to meet the manufacturer's design specifications, a product asserted to have a defective design meets the manufacturer's design specifications but raises the question whether the specifications themselves create unreasonable risks. Answering that question requires reference to a standard outside the specifications. Subsection (b) adopts a reasonableness ("risk-utility balancing") test as the standard for judging the defectiveness of product designs. More specifically, the test is whether a reasonable alternative design would, at reasonable cost, have reduced the foreseeable risks of harm posed by the product and, if so, whether the omission of the alternative design by the seller or a predecessor in the distributive chain rendered the product not reasonably safe. (This is the primary, but not the exclusive, test for defective design. See Comment *b.*) Under prevailing rules concerning allocation of burden of proof, the plaintiff must prove that such a reasonable alternative was, or reasonably could have been, available at time of sale or distribution. See Comment *f.*

Assessment of a product design in most instances requires a comparison between an alternative design and the product design that caused the injury, undertaken from the viewpoint of a reasonable person. That approach is also used in administering the traditional reasonableness standard in negligence. See Restatement, Second, Torts § 283, Comment *c.* The policy reasons that support use of a reasonable-person perspective in connection with the general negligence standard also support its use in the products liability context.

How the defendant's design compares with other, competing designs in actual use is relevant to the issue of whether the defendant's design is defective. Defendants often seek to defend their product designs on the ground that the designs conform to the "state of the art." The term "state of the art" has been variously defined to mean that the product design conforms to industry custom, that it reflects the safest and most advanced technology developed and in commercial use, or that it reflects technology at the cutting edge of scientific knowledge. The confusion brought about by these various definitions is unfortunate. This Section states that a design is defective if the product could have been made safer by the adoption of a reasonable alternative design. If such a design could have been practically adopted at time of sale and if the omission of such a design rendered the product not reasonably safe, the plaintiff establishes defect under Subsection (b). When a defendant demonstrates that its product design was the safest in use at the time of sale, it may be difficult for the plaintiff to prove that an alternative design could have been practically adopted. The defendant is thus allowed to introduce evidence with regard to industry practice that bears on whether an alternative design was practicable. Industry practice may also be relevant to whether the omission of an alternative design rendered the product not reasonably safe. While such evidence is admissible, it is not necessarily dispositive. If the plaintiff introduces expert testimony to establish that a reasonable alternative design could practically have been adopted, a trier of fact may conclude that the product was defective notwithstanding that such a design was not adopted by any manufacturer, or even considered for commercial use, at the time of sale.

Early in the development of products liability law, courts held that a claim based on design defect could not be sustained if the dangers presented by the product were open and obvious. Subsection (b) does not recognize the obviousness of a design-related risk as precluding a finding of defectiveness. The fact that a danger is open and obvious is relevant to the issue of defectiveness, but does not necessarily preclude a plaintiff from establishing that a reasonable alternative design should have been adopted that would have reduced or prevented injury to the plaintiff.

The requirement in Subsection (b) that the plaintiff show a reasonable alternative design applies in most instances even though the plaintiff alleges that the category of product sold by the defendant is so dangerous that it should not have been marketed at all. See Comment *e*. Common and widely distributed products such as alcoholic beverages, firearms, and above-ground swimming pools may be found to be defective only upon proof of the requisite conditions in Subsection (a), (b), or (c). If such products are defectively manufactured or sold without reasonable warnings as to their danger when such warnings are appropriate, or if reasonable alternative designs could have been adopted, then liability under §§ 1 and 2 may attach. Absent proof of defect under those Sections, however, courts have not imposed liability for categories of products that are generally available and widely used and consumed, even if they pose substantial risks of harm. Instead, courts generally have concluded that legislatures and administrative agencies can, more appropriately than courts, consider the desirability of commercial distribution of some categories of widely used and consumed, but nevertheless dangerous, products.

Illustrations:

3. ABC Co. manufactured and sold a high-speed printing press to XYZ Printers, by whom Robert is employed. The press includes a circular plate cylinder that spins at a very high speed. On occasion, a foreign object, known in the trade as a "hickie," finds its way onto the plate of the unit, causing a blemish or imperfection on the printed page. To remove a hickie, it is customary practice for an employee to apply a piece of plastic to the printing plate while it is spinning. Robert performed this practice, known as "chasing the hickie," and while doing so suffered serious injuries to his hand. All employees, including Robert, knew that chasing the hickie was a dangerous procedure. Plaintiff's expert testifies that a safety-guard at the point of operation, which could have prevented Robert's injury, was both technologically and economically feasible and is utilized in similar machinery without causing difficulty. The fact that the danger is open and obvious does not bar the design claim against ABC.

4. XYZ Co. manufactures above-ground swimming pools that are four feet deep. Warnings are embossed on the outside of the pools in large letters stating "DANGER—DO NOT DIVE—SHALLOW WATER." In disregard of the warnings, Mary, age 21, dove head first into an XYZ pool and suffered serious injury. Expert testimony establishes that when Mary's outstretched hands hit the pool's slippery vinyl bottom her hands slid apart, causing her to strike her head against the bottom of the pool. For the purposes of this Illustration it is assumed that the warnings were adequate and that the only issue is whether the above-ground pool was defectively designed because the bottom was too slippery. All the expert witnesses agree that the vinyl pool liner that XYZ utilized was the best and safest liner available and that no alternative, less slippery liner was feasible. Mary has failed to establish defective design under Subsection (b).

e. Design defects: possibility of manifestly unreasonable design. Several courts have suggested that the designs of some products are so manifestly unreasonable, in that they have low social utility and high degree of danger, that liability should attach even absent proof of a reasonable alternative design. In large part the problem is one of how the range of relevant alternative designs is described. For example, a toy gun that shoots hard rubber pellets with sufficient velocity to cause injury to children could be found to be defectively designed within the rule of Subsection (b). Toy guns unlikely to cause injury would constitute reasonable alternatives to the dangerous toy. Thus, toy guns that project ping-pong balls, soft gelatin pellets, or water might be found to be reasonable alternative designs to a toy gun that shoots hard pellets. However, if the realism of the hard-pellet gun, and thus its capacity to cause injury, is sufficiently important to those who purchase and use such products to justify the court's limiting consideration to toy guns that achieve realism by shooting hard pellets, then no reasonable alternative will, by hypothesis, be available. In that instance, the design feature that defines which alternatives are relevant—the realism of the hard-pellet gun and thus its capacity to injure—is precisely the feature on which the user places value and of which the plaintiff complains. If a court were to adopt this characterization of the product, and deem the capacity to cause injury an egregiously unacceptable quality in a toy for use by children, it could conclude that liability should attach without proof of a reasonable alternative design. The court would declare the product design to be defective and not reasonably safe because the extremely high degree of danger posed by its use or consumption so substantially outweighs its negligible social utility that no rational, reasonable person, fully aware of the relevant facts, would choose to use, or to allow children to use, the product.

Illustration:

5. ABC Co. manufactures novelty items. One item, an exploding cigar, is made to explode with a loud bang and the emission of smoke. Robert purchased the exploding cigar and presented it to his boss, Jack, at a birthday party arranged for him at the office. Jack lit the cigar. When it exploded, the heat from the explosion lit Jack's beard on fire causing serious burns to his face. If a court were to recognize the rule identified in this Comment, the finder of fact might find ABC liable for the defective design of the exploding cigar even if no reasonable alternative design was available that would provide similar prank characteristics. The utility of the exploding cigar is so low and the risk of injury is so high as to warrant a conclusion that the cigar is defective and should not have been marketed at all.

f. Design defects: factors relevant in determining whether the omission of a reasonable alternative design renders a product not reasonably safe. Subsection (b) states that a product is defective in design if the omission of a reasonable alternative design renders the product not reasonably safe. A broad range of factors may be considered in determining whether an alternative design is reasonable and whether its omission renders a product not reasonably safe. The factors include, among others, the magnitude and probability of the foreseeable risks of harm, the instructions and warnings accompanying the product, and the nature and strength of consumer expectations regarding the product, including expectations arising from product portrayal and marketing. See Comment *g*. The relative advantages and disadvantages of the product as designed and as it alternatively could have been designed may also be considered. Thus, the likely effects of the alternative design on production costs; the effects of the alternative design on product longevity, maintenance, repair, and esthetics; and the range of consumer choice among products are factors that may be taken into account. A plaintiff is not necessarily required to introduce proof on all of these factors; their relevance, and the relevance of other factors, will vary from case to case. Moreover, the factors interact with one another. For example, evidence of the magnitude and probability of foreseeable harm may be offset by evidence that the proposed alternative design would reduce the efficiency and the utility of the product. On the other hand, evidence that a proposed alternative design would increase production costs may be offset by evidence that product portrayal and marketing created substantial expectations of performance or safety, thus increasing the probability of foreseeable harm. Depending on the mix of these factors, a number of variations in the design of a given product may meet the test in Subsection (b). On the other hand, it is not a factor under Subsection (b) that the imposition of liability would have a negative effect on corporate earnings or would reduce employment in a given industry.

When evaluating the reasonableness of a design alternative, the overall safety of the product must be considered. It is not sufficient that the alternative design would have reduced or prevented the harm suffered by the plaintiff if it would also have introduced into the product other dangers of equal or greater magnitude.

While a plaintiff must prove that a reasonable alternative design would have reduced the foreseeable risks of harm, Subsection (b) does not require the plaintiff to produce expert testimony in every case. Cases arise in which the feasibility of a reasonable alternative design is obvious and understandable to laypersons and therefore expert testimony is unnecessary to support a finding that the product should have been designed differently and more safely. For example, when a manufacturer sells a soft stuffed toy with hard plastic buttons that are easily removable and likely to choke and suffocate a small child who foreseeably attempts to swallow them, the plaintiff should be able to reach the trier of fact with a claim that buttons on such a toy should be an integral part of the toy's fabric itself (or otherwise be unremovable by an infant) without hiring an expert to demonstrate the feasibility of an alternative safer design. Furthermore, other products already available on the market may serve the same or very similar function at lower risk and at comparable cost. Such products may serve as reasonable alternatives to the product in question.

In many cases, the plaintiff must rely on expert testimony. Subsection (b) does not, however, require the plaintiff to produce a prototype in order to make out a prima facie case. Thus, qualified expert testimony on the issue suffices, even though the expert has produced no prototype, if it reasonably supports the conclusion that a reasonable alternative design could have been practically adopted at the time of sale.

The requirements in Subsection (b) relate to what the plaintiff must prove in order to prevail at trial. This Restatement takes no position regarding the requirements of local law concerning the adequacy of pleadings or pretrial demonstrations of genuine issues of fact. It does, however, assume that the plaintiff will have the opportunity to conduct reasonable discovery so as to ascertain whether an alternative design is practical.

A test that considers such a broad range of factors in deciding whether the omission of an alternative design renders a product not reasonably safe requires a fair allocation of proof between the parties. To establish a prima facie case of defect, the plaintiff must prove the availability of a technologically feasible and practical alternative design that would have reduced or prevented the plaintiff's harm. Given inherent limitations on access to relevant data, the plaintiff is not required to establish with particularity the costs and benefits associated with adoption of the suggested alternative design.

In sum, the requirement of Subsection (b) that a product is defective in design if the foreseeable risks of harm could have been reduced by a reasonable alternative design is based on the commonsense notion that liability for harm caused by product designs should attach only when harm is reasonably preventable. For justice to be achieved, Subsection (b) should not be construed to create artificial and unreasonable barriers to recovery.

The necessity of proving a reasonable alternative design as a predicate for establishing design defect is, like any factual element in a case, addressed initially to the courts. Sufficient evidence must be presented so that reasonable persons could conclude that a reasonable alternative could have been practically adopted. Assuming that a court concludes that sufficient evidence on this issue has been presented, the issue is then for the trier of fact. This Restatement takes no position regarding the specifics of how a jury should be instructed. So long as jury instructions are generally consistent with the rule of law set forth in Subsection (b), their specific form and content are matters of local law.

Illustrations:

6. Andrea, age four, suffered serious burns when she got out of bed one night to go to the bathroom and tripped on the electric cord connected to a hot-water vaporizer. When Andrea tripped on the cord, the vaporizer separated into its three component parts—a large, wide-mouthed glass jar, a metal pan, and a plastic top-heating unit. The plastic top-heating unit was not secured to the jar. When it came off, the hot water in the jar poured out, causing Andrea's burns. In an action alleging defective design of the vaporizer for not securing the top unit to the jar, the following factors are relevant: (1) the foreseeability that the vaporizer might be accidentally tipped over; (2) the overall safety provided by an alternative design that secures the heating unit to the receptacle holding the water; (3) consumer knowledge or lack thereof that the water in the glass jar is scalding hot; (4) the added cost of the safer alternative design; and (5) the relative convenience of a vaporizer with a lift-off cap. If Andrea offers expert testimony based on a reasonable analysis of these factors and such testimony is sufficient to allow reasonable persons to conclude that the omission of the alternative design renders the product not reasonably safe, the question of defectiveness is for the trier of fact. Whether instructions to the trier of fact should include specific reference to these factors is beyond the scope of this Restatement and should be determined under local law.

7. The same facts as Illustration 6, except that the safety feature that will secure the top-heating unit to the jar and prevent the water from spilling is a component that will add $5 to the cost of the vaporizer. Although the increase in cost to consumers is a relevant consideration, the impact of a finding of defectiveness on the general economy or on the profitability of the vaporizer manufacturer is not a factor to be considered in deciding whether the alternative safer design is reasonable.

8. XYZ Corp. designs and markets a new television antenna for home use that utilizes the electrical system in the buyer's home as the main signal receptor. The new antenna improves reception compared with traditional television antennas, but also

introduces significant risks of electrical shock and electrocution. XYZ markets the new antenna with warnings about these risks, and emphasizes the benefits of improved reception to be derived from using the electrical wiring system. Fred buys one of the new antennas and installs it in his home. Two months later Fred suffers serious electrical burns while changing channels on his television set. Fred brings an action against XYZ, claiming that the design of the new television antenna is defective. At trial, Fred relies on the availability of traditional television antennas that are not connected with electrical systems to show that reasonable alternative designs could have been adopted by the manufacturer.

In connection with proving that the defendant's design is defective under Subsection (b), Fred is not confined to offering variations of television antennas that rely on electrical wiring systems. The feature of XYZ's design that presents the risk of electrocution—incorporating pre-existing electrical wiring systems—is merely a means of achieving the objective of improved television reception. That feature does not, in itself, provide consumers with intrinsic benefits other than its effects on reception. Merely because the defendant chooses to emphasize that feature in its marketing does not prevent the plaintiff from proving that the increases in risk generated by that feature more than outweigh any increases in reception when compared with traditional antenna systems.

9. John was driving a compact automobile manufactured by the ABC Auto Company when he lost control and collided with a tree. John suffered serious injuries. John brings a products-liability claim against ABC, arguing that the design of his car is defective in that it does not offer the same level of crashworthiness as does a full-size automobile. John's experts admit that reducing the size of an automobile unavoidably increases the risk of injuries to occupants in collisions. John can identify no specific feature of the ABC automobile that could have been designed differently so as to be safer without increasing its size and substantially reducing its desirable characteristics of lower cost and lower fuel economy. John has not established a defect within the meaning of Subsection (b). Although ABC's design is less safe than larger vehicles, the only way to make it safer, on John's own proof, is to make it larger, and the costs of doing that are unacceptably great. Moreover, eliminating smaller automobiles from the market would unduly restrict the range of consumer choice among automobile designs. Thus, the ABC design is not, by reason of its being smaller than other automobiles, "not reason-

ably safe." Given that the risks and benefits associated with relative automobile size are generally known, decisions regarding which sizes to purchase and use should be left to purchasers and users in the market.

10. ABC Armour Co. manufactures bullet-proof vests for use by police and security personnel. ABC offers several models, some providing front and back protection only, and others providing wrap-around protection. State A highway patrol officials chose to purchase the model that provides front and back protection only. They did so because that model is less expensive, allows greater flexibility of movement, and is more comfortable. Robert, a state trooper, was shot and killed while making a routine traffic arrest. The bullet entered the side of his body, where the vest did not provide protection. Robert's legal representative argues that the design of the vest is defective because it does not provide wrap-around coverage. Robert has not established a defect within the meaning of Subsection (b). The mere fact of the availability of a wrap-around vest does not render defective the vest that provides only front-and-back protection. Although the wrap-around design is somewhat safer, it is also more costly to buy and use. Moreover, the differences in advantages and disadvantages are sufficiently understood by consumers that omission of the wrap-around feature does not render the front-and-back design not reasonably safe. To subject sellers to liability based on that design would unduly restrict the range of consumer choice among products.

g. Consumer expectations: general considerations. Under Subsection (b), consumer expectations do not constitute an independent standard for judging the defectiveness of product designs. Courts frequently rely, in part, on consumer expectations when discussing liability based on other theories of liability. Some courts, for example, use the term "reasonable consumer expectations" as an equivalent of "proof of a reasonable, safer design alternative," since reasonable consumers have a right to expect product designs that conform to the reasonableness standard in Subsection (b). Other courts, allowing an inference of defect to be drawn when the incident is of a kind that ordinarily would occur as a result of product defect, observe that products that fail when put to their manifestly intended use disappoint reasonable consumer expectations. See § 3. However, consumer expectations do not play a determinative role in determining defectiveness. See Comment *h.* Consumer expectations, standing alone, do not take into account whether the proposed alternative design could be implemented at reasonable cost, or whether an alternative design would provide greater overall safety. Nevertheless, consumer expectations about product performance and the dangers attendant to product use affect how risks are perceived and relate to foreseeability and frequency of the risks of harm, both of which are relevant under Subsection (b). See Comment *f*. Such expectations are often influenced by how products are portrayed and marketed and can have a significant impact on consumer behavior. Thus, although consumer expectations do not constitute an independent standard for judging the defectiveness of product designs, they may substantially influence or even be ultimately determinative on risk-utility balancing in judging whether the omission of a proposed alternative design renders the product not reasonably safe.

Subsection (b) likewise rejects conformance to consumer expectations as a defense. The mere fact that a risk presented by a product design is open and obvious, or generally known, and that the product thus satisfies expectations, does not prevent a finding that the design is defective. But the fact that a product design meets consumer expectations may substantially influence or even be ultimately determinative on risk-utility balancing in judging whether the omission of a proposed alternative design renders the product not reasonably safe. It follows that, while disappointment of consumer expectations may not serve as an independent basis for allowing recovery under Subsection (b), neither may conformance with consumer expectations serve as an independent basis for denying recovery. Such expectations may be relevant in both contexts, but in neither are they controlling.

h. Consumer expectations: food products and used products. With regard to two special product categories consumer expectations play a special role in determining product defect. See § 7 (food products) and § 8 (used products). On occasion it is difficult to determine whether a given food component is an inherent aspect of a product or constitutes an adulteration of the product. Whether, for example, a fish bone in commercially distributed fish chowder constitutes a manufacturing defect within the meaning of § 2(a) is best determined by focusing on reasonable consumer expectations.

Regarding commercially distributed used products, the rules set forth in § 2 are not adequate to the task of determining liability. Variations in the type and condition of used products are such that the stringent rules for imposition of liability for new products are inappropriate. On occasion the seller of a used product may market the product in a manner that would cause a reasonable person in the position of the buyer to expect the used product to present no greater risk of defect than if it were new; or a used product may be remanufactured, justifying heightened seller's responsibility. In these limited settings it is appropriate to treat the sale under rules similar to those applicable to new products. See §§ 8(b) and 8(c).

i. Inadequate instructions or warnings. Commercial product sellers must provide reasonable instructions and warnings about risks of injury posed by products. Instructions inform persons how to use and consume products safely. Warnings alert users and consumers to the existence and nature of product risks so that they can prevent harm either by appropriate conduct during use or consumption or by choosing not to use or consume. In most instances the instructions and warnings will originate with the manufacturer, but sellers down the chain of distribution must warn when doing so is feasible and reasonably necessary. In any event, sellers down the chain are liable if the instructions and warnings provided by predecessors in the chain are inadequate. See Comment *o*. Under prevailing rules concerning allocation of burdens of proof, plaintiff must prove that adequate instructions or warnings were not provided. Subsection (c) adopts a reasonableness test for judging the adequacy of product instructions and warnings. It thus parallels Subsection (b), which adopts a similar standard for judging the safety of product designs. Although the liability standard is formulated in essentially identical terms in Subsections (b) and (c), the defectiveness concept is more difficult to apply in the warnings context. In evaluating the adequacy of product warnings and instructions, courts must be sensitive to many factors. It is impossible to identify anything approaching a perfect level of detail that should be communicated in product disclosures. For example, educated or experienced product users and consumers may benefit from inclusion of more information about the full spectrum of product risks, whereas less-educated or unskilled users may benefit from more concise warnings and instructions stressing only the most crucial risks and safe-handling practices. In some contexts, products intended for special categories of users, such as children, may require more vivid and unambiguous warnings. In some cases, excessive detail may detract from the ability of typical users and consumers to focus on the important aspects of the warnings, whereas in others reasonably full disclosure will be necessary to enable informed, efficient choices by product users. Product warnings and instructions can rarely communicate all potentially relevant information, and the ability of a plaintiff to imagine a hypothetical better warning in the aftermath of an accident does not establish that the warning actually accompanying the product was inadequate. No easy guideline exists for courts to adopt in assessing the adequacy of product warnings and instructions. In making their assessments, courts must focus on various factors, such as content and comprehensibility, intensity of expression, and the characteristics of expected user groups.

Depending on the circumstances, Subsection (c) may require that instructions and warnings be given not only to purchasers, users, and consumers, but also to others who a reasonable seller should know will be in a position to reduce or avoid the risk of harm. There is no general rule as to whether one supplying a product for the use of others through an intermediary has a duty to warn the ultimate product user directly or may rely on the intermediary to relay warnings. The standard is one of reasonableness in the circumstances. Among the factors to be considered are the gravity of the risks posed by the product, the likelihood that the intermediary will convey the information to the ultimate user, and the feasibility and effectiveness of giving a warning directly to the user. Thus, when the purchaser of machinery is the owner of a workplace who provides the machinery to employees for their use, and there is reason to doubt that the employer will pass warnings on to employees, the seller is required to reach the employees directly with necessary instructions and warnings if doing so is reasonably feasible.

In addition to alerting users and consumers to the existence and nature of product risks so that they can, by appropriate conduct during use or consumption, reduce the risk of harm, warnings also may be needed to inform users and consumers of nonobvious and not generally known risks that unavoidably inhere in using or consuming the product. Such warnings allow the user or consumer to avoid the risk warned against by making an informed decision not to purchase or use the product at all and hence not to encounter the risk. In this context, warnings must be provided for inherent risks that reasonably foreseeable product users and consumers would reasonably deem material or significant in deciding whether to use or consume the product. Whether or not many persons would, when warned, nonetheless decide to use or consume the product, warnings are required to protect the interests of those reasonably foreseeable users or consumers who would, based on their own reasonable assessments of the risks and benefits, decline product use or consumption. When such warnings are necessary, their omission renders the product not reasonably safe at time of sale. Notwithstanding the defective condition of the product in the absence of adequate warnings, if a particular user or consumer would have decided to use or consume even if warned, the lack of warnings is not a legal cause of that plaintiff's harm. Judicial decisions supporting the duty to provide warnings for informed decisionmaking have arisen almost exclusively with regard to those toxic agents and pharmaceutical products with respect to which courts have recognized a distinctive need to provide risk information so that recipients of the information can decide whether they wish to purchase or utilize the product. See § 6, Comment *d.*

Illustration:

11. ABC Adhesives Inc. manufactures a chemical adhesive for home use. Sandra purchased a gallon for use in laying tile in her kitchen. The label on the container warned in large letters that fumes from the adhesive were flammable and toxic, that the product should be used with adequate ventilation, and that all sources of fire should be extinguished. Sandra opened the windows in her kitchen, but did not extinguish the pilot light in her gas stove. When she had partly completed laying the tile, the pilot light suddenly ignited the fumes from the adhesive, causing Sandra serious burns. In an action against ABC, Sandra contends that the warnings were inadequate in failing specifically to state that gas-stove pilot lights should be extinguished. Whether the warning actually given was reasonable in the circumstances is to be decided by the trier of fact.

j. Warnings: obvious and generally known risks. In general, a product seller is not subject to liability for failing to warn or instruct regarding risks and risk-avoidance measures that should be obvious to, or generally known by, foreseeable product users. When a risk is obvious or generally known, the prospective addressee of a warning will or should already know of its existence. Warning of an obvious or generally known risk in most instances will not provide an effective additional measure of safety. Furthermore, warnings that deal with obvious or generally known risks may be ignored by users and consumers and may diminish the significance of warnings about non-obvious, not-generally-known risks. Thus, requiring warnings of obvious or generally known risks could reduce the efficacy of warnings generally. When reasonable minds may differ as to whether the risk was obvious or generally known, the issue is to be decided by the trier of fact. The obviousness of risk may bear on the issue of design defect rather than failure to warn. See Comments *d* and *g*.

Illustration:

12. XYZ Ladder Co. manufactures kitchen step ladders for home use. Sid used an XYZ ladder to post a sign above the door of his home office, unaware that his five-year-old son was playing in the office. While Sid was standing on the ladder, his son suddenly opened the door, which struck the ladder. Sid fell off the ladder and suffered a fractured hip. There were no warnings on the ladder, nor in the instruction booklet that came with it, not to use the ladder in front of an unlocked door. The danger should be obvious to foreseeable product users. No reasonable trier of fact would find XYZ liable for failing to warn about it and the court should rule for XYZ as a matter of law.

k. Warnings: adverse allergic or idiosyncratic reactions. Cases of adverse allergic or idiosyncratic reactions involve a special subset of products that may be defective because of inadequate warnings. Many of these cases involve nonprescription drugs and cosmetics. However, virtually any tangible product can contain an ingredient to which some persons may be allergic. Thus, food, nonprescription drugs, toiletries, paint, solvents, building materials, clothing, and furniture have all been involved in litigation to which this Comment is relevant. Prescription drugs and medical devices are also capable of causing allergic reactions, but they are governed by § 6.

The general rule in cases involving allergic reactions is that a warning is required when the harm-causing ingredient is one to which a substantial number of persons are allergic. The degree of substantiality is not precisely quantifiable. Clearly the plaintiff in most cases must show that the allergic predisposition is not unique to the plaintiff. In determining whether the plaintiff has carried the burden in this regard, however, the court may properly consider the severity of the plaintiff's harm. The more severe the harm, the more justified is a conclusion that the number of persons at risk need not be large to be considered "substantial" so as to require a warning. Essentially, this reflects the same risk-utility balancing undertaken in warnings cases generally. But courts explicitly impose the requirement of substantiality in cases involving adverse allergic reactions.

The ingredient that causes the allergic reaction must be one whose danger or whose presence in the product is not generally known to consumers. When both the presence of an allergenic ingredient in the product and the risks presented by such ingredient are widely known, instructions and warnings about that danger are unnecessary. When the presence of the allergenic ingredient would not be anticipated by a reasonable user or consumer, warnings concerning its presence are required. Similarly, when the presence of the ingredient is generally known to consumers, but its dangers are not, a warning of the dangers must be given.

Finally, as required in Subsection (c), warnings concerning risks of allergic reactions that are not reasonably foreseeable at the time of sale need not be provided. See Comment *m*.

Illustration:

13. XYZ produces an over-the-counter nonprescription medicine containing aspirin, a well-known allergen to which a substantial minority of persons are sensitive. XYZ may reasonably assume that those who are allergic to aspirin are aware of their allergy or that, if they are not aware, warnings of possible allergic

reactions would not be heeded. Thus, it is necessary to warn only of the fact that the medicine contains aspirin.

l. Relationship between design and instruction or warning. Reasonable designs and instructions or warnings both play important roles in the production and distribution of reasonably safe products. In general, when a safer design can reasonably be implemented and risks can reasonably be designed out of a product, adoption of the safer design is required over a warning that leaves a significant residuum of such risks. For example, instructions and warnings may be ineffective because users of the product may not be adequately reached, may be likely to be inattentive, or may be insufficiently motivated to follow the instructions or heed the warnings. However, when an alternative design to avoid risks cannot reasonably be implemented, adequate instructions and warnings will normally be sufficient to render the product reasonably safe. Compare Comment *e*. Warnings are not, however, a substitute for the provision of a reasonably safe design.

The fact that a risk is obvious or generally known often serves the same function as a warning. See Comment *j*. However, obviousness of risk does not necessarily obviate a duty to provide a safer design. Just as warnings may be ignored, so may obvious or generally known risks be ignored, leaving a residuum of risk great enough to require adopting a safer design. See Comment *d*.

Illustration:

14. Jeremy's foot was severed when caught between the blade and compaction chamber of a garbage truck on which he was working. The injury occurred when he lost his balance while jumping on the back step of the garbage truck as it was moving from one stop to the next. The garbage truck, manufactured by XYZ Motor Co., has a warning in large red letters on both the left and right rear panels that reads "DANGER—DO NOT INSERT ANY OBJECT WHILE COMPACTION CHAMBER IS WORKING—KEEP HANDS AND FEET AWAY." The fact that adequate warning was given does not preclude Jeremy from seeking to establish a design defect under Subsection (b). The possibility that an employee might lose his balance and thus encounter the shear point was a risk that a warning could not eliminate and that might require a safety guard. Whether a design defect can be established is governed by Subsection (b).

m. Reasonably foreseeable uses and risks in design and warning claims. Subsections (b) and (c) impose liability only when the product is put to uses that it is reasonable to expect a seller or distributor to foresee. Product sellers and distributors are not required to foresee and take precautions against every conceivable mode of use and abuse to which their products might be put. Increasing the costs of designing and marketing products in order to avoid the consequences of unreasonable modes of use is not required.

In cases involving a claim of design defect in a mechanical product, foreseeability of risk is rarely an issue as a practical matter. Once the plaintiff establishes that the product was put to a reasonably foreseeable use, physical risks of injury are generally known or reasonably knowable by experts in the field. It is not unfair to charge a manufacturer with knowledge of such generally known or knowable risks.

The issue of foreseeability of risk of harm is more complex in the case of products such as prescription drugs, medical devices, and toxic chemicals. Risks attendant to use and consumption of these products may, indeed, be unforeseeable at the time of sale. Unforeseeable risks arising from foreseeable product use or consumption by definition cannot specifically be warned against. Thus, in connection with a claim of inadequate design, instruction, or warning, plaintiff should bear the burden of establishing that the risk in question was known or should have been known to the relevant manufacturing community. The harms that result from unforeseeable risks—for example, in the human body's reaction to a new drug, medical device, or chemical—are not a basis of liability. Of course, a seller bears responsibility to perform reasonable testing prior to marketing a product and to discover risks and risk-avoidance measures that such testing would reveal. A seller is charged with knowledge of what reasonable testing would reveal. If testing is not undertaken, or is performed in an inadequate manner, and this failure results in a defect that causes harm, the seller is subject to liability for harm caused by such defect.

Illustration:

15. ABC Adhesives Inc. manufactures a chemical adhesive for use in laying ceramic tile. Recently it has become known that prolonged use of its ceramic adhesive over many years by diabetics can cause severe aggravation of the diabetic condition. Diabetics who have been using the ABC adhesive and have suffered serious aggravation of their condition bring an action against ABC for failing to warn about the risks of prolonged product use. However, it cannot be established that, at the time ABC's product was distributed, special risks to diabetics were reasonably foreseeable or that reasonable testing of the product would have led to the discovery of the risks. ABC is not liable since the risks attendant to such product use were not reasonably foreseeable.

n. Relationship of definitions of defect to traditional doctrinal categories. The rules in this Section and in other provisions of this

Chapter define the bases of tort liability for harm caused by product defects existing at time of sale or other distribution. The rules are stated functionally rather than in terms of traditional doctrinal categories. Claims based on product defect at time of sale or other distribution must meet the requisites set forth in Subsection (a), (b), or (c), or the other provisions in this Chapter. As long as these requisites are met, doctrinal tort categories such as negligence or strict liability may be utilized in bringing the claim.

Similarly, a product defect claim satisfying the requisites of Subsection (a), (b), or (c), or other provisions in this Chapter, may be brought under the implied warranty of merchantability provisions of the Uniform Commercial Code. It is recognized that some courts have adopted a consumer expectations definition for design and failure-to-warn defects in implied warranty cases involving harm to persons or property. This Restatement contemplates that a well-coordinated body of law governing liability for harm to persons or property arising out of the sale of defective products requires a consistent definition of defect, and that the definition properly should come from tort law, whether the claim carries a tort label or one of implied warranty of merchantability.

In connection with a claim under §§ 1 and 2 and related provisions of this Restatement, the evidence that the defendant did or did not conduct adequately reasonable research or testing before marketing the product may be admissible (but is not necessarily required) regardless of whether the claim is based on negligence, strict liability, or implied warranty of merchantability. Although a defendant is held objectively responsible for having knowledge that a reasonable seller would have had, the fact that the defendant engaged in substantial research and testing may help to support the contention that a risk was not reasonably foreseeable. Conversely, the fact that the defendant engaged in little or no research or testing may, depending on the circumstances, help to support the contention that, had reasonable research or testing been performed, the risk could have been foreseen. Moreover, as long as the requisites in Subsection (a), (b), or (c), or other provisions in this Chapter, are met, the plaintiff may in appropriate instances—for example, in connection with comparative fault or punitive damage claims—show that the defect resulted from reckless, willfully indifferent, or intentionally wrongful conduct of the defendant.

A separate and more difficult question arises as to whether a case should be submitted to a jury on multiple theories of recovery. Design and failure-to-warn claims may be combined in the same case because they rest on different factual allegations and distinct legal concepts. However, two or more factually identical defective-design claims or two or more factually identical failure-to-warn claims should not be submitted to the trier of fact in the same case under different doctrinal labels. Regardless of the doctrinal label attached to a particular claim, design and warning claims rest on a risk-utility assessment. To allow two or more factually identical risk-utility claims to go to a jury under different labels, whether "strict liability," "negligence," or "implied warranty of merchantability," would generate confusion and may well result in inconsistent verdicts.

In proceedings in which multiple theories are alleged, the Restatement leaves to local law the question of the procedural stage in a tort action at which plaintiff must decide under which theory to pursue the case.

A different approach may be appropriate for claims based on manufacturing defects, since the rule set forth in Subsection (a) does not require risk-utility assessment while a negligence claim does. That is, the two types of manufacturing defect claims are based on different factual predicates. Negligence rests on a showing of fault leading to product defect. Strict liability rests merely on a showing of product defect. When a plaintiff believes a good claim for the negligent creation of (or failure to discover) a manufacturing defect may be established, the plaintiff may assert such a claim in addition to a claim in strict liability under Subsection (a). The plaintiff in such a case should have the opportunity to prove fault and also to assert the right to recover based on strict liability. However, clearly it would be inconsistent for a trier of fact to find no manufacturing defect on a § 2(a) claim and yet return a verdict of liability because the defendant was negligent in having poor quality control. What must be shown under either theory is that the product in question did, in fact, have a manufacturing defect at time of sale that contributed to causing the plaintiff's harm.

In connection with manufacturing defects, a § 2(a) tort claim and an implied warranty of merchantability claim rest on the same factual predicate—the sale by the defendant of a product that departs from the manufacturer's specifications irrespective of anyone's fault. Thus, these two claims are duplicative and may not be pursued together in the same case.

The same analysis applies to claims against a nonmanufacturing supplier. The supplier can be held liable as the seller of a defective product under § 2(a) or can be held liable under a negligence theory for failing reasonably to inspect a product or for negligently introducing a defect into the product. Since these claims are based on different factual predicates, the plaintiff may bring actions in both strict liability and negligence. Again, of course, recovery under either theory requires a finding of defect.

The plaintiff in the nonmanufacturing-supplier case should, once again, not be free to submit a case to a jury based on both the implied warranty of merchantability and strict liability theories since they rest on the same factual base—the sale by the supplier of a defective product regardless of fault. The theories are thus duplicative and do not constitute valid separate claims that may be given to the trier of fact in the same case.

In all instances set forth above in which claims are duplicative, if one or the other theory presents an advantage to the plaintiff—in connection with the statute of limitations, for example—the plaintiff may pursue the more advantageous theory. But the trier of fact may not consider both theories on the same facts.

Plaintiffs may, consistent with the foregoing principles, join claims based on product defect existing at time of sale or other distribution and claims based on theories of recovery that do not rest on a premise of product defect at time of sale. Claims based on misrepresentation, express warranty, and implied warranty of fitness for particular purpose, in particular, are not within the scope of this Chapter and thus are unaffected by it.

Finally, negligence retains its vitality as an independent theory of recovery for a wide range of product-related, harm-causing behavior not involving defects at time of sale. This Restatement includes several such topics in later Chapters, including post-sale failure to warn (see § 10); post-sale failure to recall (see § 11); and a successor's liability for its own failure to warn (see § 13). Other topics are covered in the Restatement, Second, of Torts. Thus, for example, negligent entrustment is treated in § 390. Liability for negligent service, maintenance, or repair, or negligent overpromotion of a product, is governed by the rules set forth in §§ 291 et seq.

Illustrations:

16. A bottle of soda exploded in Bob's hand, causing harm. The soda was manufactured by LMN Bottlers, against whom Bob brings an action in tort. Bob's expert testifies that the bottle contained a manufacturing defect that caused the explosion. The expert also testifies that LMN's quality control efforts are below levels that reasonably prudent bottlers should maintain. Bob may rely on both strict liability and negligence theories.

17. Same facts as Illustration 6, but plaintiff presents no evidence that a reasonable alternative vaporizer design was available at the time of sale that would secure the top heating unit to the glass jar so that water would not escape when the vaporizer tipped over. Plaintiff nonetheless claims that the defendant is

strictly liable because the product design caused her harm. Plaintiff has failed to establish an alternative design as required by Subsection (b). Her claim for recovery under a theory of strict liability thus fails.

18. Ray's automobile overturned while turning a corner, causing Ray to suffer harm. Ray brings an action against the manufacturer, alleging that the automobile was defectively unstable in design and also that the manufacturer should have warned of the automobile's instability in turning. The design and warning claims are independent. Ray may plead and prove either or both as grounds for recovery.

19. Same facts as Illustration 18, except that Ray asserts a claim for defectively unstable design alleged to be the result of negligence and a factually identical claim of defectively unstable design based on strict liability. A court should not allow Ray to submit both claims to the trier of fact.

o. Liability of nonmanufacturing sellers for defective design and defects due to inadequate instructions or warnings. Nonmanufacturing sellers such as wholesalers and retailers often are not in a good position feasibly to adopt safer product designs or better instructions or warnings. Nevertheless, once it is determined that a reasonable alternative design or reasonable instructions or warnings could have been provided at or before the time of sale by a predecessor in the chain of distribution and would have reduced plaintiff's harm, it is no defense that a nonmanufacturing seller of such a product exercised due care. Thus, strict liability is imposed on a wholesale or retail seller who neither knew nor should have known of the relevant risks, nor was in a position to have taken action to avoid them, so long as a predecessor in the chain of distribution could have acted reasonably to avoid the risks. See Comment *a.* For exceptions to the general rule regarding the liability of a nonmanufacturer seller, see § 1, Comment *e.*

p. Misuse, modification, and alteration. Product misuse, modification, and alteration are forms of post-sale conduct by product users or others that can be relevant to the determination of the issues of defect, causation, or comparative responsibility. Whether such conduct affects one or more of the issues depends on the nature of the conduct and whether the manufacturer should have adopted a reasonable alternative design or provided a reasonable warning to protect against such conduct.

Under the rule in Subsection (b), liability for defective design attaches only if the risks of harm related to foreseeable product use could have been reduced by the adoption of a reasonable alternative design. Similarly, under the rule in Subsection (c), liability for failure to instruct or warn attaches only if the risks presented by the product could have been reduced by the adoption of reasonable instructions or warnings. Foreseeable product misuse, alteration, and modification must also be considered in deciding whether an alternative design should have been adopted. The post-sale conduct of the user may be so unreasonable, unusual, and costly to avoid that a seller has no duty to design or warn against them. When a court so concludes, the product is not defective within the meaning of Subsection (b) or (c).

A product may, however, be defective as defined in Subsection (b) or (c) due to the omission of a reasonable alternative design or the omission of an adequate warning, yet the risk that eventuates due to misuse, modification, or alteration raises questions whether the extent or scope of liability under the prevailing rules governing legal causation allow for the imposition of liability. See § 15.

Moreover, a product may be found to be defective and causally responsible for plaintiff's harm but the plaintiff may have misused, altered, or modified the product in a manner that calls for the reduction of plaintiff's recovery under the rules of comparative responsibility. Thus, an automobile may be defectively designed so as to provide inadequate protection against harm in the event of a collision, and the plaintiff's negligent modification of the automobile may have caused the collision eventuating in plaintiff's harm. See § 17.

It follows that misuse, modification, and alteration are not discrete legal issues. Rather, when relevant, they are aspects of the concepts of defect, causation, and plaintiff's fault. Jurisdictions differ on the question of who bears the burden of raising and introducing proof regarding conduct that constitutes misuse, modification, and alteration. The allocation of burdens in this regard is not addressed in this Restatement and is left to local law.

Illustration:

20. The ABC Chair Co. manufactures and sells oak chairs. The backs of the chairs have five horizontal wooden bars shaped to the contour of the human back. John, a college student, climbed up to the top bar of an ABC chair to reach the top shelf of a bookcase. The chair tipped and John fell, suffering serious harm. John brings an action against ABC, alleging that the chair should either have had the stability to support him when standing on the top bar or have had a differently designed back so that he could not use the bars for that purpose. The ABC chair is not defectively designed. John's misuse of the product is so unreasonable that the risks it entails need not be designed against.

q. Causation. Under § 1, the product defect must have caused harm to the plaintiff. See §§ 17 and 18.

r. Warranty. Liability for harm caused by product defects imposed by the rules stated in this Chapter is tort liability, not liability for breach of warranty under the Uniform Commercial Code (U.C.C.). Courts may characterize claims under this Chapter as claims for breaches of the implied warranty of merchantability. But in cases involving defect-caused harm to persons or property, a well-coordinated body of law dealing with liability for such harm arising out of the sale of defective products would adopt the tort definition of product defect. See Comment *n*.

REPORTERS' NOTE

Comment a. Rationale. Strict liability for harm caused by manufacturing defects has been supported on the ground that it promotes investment in product safety. See, e.g., Hoven v. Kelble, 256 N.W.2d 379, 391 (Wis. 1977) ("Strict liability is an effective deterrent; it deters the creation of unnecessary risks, or to put it positively, strict liability is an incentive to safety."). Strict liability also has been justified on the ground that it reduces the consumption of unreasonably risky products by increasing their cost and so placing them at a disadvantage in the market. See, e.g., G. Calabresi, The Cost of Accidents 68–75 (1970); McKean, Products Liability: Trends and Implications, 38 U. Chi. L. Rev. 3, 41–42 (1970). Another objective traditionally thought to be promoted by strict liability is the reduction of transaction costs, which include the costs of operating the accident reparation system. See, e.g., Calabresi, supra, at 27.

The foregoing rationales may be said to be "instrumental," in the sense that they reflect the view that tort liability is a means of achieving a more efficient allocation of resources. In addition to these instrumental objectives, strict liability has been justified on fairness grounds because the product containing a hidden manufacturing defect that causes harm disappoints the consumer's or user's reasonable expectations with regard to safety. See generally Hubbard, Reasonable Human Expectations: A Normative Model for Imposing Strict Liability, 29 Mercer L. Rev. 465 (1978). See also Jerry v. Borden Co., 358 N.Y.S.2d 426, 431–32 (N.Y.App.Div. 1974) (Because consumers rely on suppliers for protection, fairness requires that they be allowed to recover when that protection is not provided.).

Strict liability also has been supported by the argument that, in distributing its products, some of which are certain to contain hidden manufacturing defects, the producer may be said to be deliberately taking the physical well-being of those who are injured by defective products. See generally Cowan, Some Policy Bases of Products Liability, 17 Stan. L. Rev. 1077, 1087–92 (1965). See also LeBel, Intent and Recklessness as Bases of Products Liability: One Step Back, Two Steps Forward, 32 Ala. L. Rev. 31, 67 (1980) (The author refers to "the sense of outrage, frustration, and demoralization that accompanies the realization that the lives or physical well-being of a certain number of people have been written off by a manufacturer in pursuit of an economically efficient allocation of resources."). Strict liability for manufacturing defects also has been justified on fairness grounds because it arguably causes the financial burden of accidents to be borne by those who benefit directly from the product and do not suffer harm. Thus, the Illinois Supreme Court in Suvada v. White Motor Co., 210 N.E.2d 182, 186 (Ill.1965), concluded that the manufacturer should be strictly liable because it profits from its activity, which inevitably involves defect-caused harm to others.

While the strict liability standard of § 2(a) is the superior standard for assessing liability for harm caused by manufacturing defects, the "risk-utility" balancing of costs and benefits embraced by §§ 2(b) and 2(c) is the proper method of defining defects in design, instructions, and warnings. This important point is explained by Professor David Owen in Defectiveness Restated: Exploding the "Strict" Products Liability Myth, 1996 U. Ill. L. Rev. 743, 754–755:

> [S]ince the degree of risk or safety in every product design is counterbalanced by considerations such as cost, utility, and aesthetics, the basis of responsibility for design choices logically should be based on the principle of optimality inherent in the philosophical notion of utility and in the economic concept of efficiency. That is, the goal of both design engineers and the law should be to promote in products an ideal *balance* of product usefulness, cost, and safety.
>
> ... The concept of negligence has been based on the notion of "reasonableness," predicated on the idea that proper decisions involve selecting the proper *balance* of expected benefits and costs. Learned Hand, of course, memorialized the essence of this concept in his celebrated B<PL → N negligence formula in *United States v. Carroll Towing Co.* This type of "cost-benefit" or "risk-utility" analysis may be problematic if relied upon excessively as a mechanical device for producing automatic "right" answers, but it nicely describes the decisional calculus that lies at the heart of products liability law in particular and accident law in general.

The rationale supporting the risk-utility-based standards for defectiveness in design and failure-to-warn cases is implicit in those standards. Liability is imposed whenever the designer or marketer of a product is in a relatively better position than are users and consumers to minimize product-related risks. This theme is developed at some length in Henderson & Twerski, Closing the American Products Liability Frontier: The Rejection of Liability Without Defect, 66 N.Y.U. L. Rev. 1263 (1991). In that article, the Reporters argue that the requirement that the plaintiff establish defectiveness in design and warning cases is necessary to create appropriate incentives to cause users and consumers to engage in safe use and consumption of products. Users and consumers are relatively helpless with respect to harm caused by hidden manufacturing defects; but they are more often better risk minimizers than are product sellers with respect to generic risks involving the inherent design of products. Thus, users of knives are thought to be the appropriate actors to bear legal responsibility for the harm caused by the sharpness of such products. Liability for knife-related accidents unrelated to manufacturing defects should not be imposed on commercial sellers, who have no opportunity to design or market knives that are incapable of causing injury.

Why strict liability (without reference to risk-utility trade-offs) is appropriate in manufacturing defect (and misrepresentation) cases, but not in design and warning cases, is explained in terms of moral theory in Owen, The Moral Foundations of Product Liability Law: Toward First Principles, 68 Notre Dame L. Rev. 427 (1993). Professor Owen describes how principles of freedom and equality support these differences in classification, approach, and outcome. See also Owen, Products Liability: Principles of Justice for the 21st Century, 11 Pace L. Rev. 63 (1990), and Owen, The Fault Pit, 26 Ga. L. Rev. 703 (1992).

Comment b. The nonexclusiveness of the definitions of defect in this Section. The most important application of this Comment is to cases involving allegedly defective designs. Subsection 2(b) sets forth the general rule, applicable to most design defect cases, requiring that the plaintiff establish a reasonable alternative design in order to make out a prima facie case. This Comment emphasizes that in some instances the plaintiff may establish a design defect without proof of a reasonable alternative design. These instances are specifically covered in § 2, Comment *e*, and §§ 3 and 4. When § 2(b) is read in conjunction with these other provisions that allow other avenues for determining defective design, it reflects a substantial body of case law suggesting that a reasonable alternative design is the predominant, yet not exclusive, method for establishing defective design.

Consider, for example, statements in numerous cases that evidence of a reasonable alternative design is normally required but is not invariably required in all cases. This statement is often accompanied by a footnote stating that in some cases a product may be judged not reasonably safe because it should be removed from the market rather than be redesigned. See, e.g., Wilson v. Piper Aircraft Corp., 577 P.2d 1322, 1326–27 and n. 5 at 1328 (Or.1978); Armentrout v. FMC Corp., 842 P.2d 175, 184–85 and n. 11 at 185 (Colo.1992); Banks v. ICI Americas, Inc., 450 S.E.2d 671, 674–675 (Ga.1994); Kallio v. Ford Motor Co., 407 N.W.2d 92, 96–97 (Minn. 1987). Section 2, Comment *e*, leaves open the possibility that courts may conclude that a product is manifestly unreasonable because the extremely high degree of danger posed by its use or consumption outweighs its negligible social utility. The cases cited above leave open in dicta the possibility that when this test is met the courts might not require a reasonable alternative design. This Restatement recognizes this possibility and is thus consistent with the cases set forth.

Similarly, statements in cases that the availability of a reasonable alternative design is one factor among many in considering whether a product meets risk-utility guidelines can only be understood in the context of reasonable alternative design as set forth in § 2(b) and Comment *e*. In judging a product under risk-utility guidelines there are only two options. Either the product should have been reasonably designed to avoid the risk of foreseeable injury or the product should not have been marketed at all. The former invokes reasonable alternative design and the latter Comment *e*.

Many cases take the position that one need not prove a reasonable alternative design when the incident that harmed the plaintiff is of a kind that ordinarily occurs as a result of product defect. When a relatively new product fails in its manifestly intended function, it may in the absence of proof of other causes of the failure, be found to be defective without the necessity of establishing whether the defect was a manufacturing defect or a design defect. This is the position taken by § 3. Thus, these cases are totally consistent with the approach taken by this Restatement.

Finally, when a product design is in violation of a safety statute or regulation, there is no necessity to prove an alternative design in order to establish defect. Section 4 makes it clear that a product design that is in violation of safety standards is defective per se.

This Restatement, especially its first four Sections, must be read together, as an integrated whole. The concept of defect is too nuanced to be set forth in a single Section. When read in its totality the Restatement reflects the strong majority of cases. To be sure, in most cases a plaintiff must establish a reasonable alternative design to make out a design defect. But § 2(b) is not the only road to victory in design cases. Section 2, Comment *e*, and §§ 3 and 4 are alternative grounds for establishing defect. When the facts call for their application a plaintiff need not establish a reasonable alternative design in order to establish defect.

Comment c. Manufacturing defects. For authority that a manufacturing defect is a departure from a manufacturer's own design specification for that product, see, e.g., Caterpillar Tractor Co. v. Beck, 593 P.2d 871, 881 (Alaska 1979) (deviation from the manufacturer's norm); Barker v. Lull Eng'g Co., 573 P.2d 443, 454 (Cal.1978) ("defective product differs from the manufacturer's intended result or other ostensible identical units of the same product line"); Banks v. ICI Americas, Inc., 450 S.E.2d 671, 673 (Ga.1994) (In a manufacturing defect case " . . . it is assumed that the design of the product is safe and had the product been manufactured in accordance with the design it would have been safe for consumer use."); La. Rev. Stat. Ann. § 9:2800.55 (West 1988) ("product deviated in a material way from the manufacturer's specifications or performance standards for the product or from otherwise identical products manufactured by the same manufacturer."); Singleton v. International Harvester Co., 685 F.2d 112, 115 (4th Cir.1981) (applying Maryland law) ("In manufacturing defect cases, the plaintiff proves that the product is defective by simply showing that it does not conform to the manufacturer's specifications."); Back v. Wickes Corp., 378 N.E.2d 964, 970 (Mass.1978) (deviation from the manufacturer's design standard); Prentis v. Yale Mfg. Co., 365 N.W.2d 176, 182 (Mich.1984) ("In the case of a 'manufacturing defect,' the product may be evaluated against the manufacturer's own production standards, as manifested by that manufacturer's other like products."); Miss. Code Ann. § 11–1–63 (1993) (product "deviated in a material way from the manufacturer's specifications or from otherwise identical units manufactured to the same manufacturing specifications"); Rix v. General Motors Corp., 723 P.2d 195, 200 (Mont.1986) (product is flawed or defective because it was not constructed correctly by the manufacturer; product does not conform to its intended design); Thibault v. Sears, Roebuck & Co., 395 A.2d 843, 846 (N.H.1978) ("defect is an accidental variation caused by a mistake in the manufacturing process; . . . product does not 'conform to the great majority of products manufactured in accordance with that design'"); N.J. Stat. Ann. § 2A:58C–2 (West 1987) (product " . . . deviated from the design specifications, formulae, or performance standards of the manufacturer or from otherwise identical units manufactured to the same manufacturing specifications or formulae . . ."); Voss v. Black & Decker Mfg. Co., 450 N.E.2d 204, 207 (N.Y. 1983) (mistake in the manufacturing process). In an earlier opinion, Caprara v. Chrysler Corp., 417 N.E.2d 545, 552 (N.Y.1981), Judge Jasen (the author of *Voss*), writing for the dissent, described a manufacturing defect as follows: " . . .[A] defectively manufactured product is flawed because it is misconstructed without regard to whether the intended design of the manufacturer was safe or not."; Ohio Rev. Code Ann. § 2307.74 (Anderson 1991) (" . . . deviated in a material way from the design specifications, formula, or performance standards of the manufacturer, or from otherwise identical units manufactured to the same design specifications, formula, or performance standards . . ."); Wash. Rev. Code Ann. § 7.72.030(2)(a) (West 1992) (" . . . product deviated in some material way from the design specifications or performance standards of the manufacturer, or deviated in some material way from otherwise identical units of the same product line."). See also Model Uniform Product Liability Act § 104(A); Prosser & Keeton On the Law of Torts 695 (5th ed. 1984) (manufacturing flaw causes the product to be more dangerous than it was designed to be); Owen, The Moral Foundations of Products Liability: Toward First Principles, 68 Notre Dame L. Rev. 427, 500–506 (1993) (strict liability is morally defensible for manufacturing defects, but not for design and failure to warn).

Comment d. Design defects: general considerations. This is by far the longest Reporters' Note to any Comment in this Restatement, and therefore a special format is appropriate. The Note is divided into the following subparts:

I. Introductory Overview

Comment *b* and the Reporters' Note to that Comment make clear that, under the approach reflected in this Restatement, proof of a reasonable alternative design is not an absolute requirement in every case. When a plaintiff in a design case successfully invokes § 3 by proving product malfunction, an inference of design defect is justified without proof of a reasonable alternative design. And when a plaintiff shows that the design fails to conform to an applicable safety statute or regulation under § 4, the same conclusion follows. Moreover, when a court is willing to impose liability on the seller or other distributor of an egregiously dangerous product under Comment *e* to § 2, design-based liability is appropriate even if no reasonable alternative design was available to the defendant. Thus, commentators who criticize this Restatement on the ground that § 2(b) imposes an absolute requirement that claims of defective design must always be supported by proof of a reasonable alternative design are either reacting to portions of earlier drafts taken out of context or are simply wrong. Not surprisingly, almost all of the decisions upon which critics rely to demonstrate that a reasonable alternative design is not always required fall within the alternative grounds for design-based liability explicitly recognized in §§ 3 and 4 and in Comment *e* to § 2.

It follows that the discussion of the case law about to be undertaken primarily addresses the question of what legal standard courts apply when the circumstances described in §§ 3 and 4, and Comment *e* to § 2, are not available to the plaintiff. What standard, in other words, do American courts apply in the majority, but by no means in all, of the design cases that come before them? Jurisdictions vary in their responses to this question. But whatever the response in a given case may be, it is assumed throughout the following discussion that product malfunction (§ 3), violation of safety regulation (§ 4), and egregiously dangerous design (§ 2, Comment *e*), are not involved on the facts of the case before the court.

Before turning to the reported decisions themselves, it will be useful to describe the four general categories into which the cases are grouped. FIRST are the jurisdictions that explicitly require a plaintiff to whom the important alternative bases of liability described above are not available to prove that a reasonable alternative design would have reduced or avoided the plaintiff's harm. SECOND are the jurisdictions that apply a general risk-utility test for defective design without explicitly requiring proof of a reasonable alternative design. Recognition of a risk-utility standard for judging the defectiveness of product designs implicitly commits the court to the requirement of a reasonable alternative design. THIRD are the jurisdictions that purport to rely on a consumer expectations test but in fact engage in a risk-utility analysis that, as with the SECOND approach, implicitly commits the court to a reasonable alternative design requirement. And FOURTH are the jurisdictions, relatively few in number, that apply a true consumer expectations test, independent of risk-utility, without requiring proof of a reasonable alternative design.

Taken together, the FIRST, SECOND, and THIRD of these approaches require, either explicitly or implicitly, the plaintiff to establish the availability of a reasonable alternative design in cases not involving product malfunction, safety standard violation, or egregiously dangerous design. Taken together, they represent the overwhelming majority of American jurisdictions. Admittedly the FOURTH category of decisions in which consumer expectations, standing alone, determine defective design does not support the position reflected in § 2(b). But the FOURTH approach—reliance on consumer expectations standing apart from risk-utility—is recognized in only a small minority of jurisdictions.

II. Summary of American Case Law on the General Test for Defective Product Design

A. Jurisdictions That Explicitly Require Proof of a Reasonable Alternative Design in Cases Not Covered by § 3 or § 4 or Comment *e* to § 2.

Alabama law unequivocally requires proof of a reasonable alternative design in cases not covered by § 3 or § 4 or Comment *e* to § 2. Summary judgment has been granted for defendants in numerous cases where this requirement is not met. The leading case is General Motors Corp. v. Edwards, 482 So.2d 1176 (Ala.1985). The Alabama high court said that:

> In order to prove defectiveness, the plaintiff must prove that a safer, practical, alternative design was available to the manufacturer at the time it manufactured the automobile. The existence of a safer, practical, alternative design must be proved by showing that:
>
> (a) The plaintiff's injuries would have been eliminated or in some way reduced by use of the alternative design, and that;
>
> (b) taking into consideration such factors as the intended use of the vehicle, its styling, cost, and desirability, its safety aspects, the foreseeability of the particular accident, the likelihood of injury, and the probable seriousness of the injury if that accident occurred, the obviousness of the defect, and the manufacturer's ability to eliminate the defect, the utility of the alter-

native design outweighed the utility of the design actually used.

Id. at 1191. This rule has been consistently applied in the Alabama courts. See Townsend v. General Motors Corp., 642 So.2d 411 (Ala.1994) (summary judgment granted for defendants as plaintiff's expert testimony did not establish viability of an alternative design of a compaction unit on a garbage truck); Vines v. Beloit Corp., 631 So.2d 1003, 1006 (Ala.1994) (summary judgment granted to defendants when plaintiffs failed to show reasonable alternative design for machine that processes pulp wood into paper); Bean v. BIC Corp., 597 So.2d 1350, 1352 (Ala.1992) ("The scope of a manufacturer's legal duty [for defective design], therefore, depends upon two factors: (1) the foreseeability of the danger; and (2) the feasibility of an alternative design that averts that danger."); Beech v. Outboard Marine Corp., 584 So.2d 447, 450 (Ala.1991) (In answering a question certified by the United States District Court, the Alabama Supreme Court held that failure to prove that a safer, practical, alternative design was available was a bar to a cause of action for defective design under both the Alabama Extended Manufacturer Liability Doctrine (AEMLD) and negligence.); see also Richards v. Michelin Tire Corp., 21 F.3d 1048, 1056 (11th Cir.1994) (applying Alabama law) ("To prove defectiveness under Alabama law, a plaintiff must prove that a safer, practical, alternative design was available to the manufacturer at the time it manufactured its product." Although the claim was based on negligent design, the court drew no distinction between negligence and strict liability.); Elliott v. Brunswick Corp., 903 F.2d 1505, 1507 (11th Cir.1990) (applying Alabama law) (court affirmed directed verdict for defendant since plaintiff failed to prove existence of a safer alternative design that was practical), cert. denied, 498 U.S. 1048, 111 S.Ct. 756, 112 L.Ed.2d 776 (1991).

In Graham v. Sprout–Waldron & Co., 657 So.2d 868 (Ala.1995), the court did set forth the consumer expectations test as relevant to the issue of defect, as do Comments *f* and *g* to § 2 of this Restatement. The case involved a residue bin for corn byproducts whose dangers were well known to all who worked on them. The court emphasized that plaintiff had presented insufficient evidence that the alternative design it offered would have made the bins any safer. In light of the clear consumer expectations with regard to the known danger and the lack of a reasonable alternative design, the court affirmed the trial court's grant of summary judgment to the manufacturer.

In **Delaware**, the Uniform Commercial Code governs liability in all sales transactions. Although the implied warranty of merchantability does not require the establishment of fault, the Delaware court has engrafted a reasonableness test to determine whether a product was "fit for the ordinary purposes for which it was sold." The earliest case setting forth this requirement is Nacci v. Volkswagen of America, Inc., 325 A.2d 617 (Del.Super.Ct.1974), which held that:

> The manufacturer must exercise reasonable care to produce a product which does not create an unreasonable risk of causing physical harm to those whom he should expect to be endangered by its probable use.... One facet of this requirement is that the manufacturer have a formula, plan or design

> which would produce an article which is safe for its reasonable use....
>
> A number of tests have been devised to determine whether a particular situation renders an automobile manufacturer liable.... I conclude that the proper test is whether the design has created a risk of harm which is so probable that an ordinary prudent person, acting as a manufacturer, *would pursue a different available design* which would substantially lessen the probability of harm.

Id. at 620 (emphasis added) (citations omitted). In several recent cases, evidence of alternative designs was presented by the plaintiff and was an important reason for the denial of summary judgment motions made by the defendant. See, e.g., Betts v. Robertshaw Controls Co., CIV. A No. 89C-08-028, 1992 WL 436727 (Del. Sup.Ct.Dec. 28, 1992) ("Feasibility of designing a safer product must be determined at the time the product was designed."); Evans v. FMC Corp., CIV. A. No. 89C-AU27, 1992 WL 51872 (Del.Sup.Ct.Mar. 9, 1992); Hammond v. Colt Indus. Operating Corp., 565 A.2d 558, 560 (Del.Super.Ct.1989).

The law applicable in the **District of Columbia** is also generally consistent with the requirements of this Restatement. Thus the court in Hull v. Eaton, 825 F.2d 448, 454 (D.C.Cir. 1987) (applying District of Columbia law), upheld summary judgment granted to defendant on the grounds that the design proffered by plaintiff was not a reasonable alternative to that originally chosen. The court looked to Maryland law for guidance in the absence of controlling District of Columbia case law. In doing so, it set forth the following test:

> We believe that the District of Columbia would follow the risk/utility balancing test referred to by the Maryland courts. Under that test a manufacturer is strictly liable for damage caused by his product if there was a feasible way to design a safer product and an ordinary consumer would conclude that the manufacturer ought to have used that alternative design.

Id. In Warner Fruehauf Trailer Co., Inc. v. William Boston, 654 A.2d 1272 (D.C.1995), the court began by stating that "[i]n general, the plaintiff must 'show the risks, costs and benefits of the product in question and alternative designs,' and 'that the magnitude of the danger from the product outweighed the costs of avoiding the danger.'" Id. at 1276 (citing Hull v. Eaton Corp., 825 F.2d 448, 453). The court then indicated in a footnote that in some cases a consumer expectation test might be warranted. *Fruehauf*, 654 A.2d at 1276 n.9.

More recently, in Ferguson v. F.R. Winkler GMBH & Co., 79 F.3d 1221 (D.C.Cir.1996), the court began its analysis by emphasizing the risk-utility, reasonable alternative design aspect of the *Fruehauf* case.

In **Illinois** the statute mandates that plaintiff establish a reasonable alternative design. 735 Ill. Comp. Stat. Ann. § 5/2-2104 (West 1993 & Supp. 1996) provides that:

> If the design of a product or product component is in issue in a products liability action, the design shall be presumed to be reasonably safe unless, at the time the product left the control of the manufacturer, a practical and technically feasible alternative design was available that would have prevented the harm

> without significantly impairing the usefulness, desirability, or marketability of the product. An alternative design is practical and feasible if the technical, medical, or scientific knowledge relating to safety of the alternative design was, at the time the product left the control of the manufacturer, available and developed for commercial use and acceptable in the marketplace.

In Best v. Taylor Machine Works, and Isbell v. Union Pacific Railroad Co., 689 N.E.2d 1057 (Ill.1997), the Illinois Supreme Court held the tort reform statute to be unconstitutional as a violation of the state constitutional provision against "special legislation." It is important to note that the provision requiring a plaintiff to establish a reasonable alternative design might, standing alone, not have been found unconstitutional. However, the court held that the other provisions of the bill that it found to be unconstitutional were essential to the legislative policy and thus could not be severed from the Act.

The statute in **Indiana** articulates a reasonable consumer expectations test. Ind. Code Ann. § 33–1–1.5–2.5 (West 1994). However, Indiana courts in practice have required proof of a reasonable alternative design for maintenance of an action sounding in defective design. Jackson v. Warrum, 535 N.E.2d 1207, 1220 (Ind.Ct.App. 1989) (court held that a "burden of proof scheme" required that "plaintiff must prove that a feasible safer alternative product design existed"); see also Miller v. Todd, 551 N.E.2d 1139, 1141–42 (Ind.1990) (applying risk-utility analysis); Rogers v. R.J. Reynolds Tobacco Co., 557 N.E.2d 1045, 1051 n. 6 (Ind.Ct.App.1990) ("A defective design is one which makes the product inadequate or unsafe relative to alternative design choices." (citation omitted)); Pries v. Honda Motor Co., Ltd., 31 F.3d 543, 545 (7th Cir.1994) (applying Indiana law) (in crashworthiness case where issue was safety of automobile design, court cited to Restatement Third, Torts: Products Liability, Tentative Draft No. 1 (1994) § 2(b) and Comment *c*, and said "[t]o demonstrate a defect, the plaintiff must compare the costs and benefits of alternative designs"); Whitted v. General Motors Corp., 58 F.3d 1200, 1206 (7th Cir.1995) (applying Indiana law) (court said that, although Indiana statute sets forth a consumer expectation test:

> [i]n questioning the propriety of a product's design, we have said that the law requires more than mere assertion: "That a product failed in a particular accident does not necessarily show 'defect,' however." "Indiana requires the plaintiff to show that another design not only could have prevented the injury but also was cost-effective under general negligence principles" . . . The appropriate evidence for demonstrating that a particular seat belt design could have prevented an injury would be, for example, a study of failures for that design. To allege that a manufacturer breached its duty to design a safe product under strict liability, a claimant must offer a safer, more practicable product design than the design in question. Accordingly, since [plaintiff] failed to present evidence that the product was flawed in its design and he failed to illustrate that a better design was cost-effective, summary judgment was properly issued as to the claim of design defect. Id. (citations omitted)).

Louisiana has codified the requirement of proof of a reasonable, safer alternative design in design defect cases in its Products Liability Act, which states that:

> A product is unreasonably dangerous in design if, at the time the product left its manufacturer's control:
>
> (1) There existed an alternative design for the product that was capable of preventing the claimant's damage; and
>
> (2) The likelihood that the product's design would cause the claimant's damage and the gravity of that damage outweighed the burden on the manufacturer of adopting such alternative design and the adverse effect, if any, of such alternative design on the utility of the product. An adequate warning about a product shall be considered in evaluating the likelihood of damage when the manufacturer has used reasonable care to provide the adequate warning to users and handlers of the product.

La. Rev. Stat. § 9:2800.56 (West 1988).

Maryland law supports the positions taken by §§ 2 and 3. The Maryland courts recognize that strict liability may apply in cases of "inherently unreasonable risks" without establishing the specific nature of the defect and without undertaking risk-utility balancing. In Phipps v. General Motors Corp., 363 A.2d 955 (Md.1976), the court elaborated on this point:

> [T]here are those kinds of conditions which, whether caused by design or manufacture can never be said to involve a reasonable risk. For example, the steering mechanism of a new automobile should not cause the car to swerve off the road; . . . the drive shaft of a new automobile should not separate from the vehicle when it is driven in a normal manner; . . . the brakes of a new automobile should not suddenly fail; . . . and the accelerator of a new automobile should not stick without warning, causing the vehicle to suddenly accelerate. Conditions like these, even if resulting from the design of the products, are defective and unreasonably dangerous without the necessity of weighing and balancing the various factors involved.

Id. at 959; see also Ziegler v. Kawasaki Heavy Indus., 539 A.2d 701, 705 (Md.Ct.Spec.App.1988) (The court explains that " 'an inherently unreasonable risk' type of design defect is similar to a manufacturing defect because in both the product does not function as the manufacturer intended."). The Reporters interpret these comments as consistent with the position taken in § 3 of this Restatement.

Several cases support the view that the "inherently unreasonable risk" category is limited to those situations arising under § 3, and that the typical design defect case requires risk-utility balancing. *Ziegler*, 539 A.2d at 705; see also Singleton v. Int'l Harvester Co., 685 F.2d 112, 114–15 (4th Cir.1981) (applying Maryland law). When a product does not present an inherently unreasonable risk, the Maryland courts use risk-utility balancing to establish the standard for defect and require that the plaintiff prove a feasible alternative design. See *Ziegler*, 539 A.2d at 705 (adopting risk-utility and rejecting a consumer expectation test); Valk Mfg. v. Rangaswamy, 537 A.2d 622, 626–27 (Md.Ct.Spec.App.1988), rev'd on other grounds, 562 A.2d 1246 (Md.1989). Furthermore, it is the plaintiff's burden to prove a feasible alternative design as a necessary predicate to establishing a design defect, as was made clear in *Ziegler*:

> In order to create a jury issue on Kawasaki's liability for defective design, Ziegler was required but failed to produce evidence showing "the technological feasibility of manufacturing a product with the suggested safety device at the time the suspect product was manufactured; the cost of production of the suggested device; price to the consumer, including that of the suggested device; and the chances of consumer acceptance of a model incorporating such features."

539 A.2d at 707. See also *Singleton*, 685 F.2d at 115–16; Troja v. Black & Decker Mfg., 488 A.2d 516, 519 (Md. Ct.Spec.App.1985).

The leading case in **Massachusetts** on defective design is Uloth v. City Tank Corp., 384 N.E.2d 1188 (Mass. 1978). The case was brought on a negligence theory; the court held that there was "a case for the jury if the plaintiff can show an available design modification which would reduce the risk without undue cost or interference with the performance of the machinery." Id. at 1193; see also Back v. Wickes Corp., 378 N.E.2d 964, 970 (Mass.1978) (In a warranty case, the court preliminarily observed that the state's law of warranty was "congruent in nearly all respects with the principles expressed in Restatement, Second, of Torts § 402A (1965)," and went on to hold that the inquiry would put heavy emphasis on "the mechanical feasibility of a safer alternative design, the financial cost of an improved design, and the adverse consequences to the product and to the consumer that would result from an alternative design."); Fahey v. Rockwell Graphic Sys., Inc., 482 N.E.2d 519, 525 (Mass.App.Ct.1985). Reviewing Massachusetts authority, the United States Court of Appeals in Kotler v. American Tobacco Co., 926 F.2d 1217 (1st Cir.1990), vacated, 505 U.S. 1215, 112 S.Ct. 3019, 120 L.Ed.2d 891 (1992) (vacated on the issue of federal preemption in the field of cigarette labeling), succinctly summarizes the requirement of proof of a reasonable alternative design in the state:

> We are aware of no Massachusetts case in which liability attached in the absence of evidence that some different, arguably safer, alternative design was possible. In a design defect case premised on negligence, the existence of a safer alternative design is a sine qua non for the imposition of liability. It follows, we think, that a design defect case premised on breach of warranty is, in Massachusetts, similarly dependent on proof of a safer alternative design—a design which reasonably could, or should, have been adopted.

Id. at 1225 (citations omitted).

Smith v. Ariens Co., 377 N.E.2d 954 (Mass.1978), raises the question whether it is always necessary to present expert testimony to support a finding of design defect. In that case the plaintiff was injured when she fell from a snowmobile and her face came down and hit a brake bracket that had two sharp metal protrusions, which caused serious injury to her. The court concluded that it is within the province of a jury based on its own lay knowledge to conclude that "windshield metal protrusions on the handle bar of a snowmobile constitute a defect in design." Id. at 957–58. The court's version is consistent with the position set forth in § 2, Comment *f*, that in some cases the feasibility of an alternative design is sufficiently clear that expert testimony is not necessary to support the proposition.

Michigan has explicitly rejected the consumer expectations test as the general standard for defective design in cases not involving product malfunction (§ 3) and has adopted a pure risk-utility analysis for design defect cases, regardless of whether the case was based on strict liability (or implied warranty of merchantability) or negligence. See Prentis v. Yale Mfg., 365 N.W.2d 176, 184 (Mich.1984). As a practical matter, the plaintiff cannot establish a prima facie case of design defect without producing evidence of a reasonable alternative design. In Owens v. Allis–Chalmers Corp., 326 N.W.2d 372, 378–79 (Mich.1982), the failure of the plaintiff to produce evidence of the practicality and cost-effectiveness of a proffered alternative design was grounds for upholding a directed verdict for the defendant; accord, Scott v. Allen Bradley, 362 N.W.2d 734, 737 (Mich.Ct.App. 1984) ("Owens established that the plaintiff must present evidence concerning the magnitude of the risks involved *and* the reasonableness of any proposed alternative design." (emphasis added)). The Michigan Court of Appeals in Reeves v. Cincinnati, Inc., 439 N.W.2d 326, 329 (1989), summarized the elements of a prima facie case of failure to provide adequate safety devices:

> A prima facie case of a design defect premised upon the omission of a safety device requires first a showing of the magnitude of foreseeable risks, including the likelihood of occurrence of the type of accident precipitating the need for the safety device, and the severity of the injuries sustainable from such an accident. It *secondly requires a showing of alternative safety devices and whether those devices would have been effective as a reasonable means of minimizing the foreseeable risk of danger.* This latter showing may entail an evaluation of the alternative design in terms of its additional utility as a safety measure and its trade-offs against the costs and effective use of the product. (Emphasis added).

See also Phillips v. Hardware Wholesalers, Inc., 762 F.2d 46, 47 (6th Cir. 1985) (applying Michigan law); Foster v. Caterpillar Tractor Co., 714 F.2d 654, 657 (6th Cir.1983) (applying Michigan law); Zettle v. Handy Mfg., 837 F.Supp. 222, 225 (E.D.Mich.1992); Gawenda v. Werner Co., 932 F.Supp. 183 (E.D.Mich.1996).

Mississippi has established by statute that proof of a reasonable alternative design is necessary in order to maintain an action alleging a design defect. Miss. Code Ann. § 11–1–63 (1993) (Plaintiff must prove that "there existed a feasible design alternative that would to a reasonable probability have prevented the harm. A feasible design alternative is a design that would to a reasonable probability have prevented the harm without impairing the utility, usefulness practicality or desirability of the product to users or consumers.").

New Jersey has also established a reasonable alternative design requirement by statute. N.J. Rev. Stat. § 2A:58c–3a.(1) (1987) (setting up as a defense that a manufacturer shall not be liable if, "At the time the product left the control of the manufacturer, there was not a practical and technically feasible alternative design that would have prevented the harm without substantially impairing the reasonably anticipated or intended function of the product . . ." However, note the very narrow exception established in subsections b(1), (2), (3), applying only to situations in which the product is "egregiously unsafe," beyond the knowledge of the average consumer or posing a serious risk to third parties or their property, *and* "has little or no usefulness." See discussion, infra.).

An intermediate court in New Jersey reached the following conclusion:

> [The] conclusion [that in most cases a reasonable alternative design is required] is reinforced by the current tentative draft of the proposed Restatement, Third, of Torts, which endorses the position that a plaintiff in a design-defect products liability action must show the existence of reasonable alternative design:
>
> A product is defective in design when foreseeable risks of harm posed by the product could have been reduced by the adoption of a reasonable alternative design by the seller or a predecessor in the commercial chain of distribution and the omission of the alternative design renders the product not reasonably safe....
>
> [Restatement Third, Torts: Products Liability § 2(b) (Tentative Draft No. 1, 1994).] Under this provision, "[t]o establish a prima facie case of defect, plaintiff must prove the availability of a technologically feasible and practical alternative design that would have reduced or prevented plaintiff's harm." Id., Cmt. *d* at 20.

Smith v. Keller Ladder Co., 645 A.2d 1269, 1271 (N.J. Super. Ct. App. Div. 1994).

In a more recent case, Grzanka v. Pfeifer, 694 A.2d 295 (N.J.Super.Ct.App.Div.1997), § 2(b) appears to have been implicitly adopted by a New Jersey intermediate court as the proper standard of liability in a design defect case. In that case, the plaintiffs were injured when their motorcycle collided with a car in the middle of an intersection. Apparently, the traffic light located at the intersection where the collision occurred was rendered inoperable by vandals. The plaintiffs claimed that the traffic light was defectively designed because it should have been equipped with a locked case and padlock in order to protect against such vandalism. However, the plaintiffs failed to offer any admissible proof that the vandalism in this case should have been foreseeable to the manufacturer at the time the traffic light left the manufacturer's hands. In upholding the trial court's granting of summary judgment for the manufacturer, the intermediate court explained:

> Plaintiffs did come forward with an allegedly reasonable alternative design to protect against the tampering and vandalism in this case.... Yet there is a second aspect to the "reasonable alternative design" test. Without proof of a reasonably foreseeable risk, so that "the omission of the alternative design renders the product not reasonably safe," plaintiffs' alternative design fails to meet the full test of Restatement § 2(b).

Id. at 303 (Citations omitted).

The **New York** Court of Appeals imposed the requirement of a reasonable alternative design in Voss v. Black & Decker Manufacturing, 450 N.E.2d 204, 208 (N.Y.1983) ("The plaintiff, of course, is under an obligation to present evidence that the product, as designed, was not reasonably safe because there was substantial likelihood of harm and it was feasible to design the product in a safer manner."). See also Garcia v. Rivera, 553 N.Y.S.2d 378, 380 (N.Y.App.Div.1990) ("In establishing that the design in question is defective, the plaintiff must offer proof of an alternative safer design, practicable under the circumstances."); Burgos v. Lutz, 512 N.Y.S.2d 424, 425 (N.Y.App.Div.1987). In Denny v. Ford Motor Co., 662 N.E.2d 730, 736 (N.Y.1995), the New York Court of Appeals affirmed risk-utility balancing and the *Voss* line of cases as governing a cause of action based in tort. It did, however, recognize that a consumer expectations test would govern under U.C.C. § 2–314(2)(c). The court held that "[a]s long as that legislative source of authority exists, we are not free to merge the warranty cause of action with its tort-based sibling regardless of whether, as a matter of policy, the contract-based warranty claim *may fairly be regarded as a historical relic that no longer has any independent substantive value*." Id. (emphasis added). See also the discussion on *Denny* in the Reporters' Note to Comment *n*.

Although **Pennsylvania** case law governing products liability is sometimes difficult to decipher, a careful analysis of Pennsylvania's appellate decisions suggests that its law may be read to be consistent with the rules set forth in § 2. The leading case in Pennsylvania is Azzarello v. Black Bros. Co., 391 A.2d 1020 (Pa. 1978). In this important decision, the Supreme Court held that a jury should not be given an instruction regarding the "unreasonable danger" of a product. Quoting at length from Dean Wade, the court indicated that risk-utility balancing is for the court. The court said:

> Furthermore, we must not lose sight of the fact that regardless of the utility of the Restatement formulation in predicting responsibility, it is primarily designed to provide guidance for the bench and bar, and not to illuminate the issues for laymen. As Dean Wade aptly observed:
>
>> "The problem here is similar to that in negligence. The Restatement of Torts has analyzed negligence, described it as a balancing of the magnitude of the risk against the utility of the risk, and listed the factors which go into determining the weight of both of these elements. This analysis is most helpful and can be used with profit by trial and appellate judges, and by students and commentators. But it is not ordinarily given to the jury. Instead, they are told that negligence depends upon what a reasonable prudent man would do under the same or similar circumstances. Occasionally, when one of the factors has especial significance, it may be appropriate for the judge to make reference to it in suitable language." (footnote omitted)
>
> Wade, supra, 44 Miss. L.J. at 840.
>
> Thus the mere fact that we have approved Section 402A, and even if we agree that the phrase "unreasonably dangerous" serves a useful purpose in predicting liability in this area, it does not follow that this language should be used in programming the issues for the jury's consideration. Should an ill-conceived design which exposes the user to the risk of harm entitle one

> injured by the product to recover? Should adequate warnings of the dangerous propensities of an article insulate one who suffers injuries from those propensities? When does the utility of a product outweigh the unavoidable danger it may pose? These are questions of law and their resolution depends upon social policy....

Azzarello at 1026. The court then approved the following jury instruction:

> The [supplier] of a product is the guarantor of its safety. The product must, therefore, be provided with every element necessary to make it safe for [its intended] use, and without any condition that makes it unsafe for [its intended] use. If you find that the product, at the time it left the defendant's control, lacked any element necessary to make it safe for [its intended] use or contained any condition that made it unsafe for [its intended] use, then the product was defective, and the defendant is liable for all harm caused by such defect.

Id. at 1027 n.12.

Several points need to be made. First, simply because the court has reserved to itself risk-utility balancing does not mean elimination of the plaintiff's obligation to prove that the product that caused injury was not reasonably safe. To make a prima-facie case, the plaintiff must satisfy the court that risk-utility parameters have not been met. Second, the jury instructions speak of a product being "provided with every element necessary to make it safe for its intended use." Although the Reporters, joined by most critics, find this language unduly harsh, it does point to the need to prove the existence of a way to make the product safer; otherwise, how would the presence or absence of an "element necessary to make it safe" be determined? The need for establishment of an alternative design is manifest. Third, Comment *f* leaves to the several states the decision as to how to phrase jury instructions. The rule set forth in § 2(b) is a rule of law, addressed to the court; once sufficient evidence to satisfy risk-utility has been presented to the court, the text of jury instruction is for each state to decide.

Recent cases applying Pennsylvania law support the position that proof of a reasonable alternative design is a required element of a prima facie case of design defect. In Habecker v. Clark Equip. Co., 942 F.2d 210 (3d Cir.1991), the court said:

> It is important to distinguish evidence of what safety features were *feasible* at the time a product was designed, from evidence of what safety features were *known to be desirable* at that time. Evidence of the first must be admissible in a crashworthiness case. Liability is imposed on a manufacturer in a crashworthiness case for a design defect because an alternative, *feasible*, safer design would have lessened or eliminated the injury plaintiff suffered. *If no such alternative feasible design existed when the product was manufactured, then the design cannot be said to be "defective," even if more recent technology has rendered a safer design feasible.* Therefore, the fact finder can only determine whether a particular design was defective after hearing evidence about what designs were feasible at the time the product was manufactured and whether they were in fact safer.

942 F.2d at 215 (last emphasis added, citations omitted); see also Habecker

v. Clark Equip. Co., 36 F.3d 278 (3d Cir.1994) (*Habecker II*).

In Surace v. Caterpillar, Inc., 111 F.3d 1039 (3d Cir. 1997), a construction worker was injured when a pavement profiler ran over his foot. He alleged that the profiler was defectively designed because its back-up alarms were susceptible to "habituation," a condition by which persons become immune to certain stimuli through repetition and exposure. The plaintiff attempted to introduce expert testimony concerning an alternative safety mechanism (a lockout/tagout device), but the trial court excluded the testimony and granted the manufacturer's motion for summary judgment. The Third Circuit found that Pennsylvania would apply a risk-utility analysis:

> '[f]urthermore, Dean John Wade's article setting forth the risk-utility analysis was cited favorably throughout the *Azzarello* decision . . . That fact, coupled with its long hegemony in Pennsylvania—risk-utility analysis has been used by state and federal trial courts since at least 1985 without comment by the Pennsylvania Supreme Court—satisfies us that the Supreme Court would adopt it.'

Id. at 1045.

The federal court of appeals went on to reverse the district court's decision and remand the case, expressing its conclusion in terms that clearly embrace the reasonable alternative design concept: "[w]hile it would have been preferable for [plaintiff's expert] to have proffered design drawings or developed a prototype of the device, his testimony was sufficient for purposes of the threshold risk-utility calculus to make a showing of the feasibility of a lockout/tagout device" Id. at 1049.

A similar note was struck in Ballarini v. Clark Equipment Co., 841 F.Supp. 662 (E.D.Pa.1993). In *Ballarini*, the plaintiff alleged that a forklift was defective because it did not come equipped with an interlock device that would put the vehicle into neutral when the operator left the driver's seat. Citing *Habecker*, discussed supra, the court said that "it was particularly important for plaintiff to present a feasible alternative to the forklift's existing safety features." Id. at 665. After reviewing the evidence, the court concluded that the plaintiff's expert failed to establish the feasibility of an alternative design and, consequently, that a verdict should have been directed for the defendant. Id. at 666. In Williams v. Crompton and Knowles Corp., No. CIV. A. 92–4605 1994 WL 71283 (E.D.Pa.1994), the plaintiff alleged that a wrapping machine was defectively designed. Prior to evaluating the sufficiency of the evidence offered to make out a prima facie case for design defect, the court said that "[s]ince this is a design defect case, plaintiffs are also required to demonstrate that a feasible alternative design is possible which eliminates the hazard yet permits the essential functions of the purportedly defective design to be accomplished." Id. See also Fritchey v. Rhone–Poulenc, Inc., No. 95–1983, 1996 WL 240009 (E.D.Pa. Feb.16, 1996) (worker slipped and fell on a colorless chemical in a waste water treatment plant. Court granted defense motion for directed verdict because plaintiff had presented no evidence that a reasonably safer alternative was available that would perform the same design function and allow for coloration that would be visible on a host of different types of floors in waste treatment plants); Wallace v. Tesco Eng'g, Inc., Prod. Liab.Rep. (CCH) P 14523 (E.D.Pa. 1996) (employee who slipped and fell on oil brought claim of design defect of assembly line for failing to have an adequate oil drainage system; court granted directed verdict because the suggested alternative design offered by plaintiff was not shown to be safer).

Recent state cases in **Pennsylvania** are in agreement with the requirement of a reasonable alternative design. Fitzpatrick v. Madonna, 623 A.2d 322 (Pa.Super.Ct.1993), was a wrongful death action brought by the representatives of a swimmer killed by a propeller on a carelessly operated boat. The trial court entered judgment for the plaintiffs on the defective design claim, and the manufacturer appealed. The court on appeal performed a risk-utility balance, considering the seven Wade factors, and decided that, as the utility of the propeller outweighed its risks and no feasible alternative was available, it was not defectively designed. Id. at 326. The court concluded that the case should not have been submitted to the jury and reversed the judgment. Id. at 327. The court thus followed *Azzarello* in performing risk-utility balancing itself before allowing a case to go to a jury for its determination under the severe *Azzarello* instruction.

In evaluating Pennsylvania cases, one must be careful to distinguish the standard for identifying design defects from the variety of proof that the plaintiff must introduce, through expert testimony, to establish a breach of that standard. In DiFrancesco v. Excam Inc., 642 A.2d 529 (Pa.Super.Ct.1994), the plaintiff was severely injured when the derringer hand pistol he was carrying in his sweater pocket discharged when the hammer was inadvertently bumped. The plaintiff introduced expert testimony on this point, as the court observed:

> Plaintiff's witnesses . . . were qualified as experts and were properly allowed to testify on design alternatives for the [defendant's] derringer. . . . Plaintiff's experts testified at length about feasible and safer design alternatives that would eliminate the problems that made the derringer unsafe for its intended use. [One expert] testified, for example, that there were a number of patents in existence for mechanisms that would make the derringer safer.

Id. at 532, 534.

Responding to the defendant's argument that no existing comparable weapon contained such mechanisms, the court concluded: "[a]lthough [plaintiff's expert] was unaware of any derringer on the market that had the safety mechanism he recommended, he was positive such a mechanism could be incorporated into the derringer design." Id. at 534.

Thus, *DiFrancesco* supports, rather than contradicts, the requirement that the plaintiff must show a reasonable alternative design. Moreover, the Comments to § 2 are careful to distinguish between the legal standard and the nature of the plaintiff's required proof in a design defect case. See Comment *f. DiFransesco* clearly embraces this Restatement's position in § 2.

Several other Pennsylvania cases support the position taken in § 2(b). Although *Azzarello* mandates that a court perform risk-utility balancing, it is impermissible for a court to make the judgment that, absent a defect, a product is so inherently dangerous that it should not have been marketed. This approach was advocated by the plaintiff in Hite v. R. J. Reynolds Tobacco Co., 578 A.2d 417 (Pa.Super.Ct.1990). The court, in rejecting the claim, said:

> Appellant in the instant case does not contend that a better design is available for the cigarette company's product. She contends only that appellee's product is so inherently dangerous that the manufacturer should be made liable for the mischief it causes. She would accomplish this by applying the risk-utility approach to design defect cases. Thus far, however, the Pennsylvania courts have resisted such an approach in design defect cases....
>
> The federal courts have recognized the Pennsylvania Supreme Court's refusal to embrace the risk-utility analysis and have held that cigarette claims based upon such an approach are not cognizable in Pennsylvania. In Miller v. Brown & Williamson Tobacco Corp., 679 F.Supp. 485 (E.D.Pa.1988), the court held that under Pennsylvania law the risk-utility theory of liability was inapplicable; and, therefore, an action against a cigarette manufacturer for death caused by cigarette smoking on grounds that cigarettes gave no benefit to society but imposed great risk could not be maintained. Similarly, in *Gunsales v. Celotex Corp.*, supra, the United States District Court for the Eastern District of Pennsylvania reasoned that the risk-utility test had not been adopted in Pennsylvania and held that tobacco was not per se a "defective" product merely because it caused or increased the risk of lung cancer and other life threatening diseases....

Id. at 421.

The most important difference between Pennsylvania law and the position in §§ 2(b) and 2(c) is that Pennsylvania does not require a finding that specific risks arising out of a foreseeable product use were reasonably knowable by the defendant. See Carrecter v. Colson Equip. Co., 499 A.2d 326, 330–31 (Pa.Super.Ct.1985); Dambacher v. Mallis, 485 A.2d 408, 424 (Pa.Super.Ct.1984). However, if in fact, at the time of trial, a product design meets risk-utility norms, the product is simply not defective. This view, that liability may be imposed even if risks are unforeseeable, is held in a small minority of states. See IV.B, infra. In mechanical defect cases Comment *m* notes that risks arising out of foreseeable uses of a product are generally knowable and that it typically can be assumed that they were known to the manufacturer. Furthermore, Comment *d* provides that there is no absolute state-of-the-art defense, and that a plaintiff is always free to prove that an alternative design was both practical and feasible. The plaintiff is not precluded from proving the viability of an alternative design merely because it had not been previously commercially adopted or constructed by any manufacturer.

In sum, when one views Pennsylvania law in its broad sweep, both risk-utility analysis and the need to introduce evidence of a reasonable alternative are well-established and consistent with the views of this Restatement. The harsh language of the Pennsylvania jury instruction does not set forth the rules for a prima facie case of defect. The instructions are the prism through which the Pennsylvania courts wish the jury to judge cases once a prima facie case has been established.

Nevertheless, the Third Circuit has bemoaned the Pennsylvania high court's failure to clear up the confusion surrounding its pronouncements regarding defective product design: "[W]e regret that the [Pennsylvania] Supreme Court has not yet spoken definitively on the matter of risk-utility analysis or its component factors. Since it is almost twenty years since *Azzarello*, we hope that the Court will speak definitively soon." Surace v. Caterpillar, Inc., 111 F.3d 1039 (3d Cir. 1997).

Texas rejected the consumer expectations test as a general standard for evaluating most design defect claims and adopted risk-utility balancing in Turner v. General Motors Corp., 584 S.W.2d 844, 847 (Tex. 1979). Texas courts have long given heavy weight to the production of reasonable alternative design evidence in the evaluation of a prima facie case of design defect. See, e.g., Boatland of Houston, Inc. v. Bailey, 609 S.W.2d 743, 746 (Tex.1980) ("Because defectiveness of the product in question is determined in relation to safer alternatives, the fact that its risks could be diminished easily or cheaply may greatly influence the outcome of the case."); Cantrell v. Hennessy Indus., 829 S.W.2d 875, 877 (Tex.Ct.App.1992) ("Courts must determine whether a product is defectively designed in relation to safer alternatives."), cert. denied, 508 U.S. 912, 113 S.Ct. 2347, 124 L.Ed.2d 256 (1993). The longstanding reasonable alternative design requirement in Texas has been codified by statute:

> The burden is on the claimant to prove that ... there was a safer alternative design.... "Safer alternative design" means a product design other than the one actually used that in reasonable probability ... would have prevented or significantly reduced the risks of the claimant's personal injury, property damage, or death without substantially impairing the product's utility; and was economically and technologically feasible at the time the product left the control of the manufacturer or seller....

Tex. Civ. Prac. & Rem. Code Ann. § 82.005 (West 1993).

Utah case law also makes the reasonable alternative design requirement clear. Allen v. Minnstar, Inc., 8 F.3d 1470, 1479 (10th Cir.1993) (applying Utah law) ("Plaintiff did bear the burden of showing that an alternative, safer design, practicable under the circumstances, was available at the time the boat and engine were sold.").

In **West Virginia**, the Supreme Court of Appeals has adopted the standard of reasonable safety, as determined "by what a reasonably prudent manufacturer's standards *should have been* at the time the product was made." Morningstar v. Black & Decker Mfg., 253 S.E.2d 666, 683 (W.Va. 1979) (emphasis added). This language can only be read to require the production of evidence on reasonable alternative design, to gauge what "should have been." Indeed, in Church v. Wesson, 385 S.E.2d 393 (W.Va.1989), the court upheld a directed verdict for defendant, in a strict liability context, on the ground that the plaintiff had failed to establish feasibility of a proffered alternative design. Id. at 396. ("We find that appellant failed to establish a prima facie right of recovery.... [Witness] suggested that [a certain design] may have been a more appropriate [one, but] it was undisputed that the [alternative] was not feasible.... ").

As explained earlier, merely because a state recognizes the possibility that proof of a reasonable alternative design may not be required in every case does not mean that such a showing is not required in most cases. Thus, decisions in a number of jurisdictions support the proposition that proof of a reasonable alternative design is necessary as a general rule to support a claim for design defect, while recognizing, in dicta, that there may be instances when a product has both such negligible utility and such a high degree of risk that, regardless of alternatives, the product should not have been marketed at all. This position is reflected in § 2, Comment *e* and is perfectly consistent with this Restatement.

Oregon was perhaps the first state to couple a reasonable alternative design requirement with a realization that in a small class of cases it might not be absolute. The leading case is Wilson v. Piper Aircraft Corp., 577 P.2d 1322, 1326–27 (Or.1978). The Oregon Supreme Court first stated the general test as follows: "The court is to determine, and to weigh in the balance, whether the proposed alternative design has been shown to be practicable. [It] should not permit an allegation of design defect to go to the jury unless there is sufficient evidence upon which to make this determination." It then described the case at hand: "Plaintiff's allegations amount to a contention that an airplane furnished with a standard aircraft engine is defective because an engine of a different type, or with a different carburetor system, would be safer in one particular." Finally, it found the plaintiff's allegations lacking, stating that "It is not proper to submit such allegations to the jury unless the court is satisfied that there is some evidence from which the jury could find the suggested alternatives are not only technically feasible but also practicable in terms of cost and the over-all design and operation of the product," and emphasizing that "It is part of the *required proof* that a design feature is a 'defect' to present such evidence." (emphasis added).

See also Wood v. Ford Motor Co., 691 P.2d 495, 498 (Or.Ct.App.1984) (The court first stated the test as whether "a reasonably prudent manufacturer would have so designed and sold the product in question had it known of the risk which injured plaintiff." (citation omitted). It then cited *Wilson* for the proposition that "[w]hen the utility of the product is great and the magnitude of the risk is limited, one of the most crucial factors in determining what a reasonably prudent manufacturer would do is whether it is possible to eliminate the unsafe characteristic of the product without impairing its usefulness or making it too expensive.... Plaintiff must show that an alternative safer design, practicable under the circumstances, was available" and concluded that when the practicability of the alternative "cannot be properly weighed solely on the basis of inference and common knowledge" evidence must be presented to bear on both its technical and practical feasibility.). Id. Thus, *Wilson* and *Wood* both make the point that the need to introduce evidence of a reasonable safer, alternative design is crucial in connection with products that have significant social utility (e.g., airplanes and automobiles).

Regarding the Comment *e* point, the court in *Wilson* left open the possibility that it might choose to impose liability without an alternative design:

> As pointed out above, the court's task is to weigh the factors bearing on the utility and the magnitude of the risk and to determine whether, on balance, the case is a proper one for submission to the jury. In this case we focus on the practicability of a safer alternative design and hold that the evidence was insufficient to permit the trial judge to consider that factor. Our holding should not be interpreted as a requirement that this factor must in all cases weigh in plaintiff's favor before the case can be submitted to the jury. There might be cases in which the jury would be permitted to hold the defendant liable on account of a dangerous design feature even though no safer design was feasible (or there was no evidence of a safer practicable alternative). If, for example, the danger was relatively severe and the product had only limited utility, the court might properly conclude that the jury could find that a reasonable manufacturer would not have introduced such a product into the stream of commerce. We hold here only that, given the nature of the product and the defects alleged, it was improper to submit the issue of a defect in the engine design to the jury in the absence of appropriate evidence that the safer alternative design was practicable.

Wilson, 577 P.2d at 1328 n.5. In sum, except for situations coming under the aegis of the foregoing footnote, the Oregon cases cited not only require proof of a reasonable alternative design but demand a high threshold of evidence to support the conclusion that it would be as practical and efficient as the challenged design. See also Glover v. BIC Corp., 6 F.3d 1318, 1330–32 (9th Cir.1993) (applying Oregon law). It appears that Oregon's requirements may exceed those set forth in § 2, Comment *e*.

Courts in other states have followed Oregon's path in this regard. Thus, in Ortho Pharmaceutical Corp. v. Heath, 722 P.2d 410 (Colo.1986), overruled in part by Armentrout v. FMC Corp., 842 P.2d 175 (Colo.1992) (overruled solely on the issue of placement of the burden of proof for design defect), **Colorado** adopted risk-utility as the governing mode of analysis for design defect cases. The court expanded upon this theme in Camacho v. Honda Motor Co.:

> These considerations strongly suggest that the consumer contemplation concept embodied in [C]omment *i*, while illustrative of a particular problem, does not provide a satisfactory test for determining whether particular products are in a defective condition unreasonably dangerous to the user or consumer. In the final analysis, the principle of products liability contemplated by [S]ection 402A is premised upon the concept of enterprise liability for casting defective products into the stream of commerce.

741 P.2d 1240, 1246 (Colo.1987) (citation omitted), cert. dismissed, 485 U.S. 901, 108 S.Ct. 1067, 99 L.Ed.2d 229 (1988); see also White v. Caterpillar, Inc., 867 P.2d 100, 105 (Colo.Ct. App.1993) (At trial, plaintiff introduced evidence bearing on benefits and risks of equipping a product with a safety device; judge instructed jury to consider only whether its omission created a "risk of harm which would not ordinarily have been expected,"

after which jury found for defendant. Plaintiff appealed, and the appellate court reversed because the instruction "improperly directed the jury to consider whether the product created a risk of harm which would not ordinarily have been expected, rather than whether the risks associated with [the product] outweigh its benefits."). It is clear that consumer expectations are a relevant and often very important factor in risk-utility analysis in Colorado. Armentrout v. FMC Corp., 842 P.2d 175, 184–85 n. 10 (Colo.1992). However, the high court has further noted that:

> Exclusive reliance upon consumer expectations is a particularly inappropriate means of determining whether a product is unreasonably dangerous under [S]ection 402A where both the unreasonableness of the danger in the design defect and the efficacy of alternative designs in achieving a reasonable degree of safety must be defined primarily by technical, scientific information.

Camacho, 741 P.2d at 1246–47.

Although in *Armentrout*, its latest pronouncement on the issue, the Colorado court takes the position that "[t]he existence of a feasible alternative is a factor in the risk-benefit analysis of the unreasonable dangerousness of the product design," 842 P.2d at 184–85, it also cites to Wilson v. Piper Aircraft Corp., 577 P.2d at 1328 n.5, for the proposition that "[e]vidence of a feasible design alternative is not always necessary." *Armentrout*, 842 P.2d at 185 n.11 (full text of *Wilson*, n.5 quoted). This reliance on *Wilson* is significant. It would appear that the only exceptions to the reasonable alternative design requirement in Colorado are those cases where, per *Wilson*, the product has negligible utility and high risk. If this is so, then Colorado law is consistent with the position of this Restatement, § 2, Comments *d* and *e*. It should also be noted that the position of the Colorado court that a jury need not be instructed on reasonable alternative design is also consistent with the position taken in § 2, Comment *f*.

A recent case decided by the **Georgia** Supreme Court, citing a Preliminary Draft of Restatement Third, Torts: Products Liability, emphasized the importance of the reasonable alternative design requirement in design defect litigation. In Banks v. ICI Americas, Inc., 450 S.E.2d 671, 674 (Ga.1994), the court adopted risk-utility balancing as the governing test for design litigation. In doing so the court said:

> Numerous lists of factors to be considered by the trier of fact in balancing the risk of the product against the utility or benefit derived from the product have been compiled by various authorities. One factor consistently recognized as *integral to the assessment of the utility of a design* is the availability of alternative designs, in that the existence and feasibility of a safer and equally efficacious design diminishes the justification for using a challenged design.... The alternative safer design factor reflects the reality that
>
> > [i]t often is not possible to determine whether a safer design would have averted a particular injury without considering whether an alternative design was feasible. The essential inquiry, therefore, is whether the design chosen was a reasonable one from among the feasible choices of which the manufacturer was

aware or should have been aware.

2 Am. L. Prod. Liab., ... § 28:14, p. 28. *Indeed, the reasonableness of choosing from among various alternative product designs and adopting the safest one if it is feasible is considered the "heart" of design defect cases, since it is only at their most extreme that design defect cases reflect the position that a product is simply so dangerous that it should not have been made available at all.* (Emphasis added).

The position adopted by the Georgia high court recognizes that, except for the "most extreme" instance, when a court determines that the product is so dangerous that it should not have been sold at all, it is necessary to prove a reasonable alternative design. This position is supported by § 2(b) and Comment *e* thereto.

In Holm v. Sponco Manufacturing., 324 N.W.2d 207, 212–13 (Minn.1982), **Minnesota** rejected the consumer expectations test and adopted risk-utility balancing as the governing rule for design defect litigation. Minnesota recognizes that, in general, the plaintiff has the burden of showing a reasonable, safer alternative design, but notes that there may be rare cases in which that requirement does not apply. Thus, in Kallio v. Ford Motor Co., 407 N.W.2d 92, 96 (Minn.1987), the court stated that, in establishing that a product was unreasonably dangerous, "a factor bearing upon the requirement ... will be the existence or non-existence of a feasible alternative design.... The plaintiff *ordinarily* has the burden of showing the existence of an alternative design that was safer." (Emphasis added.) Amplifying this point in a lengthy footnote, the court said:

Examination of our cases ... [alleging] defective design demonstrates that, as a practical matter, successful plaintiffs, almost without fail, introduce evidence of an alternative safer design. See, e.g., Bilotta v. Kelley, 346 N.W.2d 616, [622] (Minn.1984) (plaintiff presented evidence of manufacturer's actual alternative design of dockboard); Hudson v. Snyder Body, Inc., 326 N.W.2d 149, [152] (Minn.1982) (plaintiff presented evidence that a portion of the release mechanism of a hydraulic bed dumptruck was superfluously long, creating the defect); Busch v. Busch Constr., Inc., 262 N.W.2d 377, [382] (Minn.1977) (plaintiff presented evidence that a turn signal's use of a plastic yoke inside of a locking steering column required a design allowing a greater clearance radius than the manufacturer's design had allowed); McCormack v. Hankscraft Co., 278 Minn. 322, 154 N.W.2d 488, 498 (Minn. 1967) (plaintiff presented evidence that the cover of a vaporizer should have been secured so that it would prevent water in the vaporizer's jar from simultaneously discharging if the vaporizer should tip over).

Id. n.6 at 96.

The Minnesota high court in *Kallio* did not require that in all cases a reasonable alternative design be presented to the jury as an essential element in finding defect. This is consistent with the position taken in the *Wilson* footnote and in § 2, Comment *e*. The court said that "although *normally* evidence of a safer alternative design will be presented initially by the plaintiff, it is not necessarily required in all cases." Id. at 96–97 (emphasis added). The court exemplified this exception by citing Wilson v. Piper Aircraft Corp., 577 P.2d at 1328 n.5, stating that "[c]onceivably, rare cases may exist where the product may be judged unreasonably dangerous because it should be removed from the market rather than be redesigned." (Citations omitted).

A fair reading of Minnesota law is that for the majority of design defect cases proof of a reasonable alternative is necessary. It is not, however, necessary to instruct a jury on a reasonable alternative design requirement; a general instruction on risk-utility is required by the court. In rare cases, when a product has negligible utility and high risk, the reasonable alternative design requirement is not imposed. The position of the Minnesota courts is thus fully consistent with both the black letter of § 2 and Comments *d*, *e*, and *f*. A leading authority on Minnesota products liability law agrees. See Steenson, The Restatement (Third) of Torts and Minnesota Products Liability Law: Liability Standards, 24 Wm. Mitchell L. Rev. 1 (1997).

Montana decisions support the proposition that to maintain a claim of design defect a plaintiff must prove that a reasonable alternative design could have been adopted that would have reduced the harm. In Rix v. General Motors Corp., 723 P.2d 195, 202 (Mont.1986), the court said that "[a] design is defective if at the time of manufacture an alternative designed product would have been safer than the original designed product and was both technologically feasible and a marketable reality." Earlier in the decision, the court emphasized that this rule applied "when a manufactured product is claimed to be unreasonably dangerous because a safer alternative was available to the manufacturer." Id. The court left open the question of how it would rule if no alternative design was technologically feasible, citing O'Brien v. Muskin, 463 A.2d 298, 306 (N.J.1983) (court held that a design could be found to be defective even if no feasible alternative was available). Even if the Montana court were to follow *O'Brien*, in the ordinary design defect case a reasonable alternative design would have to be proven; *O'Brien*, on its own terms, allows for dispensing with the alternative design requirement only when the product has minimal social utility. Id. (Some products "are so dangerous and of such little use that under the risk-utility analysis, a manufacturer would bear the cost of liability of harm to others."); see also Krueger v. General Motors Corp., 783 P.2d 1340, 1345 (Mont.1989) (court reiterated the need for a reasonable alternative design).

North Carolina also requires that a plaintiff seeking to establish liability on the basis of a design defect must prove the existence of a safer alternative design. N.C. Gen. Stat. § 99B–6 (1995) provides:

> (a) No manufacturer of a product shall be held liable . . . for . . . inadequate design . . . unless the claimant proves that at the time of its manufacture the manufacturer acted unreasonably in designing or formulating the product, that this conduct was a proximate cause of the harm for which damages are sought, and also proves one of the following:
>
> (1) At the time the product left the control of the manufacturer, the *manufacturer unreasonably failed to adopt a safer, practical, feasible, and otherwise reasonable alternative design* . . . that could

then have been adopted and that would have prevented or substantially reduced the risk of harm without substantially impairing the usefulness, practicality, or desirability of the product.

(2) ... the design ... of the product was so unreasonable that a reasonable person, aware of the relevant facts, would not use or consume a product of this design. (emphasis added).

While the North Carolina courts have yet to reach the issue, it seems reasonable to assume that subsection (a)(2) of the foregoing statute will serve as an acceptable basis for design-defect liability only in very rare instances (i.e. Comment *e* cases). The use of the language "so unreasonable," coupled with the fact that North Carolina has already expressed an aversion to strict liability in products-liability actions, see N.C. Gen. Stat. § 99B-1.1 (1995), lends support to this position.

Ohio law on these issues is unclear. An Ohio statute provides that, whether proceeding on a risk-utility or consumer expectations theory of design defect, it is a *sine qua non* to maintenance of the action that plaintiff prove the existence of a reasonable alternative design. Ohio Rev. Code Ann. § 2307.75 (A)-(F) (Anderson 1993) (Subsection (A) allows alternate theories of recovery, including disappointment of consumer expectations. Subsection (F) provides that a product is not defective in design if "a practical and technically feasible alternative design ... was not available that would have prevented the harm ... without substantially impairing the usefulness or intended purpose of the product, unless the manufacturer acted unreasonably in introducing the product into trade or commerce."). It should be noted that Subsection (F) provides a caveat to the reasonable alternative design requirement, dispensing with it when "[t]he manufacturer acted unreasonably in introducing the product into trade or commerce." If this caveat is not narrowly construed by the Ohio courts, it is evident that it will devour the rule itself; a plaintiff would be free in every case to argue that the design was unreasonable and that the manufacturer thus acted unreasonably, by definition, in introducing it into commerce. A more reasonable construction is that the legislature sought to reflect the sense of Wilson v. Piper Aircraft Corp., 577 P.2d at 1328 n.5, i.e., that a manufacturer acts unreasonably in introducing a product into commerce when the product has negligible utility and very high risk potential. Thus, the Ohio statute may well be consistent with the position taken in § 2, Comments *d* and *e*.

B. Jurisdictions That Apply a Risk-Utility Test for Defective Design, Thereby Implicitly Requiring Proof of a Reasonable Alternative Design Without Explicitly Doing So

Case law in some jurisdictions, while not explicitly requiring proof of an alternative in design cases, asserts that defective design is to be determined by risk-utility balancing. Under risk-utility balancing the likelihood and magnitude of foreseeable harm is balanced against the burden of precaution against the anticipated harm. In a products-liability setting involving product design, the plaintiff's burden of precaution against the harm can only be either adoption of a reasonable safer alternative design or a decision that, even absent an alternative design, the product should not have been marketed at all. The former statement of the burden is expressed in terms of the omission of the safer alternative rendering the particular product design defective; the latter is expressed in terms of the product being inherently socially unacceptable. The latter position, of course, is reflected in Comment *e* to § 2. Assuming that that unusual circumstance involving Comment *e* is not presented, application of a risk-utility approach to defective design must involve the question of whether a reasonable manufacturer would have adopted a safer alternative design, whether or not the court explicitly says so.

The relevant case law supports this analysis. For example, **Arizona** law is found in Dart v. Wiebe Mfg., 709 P.2d 876 (Ariz.1985) (en banc). Preliminarily, the court acknowledges that the standard for design defect is difficult to articulate; the consumer expectations test is adequate for manufacturing defects, but will only "sometimes work well" in design cases, as consumers will very often not know what to expect of a complex or unfamiliar design. Id. at 878. (The Reporters read this part of the court's analysis to be referring to the malfunction theory captured in § 3.) Therefore, the court opts for a risk-utility test, using the factors suggested by Dean Wade in the more frequent situations not involving malfunction, in which consumer expectations are inadequate to measure defectiveness. Id. at 879. In addition, Arizona draws a sharp distinction between negligence and strict liability, applying knowledge available at time of trial for strict liability, and at time of sale for negligence. Id. at 880–82. In sum, it is probable that the situations in which Arizona will apply the consumer expectations test are those covered by § 3, and that risk-utility analysis will be applied in all others. As we have explained, risk-utility unavoidably implies that the manufacturer should have either adopted a reasonable alternative design (§ 2(b)), or not sold the product at all (Comment *e*).

The leading case in **Florida** is Radiation Technology, Inc. v. Ware Construction Co., 445 So.2d 329 (Fla. 1983), in which the importance of reasonable alternative design evidence in Florida risk-utility analysis was described as follows:

> With the adoption of strict liability . . . the phrase [inherently dangerous] became largely passe except as a rhetorical device to persuade a jury that a product contained a defect or inherent characteristic which posed a danger to users or bystanders. Under strict liability, the Restatement, Second, of Torts, [S]ection 402A (1965) refers to products which are "unreasonably dangerous to the user or consumer or to his property" regardless of privity. The term "unreasonably dangerous" more accurately depicts liability of a manufacturer or supplier in that it balances the likelihood and gravity of potential injury against the utility of the product, *the availability of other, safer products to meet the same need,* the obviousness of the danger, public knowledge and expectation of the danger, the adequacy of instructions and warnings on safe use, *and the ability to eliminate or minimize the danger without seriously impairing the product or making it unduly expensive.* Thus, an unsafe product, whether it be

> characterized as inherently dangerous or unavoidably dangerous, would not necessarily be an unreasonably dangerous product.

Id. at 331 (emphasis added). The above-cited language regarding the importance of reasonable alternative design evidence is consistent with prior Florida cases. See, e.g., Husky Indus. v. Black, 434 So.2d 988, 995 (Fla. Dist.Ct.App.1983) (Court decides case for defendant on absence of an alternative design: "what is missing here is any showing . . . that if the can had been any other color or made of any other material, it would not have exploded. There is simply nothing from which a trier of fact could infer that the color of the can was a defect."), and has subsequently been relied upon by the Florida courts. See, e.g., Light v. Weldarc Co., Inc., 569 So.2d 1302, 1304 (Fla.Dist.Ct.App.1990) ("The term 'unreasonably dangerous' more accurately depicts liability of a manufacturer or supplier in that it balances the likelihood and gravity of potential injury against the utility of the product, the availability of other, safer products to meet the same need, the obviousness of the danger . . . and the ability to eliminate or minimize the danger without seriously impairing the product. . . . ").

Several federal courts sitting in diversity have suggested that Florida also recognizes a consumer expectations test, relying primarily on Florida standard jury instructions. See, e.g., Taylor v. General Motors Corp., 875 F.2d 816, 818 (11th Cir.1989) (applying Florida law), cert. denied, 494 U.S. 1065, 110 S.Ct. 1781, 108 L.Ed.2d 783 (1990); Norton v. Snapper Power Equip., 806 F.2d 1545, 1548–49 (11th Cir.1987) (applying Florida law); Pulte Home Corp., Inc. v. Ply Gem Indus., Inc., 804 F.Supp. 1471, 1486–87 (M.D.Fla.1992) (applying Florida law). But actual Florida court holdings regarding what a plaintiff must prove to reach the jury do not support this *Erie*-educated guess by federal courts applying Florida law.

At first glance, **Kansas** may appear to apply a consumer expectations test to establish a defective design. However, Kansas applies consumer expectations only in jury instructions and embraces a risk/utility test to determine the sufficiency of evidence presented at trial.

In Lester v. Magic Chef, Inc., 641 P.2d 353 (Kan. 1982), the plaintiff argued that the trial court erred when it instructed the jury that it could find a design defect by applying a consumer expectations test. The Supreme Court of Kansas rejected this argument and held that the trial court did not err when it instructed the jury solely on the basis of the consumer expectations test.

Similarly, in Barnes v. Vega Industries, 676 P.2d 761 (Kan.1984), the Supreme Court found that the consumer expectations test was appropriate for jury instructions. The Court held that "it was not error for the trial court, in its instruction, to define unreasonably dangerous in accordance with the Restatement (Second) of Torts § 402A, Comment *i*, (1965)—the consumer expectation test." Id. at 763.

In Siruta v. Hesston Corp., 659 P.2d 799 (Kan.1983), a farmer lost his left arm when he was examining a hay baler and was pushed into the machine when a belt snapped and whipped him in the back. The plaintiff presented evidence of safer alternative designs by calling expert witnesses who testified that a guard on the belts and rollers would have prevented the plaintiff's injuries. The Supreme Court held that the evidence of the alternative designs was properly admitted: "[i]n products liability cases, the plaintiff in sustaining its burden to prove that a product is defectively designed may properly show the feasibility of a safer design." Id. at 808. Thus, after *Siruta*, it was clear that Kansas would instruct a jury as per a consumer expectations test but, in deciding whether the plaintiff should reach the jury with a claim based on design defect, a plaintiff must establish the existence of a reasonable alternative design.

This was the tone of the Kansas high court in Betts v. General Motors Corps., 689 P.2d 795 (Kan.1984). This case represents the Supreme Court of Kansas's last clear attempt to define the boundaries of design defect. The plaintiffs alleged that General Motors defectively designed the 1973 Monte Carlo by placing the fuel tank in a location where it was likely to rupture in a collision. The Supreme Court again found that the trial court did not err in instructing the jury according to the consumer expectations test. It also found that a risk/utility test was more appropriate for the evidentiary portion of the trial:

> The contention of the plaintiffs that the trial court excluded certain relevant evidence because it applied the consumer expectations test is wholly without merit. The instruction given to the jury setting forth the test to be applied in determining whether a product is unreasonably dangerous really has nothing to do with the scope of evidence offered at the trial. In a products liability case involving a claimed design defect, the parties at the trial may present evidence as to the degree of the likelihood of harm from an intended and reasonably foreseeable use of the product and the feasibility of a safer design. Likewise, evidence may be introduced as to the importance of the need or needs served by the product and its design, the technical and economic feasibility and practicality of serving those needs with a safer design, and the availability of other products, if any, to serve the same needs.

Id. at 801.

As the *Betts* court made clear, the instructions a court gives to a jury are irrelevant to the burden of proof a plaintiff must meet in order to show a defective design. In Kansas, a plaintiff must first pass a risk/utility test to show a defective design before the case can proceed to the jury. This Restatement does not address appropriate jury instructions; it leaves the issue to local law. The reasonable alternative design requirement of § 2 is intended to represent the standard a court would apply in determining whether a plaintiff has met the evidentiary burden. Therefore, Kansas's application of a risk/utility test (and its implicit reasonable alternative design requirement) in the evidentiary portion of a trial is entirely consistent with this Restatement.

In Jenkins v. Amchem Prods., 886 P.2d 869 (Kan.1994), the Kansas high court recently struggled with the division between the standard for jury instructions and the separate standard for the plaintiff's burden of proof in design defect cases. In *Jenkins*, a farmer alleged that the defendant's 2, 4–D herbicide products (which contained cholorophenoxy herbicides) caused or contributed to his development of non-Hodgkin's lymphoma. He sought recovery under failure to warn and design defect theories. The trial court granted summary judgment for the manufacturer because the claims were preempted by the Federal Insecticide, Fungiccide & Rodenticide Act (FIFRA), 7 U.S.C.A. § 136 *et seq.* (1988). However, the trial court ruled that if the design defect claim had not been preempted and the plaintiff had proven that the defendant's products cause cancer, then he would have met his evidentiary burden without having to prove a specific defect.

On appeal, the Kansas Supreme Court held that FIFRA preempted the plaintiff's failure to warn claim, but not the design defect claim. In evaluating the design defect claim, the Kansas Supreme Court rejected the trial court's application of res ipsa loquitur and held that the plaintiff must show a specific defect in a design case. In determining the appropriate test a plaintiff must meet to show a specific defect however, the court (in dictum) appeared to confuse the jury instruction standard of *Lester* with the burden of proof standard set down in *Siruta*:

> [g]enerally, evidence of a safer alternative design seems to lend itself to a risk-benefit analysis. The risk-benefit analysis looks in part to whether there is a safer feasible alternative, whether such an alternative is cost effective, and whether there are risks associated with the alternative design. Evidence of a safer alternative design seems to have no place under the consumer expectations test, which merely looks to whether the product was more dangerous than the ordinary consumer expected. However, *Siruta* clearly approves proof of a safer alternative design in design defect cases.... It is clear from *Siruta* that even though Kansas has adopted the consumer expectations test, evidence of a feasible alternative design is admissible in design defect cases, though it is probably not required.

Id. at 890 (citations omitted). The *Jenkins* court then failed to suggest which standard the plaintiff should meet and simply held that: "[p]laintiff has failed to identify what aspect of defendants' products was defectively designed. Therefore, plaintiff cannot prevail on a strict liability design defect claim." Id.

Although the *Jenkins* court was unsure of which standard it would apply to a design defect case, it seems clear that the Kansas Supreme Court would have to confront the *Betts* rationale if it is faced with a case in which a plaintiff attempts to prove a specific defect. Since the high court's confusion in *Jenkins* was contained in mere dictum, the *Betts* court's adherence to a risk-utility test is still the law in Kansas.

Kentucky has characterized its risk-utility standard as that of whether an "ordinarily prudent company ... being fully aware of the risk, would not have put [the product] on the market." Nichols v. Union Underwear Co., 602 S.W.2d 429, 433 (Ky. 1980); see also Montgomery Elevator Co. v. McCullough, 676 S.W.2d 776, 780–81 (Ky.1984). In Ingersoll–Rand Co. v. Rice, 775 S.W.2d 924, 928–29 (Ky.Ct.App.1988), the court indicated that no issue of strict liability would go to the jury unless plaintiff could establish an alternative design that was feasible and would have prevented injury. See also Tobin v. Astra Pharm. Prods., Inc., 993 F.2d 528, 536 (6th Cir.1993) (applying Kentucky law) ("Under Kentucky law, the test for whether a product is in a defective condition and unreasonably dangerous to the user is whether an ordinarily prudent manufacturer, being fully aware of the risks, would have placed the product on the market."), cert. denied, 510 U.S. 914, 114 S.Ct. 304, 126 L.Ed.2d 252 (1993).

Maine, too, is solidly in the risk-utility camp. St. Germain v. Husqvarna Corp., 544 A.2d 1283, 1286 (Me. 1988) (court rejected consumer expectations and adopted risk-utility analysis for design defect cases; heavy emphasis placed on proffered reasonable alternative design in overruling trial court's directed verdict for defendant). See also Guiggey v. Bombardier, et al., 615 A.2d 1169, 1172 (Me. 1992) ("To determine whether a product is defectively dangerous, we balance the danger presented by the product against its utility.").

Missouri instructs juries to determine design defectiveness on the basis of whether the defendant's design is "unreasonably dangerous," without further elaboration; but the reported cases reveal that, in assessing the sufficiency of the plaintiff's proof, courts determine whether a reasonable alternative design has been made out. See Nesselrode v. Executive Beechcraft, Inc., 707 S.W.2d 371, 378 (Mo.banc.1986) (standard is "unreasonably dangerous;" "a key element of plaintiff's theory of defective design was the feasibility of an alternative design—which would have guarded against reverse installation"). See also Wilson v. Danuser Machine Co., Inc., 874 S.W.2d 507, 512 (Mo.App.1994) (no need to prove malfunction; plaintiff's expert testified that hazard "was easily remedied by use of a proper design").

New Hampshire has not spoken definitively as to whether the plaintiff must show that a reasonable alternative design could have been adopted that would have reduced the harm. However, the language in Thibault v. Sears, Roebuck & Co., 395 A.2d 843 (N.H.1978), strongly suggests that, as a practical matter, such a showing is necessary. *Thibault* adopted risk-utility as the governing standard for design defect, and applied the test as follows:

> The utility of the product must be evaluated from the point of view of the public as a whole, because a finding of liability for defective design could result in the removal of an entire product line from the market.... In weighing utility and desirability against danger, courts should also consider whether the risk of danger could have been reduced without significant impact on product effectiveness and manufacturing cost. For example, liability may attach if the manufacturer did not take available and reasonable steps to lessen or eliminate the danger of even a significantly useful and desirable product.

Id. at 846. This language strongly suggests that production of evidence of a reasonable alternative design is required.

The leading case in **New Mexico** is Brooks v. Beech Aircraft Corp., 902 P.2d 54 (N.M.1995). *Brooks* attributes a time-of-trial knowledge to defendant, but, given that knowledge, applies a risk-utility test to the issue of design defect. In *Brooks*, the New Mexico court stated that it would charge a manufacturer with knowledge of risk available at time of trial regardless of whether it was available to defendant at time of sale. (This is the "state of the art" issue discussed in IV.B, infra.) Nonetheless, the court clearly adopted a risk-utility analysis as the grounds for deciding whether a product was unreasonably dangerous. Id. at 61–62. It should be noted that the court said:

> In most instances a manufacturer is aware of the risks posed by any given design and of the availability of an alternative design. This case is a perfect example; Dr. Snyder testified that Beech had developed and used a workable shoulder harness prior to the design and manufacture of Mr. Brook's plane. Thus we disagree with the premise that fairness requires the rejection of strict liability in design cases; when the manufacturer is aware of product risk and alternative designs at the time of supply, it is certainly not unfair to judge the manufacturer's design according to principles of strict liability rather than by conduct at the time of supply.

Id. at 63. The court then concluded:

> If in some future case we are confronted directly with a proffer of evidence on an advancement or change in the state of the art that was neither known nor knowable at the time the product was supplied, we may at that time reconsider application of a state-of-the-art defense to those real circumstances, properly developed under the proffer with applicable briefs and argument.

Id.

South Carolina described its version of risk-utility balancing in Claytor v. General Motors Corp., 286 S.E.2d 129, 132 (S.C.1982) ("In the final analysis, we have another of the law's balancing acts and numerous factors must be considered, including the usefulness and desirability of the product, the cost involved for added safety, the likelihood and potential seriousness of injury, and the obviousness of danger.").

Virginia has not adopted strict products liability in tort, but an action for breach of implied warranty of merchantability provides the substantial equivalent. Virginia case law repeatedly has expressed the concept of reasonable safety. See, e.g., Featherall v. Firestone Tire & Rubber Co., 252 S.E.2d 358 (Va.1979); Turner v. Manning, Maxwell & Moore, Inc., 217 S.E.2d 863 (Va.1975); see also Marshall v. H.K. Ferguson Co., 623 F.2d 882 (4th Cir.1980) (applying Virginia law); Dreisonstok v. Volkswagenwerk, A.G., 489 F.2d 1066, 1073 (4th Cir. 1974) (applying Virginia law) (manufacturer owes a duty to adopt reasonably safer alternative designs); Lemons v. Ryder Truck Rental, Inc., 906 F.Supp. 328 (W.D.Va.1995) (applying Virginia law) (court found that in the absence of proof of a technically feasible and desirable alternative design, plaintiff cannot establish that a defect in the product caused the harm).

C. Jurisdictions That Apply a Consumer Expectations Test Based on Risk–Utility, Thereby Implicitly Requiring Proof of a Reasonable Alternative Design in Most Cases

A few courts set forth the test for defective design using consumer expectations rhetoric, but then apply risk-utility balancing to determine whether reasonable expectations are met. As explained in the preceding Section, adoption of risk-utility analysis unavoidably commits a court to a reasonable alternative design requirement in cases not involving § 3 or Comment *e* to § 2.

A paradigmatic example of a state adopting this approach is **Connecti-**

cut. In Potter v. Chicago Pneumatic Tool Co., 694 A.2d 1319 (Conn.1997), the Connecticut Supreme Court states that "[the] 'consumer expectation' standard is now well established in Connecticut strict products liability decisions," and seemingly rejects the reasonable alternative design approach as the basic test for defective design. (See discussion below) But then the court notes:

> . . . we nevertheless recognize that there may be instances in which an ordinary consumer may not be able to form expectations of safety. In such cases, a consumer's expectations may be viewed in light of various factors that balance the utility of the product's design with the magnitude of its risks. We find persuasive the reasoning of those jurisdictions that have modified their formulation of the consumer expectation test by incorporating risk-utility factors into the ordinary consumer expectation analysis.

Id. at 1333 (citations omitted). Although the Court's opinion asserts otherwise, this holding inevitably steers Connecticut toward the reasonable alternative design requirement set forth in this Restatement. Indeed, this fact was not lost on one of the Justices who decided the case. Justice Berdon, in a concurring opinion, expresses concern about this very issue. He points out that "adopting such a risk-utility test for 'complex product designs' sounds dangerously close to requiring proof of the existence of 'a reasonable alternative design.' " Id. at 1356.

The *Potter* decision is also interesting in that it sheds light on how courts may interpret, and possibly misinterpret, the provisions of this Restatement dealing with defective product designs. On its facts, the claim in the *Potter* case was clearly one for the jury under § 2(b). The plaintiffs were workers who alleged that they had been injured by the defendant manufacturer's failure to adopt safety devices in its industrial hand tools that would have reduced the levels of vibration. The plaintiffs introduced credible evidence of reasonable alternative designs that would have prevented their injuries. Indeed, the defendant's tools did not even meet promulgated industry safety standards in this regard. Understandably, the trial court gave the case to the jury and the jury returned verdicts in favor of the plaintiffs. Inexplicably, the defendant appears to have argued on appeal, relying on an earlier draft of the Restatement, that proof of an alternative design was an absolute requirement under the Restatement and that the plaintiffs had failed to introduce such proof. The defendant, however, was clearly wrong on both counts. Under this Restatement proof of an alternative design is *not* required in every case (see the discussion of Comment *b* at the outset of this Note); and, in any event, the plaintiff's proof of a feasible, safer alternative in the *Potter* case was more than adequate. But given the defendant's apparent insistence on appeal that the Restatement Third, (then in early draft) imposes an "absolute" requirement in this regard, the Court rejected both the defendant's argument and the early draft of this Restatement.

That the Connecticut Supreme Court's analysis in *Potter* is, in actuality, perfectly consistent with this Restatement is clear from that portion of the court's opinion that considers the circumstances in which proof of a reasonable alternative design is not necessary. The court identifies two such circumstances: (1) when a product malfunctions, the existence of a defect may be inferred; and (2) a product design may be so dangerous that it should not be sold at all, even if a reasonable alternative design is not available. As indicated throughout this Reporters' Note, both of these alternatives to providing a reasonable alternative design are embraced in this Restatement. Product malfunction is recognized in § 3; and the "should not be sold at all" circumstance is recognized in Comment *e* to § 2. Having pointed to both of these possibilities, the Court concludes: "[a]ccordingly, we decline to adopt the requirement [embodied in the Restatement Third,] that a plaintiff must prove a feasible alternative design as a *sine qua non* to establishing a prima facie case of design defect." (Emphasis added.)

Given that the foregoing conclusion by the court is perfectly consistent with this Restatement as finally promulgated, when the issue is next before the court, the court may find it easier to accept the Restatement as consistent with its position as articulated in *Potter*. Whatever ambiguities in the earlier draft may have misled the court in this regard, those ambiguities have since been eliminated. See § 2, Comment *b*.

Perhaps not so obviously, other states have fallen into this pattern of using "consumer expectations" rhetoric while applying risk-utility analysis. One such state is **Iowa**. See e.g., Aller v. Rodgers Machinery Mfg. Co., Inc., 268 N.W.2d 830, 834–35 (Iowa 1978) (" 'The article sold must be dangerous to an extent beyond that which would be expected by the ordinary consumer.... Proof of unreasonableness involves a balancing process. On one side of the scale is the utility of the product and on the other side is the risk of its use.' "). **Washington** also exemplifies this approach. See Seattle–First Nat'l Bank v. Tabert, 542 P.2d 774, 779 (Wash. 1975) ("In determining the reasonableness of expectations of the ordinary consumer, a number of factors must be considered. The relative cost of the product, the gravity of the potential harm from the claimed defect and the cost and feasibility of eliminating or minimizing the risk may be relevant.... "); see also Baughn v. Honda Motor Co., 727 P.2d 655, 660 (Wash.1986) ("[W]hile usually called a consumer expectations test, the *Tabert* rule actually combines the consideration of consumer expectations with an analysis of the risk and utility inherent in the product's use.").

D. Jurisdictions That Apply a Consumer Expectations Test Without Requiring Proof of a Reasonable Alternative Design

The only true rival in American products liability law to the risk-utility test (with its necessary reliance on a requirement of reasonable alternative design) in cases not involving § 3 or Comment *e* to § 2 is the consumer expectations test. In a minority of jurisdictions the failure of a product to meet consumer expectations suffices, in and of itself, to establish liability in cases predicated on design defect. These jurisdictions represent a distinct minority, and there are reasons to believe their numbers may diminish over time.

In any event, before getting to the relevant decisions, it is important to understand that a number of "false positives" exist in this regard—i.e., that there are various ways in which courts make reference to consumer expectations without committing to consumer expectations as an independent test for design defectiveness. In most instances, judicial references to consumer expectations are fully consistent with the rules of this Restatement governing defective design. For example, jury instructions often are couched in language that asks the jury to determine whether the product is not reasonably safe, is unreasonably dangerous, or fails to meet reasonable consumer expectations. The requirement that proof of a reasonable alternative design be introduced as a necessary predicate for reaching the jury in a design defect case is a rule of law for the court. Once a court finds that sufficient evidence of a reasonable alternative design has been introduced, this Restatement leaves the formulation of the jury instruction to the local law applicable in trial courts in the various states. See § 2, Comment *f.* Many states require proof of a reasonable alternative design as a prerequisite to reaching the jury, yet couch their jury instructions in more general language that often includes consumer expectations. The practice of these jurisdictions is fully compatible with the rule stated in this Section.

Moreover, as noted earlier, some courts talk of reasonable consumer expectations as the test for liability but define consumer expectations in risk-utility terms. This is merely terminological variance and is consistent with the rule of this Section. See § 2, Comment *g*. Moreover, courts often focus on consumer expectations as an important factor in risk-utility balancing. Consumer expectations are relevant in assessing the foreseeability of the harm and in evaluating the range of foreseeable uses of a product, even under a reasonable alternative design standard. See § 2, Comment *g*.

Consumer expectations are sometimes invoked by courts to defeat otherwise valid claims of defective design. Thus, in some jurisdictions, for a product meeting consumer expectations, courts take the position that liability for defective design cannot be made out even though a plaintiff seeks to establish that a reasonable safer alternative design was possible. When the consumer expectations test is applied in this manner, it simply reintroduces the "patent danger" rule as a bar to liability. The patent danger rule is specifically disapproved in this Restatement. See Section IV.C of this Reporters' Note, which demonstrates that the overwhelming majority of jurisdictions have disavowed the patent danger rule.

Finally and most importantly, in cases where courts allow a res-ipsa type of inference of defect based on the standards set forth in § 3, they often speak of the failure of the product to meet reasonable consumer expectations. This also is true of cases in which the product fails in a catastrophic fashion and the inference of defect (be it in design or manufacturing) is manifest. See § 3, Comment *b*.

This last point is critical to an understanding of what many courts are doing when they refer to consumer expectations in the context of the standard for defective design. As explained at the outset of this Reporters' Note, § 3 supplies an alternative basis for imposing liability for defective design. Thus, when a product malfunctions due to an inadequate design, courts often speak of the disappointment of consumer expectations without meaning to detract from the viability of the reasonable alternative design requirement in cases not involving malfunction, to which § 3 does not apply.

California supplies a good example of this last-described phenomenon. Originally, California adopted consumer expectations as an independent test for determining defective design. See Barker v. Lull Eng'g Co., Inc., 573 P.2d 443 (Cal.1978). Later, in Soule v. General Motors Corp., 882 P.2d 298 (Cal.1994), the California Supreme Court reexamined the role of the consumer expectations test in design defect litigation. The court recognized a limited role for the consumer expectations test but found it wholly unsatisfactory for a case involving product design of any complexity. The court said:

> In some cases, therefore, "ordinary knowledge ... as to ... [the product's] characteristics" (Rest.2d Torts, supra, § 402A, Com. *i*) ... may permit an inference that the product did not perform as safely as it should. *If* the facts permit such a conclusion and *if* the failure resulted from the product's design, a finding of defect is warranted without any further proof. The manufacturer may not defend a claim that a product's design failed to perform as safely as its ordinary consumers would expect by presenting expert evidence of the design's relative risks and benefits.
>
> However, as we noted in *Barker*, a complex product, even when it is being used as intended, may often cause injury in a way that does not engage its ordinary consumers' reasonable minimum assumptions about safe performance. For example, the ordinary consumer of an automobile simply has "no idea" how it should perform in all foreseeable situations, or how safe it should be made against all foreseeable hazards....
>
> ...
>
> As we have seen, the consumer expectations test is reserved for cases in which the *everyday experience* of the product's users permits a conclusion that the product's design violated *minimum* safety assumptions, and is thus defective *regardless of expert opinion about the merits of the design.*

Id. at 308 (emphasis added).

Also see Collazo v. Toyota Motor Corp., 937 F.Supp. 134 (D.P.R.1996) (The federal court applying the law of Puerto Rico held that it would follow the *Barker-Soule* cases in California. Applying those cases to a design defect claim with respect to an air-bag system the court held that a risk-utility test rather than the consumer expectations test must be used to gauge liability).

In two telling footnotes the court in *Soule* indicated the kinds of cases that would legitimately be covered by the consumer expectations test and those that are not within its proper purview. In n.3 the court said:

> For example, the ordinary consumers of modern automobiles may and do expect that such vehicles will be designed so as not to explode while idling at stoplights, experience sudden steering or brake failure as they leave the dealership, or roll over and catch fire in two-mile-per-hour collisions. If the plaintiff in a products liability action proved that a vehicle's design produced such a result, the jury could find forthwith that the car failed to perform as safely as its

> ordinary consumers would expect, and was therefore defective.

Id. And in n.4 the court opined:

> Plaintiff insists that manufacturers should be forced to design their products to meet the "objective" safety demands of a "hypothetical" reasonable consumer who is fully informed about what he or she *should* expect. Hence, plaintiff reasons, the jury may receive expert advice on "reasonable" safety expectations for the product. However, this function is better served by the risk-benefit prong of *Barker*. There, juries receive expert advice, apply clear guidelines, and decide accordingly whether the product's design is an acceptable compromise of competing considerations. . . .

Id.

The position of the California Supreme Court in *Soule* is therefore completely consistent with this Restatement. The cases included in n.3 under the consumer expectations test are identical to those covered under § 3, which allows an inference of defect from the occurrence of the accident event. Indeed, similar examples allowing an inference of defect are set forth in Illustrations 1 and 3 in § 3. This Restatement places these inference-of-defect cases under the more traditional rule of res ipsa loquitur rather than relying on the consumer expectations test to create the inference of defect. Res ipsa loquitur has a long and distinguished history in the law of torts and products liability, and is a more appropriate vehicle for allowing an inference of defect. See also, **Tennessee**, Ray v. BIC Corp., 925 S.W.2d 527 (Tenn.1996) (the court adopted the analysis of the California high court in *Soule* and limited the use of the consumer expectations test under the Tennessee statute to simple, non-complex products, the very kind of defect for which one could appropriately draw an inference under § 3).

These examples of "consumer-expectations-in-name-only" states having been put to one side, in a small number of jurisdictions the consumer expectations test does constitute an independent test for design defects. See, e.g. **Alaska** (Caterpillar Tractor v. Beck, 593 P.2d 871 (Alaska 1979)); **Arkansas** (French v. Grove Mfg. Co., 656 F.2d 295 (8th Cir.1981) (applying Arkansas law)); **Hawaii** (Ontai v. Straub Clinic & Hosp. Inc., 659 P.2d 734 (Haw.1983)); **Nebraska** (Kudlacek v. Fiat, 509 N.W.2d 603 (Neb. 1994)); **Oklahoma** (Lee v. Volkswagen of Am., Inc., 688 P.2d 1283, 1285 (Okla.1984) ("Plaintiffs . . . must prove . . . that the defect made the product unreasonably dangerous as defined by ordinary consumer expectations."))); and **Wisconsin** (Sumnicht v. Toyota Motor Sales, U.S.A., Inc., 360 N.W.2d 2, 16–17 (Wis.1984) ("'Thus, the test in Wisconsin of whether a product contains an unreasonably dangerous defect depends upon the reasonable expectations of the ordinary consumer' . . . A product may be defective and unreasonably dangerous even though there are no alternative, safer designs available." (citation omitted))). These holdings have been roundly criticized by the majority of leading academic commentators. It is also worthwhile noting that even in these jurisdictions, the appellate cases reveal that plaintiffs have in fact introduced evidence of a reasonable alternative design and that the evidence is deemed important in determining whether a prima facie case of defect has been established.

Until 1994, California would have been listed as a state that applied a consumer expectations test. See *Barker*, supra. However, in 1994, the California Supreme Court limited the application of the consumer expectations test to non-complex design cases. See *Soule*, supra. As discussed above, the current law in California is consistent with this Restatement. Similarly, Tennessee had been a state which employed a *Barker* analysis to design defect cases. Subsequently, however, Tennessee followed California by applying the consumer expectations test only in simple design defect cases. See *Ray*, supra. It will be interesting to see if the other states that continue to follow *Barker* (Hawaii and Alaska) will eventually adopt the subsequently developed reasoning of *Soule*, as did Tennessee.

III. Views of American Legal Scholars Regarding the General Test for Defective Design

A. Scholarship Written Prior to This Restatement (and Therefore Independently of It)

Scholarly commentary written prior to this Restatement project agrees overwhelmingly with the majority view reflected in the above-cited decisions and § 2(b) and the risk-utility/reasonable alternative design approach adopted herein. See, e.g., Madden, Products Liability vol. 1 at 299 (2d ed. 1988) ("[T]he majority rule posits that plaintiff cannot establish a prima facie case of defective design without evidence of a technologically feasible, and practicable, alternative to defendant's product that was available at the time of manufacture."). See generally Birnbaum, Unmasking the Test for Design Defect: from Negligence [to Warranty] to Strict Liability to Negligence, 33 Vand. L. Rev. 539 (1980); Epstein, Products Liability: The Search for the Middle Ground, 56 N.C. L. Rev. 643 (1976); Hoenig, Product Designs and Strict Tort Liability: Is There a Better Approach?, 8 Sw. U. L. Rev. 109 (1976); Keeton, Products Liability—Design Hazards and the Meaning of Defect, 10 Cumb. L. Rev. 293 (1979); Powers, A Modest Proposal to Abandon Strict Products Liability, 1991 U. Ill. L. Rev. 639; G. Schwartz, Foreword: Understanding Products Liability, 67 Cal. L. Rev. 435 (1979); Wade, On Product "Design Defects" and Their Actionability, 33 Vand. L. Rev. 551 (1980).

Many eminent scholars have also been sharply critical of the consumer expectations test as an independent general standard for design litigation. Dean Page Keeton, for example, argues that:

> It is quite clear that to the extent that a maker knows, or in the exercise of ordinary care should know, of a risk or hazard that users may not discover or appreciate, liability results for breach of the duty to discover what a reasonable person would disclose. This ground of liability protects users and consumers to a considerable extent from harm resulting from unappreciated dangers. It is submitted, however, that an inquiry as to whether the danger in fact of the design outweighed the benefits of the design would better protect users and consumers, without placing an undue burden on manufacturers and suppliers. The court's primary justification for the retention of the contemplation test is the ease with which the plaintiff can establish a design defect under this test by

circumstantial evidence. If a claimant proves that a product fails under circumstances the ordinary purchaser or user would not have expected, a case has been made. That is clearly so, but the question is, should it be so? I think not. If the court would permit the defendant to show under a risk-utility analysis by way of rebuttal that it would not be feasible, then the position would be supportable.

Keeton, Products Liability Design Hazards and the Meaning of Defect, 10 Cumb. L. Rev. 293, 310 (1979) (footnote omitted).

A similar note is sounded by Professor Gary Schwartz in Foreword: Understanding Products Liability, 67 Cal. L. Rev. 435 (1979), in which he roundly criticizes the consumer expectations test. Schwartz notes that:

> [T]he [consumer expectations] thesis works well if the "portrayal" is concrete enough to entail a U.C.C. express warranty or a Restatement product representation. Absent this concreteness, the thesis does not easily test out. Consider, for example, the advertisements of Datsun automobiles, advertisements that have always praised the car for both economy and quality, but with varying emphases. For several years, this advertising stressed economy through the slogan, "Datsun Saves." After a well-published change of advertising agencies, in 1977–78 Datsun's message became "We Are Driven," suggesting quality and performance. With inventories swelling in dealers' lots in fall 1978, its advertising shifted to "We Are Dealing," pointing to temporary low prices. To my mind, these changes in advertising themes, conspicuous though they are, do not justify a legal rule that measures Datsun's personal injury liability to its 1976 purchasers by standards less demanding than those applicable to its 1977–78 purchasers. Nor should Datsun's liability differ in any material respect from Toyota's ("If You Can Find a Better-Built Small Car, Buy It").

Id. at 476 n.241.

Prosser and Keeton, in The Law of Torts 699 (5th ed. 1984), make the following points about the consumer expectations test:

> The meaning is ambiguous and the test is very difficult of application to discrete problems. What does the reasonable purchaser contemplate? In one sense he does not "expect" to be adversely affected by a risk or hazard unknown to him. In another sense he does contemplate the "possibility" of unknown "side effects." In a sense the ordinary purchaser cannot reasonably expect anything more than that reasonable care in the exercise of the skill and knowledge available to design engineers has been exercised. The test can be utilized to explain most any result that a court or jury chooses to reach. The application of such a vague concept in many situations does not provide much guidance for a jury. (footnote omitted).

Professor Mary J. Davis succinctly identifies the reasons why most courts have rejected the consumer expectations test in design defect litigation. She notes:

> Few courts adhere closely to the letter of [S]ection 402A's consumer expectations test in proving design defect. The test has proved unworkable for a variety of reasons. First, it connotes a contract-based liability, encouraging the jury to

rely intuitively on principles of bargaining and warranty. Second, if the product contains a defect which is apparent or obvious, the consumer expectations arguably include the apparent danger, preventing liability and therefore discouraging product improvements which could easily and cost-effectively alleviate the danger. Third, bystanders, who are widely recognized as protected by both tort and contract theories of products liability regardless of privity, cannot be said to have any expectations about a product which causes them injury.

Perhaps the most important criticism of the consumer expectations test as it relates to design defects is the impossibility of the task it requires: to define just what an ordinary consumer expects of the technical design characteristics of a product. While it can be assumed that consumers expect a certain level of safety, how is that level defined when it comes to specific design criteria? For example, what do consumers expect of the structural soundness of one type of metal as opposed to another with slightly different characteristics that, if used, would require changes in still other aspects of the design? If the ordinary consumer can be said reasonably to expect a product to be "strong," how strong is strong? Is a general impression of strength or quality sufficient when it comes to technical design features? If so, how is that impression measurable against the actual condition of the design feature in question? These difficult questions led many courts to reject the consumer expectations test as the sole test for defective design. (Footnotes omitted).

Davis, Design Defect Liability: In Search of a Standard of Responsibility, 39 Wayne L. Rev. 1217, 1236–37 (1993).

The consumer expectations test has had a small core of academic supporters over the years prior to the Restatement Third. See generally Shapo, A Representational Theory of Consumer Protection: Doctrine, Function and Legal Liability for Product Disappointment, 60 Va. L. Rev. 1109 (1974). See also Bernacchi, A Behavioral Model for Imposing Strict Liability in Tort: The Importance of Analyzing Product Performance in Relationship to Consumer Expectation and Frustration, 47 U. Cin. L. Rev. 43 (1978); Hubbard, Reasonable Human Expectations: A Normative Model for Imposing Strict Liability for Defective Products, 29 Mercer L. Rev. 465 (1978); Rheingold, What Are the Consumer's "Reasonable Expectations"?, 22 Bus. Law. 589 (1967).

B. Scholarship Written in Direct Response to the Restatement's Reasonable Alternative Design Proposal

Many articles have been published in the law reviews in direct response to this Restatement's treatment of design defects. Often by their own admission, these pieces were produced in large measure in an effort to influence the process of deliberation that led to final approval of the Proposed Final Draft by the ALI membership in May of 1997. While these efforts were perfectly legitimate (and often proved useful to the Reporters) their sometimes pointedly adversarial nature warrants the exercise of caution in attempting to gauge scholarly reactions to the Restatement based on a "nose count" of articles published while this project was underway. See, e.g., Shapo, In Search of the Law of Products Liability: The ALI Restatement Project, 48 Vand. L. Rev. 631 (1995); Vandall, The Restatement (Third) of Torts: Products Liability Section 2(b): The Reasonable Alternative Design Requirement, 61 Tenn. L. Rev. 1407 (1994); Corboy, The Not–So–Quiet Revolution—Rebuilding Barriers to Jury Trial in the Proposed Restatement (Third) of Torts: Products Liability, 61 Tenn. L. Rev. 1043 (1994); Jankowski, Focusing On Quality and Risk: The General Role of Reasonable Alternatives in Evaluating Design and Warning Cases, 36 S. Tex. L. Rev. 283 (1995); Grossman, Category Liability and Alternative Feasible Design, 36 S. Tex. L. Rev. 385 (1995).

IV. American Case Law and Commentary on Issues Related to Design–Based Liability

A. The Concept of "Not Reasonably Safe"

Many courts have invoked the concept of "not reasonably safe" to describe defective designs and defects due to failure to instruct or warn. See, e.g., Washington State Physicians Ins. Exch. & Ass'n v. Fisons Corp., 858 P.2d 1054, 1064 (Wash. 1993) (en banc) ("A product manufacturer is subject to liability to a claimant if the claimant's harm is proximately caused by the negligence of the manufacturer in that the product was *not reasonably safe* as designed or *not reasonably safe* because adequate warnings or instructions were not provided.") (emphasis added); Affuso v. Crestline Plastic Pipe Co., Inc., 599 N.Y.S.2d 157, 158 (N.Y.App. Div.1993) ("It was plaintiffs' burden to make a threshold showing that the pipe was defective and *not reasonably safe* for the ordinary purpose for which such goods were used.... "); Jurado v. Western Gear Works, 619 A.2d 1312, 1315 (N.J.1993) (jury was asked: "Was the product as designed, manufactured or sold defective, in that it was *not reasonably safe* for its intended or reasonably foreseeable uses?") (emphasis added); Washburn v. Beatt Equip. Co., 840 P.2d 860, 864 (Wash.1992) (en banc) ("[B]y special verdict, the jury found that defendant's product was *not reasonably safe*.... ") (emphasis added); Bussell v. DeWalt Prods. Corp., 614 A.2d 622, 623 (N.J.Super.Ct.App.Div.1992) ("Jury rendered a verdict against [defendant] on the basis that the saw was *not reasonably safe* for its intended purposes.") (emphasis added); Britt–Tech Corp. v. American Magnetics Corp., 487 N.W.2d 671, 674 (Iowa 1992) ("The product was defective when it left the hands of the manufacturer because it was *not reasonably safe*.") (emphasis added). The suggestion to substitute the term "not reasonably safe" for "unreasonably dangerous" was first made by Dean John W. Wade in two articles entitled Strict Tort Liability of Manufacturers, 19 Sw. L.J. 5, 15 (1965) and On the Nature of Strict Tort Liability for Products, 44 Miss. L.J. 825, 833 (1973). He argued that the term "unreasonably dangerous" gives rise to the impression that the plaintiff must prove that the product was "unusually or extremely dangerous." The term "not reasonably safe" is less subject to misinterpretation.

In Defectiveness Restated: Exploding the "Strict" Products Liability Myth, 1996 U. Ill. L. Rev. 743, 777, Professor David Owen explains the important aspirational advantage of the "not reasonably safe" formulation of the legal standard:

> [T]he "not reasonably safe" standard adopts as the expected norm for products a *positive* standard—reasonable "safety"—replacing the old unreasonably "dangerous" negative formulation of the norm. It is true, of course, that danger inheres in every product, so that the central question of "How much safety is enough?" that arises in every design case in fact must turn on whether the amount of danger was excessive ("unreasonable") in view of a broad-based calculus of costs and benefits. Yet it may just be that the Products Liability Restatement for the twenty-first century properly elevates the norm, aspirationally, to one of (reasonable) *safety*. The actual legal test of liability is not thereby raised to concrete terms, but the new safety standard serves symbolically to provide a signal that (reasonable) product safety—as a positive goal required by the law—must now be afforded a central place in the decisional calculus of manufacturers.

B. The Concept of "State of the Art"

The term "state of the art" has been variously defined by a multitude of courts. For some it refers to industry custom or industry practice; for others it means the safest existing technology that has been adopted for use; for others it means cutting-edge technology. In requiring that plaintiff establish a reasonable alternative design it will, of course, be relevant whether such a safer design has been adopted and put to actual use. However, a plaintiff is not precluded from demonstrating that a reasonable alternative could have been practically adopted. As noted in Comment *d*, it may be very difficult for the plaintiff to demonstrate that a reasonable, safer design could have been adopted by the defendant when the evidence is that it has not been practically adopted by anyone in the industry. But there is no good reason why the plaintiff should be legally barred from making that demonstration and convincing a court of its practical adoptability.

Whether an alternative design was practically attainable depends on reasonableness and good sense. Whether resources should have been devoted to avoiding a particular hazard depends in part upon its frequency and seriousness. If the world were to stop, and focus were to be placed on any isolated hazard, a resolution to almost any problem might be attainable. There is no substitute for a healthy sense of pragmatism when facing this issue.

The authority cited in support of Comment *d* often will be indirect. For example, those courts that allow evidence of industry practice as relevant in a product design case, but not as determinative on the issue of defect, leave open the possibility that the plaintiff may convince a court that industry practice could have been improved upon. It is likely, though not certain, that they would take the position that even the safest technology in actual use could have been practically improved upon. A few states take the position that conformance with the best available technology in actual use is an absolute defense to design liability. And another handful take the position that evidence that a risk was beyond the scope of scientific knowability at the time of manufacture is inadmissible. It is with these extreme minority positions that Comment *d* disagrees. For authority allowing consideration of "state-of-the-art" evidence in determining defect, see, e.g., Elliott v. Brunswick Corp., 903 F.2d 1505 (11th Cir.1990) (applying Alabama law), reh'g denied, cert. denied sub nom. Elliott v. Mercury Marine, 498 U.S. 1048, 111 S.Ct. 756, 112 L.Ed.2d 776 (1991); Beech v. Outboard Marine Corp., 584 So.2d 447 (Ala.1991) (evidence of industry standards at the time of manufacture is relevant to whether product meets existing state of the art; court directed verdict since there was no credible evidence that an alternative design would have been practicable or safer); Sturm, Ruger & Co. v. Day, 594 P.2d 38, 44–45 (Alaska 1979), modified on other issue, 615 P.2d 621 (Alaska 1980), on reh'g, 627 P.2d 204 (1981), cert. denied, 454 U.S. 894, 102 S.Ct. 391, 70 L.Ed.2d 209 (1981), and overruled on other grounds, 703 P.2d 396, 405 (Alaska 1985) (conformance with "state-of-the-art" defined as customary practice in the industry is not a defense in a products liability action but may be considered in determining whether a product is defective); Gosewisch v. American Honda Motor Co., 737 P.2d 365, 370 (Ariz.Ct.App. 1985), opinion vacated in part (on another issue), 737 P.2d 376 (Ariz.1987) (court interpreted Arizona statute creating a "state-of-art defense" to mean that defendant may demonstrate that what plaintiff was suggesting as an alternative may not have been feasible; court said that "not every safety device for which technology exists is feasible"; presumably, if a reasonable, safer design would have been feasible liability could have been established); Raschke v. Carrier Corp., 703 P.2d 556 (Ariz.Ct.App.1985) (court found that design alternative suggested by plaintiff was not in existence and it was not proven how such a design would avoid the danger); Ark. Code Ann. § 16–116–104(a)(1) (Michie 1987) ("state of scientific and technological knowledge available to the manufacturer ... at the time product was placed on market ... may be considered as evidence"); Colo. Rev. Stat. § 13–21–403(1)(a) (1987) (compliance with the "state-of-the-art," as distinguished from injury practices, creates a presumption of non-defectiveness).

See also Fibreboard v. Fenton, 845 P.2d 1168, 1174 (Colo.1993) (en banc) (" 'state-of-the-art' would be an applicable factor in a design-defect case, if the alternative design suggested by the plaintiff was not practically feasible in light of the state-of-the-art at the time the product was manufactured"); Ind. Code § 33–1–1.5–4(b)(4) (1988) (conformance with the generally recognized state of the art at the time the product was designed is an affirmative defense to an action based in strict liability in tort); Ky. Rev. Stat. § 411.310(2) (Banks–Baldwin 1978) (a presumption exists that if product conforms to generally recognized and prevailing standards or the state of the art in existence at the time the design was prepared, it is not defective; presumption is rebuttable by a preponderance of the evidence); La. Rev. Stat. Ann. § 9:2800.56 and § 9:2800.59 (West 1991) (A manufacturer is not liable if it could not have known of the risk of harm or the availability of an alternative design.); Mich. Comp. Laws Ann. § 600.2946 (West 1986) (evidence of compliance with nongovernmental standards admissible); Rix v. General Motors Corp., 723 P.2d 195, 202 (Mont.1986) (test is whether at "the time of manufacture an alternative designed product ... was both technologically feasible and a marketable reality"); Heath v. Sears, Roebuck & Co., 464 A.2d 288, 298 (N.H.1983) (manufacturer held to a standard of technological feasibility at the time of sale or distribution); N.J. Stat. Ann. § 2A: 58C–3(1) (West 1987) (defense if technically feasible alternative was not available at time product left the control of the manufacturer); Voss v. Black & Decker Mfg. Co., 450 N.E.2d 204 (N.Y.1983) (manufacturer has duty to develop a feasible alternative design within the state of the art at the time of production); Ohio Rev. Code Ann. § 2307.75(F) (Anderson 1991) (design not defective if technically feasible alternative was not available at the time the product left the control of its manufacturer); Wood v. Ford Motor Co., 691 P.2d 495 (Or.Ct.App.1984) (plaintiff required to show technically feasible alternative design could have been implemented); Tex. Civ. Prac. & Rem. Code Ann. § 82.005 (West 1993) ("economically and technologically feasible . . . by the application of existing or reasonably achievable scientific knowledge").

A few jurisdictions recognize a defense based upon conformance with the state of the art. Of these jurisdictions, some focus on the state of the art at the time the product was designed, while others concentrate on the state of the art at the time at which the product was placed into the stream of commerce. See, e.g., Ind. Code § 33–1–1.5–4(b)(4) (1988) (conformance with the generally recognized state of the art at the time the product was designed is an affirmative defense to an action based in strict liability in tort); Iowa Code Ann. § 668.12 (West 1987) (conformance with the state of the art at the time the product was designed is a defense); Mo. Ann. Stat. § 537.764 (West 1987) (compliance with state of the art is a defense to a failure to warn claim. However, "state of the art" was defined to mean that the dangerous nature of the product was not known or could not reasonably have been discovered when the product was placed into the stream of commerce); N.J. Stat. Ann. § 2A: 58C–3.a(1) (West 1987) (defense if technically feasible alternative was not available at time product left the control of the manufacturer); Brooks v. Beech Aircraft Corp., 902 P.2d 54, 63 (N.M.1995) (court said the state of the art is not a defense, but in a conclusory paragraph backed away from this position stating that, "[i]f in some future case we are confronted directly with a proffer of evidence on an advancement or change in the state of the art that was neither known nor knowable at the time the product was supplied, we may at that time reconsider application of a state-of-the-art defense."); Ohio Rev. Code Ann. § 2307.75(F) (Anderson 1991) (design not defective if technically feasible alternative was not available at the time the product left the control of its manufacturer).

Another minority of jurisdictions hold that state-of-the-art evidence is irrelevant to the issue of product defect. See, e.g., In re Hawaii Fed. Asbestos Cases, 699 F.Supp. 233, 235–236 (D.Haw.1988), aff'd sub nom. In re Hawaii Fed. Asbestos Cases, 960 F.2d 806 (9th Cir.1992) (state-of-the-art evidence is irrelevant in a design defect or failure to warn cause of action based on strict liability); Hayes v. Ariens Co., 462 N.E.2d 273, 277 (Mass.1984) (state-of-the-art evidence is irrelevant in a failure to warn case). See also Simmons v. Monarch Mach. Tool Co., 596 N.E.2d 318, 320 n. 3 (Mass.1992); Sternhagen v. Dow Co., 935 P.2d 1139, 1147 (Mont.1997) ("Despite the adoption of the state-of-the-art defense in other jurisdictions, recognition of the defense in the Restatement (Third) of the Law of Torts: Products Liability (Proposed Final Draft, Preliminary Version) (Oct. 18, 1996), and the Chemical Companies' assertion that public policy supports adoption of the defense, we choose to continue to adhere to the clear precedent we have heretofore established . . . [N]o Montana case supports the Chemical Companies' position that evidence is admissible when a product's inherent dangers are undiscovered or undiscoverable.") Carrecter v. Colson Equip. Co., 499 A.2d 326 (Pa.Super.Ct.1985) (state-of-the-art evidence is not admissible). Also see Lewis v. Coffing Hoist Division, Duff–Norton Co., Inc., 528 A.2d 590 (Pa.1987) (evidence of industry custom not admissible).

Although courts generally agree that conformance with state of the art is not an absolute defense, they require that the alternative design proffered by the plaintiff could have been practically adopted by the manufacturer at the time of sale. See, e.g., Stanczyk v. Black & Decker, Inc., 836 F.Supp. 565 (N.D.Ill.1993) (design of miter saw not defective because there was no evidence that the alternative design proffered by the plaintiff was practical and would not have interfered with the normal operation of the power saw); Glover v. BIC Corp., 987 F.2d 1410, 1421–23 (9th Cir.1993) (applying Oregon law), aff'd in part and rev'd in part as amended on denial of reh'g, 6 F.3d 1318 (9th Cir.1993) (insufficient evidence that alternative design of cigarette lighter suggested by the plaintiff was practically feasible); Beech v. Outboard Marine Corp., 584 So.2d 447 (Ala.1991); Elliott v. Brunswick Corp., 903 F.2d 1505, 1509 (11th Cir.1990), reh'g denied, also, cert. denied sub nom. Elliott v. Mercury Marine, 498 U.S. 1048, 111 S.Ct. 756, 112 L.Ed.2d 776 (1991) (applying Alabama law) (In both *Beech* and *Elliott* claims of defective motorboat propeller designs were struck down because the alternative designs proffered were not shown to have reached the stage of being practically adoptable at the time of sale); Wilson v. Piper Aircraft Corp., 577 P.2d 1322 (Or.1978) (en banc), reh'g denied, 579 P.2d 1287 (1978) (in banc) (expert testimony failed to establish that alternative design of aircraft fuel system was practically and economically feasible); Bunn v. Caterpillar Tractor Co., 415 F.Supp. 286, 291 (W.D.Pa.1976), aff'd, 556 F.2d 564 (3d Cir.1977), cert. denied, 434 U.S. 875, 98 S.Ct. 224, 54 L.Ed.2d 154 (1977); Garst v. General Motors Corp., 484 P.2d 47, 61–62 (Kan.1971); Maxted v. Pacific Car & Foundry Co., 527 P.2d 832 (Wyo. 1974).

For a comprehensive discussion of the problems raised by state of the art, see Symposium, The Passage of Time: The Implications for Product Liability, 58 N.Y.U. L. Rev. 733 et seq. (1983). See also Robb, A Practical Approach to Use of State of the Art Evidence in Strict Products Liability Cases, 77 Nw. U. L. Rev. 1 (1982); Madden, Products Liability § 8.3 (1988); Wertheimer, Unknowable Dangers and the Death of Strict Products Liability: The Empire Strikes Back, 60 U. Cin. L. Rev. 1183, 1206–41 (1992). Also see Owen, The Moral Foundations of Products Liability Law: Toward First Principles, 68 Notre Dame L. Rev. 427, 465–67, 482–84, 490–92, 504–05 (1993).

C. The "Open and Obvious," or "Patent Danger," Rule

A strong majority of courts have rejected the "open and obvious" or "patent danger" rule as an absolute defense to a claim of design defect. The obviousness of the danger is one factor among many to consider as to whether a product design meets risk-utility norms. See, e.g., Beloit v. Harrell, 339 So.2d 992 (Ala.1976); Byrns v. Riddell, Inc., 550 P.2d 1065, 1068 (Ariz.1976) (en banc); Auburn Mach. Works Co. v. Jones, 366 So.2d 1167, 1169 (Fla.1979); Pike v. Frank G. Hough Co., 467 P.2d 229 (Cal.1970) (en banc); Camacho v. Honda Motor Ltd., 741 P.2d 1240 (Colo.1987) (en banc), reh'g denied, also, cert. dismissed, 485 U.S. 901, 108 S.Ct. 1067, 99 L.Ed.2d 229 (1988); Brown v. Clark Equip. Co., 618 P.2d 267 (Haw. 1980); Besse v. Deere & Co., 604 N.E.2d 998 (Ill.App.Ct.1992); Koske v. Townsend Eng'g Co., 551 N.E.2d 437 (Ind.1990); Siruta v. Hesston Corp., 659 P.2d 799 (Kan.1983); Nichols v. Union Underwear Co., 602 S.W.2d 429 (Ky.1980); Uloth v. City Tank Corp., 384 N.E.2d 1188 (Mass. 1978); Owens v. Allis–Chalmers Corp., 326 N.W.2d 372 (Mich.1982); Holm v. Sponco Mfg., 324 N.W.2d 207, 213 (Minn.1982); Sperry–New Holland v. Prestage, 617 So.2d 248 (Miss.1993); Miller v. Varity Corp., 922 S.W.2d 821 (Mo.Ct.App.1996); Brown v. North American Mfg. Co., 576 P.2d 711, 717 (Mont.1978); Thibault v. Sears, Roebuck & Co., 395 A.2d 843 (N.H.1978); Micallef v. Miehle Co., 348 N.E.2d 571 (N.Y. 1976); Olson v. A.W. Chesterton Co., 256 N.W.2d 530 (N.D.1977); Jones v. White Motor Corp., 401 N.E.2d 223 (Ohio Ct.App.1978); Dorsey v. Yoder Co., 331 F.Supp. 753 (E.D.Pa.1971), aff'd, 474 F.2d 1339 (3d Cir.1973); Berg v. Sukup Mfg. Co., 355 N.W.2d 833, 835 (S.D.1984); Gann v. International Harvester Co. of Canada, Ltd., 712 S.W.2d 100, 106 (Tenn.1986), appeal after remand, No. 03A01–9101–CV–20, 1991 WL 152430 (Tenn.Ct. App. August 13, 1991); Palmer v. Massey–Ferguson, Inc., 476 P.2d 713, 718 (Wash.Ct.App.1970); Caterpillar Tractor Co. v. Donahue, 674 P.2d 1276, 1283–84 (Wyo.1983). Whether a danger is open and obvious may be a question of fact for the jury. See, e.g., Battistoni v. Weatherking Prods., Inc., 676 A.2d 890 (Conn.App.Ct. 1996).

The patent danger rule appears to retain vitality in a few jurisdictions. See Griffin v. Summit Specialties, 622 So.2d 1299 (Ala.1993) (applying Georgia law); Weatherby v. Honda Motor Co., 393 S.E.2d 64 (Ga.Ct.App.1990); McCollum v. Grove Mfg., 293 S.E.2d 632, 635 (N.C.Ct.App.1982). Some courts reach similar results by utilizing the "consumer expectations test" as a bar to recovery for design defect. See, e.g., Elliott v. Brunswick Corp., 903 F.2d 1505 (11th Cir.1990) (applying Alabama law), cert. denied sub nom. Elliott v. Mercury Marine, 498 U.S. 1048, 111 S.Ct. 756, 112 L.Ed.2d 776 (1991); Beech v. Outboard Marine Corp., 584 So.2d 447 (Ala.1991); Lamke v. Futorian Corp., 709 P.2d 684, 686 (Okla.1985); Vincer v. Esther Williams All–Aluminum Swimming Pool Co., 230 N.W.2d 794, 798 (Wis. 1975); Estate of Schilling v. Blount, Inc., 449 N.W.2d 56, 58 (Wis.Ct.App. 1989).

Academic commentators have been almost unanimous in their criticism of the "open and obvious danger" rule. See, e.g., Darling, The Patent Danger Rule: An Analysis and Survey of Its Vitality, 29 Mercer L. Rev. 583 (1978); 2 Harper, James and Gray, Torts § 28.5 (1956); Marschall, An Obvious Wrong Does Not Make a Right: Manufacturer's Liability for Patently Dangerous Products, 48 N.Y.U. L. Rev. 1065 (1973).

Though the obviousness of the danger is one factor in deciding whether a product is defectively designed it can, depending on the facts, become crucial to the determination of defect. Thus, a court may direct a verdict when it is convinced that, given the obviousness of the danger, it is not reasonable to require the adoption of an alternative design. See, e.g., Dreisonstok v. Volkswagenwerk, A.G., 489 F.2d 1066, 1075–76 (4th Cir.1974) (applying Virginia law) (the obviousness of the risk of injury in a microbus without front-end engine protection was an important factor in directing verdict for defendant on design defect); Jones v. White Motor Corp., 401 N.E.2d 223, 233 (Ohio Ct.App. 1978) (court rejected patent danger rule but noted that there may be cases where, because of an obvious peril, there may be no duty as a matter of law; in most cases, however, the defectiveness issue is for the jury); Jackson v. Corning Glass Works, 538 A.2d 666 (R.I.1988) (court noted that the obviousness of the danger of stacking Corning Ware and glass lids in a pyramid was so great that verdict should be directed for defendant).

In Todd v. Societe Bic, 21 F.3d 1402, 1407, 1411–12 (7th Cir.1994), cert. denied, 513 U.S. 947, 115 S.Ct. 359, 130 L.Ed.2d 312, the court held that Illinois would refuse to apply a risk-utility test to a simple but obviously dangerous product. In that case a two-year-old was killed in a fire started by a four-year-old playmate who ignited a BIC cigarette lighter. The plaintiff argued that the lighter was unreasonably dangerous since it did not include child-resistant features. In upholding the district court's granting of summary judgment for the defendant the court said:

> [T]he seminal question in this case [is]: what does an ordinary consumer expect when he purchases a lighter? Quite obviously, the consumer expects the lighter, when activated, to provide a flame. That is exactly how the lighter in this case performed. But the lighter was used to do more. The small flame it produced was used to ignite some papers, causing a deadly fire. The ordinary consumer expects that if a lighter's flame is put to some other combustible object, a larger fire ensues. This makes a lighter dangerous. But it does not make a lighter unreasonably dangerous under the consumer contemplation test. As the Illinois Supreme Court has stated, "[v]irtually any product is capable of producing injury when put to certain uses or misuses.... Injuries are not compensable in products liability if they derive merely from those inherent properties...."
>
> No Illinois court has applied the risk-utility test to a simple but obviously dangerous product. The Illinois Supreme Court has never applied the test to such a product. An intermediate appellate court [*Scoby*] has determined that it never will. Our task in a diversity case is to predict what the state's highest court would do if presented with the same issue. [Citation.] Based on our examination of past and current Illinois case law, we agree with the appellate court ..., that the Illinois Supreme Court would not apply the risk-utility test to simple but obviously dangerous products.
>
> ... An ordinary disposable lighter is such a product. Therefore, the

district court was correct to determine that such a lighter is obviously dangerous, but not unreasonably dangerous, without reference to the risk-utility test.

In a recent case, Judge (former professor) Robert Keeton found that the obviousness of the risks may in certain circumstances bar an action on duty grounds. In Kearney v. Philip Morris, Inc., 916 F.Supp. 61 (D.Mass. 1996), an action was brought against a cigarette manufacturer for deaths to several people arising from a house fire that occurred when an intoxicated resident of the home dropped a lit cigarette on the couch and fell asleep. Plaintiffs alleged that the cigarette design was defective because an alternative design could have been adopted using a low ignition propensity that would have prevented the fire in question. The court found that defendant cigarette manufacturer breached no duty to the plaintiff. In his analysis, Judge Keeton acknowledged that Massachusetts has rejected the patent-danger rule and utilizes risk-utility analysis to decide design defect cases. The court said: "In various contexts ... Massachusetts courts ... have refused to extend the scope of liability of manufacturers to injuries resulting from common, everyday products whose obvious dangers are known to be associated with the use of the product." Id. at 73.

D. Rejection by a Majority of Jurisdictions of Liability Based on Nondefective Products That Are Nevertheless Egregiously Dangerous

The requirement that a plaintiff establish that the product that caused harm was defectively manufactured, was inadequately designed, or was not accompanied by adequate instructions or warnings, applies in most instances even when the plaintiff alleges that the product was egregiously dangerous. Comment *e* recognizes the possibility that egregiously dangerous products might be held defective for that reason alone. But a clear majority of courts that have faced the issue have refused so to hold.

For cases involving firearms, see Perkins v. F.I.E. Corp., 762 F.2d 1250, 1273 (5th Cir.1985), reh'g denied, 768 F.2d 1350 (applying Louisiana law); Shipman v. Jennings Firearms, Inc., 791 F.2d 1532, 1533–34 (11th Cir.1986) (applying Florida law); Armijo v. Ex Cam, Inc., 656 F.Supp. 771, 773 (D.N.M.1987), aff'd, 843 F.2d 406 (10th Cir.1988) (applying New Mexico law); Hilberg ex rel. Hilberg v. F.W. Woolworth Co., 761 P.2d 236, 240 (Colo.Ct.App.1988), reh'g denied, and cert. denied, also, overruled on other grounds; Casebolt v. Cowan, 829 P.2d 352 (Colo.1992); Riordan v. Int'l Armament Corp., 477 N.E.2d 1293, 1298–99 (Ill.App.Ct. 1985); Knott v. Liberty Jewelry & Loan, Inc., 748 P.2d 661, 663–64 (Wash.Ct.App.1988).

In McCarthy v. Olin Corporation, 119 F.3d 148 (2d Cir.1997), a wrongful death action on behalf of victims who were killed in Colin Ferguson's highly publicized, murderous shooting spree on the Long Island Railroad was brought against the manufacturer of the "Black Talon" bullets used by Ferguson. Black Talon ammunition incorporates a hollow point bullet that is designed to expand upon impact, exposing razor-sharp edges at a 90–degree angle to the bullet. The expansion dramatically increases the wounding power of the bullet. Plaintiffs argued that the bullets were defectively designed in that they caused more damage than would have been caused by an ordinary bullet. The claim was thus one for enhanced injury. See § 16. The heart of plaintiffs' claim of design defect was that Black Talon bullets fail the risk-utility test, which is the governing test for defect in New York. In affirming the district court's holding granting defendant's motion to dismiss, the court said that

> The purpose of risk/utility analysis is to determine whether the risk of injury might have been reduced by or avoided if the manufacturer had used a reasonable alternative design.... However, the risk of injury to be balanced with the utility is a risk not intended as the primary function of the product. There is no reason to search for an alternative safer design where the product's sole utility is to kill and maim.

Id. 119 F.3d at 155. Accord, Downs v. R.T.S. Security, Inc., 670 So.2d 434 (La.Ct.App.1996). Judge Guido Calabresi, dissenting in *McCarthy*, argued that Black Talon bullets meet the requisites set forth in § 2, Comment *e*, and qualify as "manifestly unreasonable" products due to their "extremely high degree of danger" and "negligible social utility."

For cases involving cigarettes, see American Tobacco Co. v. Grinnell, 951 S.W.2d 420 (Tex.1997); Kotler v. American Tobacco Co., 731 F.Supp. 50, 52 (D.Mass.), aff'd, 926 F.2d 1217 (1st Cir.1990), cert. granted and judgment vacated, 505 U.S. 1215, 112 S.Ct. 3019, 120 L.Ed.2d 891 (1992), on remand, 981 F.2d 7 (1st Cir.1992) (applying Massachusetts law); Gianitsis v. American Brands, Inc., 685 F.Supp. 853, 856 (D.N.H.1988) (applying New Hampshire law); Miller v. Brown & Williamson Tobacco Corp., 679 F.Supp. 485, 488 (E.D.Pa.), aff'd, 856 F.2d 184 (3d Cir.1988) (applying Pennsylvania law); Gunsalus v. Celotex Corp., 674 F.Supp. 1149, 1158–59 (E.D.Pa.1987) (applying Pennsylvania law). For a case involving minitrail bikes, see Baughn v. Honda Motor Co., 727 P.2d 655, 660 (Wash.1986) (en banc).

Notwithstanding the foregoing authority, several courts have sought to impose liability based on a risk-utility claim absent a showing that a reasonable alternative design was available. See O'Brien v. Muskin Corp., 463 A.2d 298, 306 (N.J.1983) (above-ground swimming pool with vinyl bottom may be defective based on risk-utility analysis even though no alternative design was feasible); Halphen v. Johns–Manville Sales Corp., 484 So.2d 110 (La.1986) (court concluded that an asbestos manufacturer can be held to a strict liability standard for a product that fails to meet risk-utility norms because the dangers created by its use, even if unforeseen at the time of manufacture, outweigh its utility. Id. at 114. But if a product does meet risk-utility norms on its own, and is only defective because there exists an alternative design, the manufacturer is held to a negligence-foreseeability standard. Id. at 115).

A third state appellate court may have imposed liability on the theory that the overall danger of the product outweighs its benefits. In Kelley v. R.G. Industries, Inc., 497 A.2d 1143 (Md.1985), the court held that the manufacturers of cheap handguns—"Saturday Night Specials"—could be held liable for injuries suffered by innocent third parties at the hands of criminals. Id. at 1152–59. Although earlier in the opinion the court rejected liability based on risk-utility balancing, id. at 1149, the court's imposition of liability on manufacturers for injuries caused by cheap handguns appears to condemn them because the overall utility to society of this genre of firearm is too low to justify its continued marketing. Id. at 1158. Nonetheless, at bottom *Kelley* is probably a case based primarily on a theory of negligent entrustment.

Each of these judicial attempts at imposing such liability have either been overturned or sharply curtailed by legislation. See La. Rev. Stat. Ann. § 9:2800.56(1) (West 1991) (overruling *Halphen*); Md. Code Ann., Crim. Law art. 27 § 36–I (Supp. 1990) (overruling *Kelley*); N.J. Stat. Ann. § 2A:58C–3.b(3) (West 1990) (limiting *O'Brien*).

Several states have enacted legislation that prohibits actions against firearm manufacturers for injuries resulting from the weapon's inherent danger. These states specifically allow for claims based on either defective manufacture or defective design (i.e., the failure to institute an alternative design). See, e.g., Cal. Civ. Code § 1714.4 (West 1985) (added by Proposition 51, approved by electorate on June 3, 1986); Colo. Rev. Stat. § 13–21–501 (1987); Idaho Code § 6–1410 (1990); Mont. Code Ann. § 27–1–720 (1991); Nev. Rev. Stat. § 41.131(1) (1987); Tex. Civ. Prac. & Rem. Code Ann. § 82.006 (West 1993).

Although several state legislatures have nullified judicial adoption of liability without proof of an alternative design, such nullification has limited application in two jurisdictions. In Dewey v. R.J. Reynolds Tobacco Co., 577 A.2d 1239, 1252 (N.J.1990), the court held that the New Jersey statute did not reflect the common law of the state prior to its enactment. Thus, for cases filed prior to the enactment of the statute, a risk-utility case could be established theoretically for products such as cigarettes. Since only six cigarette cases were pending in New Jersey at the time the legislation was enacted, the decision of the court allowing a risk-utility case to be made out when there is no alternative design available is only relevant to a handful of cases. Similarly, in Gilboy v. American Tobacco Co., 582 So.2d 1263 (La.1991), the court held that the 1988 Louisiana statute requiring a plaintiff to prove a reasonable alternative design in a claim alleging a design defect was prospective only. Thus, *Gilboy* could proceed to trial on the theory that the risks of cigarette smoking outweighed its utility.

Many commentators have been critical of the attempt by *O'Brien* to impose liability without establishing defect in the classical sense. See, e.g., Note, Products Liability—Strict Liability in Tort—State-of-the-Art Evidence Relevant to Risk-Utility Analysis in Design Defect Cases, 15 Seton Hall L. Rev. 120 n.5 (1984); Note, Strict Products Liability and the Risk–Utility Test for Design Defect: An Economic Analysis, 84 Colum. L. Rev. 2045 (1984); Note, Handguns and Products Liability, 97 Harv. L. Rev. 1912 (1984); Henderson and Twerski, Closing the American Products Liability Frontier: The Rejection of Liability Without Defect, 66 N.Y.U. L. Rev. 1263 (1991); Grossman, Categorical Liability: Why the Gates Should be Kept Closed, 36 S. Tex. L. Rev. 385 (1996). But others disagree. See Turley, Manufacturers' and Suppliers' Liability to Handgun Victims, 10 N. Ky. L. Rev. 41 (1982); Note, Manufacturers' Liability to Victims of Handgun Crime: A Common Law Approach, 51 Fordham L. Rev. 771 (1983); Bogus, Pistols, Politics and Products Liability, 59 U. Cin. L. Rev. 1103 (1991); Wertheimer, The

Smoke Gets in Their Eyes: Product Category Liability and Alternative Feasible Designs in the Third Restatement, 61 Tenn. L. Rev. 1429 (1994); Bogus, War on the Common Law: The Struggle at the Center of Products Liability, 60 Mo. L. Rev. 1, 30–34 (1995). Also see Symposium on Generic Product Liability, 72 Chi.-Kent L.Rev. 3 et seq. (1996).

Illustration 3 is based on Micallef v. Miehle Co., 348 N.E.2d 571 (N.Y. 1976). Illustration 4 is based on O'Brien v. Muskin Corp., 463 A.2d 298 (N.J.1983).

Comment e. Design defects: possibility of manifestly unreasonable design. Although as a general rule a plaintiff is required to establish a reasonable alternative design as set forth in § 2(b), it is important to note that several courts have suggested in dictum that in rare instances where the product has low social utility and very high risk that they might be willing to impose liability without proof of a reasonable alternative design. Because only one American jurisdiction currently recognizes such a position other than by way of dictum in cases that do not present the issue on their facts, the possibility of such a holding is not included in the black letter. But a Comment on the possibility is appropriate. Thus, Comment *e* recognizes the possibility that in such instances defect may be established without proof of a reasonable alternative design. In Wilson v. Piper Aircraft Corp., 577 P.2d 1322, 1328 n. 5 (Or.1978), the court said:

> As pointed out above, the court's task is to weigh the factors bearing on the utility and the magnitude of the risk and to determine whether, on balance, the case is a proper one for submission to the jury. In this case we focus on the practicability of a safer alternative design and hold that the evidence was insufficient to permit the trial judge to consider that factor. Our holding should not be interpreted as a requirement that this factor must in all cases weigh in plaintiff's favor before the case can be submitted to the jury. There might be cases in which the jury would be permitted to hold the defendant liable on account of a dangerous design feature even though no safer design was feasible (or there was no evidence of a safer practicable alternative). If, for example, the danger was relatively severe and the product had only limited utility, the court might properly conclude that the jury could find that a reasonable manufacturer would not have introduced such a product into the stream of commerce. We hold here only that, given the nature of the product and of the defects alleged, it was improper to submit the issue of a defect in the engine design to the jury in the absence of appropriate evidence that the safer alternative design was practicable.

See also Rix v. General Motors Corp., 723 P.2d 195, 201 (Mont.1986); Kallio v. Ford Motor Co., 407 N.W.2d 92, 97 n. 8 (Minn.1987) ("Conceivably, rare cases may exist where the product may be judged unreasonably dangerous because it should be removed from the market rather than be redesigned ..."); Armentrout v. FMC Corp., 842 P.2d 175, 185 n. 8 (Colo. 1992) (en banc).

The only jurisdiction that clearly recognizes by legislation an action for an egregiously dangerous product has done so in a very limited manner. See N.J. Stat. Ann. § 2A:58C–3(b) (West 1987). The New Jersey statute provides that the obligation to establish a "practical and technically feasible alternative design" is not required when a court makes all the following determinations based on clear and convincing evidence:

(1) The product is egregiously unsafe or ultra-hazardous;

(2) The ordinary user or consumer of the product cannot reasonably be expected to have knowledge of the product's risks, or the product poses a risk of serious injury to persons other than the user or consumer; and

(3) The product has little or no usefulness.

Appended to the legislation is an official commentary by the New Jersey Senate Judiciary Committee that indicates just how limited the exception was intended to be. The commentary notes: "It is intended that such a finding [under the exception] would be made only in genuinely extraordinary cases—for example, in the case of a deadly toy marketed for use by the young children, or of a product marketed for use in dangerous criminal activities." N.J. Senate Judiciary Committee Statement, No. 2805–L.1987, cl. 197; but see discussion in Reporters' Note to § 2, Comment *d* Part I.A regarding Ohio Rev. Code Ann. § 2307.75(F) (Anderson 1991).

Comment f. Design defect: factors relevant in determining whether the omission of reasonable alternative design renders the product not reasonably safe.

1. Subsection 2(b) requires a comparison between the actual design and the alternative proffered by the plaintiff. The availability of an alternative design does not mean that the alternative is a reasonable substitute for the actual design utilized by the manufacturer. The monetary cost of the alternative design may exceed the safety benefits to be derived from it. Furthermore, an alternative design may impose significant nonmonetary costs on product users and consumers. It may deprive a product of important features which make it desirable and attractive to many users and consumers. Courts that apply a "risk-utility" balancing test recognize that these considerations are central to the finding that a substitute design is a reasonable alternative. It is for this reason that courts take the position that the availability of a safer design does not *ipso facto* mean that the actual design is defective. This also accounts for the oft-repeated statement that a manufacturer has no obligation to provide the safest design available or provide for the ultimate in safety. See, e.g., Linegar v. Armour of Am., Inc., 909 F.2d 1150, 1154 (8th Cir.1990) (applying Missouri law); Husky Indus. v. Black, 434 So.2d 988, 991 (Fla.Dist.Ct.App.1983); Hunt v. Blasius, 384 N.E.2d 368, 372 (Ill.1978); Marchant v. Mitchell Distrib. Co., 240 S.E.2d 511, 514 (S.C. 1977). In short, whether a proffered design is a reasonable alternative can be determined only after a comparison of the relative advantages and disadvantages of the competing designs, utilizing the various factors for risk-utility balancing set forth in the Comment.

In Owen, Toward a Proper Test for Design Defectiveness: "Micro–Balancing" Costs and Benefits, 75 Tex. L. Rev. 1661, 1687 (1997), Professor David Owen explains how the key to proper design defect determinations rests upon a balance of the marginal costs and benefits of the proposed alternative design:

> In design defect litigation, the basic issue involves the following fundamental micro-balance question: *whether the manufacturer's failure to adopt a design feature proposed by plaintiff was on balance right or wrong.* A congruence between this central issue and the liability test requires that the test be focused squarely on the issue of what, in particular, allegedly was wrong with the manufacturer's design decision. More specifically, this involves the question of whether the increased costs (lost dollars, utility, and safety) of *altering* the design—in the particular manner plaintiff claims to have been reasonably necessary to the product's safety—would have been worth the safety benefits. Thus, the only factors ordinarily relevant in the risk-utility balance are the *incremental* ("marginal") precaution costs and safety benefits of adopting the particular design safety feature proposed by the plaintiff. The notion of *marginal* costs and benefits implies a move, and here the move is from the chosen design to the alternative design: the precaution costs and safety benefits involved in *altering* the chosen design in the particular fashion proposed by plaintiff—those costs and benefits (that would have been) incurred in *moving* from the manufacturer's actual chosen design to the plaintiff's hypothetical alternative design.

In sum, an alternative design is reasonable if its marginal benefits exceed its marginal costs.

2. The proposition that, in order to determine that a design is not reasonably safe, the alternative must contribute to greater overall safety needs no citation; it is axiomatic. If the alternative design proffered by the plaintiff does not make the product safer, let alone if it makes it more dangerous, such an alternative is not reasonable. In such a case the fact that the alternative design would have avoided injury in a specific case is of no moment. See Glover v. BIC Corp., 987 F.2d 1410, 1423 (9th Cir. 1993) amended and superseded on other grounds, 6 F.3d 1318 (9th Cir. 1993) (applying Oregon law); see also Richards v. Michelin Tire Corp., 21 F.3d 1048 (11th Cir.1994) (applying Alabama law).

3. In Cipollone v. Liggett Group, Inc., 644 F.Supp. 283, 286 (D.N.J. 1986), Judge Sarokin demonstrates why collateral effects on an industry are not relevant considerations in risk-utility balancing.

4. The overwhelming majority of courts place the burden of proving that a product design failed to meet risk-utility standards on the plaintiff. See, e.g., Ontai v. Straub Clinic & Hosp. Inc., 659 P.2d 734, 741–42 (Haw.1983); Hayes v. Ariens Co., 462 N.E.2d 273, 278 (Mass.1984); Kallio v. Ford Motor Co., 407 N.W.2d 92, 97 (Minn.1987); Cremeans v. International Harvester Co., 452 N.E.2d 1281, 1283–84 (Ohio 1983); Wilson v. Piper Aircraft Corp., 577 P.2d 1322, 1325 (Or.1978); Ray v. BIC Corp., 925 S.W.2d 527 (Tenn.1996). Only two courts shift the burden on risk-utility balancing to the defendant, Caterpillar Tractor Co. v. Beck, 593 P.2d 871, 878–79 (Alaska 1979); Barker v. Lull Eng'g Co., Inc., 573 P.2d 443, 455 (Cal.1978). As a practical matter, of course, once the plaintiff introduces evidence of a technologically feasible design, the defendant will address the risk-utility issues by justifying its design and demonstrating why the alternative design is not reasonable. Technically, though, the burdens of

production and persuasion are on the plaintiff.

Several courts have shed light on what elements of proof are required to establish the existence of a feasible alternative design. In Lavespere v. Niagara Machine & Tool Works, 910 F.2d 167, 183 (5th Cir.1990) (applying Louisiana law), the court held that the plaintiff was required to present evidence sufficient to enable a reasonable trier of fact to conclude that the plaintiff had established the essential elements of his claim "including that the risk avoided by the alternative design outweighed the burden of adopting that design."

In deciding that the plaintiff failed to carry the burden, the court was persuaded by the following circumstances: (1) the plaintiff offered no evidence concerning the extent of the risk that the alternative design would have avoided, such as evidence concerning the frequency of accidents like the one before the court, the economic costs entailed by those accidents, or the extent of the reduction in frequency of those accidents that would have resulted from the use of the proposed alternative design; (2) the plaintiff offered little or no evidence concerning the burden incurred by the manufacturer in switching to the alternative design; and (3) most significantly, the plaintiff offered no evidence on the loss of product utility that use of the alternative design would have occasioned. The court concluded:

> [Plaintiff's] proof of the risk that might have been avoided by the alternative design and of the burden that switching to that design would have entailed was, to say the least, incomplete. Faced with this meager evidence, no reasonable trier of fact could have concluded that the balance of those two factors tipped in favor of the risk avoided. One cannot balance items of indeterminate weight.

Id.

Thus, a plaintiff must introduce evidence from which the jury can find not only that the proposed alternative would have afforded greater safety, but also that it would not have substantially impaired the function, utility, economy, convenience, and other features that drive consumer demand for and acceptance of the product.

The Michigan Supreme Court reached a similar conclusion in Owens v. Allis–Chalmers Corp., 326 N.W.2d 372 (Mich.1982):

> Our conclusion that the plaintiff did not present a *prima facie* case is based on the lack of evidence concerning both the magnitude of the risks involved and the reasonableness of the proposed alternative design.... Even if this court could take judicial notice that the costs involved in attaching a seat belt or other designated restraint to a forklift would not be great, we cannot take judicial notice that their use by forklift drivers would be likely, practical, or more safe. Neither the costs nor the effects of the other restraints were established.

Id. at 378–79 (emphasis added).

In Wilson v. Piper Aircraft Corp., 577 P.2d 1322 (Or.1978), the court reversed a verdict for the plaintiffs because, although the plaintiffs showed the possible feasibility of the alternative engine design they proposed, they introduced no evidence of its real-world practicality in terms of cost, operation, maintenance requirements, overall performance, or safety in respects other than the carburetor icing that had caused the engine failure and crash in that case. The court observed:

> It is not proper to submit such allegations to the jury unless the court is satisfied that there is evidence from which the jury could find the suggested alternatives are not only technically feasible but also practicable in terms of cost and the over-all design and operation of the product. It is part of the required proof that a design feature is a "defect" to present such evidence.

Id. at 1327. It concluded that:

> If liability for the alleged design defects is to "stop somewhere short of the freakish and the fantastic," plaintiffs' *prima facie* case of a defect must show more than the technical possibility of a safer design.

Id. at 1326 (emphasis added) (footnote omitted).

5. Comment *f* lists among the factors a court may consider in determining whether an alternative design is reasonable and whether its omission renders a product not reasonably safe the following: (1) magnitude and probability of the foreseeable risks of harm; (2) the instructions and warnings accompanying the product; and (3) the nature and strength of consumer expectations. A recent California case is in agreement. In Hansen v. Sunnyside Products, Inc., 55 Cal. App.4th 1497 (1997), the court held that in a claim alleging defective design of a household cleaner containing hydroflouric acid, the availability of an alternative safer design was not dispositive of liability. The factfinder could consider the warnings on the bottle describing the danger of exposing a user's skin to the cleaner in risk-utility balancing to decide whether the product was unreasonably dangerous.

6. Illustration 6 is based on McCormack v. Hankscraft Co., 154 N.W.2d 488 (Minn.1967). Illustration 10 is based on Linegar v. Armour of America, 909 F.2d 1150 (8th Cir.1990) (applying Missouri law).

Comment g. Consumer expectations: general considerations. Comment *g* advances two propositions: first, that consumer expectations may not be employed as a sword in the sense that plaintiffs may not invoke the disappointment of such expectations as an independent legal standard with which to attack product designs; and, second, that consumer expectations may not be used as a shield in the sense that defendants may not invoke the satisfaction of such expectations as an independent bar to liability for dangerous product designs. Disappointment and satisfaction of reasonable consumer expectations are relevant in both contexts, but they control in neither. Research supporting both of these basic propositions is contained in the Reporters' Note to Comment *d*, IIIA and C.

Comment h. Consumer expectations: food products and used products. The authority suggesting the rule for food products and used products is found in the Reporters' Notes to § 7 and § 8 respectively.

Comment i. Inadequate instructions or warnings.

1. The general obligation to provide reasonable instructions and warnings is so widely recognized that extensive citation is unnecessary. A rich body of literature has developed on the subject of warnings. See, e.g., Noel, Manufacturer's Negligence of Design or Directions for Use of a

Product, 71 Yale L.J. 816 (1962); Noel, Products Defective Because of Inadequate Directions or Warnings, 23 Sw. L.J. 256 (1969); Twerski, Weinstein, Donaher & Piehler, The Use and Abuse of Warnings in Products Liability—Design Defect Litigation Comes of Age, 61 Cornell L. Rev. 495 (1976); Sales, The Duty to Warn and Instruct for Safe Use in Strict Tort Liability, 13 St. Mary's L. Rev. 521 (1982); Gershonowitz, The Strict Liability Duty to Warn, 44 Wash. & Lee L. Rev. 71 (1987); Madden, The Duty to Warn in Products Liability: Contours and Criticism, 89 W. Va. L. Rev 221 (1987) (comprehensive review); Henderson and Twerski, Doctrinal Collapse in Products Liability: The Empty Shell of Failure to Warn, 65 N.Y.U. L. Rev. 265 (1990); Jacobs, Toward a Process–Based Approach to Failure-to-Warn, 71 N.C. L. Rev. 121 (1992); Latin, "Good" Warnings, Bad Products and Cognitive Limitations, 41 U.C.L.A. L. Rev. 1193 (1994).

2. For authority that there is no duty to warn with regard to uses or risks that would not have been foreseen by a reasonable person, see Reporters' Note to § 2, Comment *m*.

3. For authority supporting the proposition that courts should be cautious before imposing a duty to provide overly numerous or too detailed warnings, see, e.g., Cotton v. Buckeye Gas Prods. Co., 840 F.2d 935, 937–39 (D.C.Cir.1988); Kerr v. Koemm, 557 F.Supp. 283, 288 n. 2 (S.D.N.Y.1983); Finn v. G.D. Searle & Co., 677 P.2d 1147, 1153 (Cal.1984); Broussard v. Continental Oil Co., 433 So.2d 354 (La.Ct.App.1983); Dunn v. Lederele Labs., 328 N.W.2d 576, 580–81 (Mich. Ct.App.1982). Similar reasoning would counsel against imposing a duty to warn against trivial or far-fetched risks. Such warnings would tend to debase warnings and detract the user's attention from warnings about risks of greater significance. For a discussion of these points relying on the work of cognition experts, see Schwartz and Divers, Warnings in the Workplace: The Need for Synthesis of Law and Communication Theory, 52 U. Cin. L. Rev. 28, 58–60 (1983).

4. The courts developed an informed-choice concept in products liability almost a decade after the onset of the products liability revolution. The first case to refer to an informed-choice theory was Borel v. Fibreboard Paper Products Corp., 493 F.2d 1076, 1089–90 (5th Cir.1973) (asbestos), cert. denied, 419 U.S. 869, 95 S.Ct. 127, 42 L.Ed.2d 107 (1974). Several early commentators distinguished between warnings to reduce the risk of harm—risk-reduction warnings—and warnings given simply to inform the purchaser that the use of the product involves a nonreducible risk—informed-choice warnings. See, e.g., Twerski, et al., The Use and Abuse of Warnings, 61 Cornell L. Rev. 495, 519 (1976). Others now recognize this distinction. See, e.g., M. Franklin & R. Rabin, Cases and Materials on Tort Law and Alternatives 609–11 (3d ed. 1983); J. Henderson & A. Twerski, Products Liability: Problems and Process 365, 459 (1987); McClellan, Strict Liability for Drug Induced Injuries: An Excursion Through the Maze of Products Liability, Negligence and Absolute Liability, 25 Wayne L. Rev. 1, 32 (1978). Considerable judicial authority identifies defendants' failure to provide for informed choice as a separate ground for a products liability action. Many of these cases cite the language of the Restatement, Second, of Torts § 402A, Comment *k*. See, e.g., Gra-

ham v. Wyeth Labs., 666 F.Supp. 1483, 1498 (D.Kan.1987), 906 F.2d 1399 (10th Cir.1990), cert. denied, 498 U.S. 981, 111 S.Ct. 511, 112 L.Ed.2d 523 (1990), on remand, 760 F.Supp. 1410 (D.Kan.1991); Finn v. G.D. Searle & Co., 677 P.2d 1147, 1152 (Cal.1984) (overruled on other grounds); Hamilton v. Hardy, 549 P.2d 1099, 1110 (Colo.Ct.App.1976); Ortho Pharm. Corp. v. Chapman, 388 N.E.2d 541, 555 n. 11 (Ind.Ct.App. 1979).

Comment *i* observes that judicial decisions supporting the duty to provide warnings for informed decision-making have arisen almost exclusively with regard to toxic agents and pharmaceutical products. Typically, once ingestion has taken place, consumers of these products are relatively passive and do not have an interactive relationship with the product. Case law has yet to expand the obligation to provide informed decision warnings to product risks in which the product-user relationship is more complex. For example, it would be onerous to impose a duty to warn about the relative degrees of crashworthiness of different models of automobiles. Such warnings would have to take into consideration such factors as speed, point of collision, use of seatbelts, and a myriad of other factors. If informed-decision warnings would necessarily be voluminous and incapable of consistent formulation, they would add little, if anything, to true informed choice.

5. The Restatement, Second, of Torts § 388, Comment *n*, utilizes the same factors set forth in Comment *i* in deciding whether a warning should be given directly to third persons. It has been relied on by numerous courts. See, e.g., Goodbar v. Whitehead Bros., 591 F.Supp. 552 (W.D.Va. 1984), aff'd sub nom. Beale v. Hardy, 769 F.2d 213 (4th Cir.1985) (applying Virginia law); Oman v. Johns–Manville Corp., 764 F.2d 224 (4th Cir. 1985), cert. denied, 474 U.S. 970, 106 S.Ct. 351, 88 L.Ed.2d 319 (1985) (applying Virginia law); Hegna v. E.I. duPont de Nemours and Co., 806 F.Supp. 822 (D.Minn.1992), on reconsideration, 825 F.Supp. 880 (D.Minn. 1993), aff'd sub nom. Abrams v. E.I. DuPont De Nemours and Co., 27 F.3d 571 (8th Cir.1994); Barsness v. General Diesel & Equip. Co., 383 N.W.2d 840, 845–46 (N.D.1986); Binder v. Jones & Laughlin Steel Corp., 520 A.2d 863 (Pa.Super.Ct.1987); Zacher v. Budd Co., 396 N.W.2d 122 (S.D.1986); Whitehead v. Dycho Co., 775 S.W.2d 593 (Tenn.1989).

6. Illustration 11 is based on Burch v. Amsterdam Corp., 366 A.2d 1079 (D.C.1976).

Comment j. Warnings: obvious and generally known risks. The rule that no duty is owed to warn of obvious and generally known dangers is supported by an overwhelming majority of jurisdictions. See, e.g., Lederman v. Pacific Industries, Inc., 119 F.3d 551 (7th Cir.1997) (applying Illinois law); Scallan v. Duriron Co., 11 F.3d 1249 (5th Cir.1994) (applying Louisiana law); Kelley v. Price–Macemon, Inc., 992 F.2d 1408 (5th Cir. 1993), reh'g denied, 999 F.2d 1581 (5th Cir.1993), cert. denied sub nom. Kelley v. Industrial Refrigerated Sys., Inc., 510 U.S. 1043, 114 S.Ct. 688, 126 L.Ed.2d 656 (1994); Beck v. Somerset Tech., Inc., 882 F.2d 993, 997 (5th Cir.1989) (applying Louisiana law); Wheeler v. John Deere Co., 862 F.2d 1404, 1414 (10th Cir.1988) (applying Kansas law); Phelps v. Sherwood Med. Indus., 836 F.2d 296, 303 (7th Cir.1987) (applying Indiana law); Koonce v. Quaker Safety Prods.

& Mfg. Co., 798 F.2d 700, 716–19 (5th Cir.1986), reh'g overruled, 814 F.2d 209 (5th Cir.1987) (applying Texas law); Laaperi v. Sears, Roebuck & Co., 787 F.2d 726 (1st Cir.1986) (applying Massachusetts law); Smith v. Hub Mfg., Inc., 634 F.Supp. 1505, 1508 (N.D.N.Y.1986) (applying New York law); Crow v. Manitex, Inc., 550 N.W.2d 175 (Iowa.Ct.App.1996); Payne v. Quality Nozzle Co., 643 N.Y.S.2d 623 (N.Y.App.Div.1996); Schiller v. Nat'l Presto Indus., Inc., 639 N.Y.S.2d 217 (N.Y.App.Div.1996). For a comprehensive listing of state court decisions supporting the position that a manufacturer owes no duty to warn of obvious dangers, see Glittenberg v. Doughboy Recreational Indus., 491 N.W.2d 208, 214 n. 15 (Mich.1992).

For authority supporting the proposition that there is no duty to warn of generally known risks, see, e.g., American Tobacco Co. v. Grinnell, 951 S.W.2d 420 (Tex.1997); Joseph E. Seagram & Sons, Inc. v. McGuire, 814 S.W.2d 385, 388 (Tex.1991) ("the danger of developing the disease of alcoholism from prolonged and excessive consumption of alcoholic beverages is within the ordinary knowledge common to the community."); Garrison v. Heublein, Inc., 673 F.2d 189, 192 (7th Cir.1982) ("the dangers of the use of alcohol are common knowledge to such an extent that the product cannot objectively be considered to be unreasonably dangerous"); Pemberton v. American Distilled Spirits Co., 664 S.W.2d 690 (Tenn. 1984) (no duty to warn of the commonly known danger of death from the rapid over-consumption of grain alcohol in a single sitting); Menard v. Newhall, 373 A.2d 505 (Vt.1977) (no duty to warn of hazards associated with BB gun because these hazards "are generally known and recognized"); Brown v. Sears, Roebuck & Co., 667 P.2d 750, 756 (Ariz.Ct.App. 1983) (no duty to warn of risks of a product that are within "the ordinary knowledge common to the community"; "[s]urely every adult knows that if an electrical extension cord is cut or frayed a danger of electrical shock is created"); Friedman v. Houston Sports Ass'n., 731 S.W.2d 572, 575 (Tex.Ct.App.1987) ("the general dangers inherent in baseball are part of the 'universal common knowledge' "); Morris v. Adolph Coors Co., 735 S.W.2d 578 (Tex.Ct.App.1987) (no duty to warn of risks of driving while intoxicated because there is a "general awareness" of these risks). For a recent case agreeing with the position of this Restatement in regard to open and obvious dangers and generally known risks, see Maneely v. GMC, 108 F.3d 1176 (9th Cir.1997).

Thus, the position of this Restatement is consistent with the second paragraph of Comment *j* in the Restatement, Second, of Torts § 402A, which states that:

> . . . a seller is not required to warn with respect to products, or ingredients in them, which are dangerous, or potentially so, when consumed in excessive quantity, or over a long period of time, when the danger, or potentiality of danger, is generally known and recognized. Again the dangers of alcoholic beverages are an example, as are also those of foods containing such substances as saturated fats, which may over a period of time have a deleterious effect upon the human heart.

Academic commentators are in general agreement. See, e.g., Prosser & Keeton, The Law of Torts, 686–87 (4th ed. 1984); Fischer & Powers,

Products Liability—Cases and Materials on Products Liability and Safety, 375 (2d ed. 1989); Henderson & Twerski, Doctrinal Collapse in Products Liability: The Empty Shell of Failure to Warn, 65 N.Y.U. L. Rev. 265, 306 (1990). But see Madden, The Duty to Warn in Products Liability: Contours and Criticism, 89 W. Va. L. Rev. 221, 253–57 (1987); Jacobs, Toward a Process–Based Approach to Failure to Warn, 71 N.C. L. Rev. 121 (1992) (author criticizes the obvious-danger rule and suggests the adoption of a liability rule that focuses on the procedures used by a manufacturer prior to the adoption and publication of a warning to assure that it has fully understood and adequately communicated the risks attendant to product use).

It is important to note that the Comments take the position that no duty is owed to warn about obvious dangers but reject the position that the obviousness of a danger is an automatic defense to a design defect claim. See § 2, Comments *d* and *f*. Also see Henderson & Twerski, Doctrinal Collapse, supra, 65 N.Y.U. L. Rev. at 282:

> [T]he argument for abandoning the patent danger rule in warning cases simply because the rule has been abandoned in design cases makes no sense. In a design case, the obviousness of the danger does not necessarily preclude the possibility that an alternative design could reduce the risk cost-effectively. By contrast, assuming that some risks are patently obvious, the obviousness of a product-related risk invariably serves the same function as a warning that the risk is present. Thus, nothing is to be gained by adding a warning of the danger already telegraphed by the product itself.

Comment k. Warnings: adverse allergic or idiosyncratic reactions. A clear majority of courts adopt the position articulated in Comment *k*. See, e.g., Kaempfe v. Lehn & Fink Products Corp., 249 N.Y.S.2d 840 (N.Y.App.Div.1964) (sensitivity experienced in the ratio of 1 in 150,000 customers using the spray deodorant; plaintiff was not, as a matter of law, one of a substantial number of consumers at risk); Thomas v. Amway Corp., 488 A.2d 716 (R.I.1985) (directed verdict for defendant on ground that only a small number of other users had made similar complaints about defendant's liquid soap); Presbrey v. Gillette Co., 435 N.E.2d 513 (Ill.App.Ct.1982) (no proof that defendant's spray deodorant was injurious to a number of people; no evidence that the product could sensitize "normal" users); Morris v. Pathmark Corp., 592 A.2d 331, 334 (Pa.Super.Ct.1991) ("[A]n unusual or rare idiosyncratic sensitivity on plaintiff's part provided no basis for recovery or even the requirement of a warning from the manufacturer in the absence of evidence that a significant number of persons suffered allergic reactions to the product."); Mountain v. Procter & Gamble Co., 312 F.Supp. 534 (E.D.Wis.1970) (defendants owe no duty to warn of possible allergic reactions to shampoo when only a minuscule percentage of total sales resulted in injury); Tayar v. Roux Labs., Inc., 460 F.2d 494 (10th Cir.1972) (beautician who had allergic or idiosyncratic reaction to defendant's hair rinse, which was normally safe for use by public, was not entitled to recover from manufacturer); Grau v. Procter & Gamble Co., 324 F.2d 309, 310 (5th Cir.1963) (rare inflammation of the mouth from use of toothpaste; no duty to warn: "There was no evidence that the allergy from which plaintiff suffered is one common to a substantial number of possible users."); Merrill v. Beaute Vues Corp., 235 F.2d 893 (10th Cir.1956) (plaintiff who suffered eye impairment after using defendant's home permanent wave solution had no cause as a matter of law; over 500 million similar products have been sold with only very rare ill effects). See also Booker v. Revlon Realistic Prof'l Prods., Inc., 433 So.2d 407 (La.App.Ct.1983); Crotty v. Shartenberg's-New Haven, Inc., 162 A.2d 513 (Conn.1960); Hafner v. Guerlain, Inc., 310 N.Y.S.2d 141 (N.Y.App.Div. 1970); Robbins v. Alberto–Culver Co., 499 P.2d 1080 (Kan.1972); Esborg v. Bailey Drug Co., 378 P.2d 298 (Wash. 1963). For a scholarly treatment recognizing the legitimacy of treating "small group" allergic reactions differently, see Madden, Products Liability § 10.10, p. 431 (2d ed. 1988) ("where a manufacturer's product is safe for use by most persons likely to come into contact with it but is likely to create allergic or highly unusual reaction in only a small proportion of the population, special issues arise as to the manufacturer's duty to warn the allergic or idiosyncratic individual").

A minority of courts impose a duty to warn even when the group at risk of allergic reaction is small. See, e.g., Wright v. Carter Prods., Inc., 244 F.2d 53 (2d Cir.1957) (only 373 complaints out of 82 million units of spray deodorant distributed; nevertheless, the court concludes that duties to warn may not be measured, in all cases, by solely quantitative standards); Proctor & Gamble Mfg. Co. v. Superior Ct., 268 P.2d 199 (Cal.Ct. App.1954); Zirpola v. Adam Hat Stores, Inc., 4 A.2d 73 (N.J.1939); Gober v. Revlon, Inc., 317 F.2d 47 (4th Cir.1963) (defendant liable to persons injured by nail polish even if percentage of users injured is small). Some of these decisions stress the severity of plaintiff's harm. See, e.g., Braun v. Roux Distrib. Co., 312 S.W.2d 758 (Mo.1958) (the type of injury suffered due to the susceptibility of the plaintiff had never been observed in any other person, but defendant was still under a duty to warn of the possibility of injury). See generally Madden, Products Liability § 10.10, p. 433 (2d ed. 1988) ("particularly when only a very small proportion of the population is put at risk, the severity of the illness or injury to which the warning would be directed is properly a factor in determining whether the manufacturer has a duty to warn"). Law review commentary has been sympathetic with imposing liability for allergic reaction injuries. See, e.g., Fischer, Products Liability—The Meaning of Defect, 39 Mo. L. Rev. 339, 356 n.134 (1974); Holtzman, Duty of the Manufacturer to Warn the Allergic User—An Evaluation of the "Appreciable Class" Criteria, 1982 Med. Trial Tech. Q. 171, 177; Keeton, Products Liability—Drugs and Cosmetics, 25 Vand. L. Rev. 131, 136–37 (1972); Schattman, A Cause of Action for the Allergic Consumer, 8 Hous. L. Rev. 827 (1971); Comment, Strict Liability and Allergic Drug Reactions, 47 Miss. L.J. 526 (1976); Note, Products Liability: The Allergic Plaintiff—Formulating a Cause of Action in Oklahoma, 30 Okla. L. Rev. 439 (1977). Two prominent writers suggested, however, in an early article on the subject, that allergic users should bear the losses in these cases, based on the factual assumption that they can easily avoid injury. See generally Calabresi & Bass, Right Approach, Wrong Implications: A Critique of McKean on Products Liability, 38 U. Chi. L. Rev. 74, 86 (1970).

Courts tend to be more willing to impose a duty to warn regardless of the relative size of the risk group when the product in question is a prescription drug. See, e.g., Davis v. Wyeth Labs., Inc., 399 F.2d 121, 129–30 (9th Cir.1968) ("when, in a particular case, the risk qualitatively (e.g., of death or major disability) as well as quantitatively, on balance with the end sought to be achieved, is such as to call for a true choice judgment, medical or personal, the warning must be given"); Basko v. Sterling Drug, Inc., 416 F.2d 417 (2d Cir.1969) ("the manufacturer is obligated to warn in cases where the drug may affect only a small number of idiosyncratic or hypersensitive users and the obligation attaches regardless of whether the number of persons affected can fairly be said to be 'appreciable' "). Of course, when the group at risk is so small that the risk of harm is unforeseeable, courts will deny recovery on failure to warn. See, e.g., Cudmore v. Richardson-Merrell, Inc., 398 S.W.2d 640, 644 (Tex.Ct.App.1965), cert. denied, 385 U.S. 1003, 87 S.Ct. 705, 17 L.Ed.2d 542 (1967) ("the manufacturer of a drug for human consumption or intimate bodily use should be held liable for injurious results only when such results ... [were foreseeable] in an appreciable number of persons").

Comment l. Relationship between design and instruction or warning. Many courts have noted that a manufacturer may be obligated to design away dangers when it is reasonable to do so because, given the nature of the user or the product use, it is foreseeable that warnings or obvious dangers will either not be seen or will be disregarded. In Uloth v. City Tank Corp., 384 N.E.2d 1188, 1192 (Mass. 1978), the court said:

> An adequate warning may reduce the likelihood of injury to the user of a product in some cases. We decline, however, to adopt any rule that permits a manufacturer or designer to discharge its total responsibility to workers by simply warning of the dangers of a product. Whether or not adequate warnings are given is a factor to be considered on the issue of negligence, but warnings cannot absolve the manufacturer or designer of all responsibility for the safety of the product.... [I]n some circumstances a warning may not reduce the likelihood of injury. For example, where the danger is obvious, a warning may be superfluous. A designer may have no duty to warn of such dangers....
>
> Moreover, a user may not have a real alternative to using a dangerous product, as where a worker must either work on a dangerous machine or leave his job.... Further, a warning is not effective in eliminating injuries due to instinctual reactions, momentary inadvertence, or forgetfulness on the part of a worker. One of the primary purposes of safety devices is to guard against such foreseeable situations....
>
> Balanced against the somewhat limited effectiveness of warnings is the designer's ability to anticipate and protect against possible injuries. If a slight change in design would prevent serious, perhaps fatal, injury, the designer may not avoid liability by simply warning of the possible injury. We think that in such a case the burden to pre-

> vent needless injury is best placed on the designer or manufacturer rather than on the individual user of a product.

See also Eads v. R.D. Werner Co., 847 P.2d 1370 (Nev.1993); Robinson v. G.G.C., Inc., 808 P.2d 522, 524 (Nev. 1991). For similar expressions as to the need to design away even obvious dangers see Reporters' Note to § 2, Comment *d*, Part IV.C. Much of the problem was created by unfortunate language in the Restatement, Second, of Torts § 402A, Comment *j*, which provides:

> Where warning is given, the seller may reasonably assume that it will be read and heeded; and a product bearing such a warning, which is safe for use if it is followed, is not in defective condition, nor is it unreasonably dangerous.

The Comment *j* presumption has elicited heavy criticism from a host of commentators. The sharpest and most cogent attack was mounted by Professor Howard Latin, Good Warnings, Bad Products, and Cognitive Limitations, 41 U.C.L.A. L. Rev. 1193, 1206–07 (1994). He argues that:

> The Comment *j* presumption embodies the behavioral assumption that "reasonable" users can be expected to receive, correctly interpret, and obey every comprehensible warning accompanying every product they use or encounter. Yet, people are exposed each day to innumerable risks created by appliances that may malfunction or be mishandled; by potentially toxic pollutants, food additives, and other chemical substances; by cosmetics, drugs, and cleansing agents that may be improperly applied and are inherently dangerous for some sensitive individuals; by machine tools, presses, and other industrial or occupational equipment; and by hazardous transportation and recreation devices. Indeed, almost all products present substantial risks if improperly manufactured, designed, or used. People would have to read, understand, remember, and follow innumerable product warnings to protect themselves from all product-related risks they may confront. Moreover, risk assessment is only one realm of decisionmaking and people must devote some of their limited time and attention to many other types of choices.

Professor Latin utilizes the work of cognitive theorists to demonstrate that warnings should only be used as a supplement to a design that already embodies reasonable safety and not as a substitute for it. See also Twerski, Weinstein, Donaher and Piehler, The Use and Abuse of Warnings in Products Liability: Design Defect Comes of Age, 61 Cornell L. Rev. 495, 506 (1976).

As recognized by the commentators cited above, Comment *j* of the Restatement, Second, is inconsistent with the judicial abandonment of the patent danger rule and with those cases that take the position that a warning will not absolve the manufacturer from the duty to design against dangers when a reasonable, safer design could have been adopted that would have reduced or eliminated the residuum of risk that remains even after a warning is provided.

Illustration 14 is based on Uloth v. City Tank Corp., 384 N.E.2d 1188 (Mass.1978).

Comment m. Reasonably foreseeable uses and risks in design and warning claims.

1. As a practical matter, in a claim based on design defect arising from mechanical products, a plaintiff who establishes that the product was put to a foreseeable use need not prove that the seller should have known of the risks that would materialize from such foreseeable use. This corollary is motivated by pragmatic concerns. There is no good reason to burden plaintiffs with proving the foreseeability of risks arising from foreseeable uses of mechanical products. Almost by definition, once the use is foreseeable, the risks that attend such use are foreseeable. Imputation of knowledge is limited to cases dealing with durable goods and specifically excludes prescription drugs, chemicals, and toxics from imputed knowledge. A perceptive discussion of the "imputed knowledge" issue is found in 4 Final Report of the Legal Study, Interagency Task Force on Products Liability 109–110 (1977):

> It is by now well recognized that the difference between negligence and strict liability in design defect cases is that the element of *scienter*—knowledge of the dangerous propensities of the product—is imputed to the manufacturer when strict liability is applied. Because, however, the manufacturer is held to the standard of an expert in its field, it will be a rare case indeed where the manufacturer "should not" have known of the dangers in its product although those dangers were knowable at the time of the marketing.
>
> Recognizing the convergence of the theories of negligence and strict liability in design cases, the commentators have argued that, for strict liability to be of any consequence in such cases, knowledge of risks that were unknowable at the time of marketing should be imputed to manufacturers. This, however, the courts have consistently failed to do. Although there is language in some cases which appears to indicate a leaning toward imputation of knowledge of unknowable risks upon the manufacturer, the overwhelming majority of courts have evaluated the product on the basis of what dangers could have been known at the time of marketing.

It would be instructive at this point to recount briefly the history of the concept of imputed knowledge. The idea originated in the work of two scholars who were extremely influential in the early development of American products liability law, Deans John Wade and Page Keeton. In an article entitled, Products Liability—Inadequacy of Information, 48 Tex. L. Rev. 398, 404 (1970), Dean Keeton said:

> All of these propositions can be stated perhaps in one general proposition:
>
> > if the sale of the product under all the circumstances under which it was marketed subjected the consumer or others to an unreasonable risk of harm, the seller is subject to liability, and it is not relevant that he neither knew nor could have known nor ought to have known in the exercise of ordinary care that the unreasonable risk actually existed. It is enough that had he known of the risk and dangers he would not have marketed the product at all or he would have done so differently.

Dean Wade expressed similar sentiments in his much-cited article, On the Nature of Strict Tort Liability for

Products, 44 Miss. L.J. 825, 834–35 (1973):

> The time has now come to be forthright in using a tort way of thinking and tort terminology. There are several ways of doing it, and it is not difficult. The simplest and easiest way, it would seem, is to assume that the defendant knew of the dangerous condition of the product and ask whether he was then negligent in putting it on the market or supplying it to someone else. In other words, the scienter is supplied as a matter of law, and there is no need for the plaintiff to prove its existence as a matter of fact. Once given this notice of the dangerous condition of the chattel, the question then becomes whether the defendant was negligent to people who might be harmed by that condition if they came into contact with it or were in the vicinity of it. Another way of saying this is to ask whether the magnitude of the risk created by the dangerous condition of the product was outweighed by the social utility attained by putting it out in this fashion.

Relying heavily on these two authorities, several courts have stated that a significant difference between negligence and strict liability is that knowledge of risk will be imputed in a strict liability case whereas such an imputation is improper in a case based on negligence. See, e.g., Dart v. Wiebe Mfg., Inc., 709 P.2d 876 (Ariz. 1985) (en banc); Phillips v. Kimwood Mach. Co., 525 P.2d 1033, 1037–38 (Or.1974) (en banc); Cepeda v. Cumberland Eng. Co., 386 A.2d 816, 826 (N.J.1978); Suter v. San Angelo Foundry & Mach. Co., 406 A.2d 140, 150 (N.J.1979); Brooks v. Beech Aircraft Corp., 902 P.2d 54 (N.M.1995); Ziegler v. Kawasaki Heavy Indus. Ltd., 539 A.2d 701, 705 (Md.Ct.App. 1988).

The idea has not worn well with time. In 1983, Dean Wade recanted the position he espoused earlier in his 1973 *Mississippi Law Journal* article. In a Symposium article dealing with the issues of passage of time in product-liability cases, On the Effect in Product Liability of Knowledge Unavailable Prior to Marketing, 58 N.Y.U. L. Rev. 734, 764 (1983), Wade concluded: "I now would be inclined to think there is no longer any particular value in using the assumed-knowledge language." Wade also noted that Keeton had at least partially recanted because he believed that when the issue was whether the manufacturer should be held liable for failing to institute a safer design, "a product's design should normally be measured in terms of whether or not it was feasible to do a better job in light of the technology that was available at the time of manufacture." Id. at 763. Also see Prosser and Keeton on Torts 697–98 n.21 (5th ed. 1984). Other academic commentators have, for the most part, been critical of the imputation doctrine. See, e.g., Danzon, Tort Reform and the Role of Government in Private Insurance Markets, 13 J. Legal Stud. 517 (1984); A. Schwartz, Products Liability, Corporate Structure and Bankruptcy: Toxic Substances and the Remote Risk Relationship, 14 J. Legal Stud. 689 (1985); Henderson, Coping with the Time Dimension in Products Liability, 69 Calif. L. Rev. 919 (1981). But see Page, Generic Product Risks: The Case Against Comment k and for Strict Liability, 58 N.Y.U. L. Rev. 853 (1983) and Wertheimer, Unknowable Dangers and the Death of Strict Products Liability: The Empire

Strikes Back, 60 U. Cin. L. Rev. 1183 (1992) (author criticizes the judicial abandonment of the imputation rules as inconsistent with the policy behind strict products liability; article contains an exhaustive compilation of authority supporting the position taken by the Reporters that foreseeability of risk is an absolute requisite to an action in products liability).

Given the criticism that has been leveled against the imputation of knowledge doctrine and the relatively thin judicial support for it, it is here rejected as a doctrinal matter. However, when dealing with risks of harm from foreseeable product uses involving mechanical products, it seems wasteful to impose a burden on plaintiffs to establish that manufacturers, who are judged as experts, knew or should have known of the risks arising from product use. It is for this reason that the Comments suggest that, ordinarily, risks of harm arising from foreseeable use of durable products should simply be assumed. Indeed, it is interesting that even those cases that support the imputation principle do so primarily in the context of mechanical defects. See, e.g., Phillips v. Kimwood Mach. Co., 525 P.2d 1033 (Or.1974) (en banc) (sanding machine); Cepeda v. Cumberland Eng'g. Co., Inc., 386 A.2d 816 (N.J. 1978) (pelletizing machine). Imputation, in cases where it significantly affects defendants' liabilities, appears to have little support. However, given that risks of harm concerning foreseeable uses are or should be known to manufacturers of mechanical products, such risk knowledge may ordinarily be assumed.

2. An overwhelming majority of jurisdictions supports the proposition that a manufacturer has a duty to warn only of risks that were known or should have been known to a reasonable person. See, e.g., Shell Oil Co. v. Gutierrez, 581 P.2d 271, 279 (Ariz.Ct.App.1978); but see Dart v. Wiebe Mfg., Inc., 709 P.2d 876, 881 n. 2 (1985) (en banc); Anderson v. Owens–Corning Fiberglas Corp., 810 P.2d 549 (Cal.1991) (en banc) (court held that "knowledge, actual or constructive, is a requisite for strict liability for failure to warn," and that strict liability has incorporated some well-settled rules from the law of negligence); Basko v. Sterling Drug, Inc., 416 F.2d 417, 425–26 (2d Cir. 1969) (applying Connecticut law); Fibreboard Corp. v. Fenton, 845 P.2d 1168, 1172 (Colo.1993) (en banc), reh'g denied ("We agree with the petitioners that state-of-the-art evidence is properly admissible to establish that a product is not defective and unreasonably dangerous because of a failure-to-warn. A manufacturer cannot warn of dangers that were not known to it or knowable in light of the generally recognized and prevailing scientific and technical knowledge available at the time of manufacture and distribution."); Payne v. Soft Sheen Prods., Inc., 486 A.2d 712, 721 (D.C.1985); Woodill v. Parke Davis & Co., 402 N.E.2d 194, 198 (Ill.1980). ("We perceive that requiring a plaintiff to plead and prove that the defendant manufacturer knew or should have known of the danger that caused the injury, and that the defendant manufacturer failed to warn plaintiff of that danger, is a reasonable requirement, and one which focuses on the nature of the product and the adequacy of the warning, rather than on the conduct of the manufacturer."); Olson v. Prosoco, Inc., 522 N.W.2d 284, 289 (Iowa 1994):

> After reviewing the authorities and comments on the failure to

warn question, we believe any posited distinction between strict liability and negligence principles is illusory. We fail to see any distinction between negligence and strict liability in the analyses of those jurisdictions injecting a knowledge requirement into their strict liability/failure to warn equation. The standard applied by these 'strict liability' jurisdictions is exactly the same in practice as holding defendants to an expert standard of care under a negligence theory. The burden on plaintiffs is the same. They must prove a defendant knew or should have known of potential risks associated with the use of its product, yet failed to provide adequate directions or warnings to users. With regard to those jurisdictions imputing to defendants knowledge of its product's propensity to injure as it did, we have refused in the past to impose a duty upon manufacturers to warn of unknowable dangers. (Citations omitted).

See also Johnson v. American Cyanamid Co., 718 P.2d 1318, 1324 (Kan.1986) ("In determining warning issues, the test is reasonableness. To impose liability on a manufacturer, the plaintiff must show negligence on the part of the manufacturer."); La. Rev. Stat. Ann. § 2800.57 (West 1991) ("manufacturer failed to use reasonable care to provide an adequate warning . . ."); Owens–Illinois, Inc. v. Zenobia, 601 A.2d 633, 640 (Md.1992) ("In a failure to warn case . . . negligence concepts to some extent have been grafted onto strict liability. In such cases, a majority of courts hold that an element of knowledge or 'state of the art' evidence is directly pertinent to a cause of action under § 402A of the Restatement, Second, of Torts and liability is no longer entirely strict."); Miss. Code Ann. § 11–1–63(c)(i) (1993) (in a failure to warn action, plaintiff must prove that at the time the product left the control of the manufacturer or seller, "the manufacturer or seller knew or in light of reasonably available knowledge should have known about the danger . . ."); Opera v. Hyva, Inc., 450 N.Y.S.2d 615, 618 (N.Y.App.Div. 1982) ("Where the theory of liability is failure to warn or adequately instruct, negligence and strict products liability are equivalent causes of action."); Ohio Rev. Code Ann. § 2307.76(A)(1)(a), (b) (Anderson 1991); Sterling Drug, Inc. v. Yarrow, 408 F.2d 978, 992 (8th Cir.1969) (applying South Dakota law); Borel v. Fibreboard Paper Prods. Corp., 493 F.2d 1076, 1088 (5th Cir.1973), cert. denied, 419 U.S. 869, 95 S.Ct. 127, 42 L.Ed.2d 107 (1974) (applying Texas law). See also Reporters' Note, § 2, Comment *d*, Part IV.B (state-of-the-art).

As the above citations show, courts vary considerably in the type of rhetoric they apply to failure to warn cases involving prescription drugs. However, it should be noted that while some courts may speak in terms of strict liability and others in terms of reasonableness or negligence, there is little, if any, substantive difference between their approaches. This phenomenon may be most clearly demonstrated by analyzing a fairly recent decision in the California Supreme Court. In Carlin v. Superior Court, 920 P.2d 1347, 1350 (Cal.1996), the court acknowledges " . . . that the knowledge or knowability requirement for failure to warn infuses some negligence concepts into strict liability cases." Yet, the court still insists that California's strict liability standard places a heavier burden on the manufacturer of prescription drugs. In support of this position, the court presents the following two hypotheticals:

> a reasonably prudent manufacturer might reasonably decide that the risk of harm was such as not to require a warning as, for example, if the manufacturer's own testing showed a result contrary to that of others in the scientific community. Such a manufacturer might escape liability under negligence principles. In contrast, under strict liability principles the manufacturer has no such leeway. Similarly, a manufacturer could not escape liability under strict liability principles merely because its failure to warn of a known or reasonably scientifically knowable risk conformed to an industry-wide practice of failing to provide warnings that constituted the standard of reasonable care. Id. at 1351 (Citation and footnote omitted).

These hypotheticals, of course, fall short of establishing any true distinction between California's strict liability approach to failure to warn and a typical negligence or reasonableness standard. A manufacturer cannot escape liability under negligence principles simply because its testing does not reveal the same dangers as that of the scientific community. The choice to ignore the findings of the scientific community would certainly raise a question for the trier of fact as to whether such a choice constituted negligence. In addition, a manufacturer may not avoid liability under a negligence regime by simply conforming to industry-wide standards of care. While such standards may be relevant to the issue of negligence, it is an elementary principle of tort law that conformance with such standards will never completely insulate the manufacturer from liability under a negligence regime.

Several states take the position that a defendant manufacturer is charged with knowledge available at time of trial without regard to whether the defendant knew or reasonably could have known of the risk. See In re Hawaii Fed. Asbestos Cases, 699 F.Supp. 233 (D.Hawai'i 1988), aff'd, 960 F.2d 806 (9th Cir.1992); Simmons v. Monarch Mach. Tool Co., 596 N.E.2d 318, 320 n. 3 (Mass.1992) (Massachusetts follows the rule established in Hayes v. Ariens Co., 462 N.E.2d 273, 277 (Mass.1984), that "[T]he adequacy of a warning is measured by the warning that would be given ... by an ordinarily prudent vendor who, at [time of sale], is fully aware of the risks presented by the product. A defendant vendor is held to that standard regardless of the knowledge of risks that he actually had, or reasonably should have had when the sale took place."); Dambacher v. Mallis, 485 A.2d 408 (Pa.Super.Ct.1984); Ayers v. Johnson & Johnson Baby Prods. Co., 818 P.2d 1337, 1346 (Wash.1991) (en banc) (foreseeability not an element of a failure to warn claim).

Most commentators agree with the majority rule. See, e.g., Danzon, Tort Reform and the Role of Government in Private Insurance Markets, 13 J. Legal Stud. 517 (1984); Owen, Defectiveness Restated: Exploding the "Strict" Products Liability Myth, 1996 U. Ill. L. Rev. 743, 785 ("As courts and commentators have come to recognize the inherent unworkability, illogic, and even incomprehensibility of such a doctrine in design and warnings cases, the very idea that liability in these central contexts is 'strict' has been viewed increasingly as a myth."); Owen, The Moral Foundation of Products Liability Law: Toward First Principles, 68 Notre Dame L. Rev. 427 (1993); Prosser and Keeton, The Law of Torts 697–98 (5th ed. 1984); G. Schwartz, Foreword, Understanding Products Liability, 67 Calif. L. Rev. 435, 462–63 (1979); G. Schwartz, The Vitality of Negligence and the Ethics of Strict Liability, 15 Ga. L. Rev. 963, 972–73 (1981); Wade, On the Effect in Product Liability of Knowledge Unavailable Prior to Marketing, 58 N.Y.U. L. Rev. 734 (1983). But see Page, Generic Product Risks: The Case Against Comment *k* and for Strict Liability, 58 N.Y.U. L. Rev. 853 (1983) and Wertheimer, Unknowable Dangers and the Death of Strict Products Liability: The Empire Strikes Back, 60 U. Cin. L. Rev. 1183 (1992).

Comment n. Relationship of definitions of defect to traditional doctrinal categories. Comment *n* takes the position that as long as the plaintiff establishes defect under § 2(a), (b), or (c), courts are free to utilize the concepts of negligence, strict liability, or implied warranty of merchantability as theories of liability. Conversely, failure to meet the requisites of § 2(a), (b), or (c) will defeat a cause of action under either negligence, strict liability, or the implied warranty of merchantability. Comment *n* takes note of the fact that some states, based on their own historical analysis of the implied warranty of merchantability under the Uniform Commercial Code, have adopted a consumer expectations test in design and failure to warn claims. A recent example of this phenomenon is Denny v. Ford Motor Co., 662 N.E.2d 730, 736 (N.Y.1995), in which the court said that "[a]s long as that legislative source of authority exists, we are not free to merge the warranty cause of action with its tort-based sibling regardless of whether, as a matter of policy, the contract-based warranty claim *may fairly be regarded as a historical relic that no longer has any independent substantive value.*" Id. (emphasis added). This Restatement contemplates that a single tort definition of defect will emerge regardless of the characterization of the claim as sounding in tort or in implied warranty of merchantability. For a critique of *Denny* see V. Schwartz and M. Behrens, An Unhappy Return to Confusion in the Common Law of Products Liability—Denny v. Ford Motor Co. Should Be Overturned, 17 Pace L. Rev. 359 (1997).

A related question faced by the courts is whether a plaintiff should be permitted to go to the jury on multiple theories for a single defect. For example, in a manufacturing defect case, should a court give a case to the jury under both a negligence and strict liability instruction? Or in a design or failure to warn case, should multiple theories of negligence and strict liability be given to the jury?

A fair number of courts have taken the position that in a design or failure to warn case, it is redundant (and thus inappropriate) to allow the plaintiff to go to the jury on both negligence and strict liability. See, e.g., Chestnut v. Ford Motor Co., 445 F.2d 967, 968 (4th Cir.1971) ("The standard of safety of goods imposed on the seller or manufacturer of a product is essentially the same whether the theory of liability is labeled warranty or negligence or strict tort liability: the product must not be unreasonably dangerous at the time that it leaves the defendant's possession.... "). See Jones v. Hutchinson

Mfg., Inc., 502 S.W.2d 66, 69–70 (Ky. 1973) (In a design case "the distinction between the so-called strict liability principle and negligence is of no practical significance so far as the standard of conduct required of the defendant is concerned. In either event, the standard required is reasonable care."); Prentis v. Yale Mfg. Co., 365 N.W.2d 176 (Mich.1984) ("The competing factors to be weighed under a risk-utility balancing test invite the trier of fact to consider the alternatives and risks faced by the manufacturer and to determine whether in light of these the manufacturer exercised reasonable care in making the design choices it made. Instructing a jury that weighing factors concerning conduct and judgment must yield a conclusion that does not describe conduct is confusing at best."); Halvorson v. American Hoist & Derrick Co., 240 N.W.2d 303, 307 (Minn.1976), overruled on other grounds, Holm v. Sponco. Mfg., Inc., 324 N.W.2d 207 (Minn.1982), and overruling recognized by, Bilotta v. Kelley Co., 346 N.W.2d 616 (Minn. 1984) ("If a product is not . . . defective . . . , it is not negligence to manufacture it that way."); Sprankle v. Bower Ammonia & Chem. Co., 824 F.2d 409, 413 (5th Cir.1987) (applying Mississippi law) (any "theoretical error" in failing to instruct jury on negligent failure to warn theory was harmless in view of jury's rejection of strict tort failure to warn theory); Garrett v. Hamilton Standard Controls, Inc., 850 F.2d 253, 257 (5th Cir.1988) (applying Texas law); Mather v. Caterpillar Tractor Corp., 533 P.2d 717, 719 (Ariz.Ct.App.1975) (court should withdraw the negligence count from the jury on grounds that it would be "superfluous and would tend to confuse the jurors" if included with a count for strict liability in tort).

The mischief caused by dual instructions on both negligence and strict liability is exemplified by Greiten v. LaDow, 235 N.W.2d 677, 685 (Wis.1975) (concurring opinion of Heffernan, J., subsequently elevated to "majority" status) ("there may be recovery for the negligent design of a product even though it is not unreasonably dangerous in the 402A sense") and Hasson v. Ford Motor Co., 564 P.2d 857 (Cal.1977) (en banc). A leading casebook, Keeton, Owen, Montgomery and Green, Product Safety and Liability 176 (2d ed. 1989), notes that most courts have rejected "this kind of nonsense." Nonetheless the continued use of dual theories for identical causes of action spawns such aberrations.

In Tipton v. Michelin Tire Co., 101 F.3d 1145, 1150 (6th Cir.1996), the court confronted the question whether a jury verdict finding the product to be "not defective" could be reconciled with a jury finding that the defendant was negligent in designing the product. The court held that the two findings were irreconcilable. A finding of defect is an absolute predicate for a finding of negligence. The court also noted that:

> At least one court interpreting the law of Kentucky has held that in order to hold a manufacturer liable under either strict liability or negligence, a jury must first find that the product in question was defective. Sexton ex rel. Sexton v. Bell Helmets, 926 F.2d 331 (4th Cir.), cert. denied, 502 U.S. 820, 112 S.Ct. 79, 116 L.Ed.2d 52 (1991). In *Sexton*, the Fourth Circuit stated:
>
> > Although Kentucky also imposes the traditional duty of care on

> manufacturers to make products reasonably safe, when a product liability claim is based on a *design defect*, the articulation of liability, whether based on a negligent breach of a duty of care or on strict liability, reduces to the single question of whether the product was defective.

> *Sexton*, 926 F.2d at 335 (emphasis added). In other words, proof of a defective product is essential to the product's liability or the negligence claim. According to *Sexton*, the distinction between the two claims is of "no practical significance." *Sexton*, 926 F.2d at 336 (quoting Jones v. Hutchinson Mfg., Inc., 502 S.W.2d 66, 69–70 (Ky.1973)). We agree that the two claims in this case depend on the existence of a defective product. As indicated above, however, the jury found no defective product for purposes of the strict liability claim, but did find that the product was defective for purposes of the negligence claim. That finding, we believe, is legally inconsistent....

Given the tests provided by §§ 2(b) and 2(c), there is even less reason to continue the dual theories. Since the tests speak of foreseeable risk, a plaintiff is free to introduce evidence of a defendant's conduct even in the context of a strict liability case, since what was foreseeable is relevant to the test for liability. Secondly, the standard used for liability is that the product must be "not reasonably safe." The tests in §§ 2(b) and 2(c) require a reasonableness balancing approach. Courts should not create jury confusion by allowing claims on both negligence and strict liability to go to juries when they are evaluating the reasonableness of the product and the alternative design.

In a case alleging a manufacturing defect, there is more reason for allowing the case to be presented to the jury on both negligence and strict liability theories. A plaintiff may, with some justification, argue that the negligence claim focuses on the conduct of the manufacturer whereas the strict liability claim is not subject to any risk-utility balancing. A manufacturing defect claim, unlike a design or failure to warn claim, is not subject to reasonableness balancing.

Finally, when a plaintiff can satisfy the requirements under the applicable statute governing liability for breach of implied warranty of merchantability, and a more generous statute of limitations is available under that statute than the limitations period applicable to tort claims, the plaintiff is free to advance the warranty claim. See, e.g., Fernandez v. Char–Li–Jon, Inc., 888 P.2d 471 (N.M.Ct.App.1994).

Comment o. Liability of nonmanufacturing sellers for defective design and defects due to inadequate instruction or warning. See Reporters' Note to § 1, Comment *e*.

Comment p. Misuse, modification, and alteration.

1. When a product is put to an unforeseeable use and the plaintiff claims that the product should have been designed to avoid injury when put to such a use, the courts agree that liability will not attach. There is widespread understanding that misuse in this context goes to the basic duty issue. See, e.g., Newman v. Utility Trailer and Equip. Co., 564 P.2d 674, 676–77 (Or.1977) (en banc), where the court said:

> It is obvious that trial courts are experiencing difficulty in distinguishing *foreseeability of use* from *foreseeability of the risk of harm.*

> Before a manufacturer or other seller is strictly liable for injury inflicted by a product, the product must have been put to a foreseeable use. As an example: if a shovel is used to prop open a heavy door, but, because of the way the shovel was designed, it is inadequate to the task and the door swings shut and crushes the user's hand, no responsibility for the injury results by reason of the shovel's not being designed to prop open doors since it was not reasonably foreseeable by the manufacturer or seller that it would be so used. (emphasis added).

Similar expressions concerning the duty issue pervade the case law. See, e.g., Jones v. Menard, 559 F.2d 1282, 1285 n. 4 (5th Cir.1977) (applying Louisiana law) ("[i]n inadequate warning cases misuse means that the seller had no duty to warn against unforeseeable uses of its products, while in design cases misuse means that the manufacturer had no duty to design a product so as to prevent injuries arising from unforeseeable uses of its product . . ."); Venezia v. Miller Brewing Co., 626 F.2d 188 (1st Cir.1980) (applying Massachusetts law) (no duty to design beer bottle to prevent injury when eight-year-old deliberately throws bottle against a telephone pole); Ellsworth v. Sherne Lingerie, Inc., 495 A.2d 348, 355 (Md. 1985) ("We conclude, as have most courts which have considered the issue, that 'reasonable foreseeability' is the appropriate test, and thus a seller is required to provide a product that is not unreasonably dangerous when used for a purpose and in a manner that is reasonably foreseeable.").

See also Jurado v. Western Gear Works, 619 A.2d 1312, 1318 (N.J. 1993):

> To the extent that misuse relates to the duty to design a safe product, 'a manufacturer has a duty to make sure that its manufactured products placed into the stream of commerce are suitably safe when properly used for their intended or reasonably foreseeable purposes.' . . . When someone is injured while using a product for an unforeseeable purpose or in an unforeseeable manner, the misuse sheds no light on whether the product is defective, because a manufacturer is not under a duty to protect against unforeseeable misuses . . . A manufacturer, however, has a duty to prevent an injury caused by the foreseeable misuse of its product.

Findlay v. Copeland Lumber Co., 509 P.2d 28, 31 (Or.1973) (Misuse is a "use or handling so unusual that the average consumer could not reasonably expect the product to be designed and manufactured to withstand it—a use which the seller, therefore, need not anticipate and provide for."); General Motors Corp. v. Hopkins, 548 S.W.2d 344, 349 (Tex. 1977), overruled on other grounds, Turner v. General Motors Corp., 584 S.W.2d 844 (1979); Duncan v. Cessna Aircraft Co., 665 S.W.2d 414 (Tex. 1984) ("We cannot charge the manufacturer of a knife when it is used as a toothpick and the user complains because the sharp edge cuts. A harness hook is not necessarily defective simply because it breaks while being used to hold up a 1700 pound weight.").

Academic commentators agree. See, e.g., Shapo, The Law of Product Liability § 21.08 (3d ed. 1994); Fischer and Powers, Products Liability—Cases and Materials 85 (1988); Twerski, The Many Faces of Misuse; An

Inquiry Into the Emerging Doctrine of Comparative Causation, 29 Mercer L. Rev. 403 (1978); Noel, Defective Products: Abnormal Use, Contributory Negligence and Assumption of Risk, 25 Vand. L. Rev. 93 (1972).

2. Discussion of misuse, alteration, and modification in the context of causation is found in the Reporters' Note to § 15, Comment *b*.

3. Discussion of misuse, alteration, and modification in the context of comparative responsibility is found in the Reporters' Note to § 17, Comment *c*.

§ 3. Circumstantial Evidence Supporting Inference of Product Defect

It may be inferred that the harm sustained by the plaintiff was caused by a product defect existing at the time of sale or distribution, without proof of a specific defect, when the incident that harmed the plaintiff:

(a) was of a kind that ordinarily occurs as a result of product defect; and

(b) was not, in the particular case, solely the result of causes other than product defect existing at the time of sale or distribution.

Comment:

a. History. This Section traces its historical antecedents to the law of negligence, which has long recognized that an inference of negligence may be drawn in cases where the defendant's negligence is the best explanation for the cause of an accident, even if the plaintiff cannot explain the exact nature of the defendant's conduct. See Restatement, Second, Torts § 328D. As products liability law developed, cases arose in which an inference of product defect could be drawn from the incident in which a product caused plaintiff's harm, without proof of the specific nature of the defect. This Section sets forth the formal requisites for drawing such an inference.

b. Requirement that the harm be of a kind that ordinarily occurs as a result of product defect. The most frequent application of this Section is to cases involving manufacturing defects. When a product unit contains such a defect, and the defect affects product performance so as to cause a harmful incident, in most instances it will cause the product to malfunction in such a way that the inference of product defect is clear. From this perspective, manufacturing defects cause products to fail to perform their manifestly intended functions. Frequently, the plaintiff is able to establish specifically the nature and identity of the defect and may proceed directly under § 2(a). But when the product unit involved in the harm-causing incident is lost or destroyed in the accident, direct evidence of specific defect may not be available. Under that circumstance, this Section may offer the plaintiff the only fair opportunity to recover.

When examination of the product unit is impossible because the unit is lost or destroyed after the harm-causing incident, a somewhat different issue may be presented. Responsibility for spoliation of evidence may be relevant to the fairness of allowing the inference set forth in this Section. In any event, the issues of evidence spoliation and any sanctions that might be imposed for such conduct are beyond the scope of this Restatement Third, Torts: Products Liability.

Although the rules in this Section, for the reasons just stated, most often apply to manufacturing defects, occasionally a product design causes the product to malfunction in a manner identical to that which would ordinarily be caused by a manufacturing defect. Thus, an aircraft may inadvertently be designed in such a way that, in new condition and while flying within its intended performance parameters, the wings suddenly and unexpectedly fall off, causing harm. In theory, of course, the plaintiff in such a case would be able to show how other units in the same production line were designed, leading to a showing of a reasonable alternative design under § 2(b). As a practical matter, however, when the incident involving the aircraft is one that ordinarily occurs as a result of product defect, and evidence in the particular case establishes that the harm was not solely the result of causes other than product defect existing at time of sale, it should not be necessary for the plaintiff to incur the cost of proving whether the failure resulted from a manufacturing defect or from a defect in the design of the product. Section 3 allows the trier of fact to draw the inference that the product was defective whether due to a manufacturing defect or a design defect. Under those circumstances, the plaintiff need not specify the type of defect responsible for the product malfunction.

It is important to emphasize the difference between a general inference of defect under § 3 and claims of defect brought directly under §§ 1 and 2. Section 3 claims are limited to situations in which a product fails to perform its manifestly intended function, thus supporting the conclusion that a defect of some kind is the most probable explanation. If that is not the case, and if no other provision of Chapter 1 allows the plaintiff to establish defect independently of the requirements in § 2 (see § 4 and Comment *e* to § 2), a plaintiff is required to establish a cause of action for defect based on proof satisfying the requirements set forth in § 2. See § 2, Comment *b*.

Illustrations:

1. John purchased a new electric blender. John used the blender approximately 10 times exclusively for making milkshakes. While he was making a milkshake, the blender suddenly

shattered. A piece of glass struck John's eye, causing harm. The incident resulting in harm is of a kind that ordinarily occurs as a result of product defect.

2. Same facts as Illustration 1, except that John accidentally dropped the blender, causing the glass to shatter. The product did not fail to function in a manner supporting an inference of defect. Whether liability can be established depends on whether the plaintiff can prove a cause of action under §§ 1 and 2.

3. Mary purchased a new automobile. She drove the car 1,000 miles without incident. One day she stopped the car at a red light and leaned back to rest until the light changed. Suddenly the seat collapsed backward, causing Mary to hit the accelerator and the car to shoot out into oncoming traffic and collide with another car. Mary suffered harm in the ensuing collision. As a result of the collision, Mary's car was set afire, destroying the seat assembly. The incident resulting in the harm is of a kind that ordinarily occurs as a result of product defect. Mary need not establish whether the seat assembly contained a manufacturing defect or a design defect.

4. Same facts as in Illustration 3, except that the seat-back assembly failed when Mary, while stopped at the red light, was rear-ended by another automobile at 40 m.p.h. Mary cannot make out liability under this Section. The product did not fail to function in a manner supporting an inference of defect since the collapse of the seat is not the kind of incident that ordinarily occurs as a result of product defect. Liability must be established under the rules set forth in §§ 1 and 2.

5. While carefully driving a new automobile at legal speed on a well-maintained road, Driver felt something crack below where the steering column connects with the dashboard. The steering wheel spun to the right and the automobile turned sharply. Before Driver could stop, the automobile crashed into a wall and Driver suffered harm. Driver has brought an action against the manufacturer of the automobile. The automobile had been driven on short trips before the accident and had 300 miles on its odometer. Driver's qualified expert witness testifies that in her opinion the accident was caused by a defect in the steering mechanism. The expert identifies four specific manufacturing and design defects that could have caused the accident, but was unable to say, on a balance of the probabilities, which of the four defects was the cause. Under this Section it is not necessary to identify the specific defect in order to draw the inference that a product defect caused the plaintiff's harm.

c. No requirement that plaintiff prove what aspect of the product was defective. The inference of defect may be drawn under this Section without proof of the specific defect. Furthermore, quite apart from the question of what type of defect was involved, the plaintiff need not explain specifically what constituent part of the product failed. For example, if an inference of defect can be appropriately drawn in connection with the catastrophic failure of an airplane, the plaintiff need not establish whether the failure is attributable to fuel-tank explosion or engine malfunction.

d. Requirement that the incident that harmed the plaintiff was not, in the particular case, solely the result of causes other than product defect existing at the time of sale. To allow the trier of fact to conclude that a product defect caused the plaintiff's harm under this Section, the plaintiff must establish by a preponderance of the evidence that the incident was not solely the result of causal factors other than defect at time of sale. The defect need not be the only cause of the incident; if the plaintiff can prove that the most likely explanation of the harm involves the causal contribution of a product defect, the fact that there may be other concurrent causes of the harm does not preclude liability under this Section. But when the harmful incident can be attributed solely to causes other than original defect, including the conduct of others, an inference of defect under this Section cannot be drawn.

Evidence may permit the inference that a defect in the product at the time of the harm-causing incident caused the product to malfunction, but not the inference that the defect existed at the time of sale or distribution. Such factors as the age of the product, possible alteration by repairers or others, and misuse by the plaintiff or third parties may have introduced the defect that causes harm.

Illustrations:

6. While driving a new automobile at high speed one night, Driver drove off the highway and crashed into a tree. Driver suffered harm. Driver cannot remember the circumstances surrounding the accident. Driver has brought an action against ABC Company, the manufacturer of the automobile. Driver presents no evidence of a specific defect. However, Driver's qualified expert presents credible testimony that a defect in the automobile must have caused the accident. ABC's qualified expert presents credible testimony that it is equally likely that, independent of any defect, Driver lost control while speeding on the highway. If the trier of fact believes the testimony of Driver's expert, then an inference of defect may be established under this Section. If, however, ABC's expert is believed, an inference of product defect may not be

drawn under this Section because Driver has failed to establish by a preponderance of the evidence that the harm did not result solely from Driver's independent loss of control at high speed.

7. Jack purchased a new ABC Electric Power Screwdriver. He inserted the bit for the appropriate screw size and turned the power button on. The bit shot out of the tool and lodged itself in Jack's arm, causing serious injury. Two weeks after purchasing the electric screwdriver, Jack believed the tool was making too much noise and brought it to the Acme Tool Repair Shop to check it out. Acme removed the mechanism that held the bit, examined it, and then reassembled it. Finding no problem, Acme returned the tool to Jack. The accident occurred the next day. On direct examination Jack's expert testifies that the accident was caused by a defect existing at time of sale. On cross-examination, however, Jack's expert admits it is equally probable that the problem with the tool was introduced by Acme. An inference that the power tool was defective at the time of sale cannot be drawn under this Section.

REPORTERS' NOTE

Comment a. History. The Restatement, Second, of Torts § 328D provides:

§ 328D. Res Ipsa Loquitur

(1) It may be inferred that harm suffered by the plaintiff is caused by negligence of the defendant when

(a) the event is of a kind which ordinarily does not occur in the absence of negligence;

(b) other responsible causes, including the conduct of the plaintiff and third persons, are sufficiently eliminated by the evidence; and

(c) the indicated negligence is within the scope of the defendant's duty to the plaintiff.

(2) It is the function of the court to determine whether the inference may reasonably be drawn by the jury, or whether it must necessarily be drawn.

(3) It is the function of the jury to determine whether the inference is to be drawn in any case where different conclusions may reasonably be reached.

Comment b. Requirement that the harm be of a kind that ordinarily occurs as a result of product defect, and Comment c. No requirement that plaintiff prove what aspect of the product was defective.

1. Case authority supports § 3 inference of defect without reference to whether it is a manufacturing defect or design defect. Under §§ 1 and 2, the plaintiff must establish one or more specific defects. Under § 3, the plaintiff need not establish a specific defect if the plaintiff meets the requisites of § 3(a) and (b). The plaintiff need not establish that the harm arose because there was either a

manufacturing defect or a design defect. The plaintiff need not prove that the product departed from its intended design or that a reasonable alternative design could have been adopted.

A huge body of case law supports this proposition. See, e.g., Dietz v. Waller, 685 P.2d 744, 745 (Ariz.1984) ("[N]o specific defect need be shown if the evidence, direct or circumstantial, permits the inference that the accident was caused by a defect"); Harrell Motors, Inc. v. Flanery, 612 S.W.2d 727, 729, (Ark.1981) ("proof of specific defect is not required when common experience tells us that the accident would not have occurred in the absence of a defect"); Stewart v. Ford Motor Co., 553 F.2d 130, 139 (D.C.Cir.1977) ("plaintiffs were allowed to ask jury to infer that the accident was caused by some unknown defect"); Cassisi v. Maytag Co., 396 So.2d 1140, 1153 (Fla.Dist.Ct.App.1981) ("immaterial that the plaintiffs failed to identify the specific cause of the malfunction since . . . the malfunction itself . . . is evidence of the product's defective condition at both the time of the injury and the time of the sale"); Stewart v. Budget Rent–A–Car Corp., 470 P.2d 240, 242 (Haw.1970) ("user's testimony on what happened is another method of proving that the product was defective"); Farmer v. International Harvester Co., 553 P.2d 1306, 1311 (Idaho 1976) ("a prima facie case may be proved by direct or circumstantial evidence"); Garrett v. Nobles, 630 P.2d 656, 658 (Idaho 1981) ("plaintiff need not prove a specific defect in order to carry burden of proof"); Holloway v. General Motors Corp., 271 N.W.2d 777 (Mich.1978) (plaintiffs were not required to prove the specific defect in the product); Western Sur. & Cas. v. General Elec. Co., 433 N.W.2d 444, 447 (Minn.App.1988) ("in a strict products liability action, a plaintiff may use circumstantial evidence to prove the existence of a defect"); Lindsay v. McDonnell Douglas Aircraft Corp., 460 F.2d 631 (8th Cir. 1972) (applying Missouri law) (fire and crash of aircraft lost at sea did not require proof of specific defect); Landahl v. Chrysler Corp., 534 N.Y.S.2d 245 (N.Y.App.Div.1988) ("plaintiff in a products liability action need not establish the precise nature of the defect in order to make out a prima facie case"); Sanders v. Quikstak, Inc., 889 F.Supp. 128, 131 (S.D.N.Y.1995) ("Under certain circumstances, however, a plaintiff need not prove a specific defect in the product at issue. Despite an absence of proof of any specific defect in a product, a jury may infer that an accident occurred because of a defect when the plaintiff has proven that the product did not perform as intended and has excluded all causes of the accident not attributable to the defendant."); Cincinnati Ins. Co. v. Volkswagen of Am., Inc., 502 N.E.2d 651 (Ohio Ct.App.1985) (plaintiff may use circumstantial evidence to show existence of defect); Henderson v. Sunbeam Corp., 46 F.3d 1151 (10th Cir. 1995) (applying Oklahoma law) (plaintiff may prove case with circumstantial evidence without identifying a particular defective component); Kridler v. Ford Motor Co., 422 F.2d 1182, 1185 (3rd Cir.1970) (applying Pennsylvania law) ("plaintiff in a suit for . . . strict liability does not have to establish a particular defect as the proximate cause of the accident"); Anderson v. Chrysler Corp., 403 S.E.2d 189 (W.Va.1991) (plaintiff need not identify the specific defect that caused the harm).

Some courts refer to the rule in this Section as the "malfunction doctrine." See, e.g., Farmer v. International Harvester Co., 553 P.2d 1306, 1311 (Idaho 1976) ("proof of malfunction is circumstantial evidence of a defect in a product since a product will not ordinarily malfunction within the reasonable contemplation of a consumer in the absence of defect"); Stackiewicz v. Nissan Motor Corp., 686 P.2d 925, 927 (Nev.1984) ("proof of an unexpected, dangerous malfunction may suffice to establish a prima facie case for the plaintiff of the existence of a product defect"); Knight v. Otis Elevator Co., 596 F.2d 84 (3d Cir.1979) (applying Pennsylvania law) (plaintiff need not prove the existence of a specific defect if plaintiff can show that the product malfunctioned in the absence of abnormal use and reasonable secondary causes); Marcus v. Anderson/Gore Homes, Inc., 498 So.2d 1051, 1052 (Fla.Dist.Ct. App.1986) ("[w]hen a product malfunctions during normal operations, a legal inference arises that the product is defective . . ."); Welge v. Planters Lifesavers Co., 17 F.3d 209, 211 (7th Cir.1994) ("If it is the kind of accident that would not have occurred but for a defect in the product, and if it is reasonably plain that the defect was not introduced after the product was sold, the accident is evidence of the defect."); see also Harkins v. Calumet Realty Co., 614 A.2d 699, 705 (Pa.Super.Ct.1992) ("malfunction theory . . . permits a plaintiff to prove a defect in a product with evidence of the occurrence of a malfunction and with evidence eliminating abnormal use or reasonable, secondary causes . . . ").

When reasonable minds could differ on the issue, courts hold that the judge should give the case to the jury. See, e.g., Marathon Battery Co. v. Kilpatrick, 418 P.2d 900 (Okla. 1965) (jury verdict for plaintiff affirmed notwithstanding four defendant's experts' testimony that some outside agency must have caused the explosion of a battery); Dietz v. Waller, 685 P.2d 744 (Ariz.1984) (to prove a product defective, a plaintiff is not required to eliminate with certainty all other possible causes of an accident, but rather to present evidence sufficient to allow the trier of fact to reasonably infer that it was more probable than not that the product was defective); Sochanski v. Sears, Roebuck & Co., 689 F.2d 45, 50 (3d Cir.1982) (applying Pennsylvania law) ("malfunction may itself . . . be sufficient evidence . . . to make the existence of a defect a jury question"); see also Troy v. Kampgrounds of Am., Inc., 581 A.2d 665 (Pa.Super.Ct.1990).

Some courts in applying the § 3 principle talk in terms of the product failing to meet "consumer expectations." See, e.g., Cassisi v. Maytag Co., 396 So.2d 1140, 1146 (Fla.Dist. Ct.App.1981) ("evidence of the nature of an accident itself may, under certain circumstances, give rise to a reasonable inference that the product was defective because the circumstances of the product's failure may be such as to frustrate the ordinary consumer's expectations of its continued performance"); Tulgetske v. R.D. Werner Co., Inc., 408 N.E.2d 492 (Ill. App.Ct.1980) (plaintiff can make out strict liability claim by proving that product failed to perform in a manner reasonably to be expected in light of its intended function); Mote v. Montgomery Ward & Co., 466 N.E.2d 593 (Ill.App.Ct.1984) (it was reasonable for the jury to conclude that there was an absence of abnormal use and that the ladder failed to perform in the manner reasonably to be expected in light of its intended function); Cincinnati Ins. Co. v. Volkswagen of Am., Inc., 502 N.E.2d 651, 654 (Ohio Ct.App.1985) (in a fire case, "the reasonable expectations of a buyer of a motor vehicle is that the main electrical cable harness of such vehicle will not start a fire"); Doyle v. White Metal Rolling & Stamping Corp., 618 N.E.2d 909, 916 (Ill.App.Ct.1993) ("[A] plaintiff may create an inference that a product was defective by direct or circumstantial evidence that: (1) there was no abnormal use of the product; (2) . . . there was no reasonable secondary cause of the injury; and (3) . . . the product failed to perform in the manner reasonably to be expected in light of its nature and intended function").

2. For authority that courts should consider the circumstances that lead to spoliation in order to preserve cases that pertain to legitimate grievances while ensuring fairness to parties who may be prejudiced by negative inferences unsubstantiated by physical evidence, see Federal Ins. Co. v. Allister Mfg. Co., 622 So.2d 1348, 1350 (Fla.App.1993) (reversal of dismissal of plaintiff's claim when plaintiff's expert inadvertently lost garage door opener suspected of being faulty; while the extreme sanction of dismissal would be available if the loss was "deliberate" or "willful," the court noted, it would be too harsh in this case); see also Gordner v. Dynetics Corp., 862 F.Supp. 1303 (M.D.Pa.1994). But see DeWeese v. Anchor Hocking Consumer & Indus. Prods. Group, 628 A.2d 421 (Pa.Super.Ct.1993); Daniels v. GNB, Inc., 629 So.2d 595 (Miss.1993). See also Burns v. Cannondale Bicycle Co., 876 P.2d 415 (Utah.Ct.App.1994) (injured party took his bike back to the store after the accident; there was conflicting evidence as to whether the bike was altered by the store at that time, but in the end there was no observable defect in the bike's brakes; the court held that despite the possibility that the store disposed of a faulty part, plaintiff had not met his burden). When no bad faith is present, courts sometimes construe spoliation as if the product had been destroyed in the accident. See Bruther v. General Elec. Co., 818 F.Supp. 1238 (S.D.Ind.1993) (light-bulb case allowed to go forward without production of the offending bulb).

Comment d. Requirement that the incident that harmed the plaintiff was not, in the particular case, solely the result of causes other than product defect existing at the time of sale. See generally Saieva v. Budget Rent–A–Car, 591 N.E.2d 507, 516 (Ill.App. Ct.1992) (summary judgment for defendant upheld where "[t]he record supports the reasonable inference that the plaintiff simply lost control of the van because he was driving at an excessive speed on a dark, wet and bumpy rural highway"); Sztubinski v. Stanton Trading Corp., 1994 WL 111353 (E.D. Pa.) (bottle opener manufacturer cannot rely on inference in impleading a bottle manufacturer where there is no proof that the bottle did not break because of the opener or some other cause); Schlier v. Milwaukee Electrical Tool Corp., 835 F.Supp. 839, 842 (E.D.Pa.1993) ("[P]laintiff's case-in-chief must . . . have been free of secondary causes or abnormal use which could account for the accident. [Based on plaintiff's own evidence, there is at least one secondary cause which could account for the accident.] ... The court determines that because plaintiff did not negate the evidence pointing to a reasonable, secondary cause for the accident, [i.e., wear and tear,] plaintiff failed to establish a prima facie case."). This burden has been interpreted with varying degrees of stringency. See, e.g., Enrich v. Windmere Corp., 616 N.E.2d 1081 (Mass.1993) (to establish an inference that more probably than not a defect in a fan had set off a fire, experts would have to conduct tests on other electrical devices, the house's wiring and fuse box, and likewise consider alternative causes); Campbell Soup Co. v. Gates, 889 S.W.2d 750, 753 (Ark.1994) ("[T]his court examined the evidence to determine to what extent the plaintiff had negated other causes of the accident and held that the proof neither went beyond suspicion or conjecture nor raised a reasonable inference that the defect was the cause of the accident."). But see Bruther v. General Electric Co., 818 F.Supp. 1238, 1242 (S.D.Ind.1993) ("The court can find no requirement that plaintiff produce an expert to bolster his allegations."); Rizzo v. Mr. Coffee, 1996 WL 68000 (N.D.Ill.). The inference of defect may not be drawn, however, from the mere fact of a product-related accident. See, e.g., Williams v. Smart Chevrolet Co., 730 S.W.2d 479 (Ark. 1987) (mere fact of an accident—car door suddenly swung open while plaintiff was driving car—standing alone, does not make out a case that product was defective; directed verdict for defendant affirmed).

That the plaintiff must establish by a preponderance of evidence that the harm was not solely the result of other causes is reflected in the Restatement, Second, of Torts § 328, Comment *f.*

> It is never enough for the plaintiff to prove that he was injured by the negligence of some person unidentified. It is still necessary to make the negligence point to the defendant. On this too the plaintiff has the burden of proof by a preponderance of the evidence; and in any case where there is no doubt that it is at least equally probable that the negligence was that of a third person, the court must direct the jury that the plaintiff has not proved his case. Again, however, the plaintiff is not required to exclude all other possible conclusions beyond a reasonable doubt, and it is enough that he makes out a case from which the jury may reasonably conclude that the negligence was, more probably than not, that of the defendant.

For authority that the product defect must exist at the time of sale or distribution, see, e.g., Franks v. National Dairy Prods. Corp., 414 F.2d 682 (5th Cir.1969) (applying Texas law) (original defect in shortening inferable from unexplained explosion during normal use); Cornell Drilling Co. v. Ford Motor Co., 359 A.2d 822 (Pa.Super.Ct.1976) (new truck inexplicably catching fire was circumstantial evidence from which to infer defective condition at time of sale) [overruled (on other grounds) by] REM Coal Co., Inc. v. Clark Equipment Co., 563 A.2d 128 (Pa.Super.Ct.1989); Dietz v. Waller, 685 P.2d 744, 748 (Ariz.1984) ("[evidence that the boat that broke up and sank] had seen only approximately 10 hours of use and was being properly operated by an experienced boatman on a clear, calm day could lead the jury to conclude that the boat's sinking was due to a manufacturing defect in the boat that existed at time of sale"); but see Walker v. General Elec. Co., 968 F.2d 116 (1st Cir.1992) (six years of trouble-free use prior to accident mitigates against inference); Woodin v. J.C. Penney Co., 629 A.2d 974 (Pa.Super.Ct.1993) (eight years of use). Cf. 1836 Callowhill St. v. Johnson Controls, Inc., 819 F.Supp. 460 (E.D.Pa. 1993) (when heating system should have functioned properly for 15 years, but failed at six years, length of use did not negate inference). Evidence that the product may have been used improperly (Henry v. General Motors Corp., 609 N.Y.S.2d 711 (N.Y.App.Div.1994); Humphreys v. General Motors Corp., 839 F.Supp. 822 (N.D.Fla.1993)) or was altered by repair people (Yielding v. Chrysler Motor Co., 783 S.W.2d 353 (Ark. 1990)) weakens the inference. Some courts place particularly strict requirements on plaintiffs seeking an inference. See, e.g., Koch v. Sports Health Home Care Corp., 54 F.3d 773 (4th Cir.1995) (applying Maryland law) (a nurse's claim that an injurious heating pack was defective was dismissed because she failed to provide evidence about the manufacturing process or account for the pack's journey between the manufacturing plant and the hospital utility room).

§ 4. Noncompliance and Compliance with Product Safety Statutes or Regulations

In connection with liability for defective design or inadequate instructions or warnings:

(a) a product's noncompliance with an applicable product safety statute or administrative regulation renders the product defective with respect to the risks sought to be reduced by the statute or regulation; and

(b) a product's compliance with an applicable product safety statute or administrative regulation is properly considered in determining whether the product is defective with respect to the risks sought to be reduced by the statute or regulation, but such compliance does not preclude as a matter of law a finding of product defect.

Comment:

a. Product safety statutes or administrative regulations. The safety statutes and administrative regulations referred to in this Section are those, promulgated by federal and state and local legislatures and agencies, intended to promote safety in the design and marketing of products. The phrase "safety statute or administrative regulation" is intended to be inclusive of all final governmental edicts and directives, issued pursuant to such statutes or regulations, that establish binding safety standards for the design and marketing of products. Because liability for manufacturing defects under §§ 1 and 2(a) is liability without fault, the violation of, or compliance with, a safety statute or regulation is not relevant to such a claim. In connection with a claim of manufacturing defect brought under common-law negligence principles, see § 2, Comment *n*, the relevance of statutory or regulatory compliance and violation should be determined according to general negligence principles.

b. Requirement that the statute or regulation be applicable. For purposes of this Section, the product safety statute or administrative regulation must have been in force and applicable at the time of sale or other distribution.

c. Requirement that the statute or regulation be relevant to the particular claim of product defect. For purposes of this Section, the safety statute or administrative regulation must be such that compliance reduces the risk that caused the plaintiff's harm. Thus, when a plaintiff complains that the design of a product should have been more stable to prevent the product from tipping over, a safety statute or regulation is relevant if it addresses the issue of stability in such a way that compliance with the statute or regulation reduces the risk of the product tipping over in the manner that caused the plaintiff's harm. This Section addresses the issue of product defectiveness. For rules governing causation, see §§ 15 and 16. For rules governing affirmative defenses, see §§ 17 and 18.

d. Noncompliance with product safety statute or administrative regulation. Subsection (a) provides that noncompliance with an applicable product safety statute or administrative regulation renders the product defective in design or defective due to inadequate instructions or warnings with respect to the risks sought to be reduced by the statute or regulation. The general rule does not apply when a regulation merely suggests, but does not require, a safety feature. The general rule also does not apply when, after sale but prior to injury, the statute or regulation is repealed or otherwise rendered invalid so as to cause the product no longer to be in noncompliance. When repeal or invalidation takes place post-injury, but prior to adjudication, the court may take the repeal or invalidation into account in deciding whether noncompliance with the statute or regulation renders the product defective. Moreover, when the statute or regulation is unclear as to its meaning or purpose, or conflicts with other safety statutes or regulations with which the product must also comply, a court may take these circumstances into account in determining whether noncompliance with the statute or regulation renders the product defective. The rule in this Subsection is based on the policy judgment that designs and warnings that fail to comply with applicable safety standards established by statute or regulations are, subject to the foregoing exceptions, by definition defective.

In contrast to Subsection (a), the parallel common-law rule governing noncompliance with safety statutes or regulations in negligence actions not involving products liability claims recognizes that noncompliance with an applicable safety statute or regulation does not constitute failure to use due care when the defendant establishes a justification or excuse for the violation. For example, if noncompliance with an administrative regulation under conditions of emergency or temporary impossibility would not constitute a violation in a direct enforcement proceeding, noncompliance alone does not prove negligence. In connection with the adequacy of product designs and warnings, however, design and marketing decisions are made before distribution to users and consumers. The product seller therefore has the option of deferring sale until statutory or regulatory compliance is achieved. Consequently, justification or excuse of the sort anticipated in connection with negligence claims generally does not apply in connection with failure to comply with statutes or regulations governing product design or warnings.

e. Compliance with product safety statute or administrative regulation. An important distinction must be drawn between the subject addressed in Subsection (b) and the matter of federal preemption of state products liability law. Subsection (b) addresses the question of whether and to what extent, as a matter of state tort law, compliance with product safety statutes or administrative regulations affects liability for product defectiveness. When a court concludes that a defendant is not liable by reason of having complied with a safety design or warnings statute or regulation, it is deciding that the product in question is not defective as a matter of the law of that state. The safety statute or regulation may be a federal provision, but the decision to give it determinative effect is a state-law determination. In contrast, in federal preemption, the court decides as a matter of federal law that the relevant federal statute or regulation reflects, expressly or impliedly, the intent of Congress to displace state law, including state tort law, with the federal statute or regulation. The question of preemption is thus a question of federal law, and a determination that there is preemption nullifies otherwise operational state law. The complex set of rules and standards for resolving questions of federal preemption are beyond the scope of this Restatement. However, when federal preemption is found, the legal effect is clear. Judicial deference to federal product safety statutes or regulations occurs not because the court concludes that compliance with the statute or regulation shows the product to be nondefective; the issue of defectiveness under state law is never reached. Rather, the court defers because, when a federal statute or regulation is preemptive, the Constitution mandates federal supremacy.

Accordingly, Subsection (b) addresses the effects of compliance with a federal statute or regulation found to be nonpreemptive. It addresses the question, under state law, of the effect that compliance with product safety statutes or regulations—federal or state—should have on the issue of product defectiveness. Subsection (b) reflects the traditional view that the standards set by most product safety statutes or regulations generally are only minimum standards. Thus, most product safety statutes or regulations establish a floor of safety below which product sellers fall only at their peril, but they leave open the question of whether a higher standard of product safety should be applied. This is the general rule, applicable in most cases.

Occasionally, after reviewing relevant circumstances, a court may properly conclude that a particular product safety standard set by statute or regulation adequately serves the objectives of tort law and therefore that the product that complies with the standard is not defective as a matter of law. Such a conclusion may be appropriate when the safety statute or regulation was promulgated recently, thus supplying currency to the standard therein established; when the specific standard addresses the very issue of product design or warning presented in the case before the court; and when the court is confident that the deliberative process by which the safety standard was established was full, fair, and thorough and reflected substantial expertise. Conversely, when the deliberative process that led to the safety standard with which the defendant's product complies was tainted by the supplying of false information to, or the withholding of necessary and valid information from, the agency that promulgated the standard or certified or approved the product, compliance with regulation is entitled to little or no weight.

f. Conduct not related to product defect. This Section deals with noncompliance and compliance with product safety statutes or regulations as they relate to the issue of product defect. Conduct involving products but not related to product defect may also be governed by statute or regulation. For example, sale of dangerous instrumentalities may be prohibited by statute or regulation, or statutes or regulations may govern such matters as post-sale warnings or recalls. When and whether liability arises when there has been noncompliance or compliance with such statutes or regulations is governed by Restatement, Second, Torts §§ 286–288C.

REPORTERS' NOTE

Comment d. Noncompliance with product safety statute or administrative regulation. The rule in Subsection (a) that noncompliance with an appropriate governmental product safety regulation renders a product defective in design or defective because of inadequate warnings or instructions finds its origin in a common-law rule holding that the unexcused omission of a statutory safety requirement is negligence per se. While §§ 2(b) and 2(c) do not explicitly talk in terms of negligence, they do incorporate the risk/utility approach that characterizes classic negligence law. See § 2, Comments *d* and *f*. Thus, the same rules that apply in determining negligence per se also apply in determining the defectiveness of a design or a marketing scheme as a matter of law. The seminal decision regarding the negligence per se rule at common law is Martin v. Herzog, 126 N.E. 814, 814–15 (N.Y.1920). In that case, Justice Cardozo of the New York Court of Appeals concluded: "We think the unexcused omission of the statutory signals is more than some evidence of negligence. It is negligence in itself. Lights are intended for the guidance and protection of other travelers on the highway. Highway Law, § 329a. By the very terms of the hypothesis, to omit, willfully or heedlessly, the safeguards prescribed by law for the benefit of another that he may be preserved in life or limb, is to fall short of the standard of diligence to which those who live in organized society are under a duty to conform. That, we think, is now the established rule in this state."

This approach was captured in the Restatement, Second, of Torts § 288B:

§ 288B. Effect of Violation

(1) The unexcused violation of the legislative enactment or an administrative regulation which is adopted by the court as defining the standard of conduct of a reasonable man, is negligence in itself.

The overwhelming majority of American courts hold that violations of product safety regulations cause products to be defective as a matter of law in cases involving both design and failure to warn. See, e.g., Ross Labs. v. Thies, 725 P.2d 1076 (Alaska 1986) (the Food, Drug and Cosmetic Act, which prohibits manufacture or sale of misbranded drugs, was designed to protect consumers of drugs from unappreciated dangers and was proper basis for drug manufacturers' or retailers' civil liability in tort); Harned v. Dura Corp., 665 P.2d 5, 12–13 (Alaska 1983) ("Applying this analysis to the case at bar, we conclude that the trial court erred in declining to instruct the jury that Dura's failure to manufacture the tank in accordance with ASME standards constituted negligence per se"; ASME Code was incorporated by reference into Alaska law at the time the tank was manufactured); Wells v. City of Vancouver, 467 P.2d 292, 295 (Wash.1970) ("The scope of the duty imposed by statutory rule is a matter of law."); Orthopedic Equip. Co., Inc. v. Eutsler, 276 F.2d 455, 461 (4th Cir.1960) ("The majority of American courts which have passed on this question, in cases arising under state laws resembling the Federal Act, have held violations [of safety statutes] to be negligence per se."); Kernan v. American Dredging Co., 355 U.S. 426, 431, 78 S.Ct. 394, 397, 2 L.Ed.2d 382 (1958) ("[A] defect resulting from a violation of . . . statute which causes the injury or death of an employee creates liability without regard to negligence.").

See also Toole v. Richardson–Merrell, Inc., 60 Cal.Rptr. 398, 409 (Cal.

Ct.App.1967) ("Appellant concedes that violation of the labelling and marketing provisions of the act may be shown to establish negligence, but argues there is a difference between violation of the labelling and marketing provisions and violation of the reporting provisions, because the labelling provisions of the statute are designed to protect the public, whereas the reporting provisions are concerned merely with raw data comprehensible only to scientists in the FDA. We find this argument unconvincing."). See generally Madden, Products Liability § 12.3 (2d ed. 1988); Wheeler, The Use of Criminal Statutes to Regulate Product Safety, 13 J. Legal Stud. 593 (1984).

American courts differ on the question of whether violation by an employer of OSHA safety regulations is relevant in an employee's products-liability action against a manufacturer for allegedly defective machinery design. See, e.g., Huber v. Niagara Mach. and Tool Works, 430 N.W.2d 465, 468 (Minn.1988) ("It was not reasonably foreseeable to Allen–Bradley that an employer would fail to comply with these OSHA regulations and therefore Allen–Bradley had no duty to warn about possible dangers of failing to provide proper point of operation safety mechanisms."). But see Widson v. International Harvester Co., Inc., 153 Cal.App.3d 45, 52, 200 Cal.Rptr. 136, 141 (Cal.Ct.App.1984) ("Cal–OSHA regulations are not applicable to nor admissible in an employee's action against a third person not his or her employer.").

A minority of jurisdictions hold that violation of a safety regulation creates merely a rebuttable presumption of negligence/defect. See, e.g., Elsworth v. Beech Aircraft Corp., 691 P.2d 630, 632 (Cal.1984) ("Section 669 of the Evidence Code sets forth the doctrine commonly called negligence per se. It provides that negligence of a person is presumed if he violated a statute or regulation of a public entity, if the injury resulted from an occurrence that the regulation was designed to prevent, and if the person injured was within the class for whose protection the regulation was adopted. This presumption may be rebutted by proof that the violator did what might reasonably be expected of a person of ordinary prudence, acting under similar circumstances, who desired to comply with the law."). Some jurisdictions hold that a statutory violation is merely evidence of negligence/defect. See, e.g., Shatz v. TEC Technical Adhesives, 415 A.2d 1188, 1193 (N.J. Super. Ct. App. Div. 1980) ("A violation of the statute and regulations under it was evidence of negligence."); Fox v. Ford Motor Company, 575 F.2d 774, 784 (10th Cir.1978) ("[I]f [jury] found that Ford had violated relevant federal safety standards, such a violation would be evidence of negligence.").

Although some commentators have suggested that the violation of a local ordinance will also support the conclusion of defectiveness as a matter of law (see American Law of Products Liability § 12:4 (1988)), in the products liability setting, local ordinances invariably relate not to the design or marketing of the product, but rather to the use of the product by one who installs, maintains, or repairs such product. See, e.g., Sanchez v. J. Barron Rice, Inc., 427 P.2d 240 (N.M. 1967) (violation of ordinance regulating plumbing or natural gas installation, maintenance, or repair and inspection is relevant in determining negligence-based liability of those engaged in such commercial activities).

In order for the violation to support a conclusion of defectiveness as a matter of law, the safety regulation in question must relate both to the risk that materializes in harm and to the person or persons who suffer that harm. See, e.g., Stanton v. Astra Pharm. Prods., Inc., 718 F.2d 553, 563–564 (3d Cir.1983) ("Under Pennsylvania law, the violation of a governmental safety regulation constitutes negligence per se if the regulation 'was, in part, intended to protect the interest of another as an individual [and] the interest of the plaintiff which was invaded . . . was one which the act intended to protect.' "); Lukaszewicz v. Ortho Pharmaceutical Corp., 510 F.Supp. 961, 964 (E.D.Wis.1981) ("The Wisconsin Supreme Court has adopted the principle embodied in that section in the following manner: . . . the current Wisconsin approach is where a statute is designed to protect a class of persons from a particular type of harm, a violation of the statute which results in that type of harm to someone in the protected class constitutes negligence per se."); Wells v. City of Vancouver, 467 P.2d 292, 295 (Wash.1970) ("The scope of the duty imposed by statutory rule is a matter of law. The duty extends only to persons in the class intended to be protected by the statute or ordinance, and only to those persons who suffer harm from a hazard which was intended to be prevented by compliance with the statute or ordinance."); Hatch v. Ford Motor Co., 163 Cal.App.2d 393, 398 (1958) ("A violation of the statute does not create liability on the part of the person violating it except towards persons whom the statute was designed to protect. Unless the person injured is within the class of persons whom the statute was designed to protect and the hazard is one which the statute was designed to protect against, no liability arises out of its violation.").

In order to be relevant to the question of product defectiveness, the safety regulation must have been promulgated prior to the time of sale. See, e.g., Lambertson v. Cincinnati Corp., 257 N.W.2d 679 (Minn.1977) (admitting a 1960 American Standard Safety Code section on power presses, while withdrawing a 1971 American national safety standard requirement and excluding a 1973 American national standard safety requirement for the construction, care, and use of power-press brakes, did not constitute an abuse of discretion in products-liability action arising from arm injuries sustained by plaintiff in a press brake manufactured by defendant inasmuch as trial court adopted a consistent approach in ruling on proffered safety standards by excluding all standards promulgated after date of manufacture of press involved in the case on the theory that defendant could not be held accountable for such standards). Even if promulgated prior to manufacture, the safety regulation must also have taken effect prior to that time. See, e.g., Frank R. Jelleff, Inc. v. Braden, 233 F.2d 671 (D.C.Cir.1956) (in action for breach of warranty in the sale of a 'brunch' coat that ignited and burned the buyer when it came in contact with an electric stove, because the injury occurred March 6, 1952, and the Flammable Fabrics Act was not approved until June 30, 1953, and by its terms was not to take effect until June 30, 1954, neither the Act nor its standards applied to the garment purchased by plaintiff).

Subsequent repeal of the safety regulation may not affect liability if the regulation was in effect at the time of the product-related accident in which plaintiff incurred injury. See, e.g., Johnson v. Chem. Supply Co., 156 N.W.2d 455, 459 (Wis.1968) ("We concur with ... the finding that the defendant was negligent per se for failure to conform to the requirements of [the statute] as it existed at the time of the accident [even though statute was repealed after the accident.]"). When the safety regulation is repealed after time of manufacture but before harm is incurred, the regulation does not support a conclusion of defectiveness. See, e.g., Martin v. Simplimatic Eng'g Corp., 390 N.E.2d 235 (Ind.Ct.App.1979) (in action brought by employee against conveyor belt assembly system designer-manufacturer for damages for injury sustained upon catching her fingers in sprocket of system, trial court properly refused to give employee's instruction pertaining to Dangerous Employment Act, since fact that such Act was repealed before employee's injury occurred meant that designer-manufacturer had not incurred any liability to employee under Act prior to its repeal).

The rule regarding negligence per se at common law provided the opportunity for the defendant to argue that the violation was excused. See, e.g., Martin v. Herzog, 126 N.E. 814, and Restatement, Second, Torts § 288B, supra. Section 288A of the Restatement, Second, of Torts sets forth the conditions under which violation is excused:

§ 288A. Excused Violations

(2) ... violation is excused when

(a) the violation is reasonable because of the actor's incapacity;

(b) he neither knows or should know of the occasion for compliance;

(c) he is unable after reasonable diligence or care to comply;

(d) he is confronted with an emergency not due to his own misconduct;

(e) compliance would involve a greater risk of harm to the actor or to others.

In the context of products liability, if the seller is competent and should know of the need for compliance, and if the sale eliminates the opportunity for the seller to react to post-sale circumstances, none of the excuses listed in § 288A is relevant. Products defendants sometimes argue that their lack of knowledge of the regulation, or the need to comply therewith, constitute excuse. But courts routinely reject such arguments. See, e.g., Bachner v. Rich, 554 P.2d 430 (Alaska 1976) (court rejected as a matter of law defendant's arguments that violation of safety code was excused because defendant believed it was in compliance and was ignorant of specific code provision).

Comment e. Compliance with product safety statute or administrative regulation. The overwhelming majority of jurisdictions hold that compliance with product safety regulation is relevant and admissible on the question of defectiveness, but is not necessarily controlling. See, e.g., O'Gilvie v. International Playtex, Inc., 821 F.2d 1438 (10th Cir.1987) (it was proper under Kansas law to give jury instruction that fact that tampon package warning was in conformity with Food and Drug Administration regulations was not a defense in strict liability action if reasonable and prudent manufacturer would have taken additional precautions); Sours v. General Motors Corp., 717 F.2d 1511, 1517 (6th Cir.1983) ("We hold that GM's alleged compliance with FMVSS 216, along with its other evidence of adherence to industry customs and standards, was properly left for the jurors to factor into the calculus that comprises reasonable design in a case of strict products liability."); Foyle v. Lederle Labs., 674 F.Supp. 530, 533 (E.D.N.C.1987) ("In summary, compliance with FDA regulations is evidence of due care but it is not controlling."); Carlin v. Superior Court, 920 P.2d 1347 (Cal. 1996) (compliance with FDA regulations is relevant in a common-law action for failure to warn); Brooks v. Beech Aircraft Corp., 902 P.2d 54, 63 (N.M.1995) ("evidence of compliance with applicable regulations is relevant to whether the manufacturer was negligent or whether the product poses an unreasonable risk of injury, but such evidence should not conclusively demonstrate whether the manufacturer was negligent or the product was defective"); Washington State Physicians Ins. Exch. & Assoc. v. Fisons Corp., 858 P.2d 1054, 1069 (Wash.1993) (Evidence of compliance with FDA regulations does not necessarily relieve a drug manufacturer of liability for failure to furnish an adequate warning of possible side effects, because the FDA regulations merely set minimum requirements.).

The Restatement, Second, of Torts § 288C adopted the approach reflected in the foregoing decisions:

§ 288C. Compliance with Legislation or Regulation

Compliance with a legislative enactment or an administrative regulation does not prevent a finding of negligence where a reasonable man would take additional precautions.

See also United Blood Servs. v. Quintana, 827 P.2d 509, 525 (Colo. 1992) ("In the instant case, UBS's compliance with the Food and Drug Administration's recommendations and with the guidelines developed by the national blood banking community was some evidence of due care, but was not conclusive proof that additional precautions were not required."); Turner v. Pointe Coupee Parish Sch. Bd., 577 So.2d 755, 756 (La.Ct.App.1991) ("Compliance (or noncompliance) with the act is simply another factor to be considered in the totality of the circumstances."); Jackson v. Spagnola, 503 A.2d 944, 949 (Pa.Super.Ct.1986) ("The introduction of [the federal automobile safety standard] into evidence was proper, although compliance by Volkswagen with the standards is 'only a piece of the evidentiary puzzle' and does not grant immunity from strict liability." Shipp v. General Motors Corp., 750 F.2d 418, 421 (5th Cir.1985)); Christou v. Arlington Park–Washington Park Race Tracks Corp., 432 N.E.2d 920, 924 (Ill.App.Ct.1982) ("Compliance with statutes and safety regulations is not conclusive evidence on the question of negligence.... It is, however, relevant to that issue."). See also Lubbock Mfg. Co. v. Perez, 591 S.W.2d 907, 914 (Tex.Civ.App.1979) ("[f]act that the Food and Drug Administration, a Federal agency, had previously approved a package insert warning did not relieve the drug company of its obligation to communicate an adequate warning to users of the dangerous drug in question"); Burch v. Amsterdam Corp., 366 A.2d 1079, 1085 (D.C.1976) ("[T]he overwhelming majority of courts presented with similar arguments in product liability cases have held that compliance with federal and state requirements for the manufacture and sale of products does not immunize a manufacturer or seller from liability.").

In holding compliance with product safety regulations is nonconclusive, courts often indicate that such safety regulations are merely "minimum standards." See, e.g., Feldman v. Lederle Labs., 625 A.2d 1066, 1070 (N.J.1993) ("[T]he FDA regulations were simply 'minimum standards'—compliance with them was mandatory, but they did not preclude Lederle from taking additional action."); Plenger v. Alza Corp., 13 Cal.Rptr.2d 811, 819 n. 7 (1992) (" '[M]ere compliance with regulations or directives as to warnings, such as those issued by the United States Food and Drug Administration here, may not be sufficient to immunize the manufacturer or supplier of the drug from liability. The warnings required by such agencies may be only minimal in nature and when the manufacturer or supplier knows of, or has reason to know of, greater dangers not included in the warning, its duty to warn may not be fulfilled.' ").

In arguing that compliance with agency-prescribed warnings should not preclude liability in tort, some commentators have noted that rule-making by agencies is often distorted by budgetary limitations, lobbying by special interests, and political pressures. See Johnson, Liberating Progress and the Free Market from the Specter of Tort Liability, 83 Nw. U. L. Rev. 1026, 1048–54 (1989).

While courts do not hold compliance with safety regulations to be conclusive, some courts give such compliance substantial weight. See, e.g., Sims v. Washex Mach. Corp., 932 S.W.2d 559 (Tex.App.1995) ("Compliance with government regulations is strong evidence, although not conclusive, that a machine was not defectively designed."). See also Miller v. Lee Apparel Co., Inc., 881 P.2d 576 (Kan.App.1994) (compliance with safety regulation supports a statutory presumption of nondefectiveness).

Although the great majority of courts find conformance with product safety regulations nonconclusive on the issue of defectiveness, courts occasionally recognize special circumstances in which conformance is conclusive on the facts of the particular case. See, e.g., Lorenz v. Celotex Corp., 896 F.2d 148 (5th Cir.1990), reh'g denied, 901 F.2d 1110 (5th Cir. 1990) (compliance with safety regulation strong and substantial evidence of lack of defect); Ramirez v. Plough, Inc., 863 P.2d 167, 176 (Cal.1993) ("Lacking the procedure and the resources to conduct the relevant inquiries, we conclude that the prudent course is to adopt for tort purposes the existing legislative and administrative standard of care on this issue."); Dentson v. Eddins & Lee Bus Sales Inc., 491 So.2d 942, 944 (Ala. 1986) ("[I]n this context, involving school transportation, an area traditionally reserved for the legislature, we find that the legislature's pronouncement is conclusive: a school bus in Alabama may not be found defective ... because it is not equipped with passenger seat belts."); Jones v. Hittle Serv., Inc., 549 P.2d 1383, 1390 (Kan.1976) ("Compliance is evidence of due care and that the conforming product is not defective, and may be conclusive in the absence of a showing of special circumstances.") (dictum); Beatty v. Trailmaster Prods., Inc., 625 A.2d 1005, 1014 (Md.1993) ("Our cases recognize ... that compliance with a statute does not necessarily preclude a finding of negligence or product defectiveness where a reasonable person would take precautions beyond the statutorily required measure. But where no special circumstances require extra caution, a court may find that conformity to the statutory standard amounts to due care as a matter of law.").

Moreover, courts frequently include compliance with product safety regulations as one factor among several justifying a directed verdict for defendant on the facts of a particular case. See, e.g., Hawkins v. Evans Cooperage Co., Inc., 766 F.2d 904, 909 (5th Cir.1985) ("It is undisputed in the present case that Olin supplied labels to Evans that warned of the dangers of TDI, that Evans was contractually bound to affix these labels to the drums, *that the labels complied with the relevant Department of Transportation regulations*, and that Evans would not have accepted the labels if they did not so comply. Midland has pointed to no authority, and we have found none, to support the contention that more was required of Olin.") (Emphasis provided). For a recent article urging greater deference to federal regulatory standards, see Ausness, The Case for a "Strong" Regulatory Compliance Defense, 55 Md. L. Rev. 1210 (1996).

TOPIC 2. LIABILITY RULES APPLICABLE TO SPECIAL PRODUCTS OR PRODUCT MARKETS

§ 5. Liability of Commercial Seller or Distributor of Product Components for Harm Caused by Products Into Which Components Are Integrated

One engaged in the business of selling or otherwise distributing product components who sells or distributes a component is subject to liability for harm to persons or property caused by a product into which the component is integrated if:

(a) the component is defective in itself, as defined in this Chapter, and the defect causes the harm; or

(b)(1) the seller or distributor of the component substantially participates in the integration of the component into the design of the product; and

(2) the integration of the component causes the product to be defective, as defined in this Chapter; and

(3) the defect in the product causes the harm.

Comment:

a. Rationale. Product components include raw materials, bulk products, and other constituent products sold for integration into other products. Some components, such as raw materials, valves, or switches, have no functional capabilities unless integrated into other products. Other components, such as a truck chassis or a multi-functional machine, function on their own but still may be utilized in a variety of ways by assemblers of other products.

As a general rule, component sellers should not be liable when the component itself is not defective as defined in this Chapter. If the component is not itself defective, it would be unjust and inefficient to impose liability solely on the ground that the manufacturer of the integrated product utilizes the component in a manner that renders the integrated product defective. Imposing liability would require the component seller to scrutinize another's product which the component seller has no role in developing. This would require the component seller to develop sufficient sophistication to review the decisions of the business entity that is already charged with responsibility for the integrated product.

The refusal to impose liability on sellers of nondefective components is expressed in various ways, such as the "raw material supplier defense" or the "bulk sales/sophisticated purchaser rule." However expressed, these formulations recognize that component sellers who do not participate in the integration of the component into the design of the product should not be liable merely because the integration of the component causes the product to become dangerously defective. This Section subjects component sellers to liability when the components themselves are defective or when component providers substantially participate in the integration of components into the design of the other products.

Illustration:

1. ABC Chain Co. manufactures chains for a wide range of uses in industrial equipment. XYZ Mach. Co. purchases chains from ABC for use in conveyor-belt systems and informs ABC that the chains will be used for that purpose. In the design of a conveyor system by XYZ, part of the chain is exposed. The conveyor system as designed and manufactured by XYZ is defective in that it should include a safety guard under the rule stated in § 2(b). XYZ sells a conveyor system to LMN Co. LMN's employee, E, while working near the conveyor, is injured when her shirt sleeve becomes entangled in the unguarded chain in the conveyor. ABC is not subject to liability to E. The chain sold by ABC is not itself defective as defined in § 2, and ABC did not participate in the integration of its chain into the design of the XYZ conveyor. XYZ is subject to liability for harm to E as the seller of a defectively designed conveyor under the rules stated in §§ 1 and 2(b).

b. Liability when a product component is defective in itself. A commercial seller or other distributor of a product component is subject to liability for harm caused by a defect in the component. See § 19, Comment *b*. For example, if a cut-off switch is sold in defective condition due to loosely connected wiring, the seller of the switch is subject to liability for harm to persons or property caused by the improper wiring after the switch is integrated into another product. Similarly, if aluminum that departs from the aluminum manufacturer's specifications due to the presence of foreign particles is utilized in the manufacture of airplane engines, the seller of the defective aluminum is subject to liability for harm to persons or property caused by the defects in the aluminum. Both the switches in the first instance and the aluminum in the second are defective as defined in § 2(a).

The same rule applies when a component is defectively designed as defined in § 2(b). For example, if motorcycle headlights intended for rugged off-road use are so designed that they fail when the motorcycle is driven over bumpy roads, they are defective within the meaning of § 2(b). Since reasonable alternative designs are available that prevent such foreseeable failures from occurring, the headlight supplier is subject to liability for harm caused by the defectively designed headlight. Indeed, a defect may be inferable under § 3. However, a component not defective in itself as defined in § 2(b) or § 3 does not become defective merely because a purchaser decides to integrate the component into another product in a way that renders the design of the integrated product defective. See Comment *e*.

The same principles apply in determining a component seller's duty to supply reasonable instructions and warnings to the component buyer. The component seller is required to provide instructions and warnings regarding risks associated with the use of the component product. See §§ 1 and 2(c). However, when a sophisticated buyer integrates a component into another product, the component seller owes no duty to warn either the immediate buyer or ultimate consumers of dangers arising because the component is unsuited for the special purpose to which the buyer puts it. To impose a duty to warn in such a circumstance would require that component sellers monitor the development of products and systems into which their components are to be integrated. See Comment *a*. Courts have not yet confronted the question of whether, in combination, factors such as the component purchaser's lack of expertise and ignorance of the risks of integrating the component into the purchaser's product, and the component supplier's knowledge of both the relevant risks and the purchaser's ignorance thereof, give rise to a duty on the part of the component supplier to warn of risks attending integration of the component into the purchaser's product. Whether the seller of a component should be subject to liability for selling its product to one who is likely to utilize it dangerously is governed by principles of negligent entrustment. See Restatement, Second, Torts § 390.

Illustrations:

2. The same facts as Illustration 1, except that one of the chains sold by ABC to XYZ contains a manufacturing defect as defined in § 2(a). XYZ installs the defective chain in the conveyor-belt system sold by XYZ to LMN. As a result of the defect, the chain breaks, causing the conveyor belt to stop abruptly. E, LMN's employee, suffers harm when the conveyor's sudden stop causes a heavy object on the conveyor to fall on E. ABC is subject to liability to E for harm caused by the sale of the defective component. XYZ is also subject to liability to E for the sale of a defective conveyor system.

3. ABC Vinyl, Inc., sells vinyl swimming-pool liners for use in above-ground swimming pools. ABC manufactures the liners without depth markers. XYZ Pools, Inc., manufactures and sells above-ground swimming pools. XYZ installs a pool with an ABC liner at the home of Roberta. Jack, while visiting Roberta, dives into the shallow portion of the pool that appears to him to be eight feet deep. In reality the water is only four feet deep. Jack hits his head on the bottom and suffers harm. If a court finds that the absence of the depth markers renders the design of the liner defective within the meaning of § 2(b), ABC is subject to liability to Jack. The fact that the liner is a component of the above-ground swimming pool and has been integrated into a specific swimming pool does not insulate ABC from liability for selling a component product that is defectively designed for all swimming-pool installations. XYZ is also subject to liability to Jack as the seller of a pool with a defectively designed liner.

4. ABC Foam Co. manufactures bulk foam with many different uses. XYZ Co. purchases bulk foam from ABC, then processes the foam and incorporates the processed foam in the manufacture of disposable dishware. ABC becomes aware that XYZ is using processed foam in the dishware. ABC and XYZ are both aware that there is a potential danger that processed foam may cause allergic skin reactions for some users. ABC is aware that XYZ is not warning consumers of this potential problem. ABC has no duty to warn XYZ or ultimate consumers of the dangers attendant to use of the processed foam for disposable dishware. The foam sold by ABC is not defective in itself as defined in this Chapter. A supplier of a component has no duty to warn a knowledgeable buyer of risks attendant to special applica-

tion of its products when integrated into another's product. ABC did not participate in the design of the disposable dishware manufactured by XYZ, and is thus not subject to liability under Subsection (b).

c. Raw materials. Product components include raw materials. See Comment *a.* Thus, when raw materials are contaminated or otherwise defective within the meaning of § 2(a), the seller of the raw materials is subject to liability for harm caused by such defects. Regarding the seller's exposure to liability for defective design, a basic raw material such as sand, gravel, or kerosene cannot be defectively designed. Inappropriate decisions regarding the use of such materials are not attributable to the supplier of the raw materials but rather to the fabricator that puts them to improper use. The manufacturer of the integrated product has a significant comparative advantage regarding selection of materials to be used. Accordingly, raw-materials sellers are not subject to liability for harm caused by defective design of the end-product. The same considerations apply to failure-to-warn claims against sellers of raw materials. To impose a duty to warn would require the seller to develop expertise regarding a multitude of different end-products and to investigate the actual use of raw materials by manufacturers over whom the supplier has no control. Courts uniformly refuse to impose such an onerous duty to warn. For a consideration of whether special circumstances may give rise to a duty on the part of raw-material sellers to warn of risks attending integration of raw materials with other components, see Comment *b.*

Illustration:

5. LMN Sand Co. sells sand in bulk. ABC Construction Co. purchases sand to use in mixing cement. LMN is aware that the improper mixture of its sand with other ingredients can cause cement to crack. ABC utilizes LMN's sand to form a cement supporting column in a building. As a result of improper mixture the cement column cracks and gives way during a mild earthquake and causes injury to the building's occupants. LMN is not liable to the injured occupants. The sand sold by LMN is not itself defective under §§ 1–4. LMN has no duty to warn ABC about improperly mixing sand for use in cement. LMN did not participate in ABC's design of the cement and is not subject to liability for harm caused by the sand as integrated into the cement.

d. Incomplete products. Product components include products that can be put to different uses depending on how they are integrated into other products. For example, the chassis of a truck can be put to a variety of different uses. A truck chassis may ultimately be used with a cement mixer or a garbage compaction unit or in a flat-bed truck.

Similarly, an engine for industrial machines may be adapted to a variety of different industrial uses. A seller ordinarily is not liable for failing to incorporate a safety feature that is peculiar to the specific adaptation for which another utilizes the incomplete product. A safety feature important for one adaptation may be wholly unnecessary or inappropriate for a different adaptation. The same considerations also militate against imposing a duty on the seller of the incomplete product to warn purchasers of the incomplete product, or end-users of the integrated product, of dangers arising from special adaptations of the incomplete product by others.

e. Substantial participation in the integration of the component into the design of another product. When the component seller is substantially involved in the integration of the component into the design of the integrated product, the component seller is subject to liability when the integration results in a defective product and the defect causes harm to the plaintiff. Substantial participation can take various forms. The manufacturer or assembler of the integrated product may invite the component seller to design a component that will perform specifically as part of the integrated product or to assist in modifying the design of the integrated product to accept the seller's component. Or the component seller may play a substantial role in deciding which component best serves the requirements of the integrated product. When the component seller substantially participates in the design of the integrated product, it is fair and reasonable to hold the component seller responsible for harm caused by the defective, integrated product. A component seller who simply designs a component to its buyer's specifications, and does not substantially participate in the integration of the component into the design of the product, is not liable within the meaning of Subsection (b). Moreover, providing mechanical or technical services or advice concerning a component part does not, by itself, constitute substantial participation that would subject the component supplier to liability. One who provides a design service alone, as distinct from combining the design function with the sale of a component, generally is liable only for negligence and is not treated as a product seller. See § 19(b).

f. Integration of the component as a cause of the harm. The mere fact that the component seller substantially participates in the integration of the component into the design of a product does not subject the seller to liability unless the integration causes the product to be defective and the resulting defect causes the plaintiff's harm. The component seller is not liable for harm caused by defects in the integrated product that are unrelated to the component. For example, a manufacturer of a component valve may substantially participate in redesigning the valve so that it can be integrated into a particular kind of tank. If the tank fails due to defective steel in the body of the tank and the failure has nothing to do with the installation of the valve, the seller of the valve is not subject to liability under Subsection (b). The valve manufacturer is not liable under Subsection (b) even if it is sufficiently involved in the design of the tank so that it would be liable for harm caused by a failure of the valve as integrated into the tank. Similarly, if a raw-material supplier offers advice about processing the material and there is no evidence that the processing advice was a cause of the allegedly defective condition, the raw-material supplier should not be subject to liability.

Illustration:

6. ABC Chemical Co. sells plastic resins in bulk. XYZ Hot Water Heater Manufacturing Co. informs ABC that XYZ wishes to purchase resin for use in making its hot-water heaters and specifies resin that can withstand heat up to 212° Fahrenheit. ABC recommends that XYZ use a certain type of resin which, in ABC's testing under specified laboratory conditions, including thickness of one-quarter inch or more, was shown to be capable of withstanding temperatures in excess of 212° Fahrenheit. ABC explains these conditions to XYZ. ABC also provides XYZ with technical support and general processing advice. XYZ purchases the recommended resin from ABC and decides upon design and processing parameters, molds the resin into a plastic part, and combines the part with other materials and parts to produce hot-water heaters. XYZ tests its hot-water heaters for safety and durability and formulates instructions and warnings to accompany them. An XYZ hot-water heater subsequently fails because the plastic walls specified by its design, one-eighth inch thick, are too thin to withstand the stress imposed by its normal operating temperatures, resulting in injury to a homeowner. ABC is not liable to the homeowner. The resin sold by ABC was not in itself defective. ABC did not substantially participate in the design, manufacture or assembly of the hot-water heater.

REPORTERS' NOTE

Comment a. Rationale. The rationale for the general rule of nonliability for sellers of nondefective components has been set forth in numerous cases. See, e.g., Crossfield v. Quality Control Equip. Co., 1 F.3d 701, 704 (8th Cir.1993) (applying Missouri law) (supplier of a chain for a chitterlings cleaning machine not liable for its use as one part of a defectively designed machine). The court reasoned:

> To impose responsibility on the supplier of the chain in the context of the larger defectively designed machine system would simply extend liability too far. This would

> mean that suppliers would be required to hire machine design experts to scrutinize machine systems that the supplier had no role in developing. Suppliers would be forced to provide modifications and attach warnings on machines that they never designed nor manufactured. Mere suppliers cannot be expected to guarantee the safety of other manufacturers' machinery.

See also Childress v. Gresen Mfg. Co., 888 F.2d 45, 49 (6th Cir.1989) (applying Michigan law) (manufacturer of a hydraulic valve held not liable for its use in a log-splitting machine). The court said:

> We observe that there is a marked difference between knowing the identity of the equipment into which a component part will be integrated and anticipating any hazardous operation by that equipment that might be facilitated by the addition of the component part. Indeed, extending the duty to make a product safe to the manufacturer of a non-defective component part would be tantamount to charging a component part manufacturer with knowledge that is superior to that of the completed product manufacturer. The law in Michigan does not go this far. The court in Jordan v. Whiting Corp. [49 Mich.App. 481, 212 N.W.2d 324 (1973)] stated, "The obligation that generates the duty to avoid injury to another which is reasonably foreseeable does not—at least yet—extend to the anticipation of how manufactured components not in and of themselves dangerous or defective can become potentially dangerous dependent upon the nature of their integration into a unit designed, assembled, installed, and sold by another." *Jordan, supra*, 49 Mich. App. at 486, 212 N.W.2d at 328.

See also Zaza v. Marquess & Nell, Inc., 675 A.2d 620, 629–34 (N.J.1996) (fabricator of a sheet-metal tank for a complex machine used to decaffeinate coffee beans held not liable where plans provided by the owner, Maxwell House, called for holes to be cut in which safety devices were to be installed at the assembly stage; these devices were never installed, and an employee of owner was injured). In reversing the Appellate Division's finding of strict liability against the defendant fabricator, the Supreme Court of New Jersey noted:

> In its recent draft, [T]he American Law Institute concluded that a component part manufacturer generally is not liable unless the component itself is defective or the component provider substantially participated in the design of the product.... [quote from Comment *a*, supra this Section, omitted].
>
> The majority of courts ... have held that a manufacturer of a component part, which is not dangerous until it is integrated by the owner into a larger system, cannot be held strictly liable to an injured employee for the failure of the owner and/or assembler to install safety devices, so long as the specifications provided are not so obviously dangerous that it would be unreasonable to follow them.
>
> * * *
>
> Holding defendant liable would impose upon a component part fabricator ... the duty to investigate whether the use of its non-defective product would be made dangerous by the integration of that product into the complex system designed

> and installed by experts. Component fabricators would become insurers for the mistakes and failures of the owners and installers to follow their own plans. Defendant would have to retain an expert to determine whether each and every integrated manufacturing system that incorporates one of its sheet metal products is reasonably safe for its intended use.

Id. at 629–34. See also Bond v. E.I. Du Pont De Nemours & Co., 868 P.2d 1114, 1120 (Colo.Ct.App.1993) (seller of Teflon not liable for its integration by manufacturer of prosthesis when the Teflon disintegrated when used as implant). The court noted:

> We further conclude DuPont had no duty to refrain from selling its product to Vitek. As already noted, there was no evidence that DuPont had actual knowledge that the Implant was unreasonably dangerous. In these circumstances, the social utility of permitting DuPont to grant relatively unrestrained access to purchasers of its product is high, especially here, because it encourages development of new products in the medical field and does not unnecessarily inhibit technological advances. Conversely, there is little social utility in placing the burden on a manufacturer of component parts or supplier of raw materials of guarding against injuries caused by the final product when the component parts or raw materials themselves were not unreasonably dangerous.

See also Shawver v. Roberts Corp., 280 N.W.2d 226, 232–33 (Wis.1979) (manufacturer of a conveyor not liable for injury caused by integration of conveyor with an electrical control system). The court found:

> There was undisputed evidence that Roberts Corporation would design and furnish only the mechanical portions of the conveyor. It was left to the Beloit Corporation to furnish the electrical systems to control the conveyor. The Roberts Corporation had no expectation that the conveyor would reach the user without substantial change, that change being the type of control system that the user would install.
>
> * * *
>
> Here, it was explicitly agreed that the conveyor was subject to further processing. The conveyor, which was inoperable without a control system, was not in itself defective. The defect was in the control system which failed to give warning or to insure that workers were off the conveyor when it was activated. Moreover, there was evidence that it was not feasible or practical for the manufacturer to include safety devices without relating them to the control system and the overall work environment.
>
> * * *
>
> For the same reasons, the duty to warn would not apply to Roberts Corporation under the facts of this case. The defect arose because of the nature and location of the controls on the conveyor. Roberts Corporation had no involvement in the design and location of the controls. The Beloit Corporation had its own engineering department, and incorporated products safety features in equipment in products it manufactured. Ordinarily there is no duty to warn members of a trade or profession about dangers generally known to that trade or profession.

For a discussion of the policy reasons behind the general rule of nonliability set forth in § 5, see Mansfield, Reflections on Current Limits on Component and Raw Material Supplier Liability and the Proposed Third Restatement, 84 Kent L.J. 221 (1995–96) (article contains exhaustive review of authority).

Comment b. Liability when a product component is defective in itself. When a component contains a manufacturing defect that causes plaintiff's harm, the fact that it was integrated into another product does not relieve the component-part manufacturer of liability. See, e.g., Bradford v. Bendix–Westinghouse Automotive Air Brake Co., 517 P.2d 406 (Colo.Ct. App.1973) (truck brake pedal assembly); Kaneko v. Hilo Coast Processing, 654 P.2d 343 (Haw.1982) (service platform); Suvada v. White Motor Co., 210 N.E.2d 182 (Ill.1965) (truck brake) overruled on other grounds, Dixon v. Chicago & N.W. Trans. Co., 601 N.E.2d 704, 711 (1992); Burbage v. Boiler Eng'g & Supply Co., 249 A.2d 563 (Pa.1969) (defective replacement valve in boiler); Jones v. Aero–Chem Corp., 680 F.Supp. 338 (D.Mont.1987) (applying Montana law) (tear gas canister valve).

Similarly, when a component is defectively designed for its designated use, liability may attach. See, e.g., Fleck v. KDI Sylvan Pools, 981 F.2d 107 (3d Cir.1992) (applying Pennsylvania law), cert. denied, 507 U.S. 1005, 113 S.Ct. 1645, 123 L.Ed.2d 267 (1993) (replacement liner for swimming pool which lacked depth markers); Dougherty v. Edward J. Meloney, Inc., 661 A.2d 375 (Pa.Super.Ct.1995) (defectively designed shut-off valve designed for use in boilers); Parkins v. Van Doren Sales, Inc., 724 P.2d 389, 392 (Wash.Ct. App.1986) (components of conveyor were defectively designed in that they always presented a risk to users).

The duty to warn immediate buyers of component parts and raw materials of risks attendant to special applications to be undertaken by the purchaser is limited. The discussion of this issue In re TMJ Implants Prods. Liab. Litig., 872 F.Supp. 1019, 1025 (D.Minn.1995), is illuminating. In granting summary judgment to DuPont, the court said:

> The focus of cases applying the raw material supplier defense is frequently on manufacturers of component parts that are combined with other parts to make a device or machine. When the machine or device operates in a defective manner, the question arises of whether the manufacturer of the component part had a duty to warn the ultimate user or to prevent the defect in some way. Many courts have concluded that, in those circumstances, the manufacturer of the component did not have such a duty.
>
> For example, the Eighth Circuit held that a supplier of parts was not liable in Crossfield v. Quality Control Equip. Co., 1 F.3d 701 (8th Cir.1993) (applying Missouri law). There, the supplier provided a chain to a manufacturer, which then used the chain as a part of a machine. *Id.* at 703. The machine malfunctioned, causing injuries to the plaintiff. The chain itself was not defective. Rather, "the dangerousness in this system came from the design of the machine, not from the chain alone. Therefore, the primary duty was owed by the designer of the machine, not the supplier of only one component part, in it-

self a non-defective element." *Id.* at 704. Under these circumstances, the court refused to extend liability to the supplier. To do so, the court pointed out, would mean that suppliers would be required to hire machine design experts to scrutinize machine systems that the supplier had no role in developing. Suppliers would be forced to provide modifications and attach warnings on machines that they never designed or manufactured. Mere suppliers cannot be expected to guarantee the safety of other manufacturers' machinery. *Id.*

The Sixth Circuit expressed similar concerns in Childress v. Gresen Mfg. Co., 888 F.2d 45 (6th Cir. 1989) (applying Michigan law). The trial court had determined that, when a component part became "potentially dangerous in its ultimate use," the mere fact that the manufacturer of the component part had knowledge of the design of the final product was not a sufficient reason to assign responsibility to the manufacturer of the component part. *Childress*, 888 F.2d at 49. Doing so would be against public policy for at least two reasons: it would encourage the component manufacturer to remain ignorant of the final design, or, alternatively, it would force it to hire experts in each client's fields of business in order to evaluate the safety of the client's products. *Id.* The appellate court agreed with the district court's reasoning, remarking that "*extending the duty to make a product safe to the manufacturer of a non-defective component part would be tantamount to charging a component part manufacturer with knowledge that is superior to that of the completed product manufacturer.* The law of Michigan does not go this far." *Id.* (Emphasis added.)

This concern is equally applicable in the instant case. DuPont merely supplied products that have multiple industrial uses. To impose liability upon DuPont for the uses to which those products are put would force DuPont to retain experts in a huge variety of areas in order to determine the possible risks associated with each potential use. *Vitek, which specialized in the field of prosthetic devices, certainly had superior knowledge regarding the risks associated with its TMJ implants. DuPont had no specialized knowledge in that field and, in fact, specifically disclaimed such knowledge.* ... (Emphasis added.)

The case law imposing a duty to warn immediate buyers of general dangers attendant to use of a raw material or component is clear. Sellers of components and raw materials have a duty to provide reasonable warnings. See, e.g., Hill v. Wilmington Chem. Corp., 156 N.W.2d 898, 902 (Minn.1968). The issue is whether the seller of a component or raw material has a duty to inform itself about specific applications of its component and a further duty to determine whether the buyer who will integrate it into another product is knowledgeable as to the dangers attendant to that specific application. No cases have been found imposing such an onerous duty. Indeed, the entire thrust of the case law is that when the product component is not defective in itself, liability only arises when the component seller substantially participates in the design of the final integrated product.

Finally, the duty is to warn only immediate buyers and not to warn users of integrated final products. See, e.g., Smith v. Walter C. Best, Inc., 927 F.2d 736 (3d Cir.1990); Goodbar v. Whitehead Bros., 591 F.Supp. 552 (W.D.Va.1984); and Jones v. Hittle Serv., Inc., 549 P.2d 1383 (Kan.1976). Also see In re TMJ Implants Prods. Liab. Litig., 872 F.Supp. 1019 (D.Minn.1995) (the court granted summary judgment in a multidistrict case in favor of the manufacturer of Teflon, a product that has numerous industrial uses and was utilized by a surgical-implant manufacturer as a component in jaw implants; the court held that in all jurisdictions a raw-material supplier or component-part manufacturer has no duty to warn consumers directly of defects in the integrated products). Other courts that have confronted the issue of direct warning to consumers in the *TMJ Implants* case are in accord. See, e.g., Kealoha v. E.I. Du-Pont de Nemours & Co., 844 F.Supp. 590, 594 (D.Haw.1994) ("Permitting plaintiffs to maintain a suit against the bulk supplier of inherently safe raw materials would lead to absurd consequences: there would be no end to potential liability if every manufacturer of nuts, bolts and screws could be held liable when this hardware was used in a defective product."); Kalinowski v. E.I. DuPont de Nemours & Co., Civ. A. No. 92–2511, 1994 WL 230832 (E.D. Pa. May 23, 1994); Klem v. E.I. DuPont De Nemours Co., 19 F.3d 997 (5th Cir.1994) (raw material supplier does not have any duty to warn of possible dangers of a mechanical product made by another company); Forest v. Vitek, 884 F.Supp. 378 (D.Nev.1993); Nowak v. E.I. Dupont De Nemours & Co., 827 F.Supp. 1334 (W.D.Mich.1993); Styck v. E.I. DuPont De Nemours & Co., No. 91–2038, 1993 WL 761301 (C.D. Ill. Nov. 12, 1993); Hoyt v. Vitek, Inc., 894 P.2d 1225 (Or.Ct.App.1995); Longo v. E.I. Dupont De Nemours & Co., 632 So.2d 1193 (La.Ct.App.1994); Bond v. E.I. DuPont De Nemours & Co., 868 P.2d 1114 (Colo.Ct.App. 1993); Mitchell v. Sky Climber, Inc., 487 N.E.2d 1374 (Mass.1986); Sperry v. Bauermeister, Inc., 804 F.Supp. 1134 (E.D.Mo.1992). Also see In re Silicone Gel Breast Implants Prods. Liab. Litig., 887 F.Supp. 1463 (N.D.Ala.1995) (manufacturer of bulk foam, which has hundreds of uses, not liable for failing to warn consumers, when its product was utilized by breast-implant manufacturers as one component in the composition of the implant); Zaza v. Marquess & Nell, Inc., 675 A.2d 620, 633 (N.J.1996) ("The prevailing view is that a manufacturer of a component part, not dangerous in and of itself, does not have a duty to warn an employee of the immediate purchaser of the component where the immediate purchaser is aware of the need to attach safety devices. Restatement, Tentative Draft No. 3 (1996) § 10 Cmt. *b*."); Hill v. Wilmington Chem. Corp., 156 N.W.2d 898 (Minn.1968), in which the manufacturer of a solvent was held not liable when the solvent was combined with other ingredients. The court held:

> This is not a case where a manufacturer of a product, through an intermediary, places the finished product upon the market. It sold its product to Wilmington who, in turn, manufactured a finished product—with Shell's product as only an ingredient—and placed the finished product on the market. Shell had no opportunity or duty to warn the ultimate consumer. It neither packaged nor placed the product on the market. Wilmington prepared the label on the package giving

> warning as to the proper use of the product. Shell's duty was to inform Wilmington of dangers inherent in the use of Sol B not known to Wilmington. If Wilmington had adequate knowledge of the dangerous propensities of the product sold by Shell, no further duty rested on Shell to give an additional warning.

156 N.W.2d at 903; House v. Armour of Am., 886 P.2d 542 (Utah.Ct.App. 1994) (seller of fibers used to weave bullet-resistant vest that does not take part in the design or assembly of the final system or product is not liable for defects in the final product if the component part itself is not defective). For a recent article taking issue with the prevailing case law, see Hager, Don't Say I Didn't Warn You Even Though I Didn't: Why the Pro–Defendant Consensus on Warning Law Is Wrong, 61 Tenn. L. Rev. 1125 (1994). Professor Hager cites Richards v. Vitek, Inc., No. 91–2–01298–2 (Sup. Ct. Clark County, Wash. Feb. 24, 1992), as an example of a decision willing to entertain a more nuanced approach to the issue of whether an upstream supplier should have a duty to warn end-users.

Illustration 3 is based on Fleck v. KDI Sylvan Pools, Inc., 981 F.2d 107 (3d Cir. 1992).

Comment c. Raw materials. See Reporters' Note to Comment *b* for relevant authority. For a recent article supporting the position set forth in § 5 see Madden, Liability of Suppliers of Natural Raw Materials and the Restatement (Third) of Torts (Products Liability): A First Step Toward Sound Public Policy, 30 U. of Mich. J. L. Ref. (March 1997). In a recent case, In re: Silicone Gel Breast Implants Products Liability Litigation, 1997 WL 858058 (N.D.Ala.1997) (unpublished opinion), the court granted General Electric's motion for summary judgment on claims arising from its sale of silicone to the manufacturers of breast implants. The court cited extensively to this Restatement (§ 5, Comments *b* and *c*) in its holding that the seller of silicone, a chemical compound that had many safe uses, should not be held liable for the use of silicone by breast implant manufacturers. Accord, Artiglio v. General Electric Co., 71 Cal. Rptr.2d 817 (Cal.App.1998) (citing to Restatement Third, Torts: Products Liability, § 5, Comments *b* and *e*.

Comment d. Incomplete products. For authority supporting this Comment, see, e.g., Zaza v. Marquess & Nell, Inc., 675 A.2d 620, 631 (N.J. 1996), discussed, supra, Reporters' Note to Comment *a*. The court in *Zaza* said:

> . . . plaintiff has provided no evidence that the quench tank was in a defective condition when it was delivered to Maxwell House or that International knew or should have known that Maxwell House was unlikely to install safety devices.
>
> Moreover, it was not feasible, practical, or reasonable for defendant, a sheet metal fabricator with no prior experience in the assembly and installation of trecar-carbon regeneration systems, to attach the safety devices to the quench tank. The safety devices could not have been incorporated into the quench tank at its factory.... [T]he work performed by Maxwell House and its assemblers in order to integrate the quench tank into the trecar-carbon regeneration system constituted a substantial change to the quench tank....

> International acted in a reasonably prudent manner in fabricating the quench tank and in delivering it to Maxwell House without incorporating the safety devices.... International manufactured the quench tank in strict accordance with the specifications provided by Maxwell House, a knowledgeable and experienced purchaser and user. International was not the designer, manufacturer, or installer of the trecarcarbon regeneration system.

See also Verge v. Ford Motor Co., 581 F.2d 384 (3d Cir.1978) (holding that chassis cab manufacturer had no duty to install back-up alarm that was needed to make the ultimate end product, a garbage truck, safe; the court held that it was not practical for the chassis cab manufacturer to install such safety devices, nor did the chassis cab manufacturer have the expertise); Trevino v. Yamaha Motor Corp., U.S.A., 882 F.2d 182 (5th Cir. 1989); Watts v. TI, Inc., 561 So.2d 1057, 1058–59 (Ala.1990) (rejecting products-liability claims against supplier of cab and chassis); Fierro v. International Harvester Co., 179 Cal. Rptr. 923, 925–26 (Cal.Ct.App.1982) (rejecting warning and design-defect claims against supplier of skeleton vehicle); Woods v. Graham Eng'g Corp., 539 N.E.2d 316, 320 (Ill.App.Ct.1989) (" ... the manufacturer is to be held liable only when it is ... responsible for the design of the final product or the component part of the product that caused the injury"); Rotzoll v. Overhead Door Corp., 681 N.E.2d 156 (Ill.App.Ct.1997) (manufacturer of automatic door is under no duty to inquire into the nature of its final use or to investigate the effectiveness of safety devices used by the installer); Davis v. Dresser Indus., Inc., 800 S.W.2d 369 (Tex.Ct.App.1990) (relieving manufacturers of oil rig components of liability when the manufacturer of the finished product decided not to install safety guards); Ruegger v. International Harvester Co., 576 N.E.2d 288, 290–91 (Ill.App.Ct.1991) ("The vehicle at issue was a standard cab-chassis used for many different purposes.... "); Bullock v. Gulf & W. Mfg., 340 N.W.2d 294 (Mich.Ct.App. 1983) (when multipurpose punch press was itself harmless until assembled with die, punch manufacturer had no duty to install safety features for any particular end use); Loos v. American Energy Savers, Inc., 522 N.E.2d 841, 845 (Ill.App.Ct.1988) (component-part manufacturer is not obligated to anticipate how a nondangerous part may become unreasonably dangerous as used in the final assembly); Molina v. Kelco Tool & Die, Inc., 904 S.W.2d 857 (Tex.Ct. App.1995) (maker of molding die manufactured in accordance with design specifications provided by the press manufacturer, which integrated the die, held not responsible for design defects in the press).

Comment e. Substantial participation in the integration of the component into the design of another product. For cases supporting liability against the component-part seller when it has substantially participated in the design of the integrated product, see, e.g., DeLeon v. Commercial Mfg. & Supply Co., 195 Cal.Rptr. 867, 872, 874 (1983); Bond v. E.I. DuPont De Nemours & Co., 868 P.2d 1114, 1118 (Colo.Ct.App.1993); Welsh v. Bowling Elec. Machinery, Inc., 875 S.W.2d 569, 572–73 (Mo.Ct.App.1994); Estate of Carey v. Hy–Temp Mfg., Inc., 702 F.Supp. 666 (N.D.Ill.1988); Stecyk v. Bell Helicopter Textron, Inc., No. 94–CU–1818, 1996 WL 153555 (E.D.Pa. Apr.1, 1996) (denying a partial summary judgment motion to bar claims against a defendant that manufactured a component because genuine issue of material fact existed as to whether defendant was involved in the design); Koonce v. Quaker Safety Prods. & Mfg. Co., 798 F.2d 700 (5th Cir.1986) (applying Texas law).

A component-part manufacturer that does not substantially participate in the integration of the product is not liable under Subsection (b). Courts frequently absolve the component-part seller in these circumstances by stating that the seller has had "no control" over the design of the integrated product. See e.g., Trevino v. Yamaha Motor Corp., 882 F.2d 182, 184–185, 186 (5th Cir.1989); Artiglio v. General Electric Co., 71 Cal.Rptr.2d 817 (Cal.App.1998); Zaza v. Marquess & Nell, Inc. 675 A.2d 620, 627 (N.J.1996); Depre v. Power Climber, Inc., 635 N.E.2d 542, 544 (Ill.App.1994); Noonan v. Texaco, Inc. 713 P.2d 160, 164 (Wyo.1986). These decisions are consistent with the thrust of Subsection (b). In all of the cited cases, the component supplier did not substantially participate in the design of the integrated product and thus would not be subject to liability. Courts appear to be using the concept of lack of "control" as a shorthand method of expressing the idea set forth in Subsection (b) and Comment *e*, i.e. a component-part seller that does not substantially participate in the integration of the component into the design of the product has no control over the decisionmaking process that brought about the defective product.

§ 6. Liability of Commercial Seller or Distributor for Harm Caused by Defective Prescription Drugs and Medical Devices

(a) A manufacturer of a prescription drug or medical device who sells or otherwise distributes a defective drug or medical device is subject to liability for harm to persons caused by the defect. A prescription drug or medical device is one that may be legally sold or otherwise distributed only pursuant to a health-care provider's prescription.

(b) For purposes of liability under Subsection (a), a prescription drug or medical device is defective if at the time of sale or other distribution the drug or medical device:

(1) contains a manufacturing defect as defined in § 2(a); or

(2) is not reasonably safe due to defective design as defined in Subsection (c); or

(3) is not reasonably safe due to inadequate instructions or warnings as defined in Subsection (d).

(c) A prescription drug or medical device is not reasonably safe due to defective design if the foreseeable risks of harm posed by the drug or medical device are sufficiently great in relation to its foreseeable therapeutic benefits that reasonable health-care providers, knowing of such foreseeable risks and therapeutic benefits, would not prescribe the drug or medical device for any class of patients.

(d) A prescription drug or medical device is not reasonably safe due to inadequate instructions or warnings if reasonable instructions or warnings regarding foreseeable risks of harm are not provided to:

(1) prescribing and other health-care providers who are in a position to reduce the risks of harm in accordance with the instructions or warnings; or

(2) the patient when the manufacturer knows or has reason to know that health-care providers will not be in a position to reduce the risks of harm in accordance with the instructions or warnings.

(e) A retail seller or other distributor of a prescription drug or medical device is subject to liability for harm caused by the drug or device if:

(1) at the time of sale or other distribution the drug or medical device contains a manufacturing defect as defined in § 2(a); or

(2) at or before the time of sale or other distribution of the drug or medical device the retail seller or other distributor fails to exercise reasonable care and such failure causes harm to persons.

Comment:

a. History. Subsections (b)(1) and (d)(1) state the traditional rules that drug and medical-device manufacturers are liable only when their products contain manufacturing defects or are sold without adequate instructions and warnings to prescribing and other health-care providers. Until recently, courts refused to impose liability based on defective designs of drugs and medical devices sold only by prescription. However, consistent with recent trends in the case law, two limited exceptions from these traditional rules are generally recognized. Subsection (d)(2) sets forth situations when a prescription-drug or medical-device manufacturer is required to warn the patient directly of risks associated with consumption or use of its product. And

Subsection (c) imposes liability for a drug or medical device whose risks of harm so far outweigh its therapeutic benefits that reasonable, properly informed health-care providers would not prescribe it.

b. Rationale. The obligation of a manufacturer to warn about risks attendant to the use of drugs and medical devices that may be sold only pursuant to a health-care provider's prescription traditionally has required warnings directed to health-care providers and not to patients. The rationale supporting this "learned intermediary" rule is that only health-care professionals are in a position to understand the significance of the risks involved and to assess the relative advantages and disadvantages of a given form of prescription-based therapy. The duty then devolves on the health-care provider to supply to the patient such information as is deemed appropriate under the circumstances so that the patient can make an informed choice as to therapy. Subsection (d)(1) retains the "learned intermediary" rule. However, in certain limited therapeutic relationships the physician or other health-care provider has a much-diminished role as an evaluator or decisionmaker. In these instances it may be appropriate to impose on the manufacturer the duty to warn the patient directly. See Subsection (d)(2).

The traditional refusal by courts to impose tort liability for defective designs of prescription drugs and medical devices is based on the fact that a prescription drug or medical device entails a unique set of risks and benefits. What may be harmful to one patient may be beneficial to another. Under Subsection (c) a drug is defectively designed only when it provides no net benefit to any class of patients. Courts have concluded that as long as a drug or medical device provides net benefits to some persons under some circumstances, the drug or device manufacturer should be required to instruct and warn health-care providers of the foreseeable risks and benefits. Courts have also recognized that the regulatory system governing prescription drugs is a legitimate mechanism for setting the standards for drug design. In part, this deference reflects concerns over the possible negative effects of judicially imposed liability on the cost and availability of valuable medical technology. This deference also rests on two further assumptions: first, that prescribing health-care providers, when adequately informed by drug manufacturers, are able to assure that the right drugs and medical devices reach the right patients; and second, that governmental regulatory agencies adequately review new prescription drugs and devices, keeping unreasonably dangerous designs off the market.

Nevertheless, unqualified deference to these regulatory mechanisms is considered by a growing number of courts to be unjustified. An approved prescription drug or medical device can present significant risks without corresponding advantages. At the same time, manufacturers must have ample discretion to develop useful drugs and devices without subjecting their design decisions to the ordinary test applicable to products generally under § 2(b). Accordingly, Subsection (c) imposes a more rigorous test for defect than does § 2(b), which does not apply to prescription drugs and medical devices. The requirement for establishing defective design of a prescription drug or medical device under Subsection (c) is that the drug or device have so little merit compared with its risks that reasonable health-care providers, possessing knowledge of risks that were known or reasonably should have been known, would not have prescribed the drug or device for any class of patients. Thus, a prescription drug or medical device that has usefulness to any class of patients is not defective in design even if it is harmful to other patients. Because of the special nature of prescription drugs and medical devices, the determination of whether such products are not reasonably safe is to be made under Subsections (c) and (d) rather than under §§ 2(b) and 2(c).

The rules imposing liability on a manufacturer for inadequate warning or defective design of prescription drugs and medical devices assume that the federal regulatory standard has not preempted the imposition of tort liability under state law. When such preemption is found, liability cannot attach if the manufacturer has complied with the applicable federal standard. See § 4, Comment *e*.

The doctrine of preemption based on supremacy of federal law should be distinguished from the proposition that compliance with statutory and regulatory standards satisfies the state's requirement for product safety. Subsections (c) and (d) recognize common-law causes of action for defective drug design and for failure to provide reasonable instructions or warnings, even though the manufacturer complied with governmental standards. For the rules governing compliance with governmental standards generally, see § 4(b).

c. Manufacturers' liability for manufacturing defects. Limitations on the liability for prescription drug and medical-device designs do not support treating drug and medical-device manufacturers differently from commercial sellers of other products with respect to manufacturing defects. Courts have traditionally subjected manufacturers of prescription products to liability for harm caused by manufacturing defects.

d. Manufacturers' liability for failure adequately to instruct or warn prescribing and other health-care providers. Failure to instruct or warn is the major basis of liability for manufacturers of prescription drugs and medical devices. When prescribing health-care providers are adequately informed of the relevant benefits and risks associated with various prescription drugs and medical devices, they can reach appropriate decisions regarding which drug or device is best for specific patients. Sometimes a warning serves to inform health-care providers of unavoidable risks that inhere in the drug or medical device. By definition, such a warning would not aid the health-care provider in reducing the risk of injury to the patient by taking precautions in how the drug is administered or the medical device is used. However, warnings of unavoidable risks allow the health-care provider, and thereby the patient, to make an informed choice whether to utilize the drug or medical device. Beyond informing prescribing health-care providers, a drug or device manufacturer may have a duty under the law of negligence to use reasonable measures to supply instructions or warnings to nonprescribing health-care providers who are in positions to act on such information so as to reduce or prevent injury to patients.

e. Direct warnings to patients. Warnings and instructions with regard to drugs or medical devices that can be sold legally only pursuant to a prescription are, under the "learned intermediary" rule, directed to health-care providers. Subsection (d)(2) recognizes that direct warnings and instructions to patients are warranted for drugs that are dispensed or administered to patients without the personal intervention or evaluation of a health-care provider. An example is the administration of a vaccine in clinics where mass inoculations are performed. In many such programs, health-care providers are not in a position to evaluate the risks attendant upon use of the drug or device or to relate them to patients. When a manufacturer supplies prescription drugs for distribution to patients in this type of unsupervised environment, if a direct warning to patients is feasible and can be effective, the law requires measures to that effect.

Although the learned intermediary rule is generally accepted and a drug manufacturer fulfills its legal obligation to warn by providing adequate warnings to the health-care provider, arguments have been advanced that in two other areas courts should consider imposing tort liability on drug manufacturers that fail to provide direct warnings to consumers. In the first, governmental regulatory agencies have mandated that patients be informed of risks attendant to the use of a drug. A noted example is the FDA requirement that birth control pills be sold to patients accompanied by a patient package insert. In the second, manufacturers have advertised a prescription drug and its indicated use in the mass media. Governmental regulations require that, when drugs are so advertised, they must be accompanied by appropriate information concerning risk so as to provide balanced advertising. The question in both instances is whether adequate warnings to the appropriate health-care provider should insulate the manufacturer from tort liability.

Those who assert the need for adequate warnings directly to consumers contend that manufacturers that communicate directly with consumers should not escape liability simply because the decision to prescribe the drug was made by the health-care provider. Proponents of the learned intermediary rule argue that, notwithstanding direct communications to the consumer, drugs cannot be dispensed unless a health-care provider makes an individualized decision that a drug is appropriate for a particular patient, and that it is for the health-care provider to decide which risks are relevant to the particular patient. The Institute leaves to developing case law whether exceptions to the learned intermediary rule in these or other situations should be recognized.

When the content of the warnings is mandated or approved by a governmental agency regulation and a court finds that compliance with such regulation federally preempts tort liability, then no liability under this Section can attach. For the rules governing compliance with governmental standards generally, see § 4(b).

f. Manufacturers' liability for defectively designed prescription drugs and medical devices. Subsection (c) reflects the judgment that, as long as a given drug or device provides net benefits for a class of patients, it should be available to them, accompanied by appropriate warnings and instructions. Learned intermediaries must generally be relied upon to see that the right drugs and devices reach the right patients. However, when a drug or device provides net benefits to no class of patients—when reasonable, informed health-care providers would not prescribe it to any class of patients—then the design of the product is defective and the manufacturer should be subject to liability for the harm caused.

A prescription drug or device manufacturer defeats a plaintiff's design claim by establishing one or more contexts in which its product would be prescribed by reasonable, informed health-care providers. That some individual providers do, in fact, prescribe defendant's product does not in itself suffice to defeat the plaintiff's claim. Evidence regarding the actual conduct of health-care providers, while relevant and admissible, is not necessarily controlling. The issue is whether, objectively viewed, reasonable providers, knowing of the foreseeable risks and benefits of the drug or medical device, would prescribe it for any class of patients. Given this very demanding objective standard, liability is likely to be imposed only under unusual circumstances. The court has the responsibility to determine when the plaintiff has introduced sufficient evidence so that reasonable persons could conclude that plaintiff has met this demanding standard.

Illustration:

1. ABC Pharmaceuticals manufactures and distributes D, a prescription drug intended to prolong pregnancy and thus to reduce the risks associated with premature birth. Patricia, six months pregnant with a history of irregular heart beats, was given D during a hospital stay in connection with her pregnancy. As a result, she suffered heart failure and required open-heart surgery. In Patricia's action against ABC, her expert testifies that, notwithstanding FDA approval of D five years prior to Patricia's taking the drug, credible studies published two years prior to Patricia's taking the drug concluded that D does not prolong pregnancy for any class of patients. Notwithstanding a finding by the trier of fact that ABC gave adequate warnings to the prescribing physician regarding the serious risks of heart failure in patients with a history of irregular heart beats, the trier of fact can find that reasonably informed health-care providers would not prescribe D for any class of patients, thus rendering ABC subject to liability.

g. Foreseeability of risks of harm in prescription drug and medical device cases. Duties concerning the design and marketing of prescription drugs and medical devices arise only with respect to risks of harm that are reasonably foreseeable at the time of sale. Imposing liability for unforeseeable risks can create inappropriate disincentives for the development of new drugs and therapeutic devices. Moreover, because actuaries cannot accurately assess unknown and unknowable risks, insuring against losses due to unknowable risks would be problematic. Drug and medical device manufacturers have the responsibility to perform reasonable testing prior to marketing a product and to discover risks and risk-avoidance measures that such testing would reveal. See § 2, Comments *a* and *m*.

Illustrations:

2. DEF Pharmaceuticals, Inc., manufactures and distributes prescription drugs. Seven years ago DEF, after years of research and testing, received permission from the FDA to market X, a drug prescribed for the treatment of low-grade infections. Three years later, Jim, age 12, began taking X on his physician's prescription for a recurring respiratory-tract infection. Jim took X for approximately one year. Two years after Jim had stopped taking X, medical research discovered that X causes loss of vision in adolescents. Prior to this discovery DEF had not warned of this risk. Jim has begun to manifest symptoms of the sort caused by the drug. No evidence suggests that DEF's testing of X was substandard, or that any reasonable drug company should have

discovered the side effects sooner than they were discovered. In a failure-to-warn action by Jim against DEF, the court should direct a verdict in favor of the defendant.

3. The same facts as Illustration 2, except that two years before Jim began taking X, medical researchers published a credible study in a leading medical journal concerning the possibility that a drug with toxicological effects very similar to X adversely affects vision in adolescents. After publication of the study suggesting a possible link between X and loss of vision in adolescents, DEF did not conduct further research or provide warnings to physicians of the risk of X causing loss of vision. Jim's expert witness testifies that a reasonable manufacturer would have tested further and that such testing would have revealed that X causes vision loss in time to have warned Jim's physician. In Jim's failure-to-warn action against DEF, the trial court should submit the issue of DEF's failure to warn to the trier of fact on appropriate instructions.

h. Liability of retail seller of prescription drugs and medical devices for defective designs and defects due to inadequate instructions or warnings. The rule governing most products imposes liability on wholesalers and retailers for selling a defectively designed product, or one without adequate instructions or warnings, even though they have exercised reasonable care in marketing the product. See § 1, Comment *e*, and § 2, Comment *o*. Courts have refused to apply this general rule to nonmanufacturing retail sellers of prescription drugs and medical devices and, instead, have adopted the rule stated in Subsection (e). That rule subjects retailers to liability only if the product contains a manufacturing defect or if the retailer fails to exercise reasonable care in connection with distribution of the drug or medical device. In so limiting the liability of intermediary parties, courts have held that they should be permitted to rely on the special expertise of manufacturers, prescribing and treating health-care providers, and governmental regulatory agencies. They have also emphasized the needs of medical patients to have ready access to prescription drugs at reasonable prices.

Illustration:

4. ABC Pharmaceuticals manufactures and distributes a prescription drug to reduce blood pressure. ABC supplies pharmacies with pamphlets explaining the risks and warning patients against drinking alcohol while taking the drug. ABC asks the pharmacies to give the pamphlets to patients when dispensing the drug. The P Pharmacy received the pamphlets but negligently failed to give them to patients. P is subject to liability to those

patients suffering injury for whom the pamphlets would have been effective in avoiding risks of usage.

REPORTERS' NOTE

Comment b. Rationale. Courts have advanced a number of reasons for exclusive reliance on the learned intermediary rule. See, e.g., West v. Searle & Co., 806 S.W.2d 608, 613–14 (Ark.1991) (provider is best assessor of relevant risks and benefits); Brown v. Superior Court, 751 P.2d 470, 478–79 (Cal.1988) (concern that increased liability would drive prices of drugs too high and make them less available); Lacy v. G.D. Searle & Co., 567 A.2d 398 (Del.1989); In re Certified Questions, 358 N.W.2d 873, 883 (Mich.1984) (Boyle, J., dissenting) (in some cases, directly warning patient "could potentially cause undue interference with the doctor-patient relationship [and] cause patient confusion"); Niemiera v. Schneider, 555 A.2d 1112, 1118 n. 3 (N.J.1989) ("The Federal Food and Drug Administration (FDA) regulates vaccine manufacturers.... The regulations are quite detailed in their setting of standards for safety, effectiveness and adequate labelling."); Gravis v. Parke–Davis & Co., 502 S.W.2d 863, 870 (Tex.App.1973) ("[The] entire system of drug distribution in America is set up so as to place the responsibility ... upon professional people"). For a useful discussion of the rule and its underlying rationale, see T. Schwartz, Consumer-Directed Prescription Drug Advertising and the Learned Intermediary Rule, 46 Food Drug Cosm. L.J. 829, 830–31 (1991).

Comment c. Manufacturers' liability for manufacturing defects. Prescription drug manufacturers are strictly liable for harm caused by manufacturing defects. See, e.g., Merck & Co. v. Kidd, 242 F.2d 592 (6th Cir.) (applying Tennessee law), cert. denied, 355 U.S. 814, 78 S.Ct. 15, 2 L.Ed.2d 31 (1957); Abbott Labs. v. Lapp, 78 F.2d 170 (7th Cir.1935); Hruska v. Parke, Davis & Co., 6 F.2d 536 (8th Cir.1925); Randall v. Goodrich–Gamble Co., 70 N.W.2d 261 (Minn.1955). Comment *k* to § 402A of the Restatement, Second, of Torts reflects this rule: "The seller of [prescription drugs], *with the qualification that they are properly prepared* and marketed, is not to be held to strict liability for unfortunate consequences attending their use" (emphasis added). See generally Madden, Products Liability § 23.3 (2d ed. 1988). Prescription drug retailers also are strictly liable for manufacturing defects. See, e.g., Tremblay v. Kimball, 77 A. 405 (Me.1910); Burgess v. Sims Drug Co., 86 N.W. 307 (Iowa 1901).

Comment d. Manufacturers' liability for failure adequately to instruct or warn prescribing and other health-care providers. The traditional rule, often referred to as the "learned intermediary rule," holds that manufacturers of prescription drugs discharge their duty of care to patients by warning the health-care providers who prescribe and use the drugs to treat them. See, e.g., DeLuryea v. Winthrop Labs., 697 F.2d 222, 228–29 (8th Cir.1983); Werner v. Upjohn Co., 628 F.2d 848, 858 (4th Cir.1980), cert. denied, 449 U.S. 1080, 101 S.Ct. 862, 66 L.Ed.2d 804 (1981); Lindsay v. Ortho Pharm. Corp., 637 F.2d 87, 91 (2d Cir.1980) (applying New York law). Accord, Salmon v. Parke, Davis

& Co., 520 F.2d 1359, 1362 (4th Cir. 1975) ("A manufacturer of an ethical drug must exercise reasonable care ... to warn physicians effectively of the drug's inherent dangers."); Basko v. Sterling Drug, Inc., 416 F.2d 417, 426 (2d Cir.1969) (applying Connecticut law) (The manufacturer of a dangerous commodity does have a duty to warn, but when the commodity is a prescription drug, that duty to warn is fulfilled by an adequate warning given to those members of the medical community lawfully authorized to prescribe, dispense, and administer drugs.); Snawder v. Cohen, 749 F.Supp. 1473, 1476 n. 3 (W.D.Ky. 1990) (applying Kentucky law); Schenebeck v. Sterling Drug, Inc., 291 F.Supp. 368 (E.D.Ark.1968) (applying Arkansas law), aff'd, 423 F.2d 919 (8th Cir.1970); Gaston v. Hunter, 588 P.2d 326, 340–41 (Ariz.Ct.App.1978); see also Walker v. Merck & Co., Inc., 648 F.Supp. 931 (M.D.Ga.1986) (applying Georgia law) (learned intermediary doctrine applied), aff'd, 831 F.2d 1069 (11th Cir.1987); Wells v. Ortho Pharm. Corp., 615 F.Supp. 262, 295 (N.D.Ga.1985) (applying Georgia law), aff'd and modified in part, 788 F.2d 741 (11th Cir.), cert. denied, 479 U.S. 950, 107 S.Ct. 437, 93 L.Ed.2d 386 (1986); Presto v. Sandoz Pharmaceuticals Corp., 487 S.E.2d 70 (Ga.Ct. App.1997); Stone v. Smith, Kline & French Labs., 447 So.2d 1301, 1303 n. 2 (Ala.1984); Brown v. Superior Court, 751 P.2d 470, 477 (Cal.1988) ("patient's expectations ... are those related to him by his physician, to whom the manufacturer directs the warnings regarding the drug's properties"); Love v. Wolf, 38 Cal.Rptr. 183 (Cal.Ct.App.1964); Buckner v. Allergan Pharms., Inc., 400 So.2d 820, 822 (Fla.Dist.Ct.App.1981); Woodill v. Parke Davis & Co., 374 N.E.2d 683, 686–87 (Ill.App.Ct.1978); Martin v. Ortho Pharm. Corp., 661 N.E.2d 352 (Ill.1996); Ortho Pharm. Corp. v. Chapman, 388 N.E.2d 541, 548 (Ind. Ct.App.1979); Moore v. Vanderloo, 386 N.W.2d 108, 115–16 (Iowa 1986); Savina v. Sterling Drug, Inc., 795 P.2d 915, 928 (Kan.1990); Kinney v. Hutchinson, 468 So.2d 714, 717–18 (La.Ct.App.1985); Miller v. Upjohn Co., 465 So.2d 42, 45 (La.Ct.App. 1985); Reeder v. Hammond, 336 N.W.2d 3, 5 (Mich.Ct.App.1983); Martin v. Hacker, 628 N.E.2d 1308, 1311 (N.Y.1993) ("Warnings for prescription drugs are intended for the physician, whose duty it is to balance the risks against the benefits of various drugs and treatments and to prescribe them and supervise their effects. The physician acts as an 'informed intermediary.' "); McEwen v. Ortho Pharms. Corp., 528 P.2d 522, 528 (Or.1974); Incollingo v. Ewing, 282 A.2d 206, 220 (Pa.1971) ("Since the drug was available only upon the prescription of a duly licensed physician, the warning requirement is not to the general public or to the patient, but to the prescribing doctor."); Pittman v. Upjohn Co., 890 S.W.2d 425 (Tenn.1994) (approval of learned intermediary rule). Pumphrey v. C.R. Bard, Inc., 906 F.Supp. 334, 338 (N.D.W.Va.1995)(noting that the learned intermediary rule adopted by this Restatement "clearly reflects the law in an overwhelming number of jurisdictions," including West Virginia).

Litigation raising the issue of design defects in medical devices has been the subject of appellate review in relatively few cases. Most of the cases that have addressed the issue have held that medical devices that require a medical provider's prescription are subject to the same rules that apply to prescription drugs. For the reasons set forth in Comments *a* and *b*, such medical devices should be subject to the rules in § 6. For authority treating medical devices as similar to prescription drugs, see Brooks v. Medtronic Inc., 750 F.2d 1227 (4th Cir.1984) (applying South Carolina law) (cardiac pacemaker); Plenger v. Alza Corp., 13 Cal.Rptr.2d 811 (Cal.Ct.App.1992) (intrauterine device); Hufft v. Horowitz, 5 Cal. Rptr.2d 377 (Cal.Ct.App.1992) (penile prosthesis); Perfetti v. McGhan Med., 662 P.2d 646 (N.M.Ct.App.1983) (mammary prosthesis); Terhune v. A. H. Robins Co., 577 P.2d 975 (Wash. 1978). For a review of the case law, see Lynn, Implantable Medical Devices: A Survey of Products Liability Case Law, 38 Med. Trial Tech. Q. 44 (1992).

Nonprescribing medical providers also must be warned. See, e.g., Holley v. Burroughs Wellcome Co., 330 S.E.2d 228, 235 (N.C.Ct.App.1985) (duty to warn doctor's assistant, a nurse anesthetist); McEwen v. Ortho Pharms. Corp., 528 P.2d 522, 529 (Or. 1974) (duty to warn extends to all members of medical profession who come into contact with patient in decisionmaking capacity).

For scholarly treatments of prescription drug liability, see generally Note, 45 Syracuse L. Rev. 1291 (1995); Britain, Product Honesty Is the Best Policy: A Comparison of Doctors' and Manufacturers' Duty to Disclose Drug Risks and the Importance of Consumer Expectations in Determining Product Defect, 79 Nw. U. L. Rev. 342 (1984); Cupp, Rethinking Conscious Design Liability for Prescription Drugs: The Restatement (Third) Standard Versus a Negligence Approach, 63 Geo. Wash. L. Rev. 76 (1994); Henderson, Prescription Drug Design Liability Under the Proposed Restatement (Third) of Torts: A Reporter's Perspective, 48 Rutgers L. Rev. 471 (1996); Ferguson, Liability for Pharmaceutical Products: A Critique of the Learned Intermediary Rule, 12 Oxford J. Legal Stud. 59 (1992); Gilgore, A Consideration of Direct-to-Consumer Advertising of Prescription Drugs and Potential Legal Problems with the Brief Summary Requirement: Is the FDA's Regulatory Authority Illusory?, 46 Food Drug Cosm. L.J. 849 (1991); Gilhooley, Learned Intermediaries, Prescription Drugs, and Patient Information, 30 St. Louis U. L.J. 633 (1986); Keeton, Some Observations About the Strict Liability of the Makers of Prescription Drugs: The Aftermath of MER/29, 56 Cal. L. Rev. 149 (1968); Maedgen & McCall, A Survey of Law Regarding the Liability of Manufacturers and Sellers of Drug Products and Medical Devices, 18 St. Mary's L.J. 395 (1986); Merrill, Compensation for Prescription Drug Injuries, 59 Va. L. Rev. 1 (1973); Pratt & Parnon, Diagnosis of a Legal Headache: Liability for Unforeseeable Defects in Drugs, 53 St. John's L. Rev. 517 (1979); Rheingold, The MER/29 Story—An Instance of Successful Mass Disaster Litigation, 56 Cal. L. Rev. 116 (1968); Schwartz, Consumer-Directed Prescription Drug Advertising and the Learned Intermediary Rule, 46 Food Drug Cosm. L.J. 829 (1991); Bukstein, Comment, Drug Products Liability: Duty to Warn, 49 U. Pitt. L. Rev. 283 (1987); Castleberry, Note, Hill v. Searle Laboratories: The Decline of the Learned Intermediary Doctrine in Favor of Direct Patient Warnings of Drug Product Risks, 43 Ark. L. Rev. 821 (1990); McGarey, Comment, Pharmaceutical Manufacturers and Consumer Directed Information—Enhancing the Safety of Prescription

Drug Use, 34 Cath. U. L. Rev. 117 (1984); T. Schwartz, Prescription Products and the Proposed Restatement (Third), 61 Tenn. L. Rev. 1357 (1994); Styles, Note, Prescription Drugs and the Duty to Warn: An Argument for Patient Package Inserts, 39 Clev. St. L. Rev. 111 (1991).

Comment e. Direct warnings to patients. Case law supports the position taken in § 6(d)(2) that warnings should be given directly to patients when the manufacturer is aware that health care medical providers will not be in a position to play the role of the learned intermediary. Many of the cases involve vaccines administered en masse at public health clinics. See, e.g., Givens v. Lederle, 556 F.2d 1341 (5th Cir.1977) (applying Florida law); Reyes v. Wyeth Labs., 498 F.2d 1264 (5th Cir.1974) (applying Texas law); Brazzell v. United States, 788 F.2d 1352 (8th Cir.1986) (swine flu vaccine); Davis v. Wyeth Labs., 399 F.2d 121 (9th Cir.1968); see also Allison v. Merck & Co., 878 P.2d 948, 959 (Nev. 1994) ("[A]lthough a manufacturer may decide to assign its duty to warn of the unsafeness of its product [a vaccine] to others [in this case, the CDC], a manufacturer cannot be relieved of ultimate responsibility for assuring that its unsafe product is dispensed with a proper warning."). See generally V. Schwartz, National Childhood Vaccine Injury Act of 1986: An Ad Hoc Remedy or a Window for the Future?, 48 Ohio St. L.J. 387 (1987).

The Institute has left to developing case law whether other exceptions to the learned intermediary rule should be recognized. Some case law supports the position that warnings should be given directly to patients when government regulations so require. See, e.g., Stephens v. G.D. Searle & Co., 602 F.Supp. 379 (E.D.Mich.1985) (applying Michigan law); MacDonald v. Ortho Pharm. Corp., 475 N.E.2d 65 (Mass.1985), cert. denied, 474 U.S. 920, 106 S.Ct. 250, 88 L.Ed.2d 258 (1985). But an equal number of decisions reject this development. See, e.g., West v. G.D. Searle & Co., 879 S.W.2d 412 (Ark. 1994); Martin v. Ortho Pharm. Corp., 661 N.E.2d 352 (Ill.1996).

Direct advertisement of prescription drugs is a relatively new phenomenon and has not yet generated case law. However, since FDA requires that drug manufacturers include in such advertisements information about side effects, contraindications, and effectiveness, the duty to include a warning in the advertisement is government-mandated. Several decisions indicate that consumer-directed advertising is a factor to be taken into account in deciding whether to apply the learned intermediary rule. See, e.g., Stephens v. G.D. Searle & Co., 602 F.Supp. 379 (E.D.Mich.1985) (applying Michigan law); Hill v. Searle Labs., 884 F.2d 1064 (8th Cir.1989); Garside v. Osco Drug, Inc., 764 F.Supp. 208, 211 n. 4 (D.Mass.1991) (applying Massachusetts law), rev'd on other grounds, 976 F.2d 77 (1st Cir.1992) (defendant failed to make required showing that physician would not have heeded warning even if adequately made; summary judgment reversed). Several commentators have urged the adoption of an exception to the learned intermediary rule in cases of direct consumer advertising of prescription drugs; see generally T. Schwartz, Consumer-Directed Prescription Drug Advertising and the Learned Intermediary Rule, 46 Food Drug Cosm. L.J. 829 (1991) ("[T]here are solid grounds for abandoning the learned intermediary rule where prescription drug manufacturers direct their advertisements to consumers."); Note, Bypassing the Learned Intermediary: Potential Liability for Failure to Warn in Direct-to-Consumer Prescription Drug Advertising, 2 Cornell J. L. & Pub. Pol'y 449, 473 (1993) (concluding that "imposition of tort liability on manufacturers who advertise directly to consumers" without adequately warning consumers of risks is appropriate).

Comment f. Manufacturers' liability for defectively designed prescription drugs and medical devices. Although courts traditionally have refused to review the reasonableness of the designs of prescription drugs and medical devices, in recent years many courts have imposed limited judicial review on this special category of products. See, e.g., Brochu v. Ortho Pharm. Corp., 642 F.2d 652, 656 (1st Cir.1981) (applying New Hampshire law) (design defect cause of action proper where an available alternative design would have provided the same benefits with far less risk); Coursen v. A. H. Robins Co., 764 F.2d 1329, 1338 (9th Cir.1985) (stating that Comment *k* to § 402A of the Restatement, Second, of Torts is an affirmative defense); Rohrbough v. Wyeth Labs., 719 F.Supp. 470, 476–77 (N.D.W.Va.1989) (applying West Virginia law), aff'd, 916 F.2d 970 (4th Cir.1990) (stating that design of vaccine is subject to ordinary risk-utility analysis); Kociemba v. G.D. Searle & Co., 695 F.Supp. 432, 433 (D.Minn.1988) (single balancing test for reasonableness determines liability for design defect); Shanks v. Upjohn Co., 835 P.2d 1189, 1193–94 (Alaska 1992) (public policies supporting strict liability for defectively designed products outweigh the policies protecting pharmaceutical companies); West v. Searle & Co., 806 S.W.2d 608, 611–13 (Ark. 1991) (manufacturer may defend against design defect case by demonstrating through risk-utility analysis that product was unavoidably unsafe); Adams v. G.D. Searle & Co., 576 So.2d 728, 732–33 (Fla.Dist. Ct.App.) (protection from design-defect liability extends only to products that pass risk-utility balancing test for reasonable design, not to all drugs and medical devices per se), cert. denied, 589 So.2d 290 (Fla. 1991); Toner v. Lederle Labs., 732 P.2d 297, 308–09 (Idaho 1987) (stating in dictum that protection from design claims will be given only on a case-by-case basis, that applicability of "unavoidably unsafe" exemption depends on whether the product's benefits outweigh the risks, and noting that Comment *k* by its terms does not give "blanket immunity" to all drugs); Savina v. Sterling Drug, Inc., 795 P.2d 915, 924 (Kan.1990) (failure to warn case; application of Comment *k* is determined on a case-by-case basis); Allison v. Merck & Co., 878 P.2d 948, 954 (Nev.1994) (strict liability appropriate even when overall benefits of drug outweigh risks); Feldman v. Lederle Labs., 479 A.2d 374, 382–83 (N.J.1984) (stating in dictum that "[d]rugs, like any other products, may contain defects that could have been avoided by better manufacturing or design"), cert. denied, 505 U.S. 1219, 112 S.Ct. 3027, 120 L.Ed.2d 898 (1992); Davila v. Bodelson, 704 P.2d 1119, 1127–28 (N.M.Ct.App.1985) ("unavoidably unsafe" exemption from strict liability appropriate when drug poses certain dangers even when properly prepared and labelled, and yet is a useful drug); White v. Wyeth Lab., 533 N.E.2d 748, 752 (Ohio 1988) (prescription drugs do not, per se, fall within Comment *k*, but will be considered on a case-by-case basis); Tansy v. Dacomed Corp., 890 P.2d 881, 886 (Okla.1994) (Comment *k* is an affirmative defense only when product has been properly manufactured, provides sufficient warning, its benefits justify its risks, and it is incapable of being made safe); Castrignano v. E.R. Squibb & Sons, 546 A.2d 775, 781 (R.I.1988) (exemption from strict liability based on design defect will be available only if drug's apparent benefits outweigh apparent risks).

Finally, some jurisdictions have adopted essentially the approach taken in § 6(c). See Tobin v. Astra Pharm. Prod., 993 F.2d 528 (6th Cir.) (applying Kentucky law) (trial court correctly instructed the jury that defective design claim could succeed if it found that a product manufacturer, aware of the risks, would not have marketed the drug), cert. denied sub nom. Duphar v. Tobin, 510 U.S. 914, 114 S.Ct. 304, 126 L.Ed.2d 252 (1993).

See also Williams v. Ciba–Geigy Corp., 686 F.Supp. 573 (W.D.La.), aff'd, 864 F.2d 789 (5th Cir.1988), in which a federal district court in Louisiana was willing to consider the possibility that the traditional bar to prescription product design review might be relaxed. Nonetheless, the court imposed a heavy burden on the plaintiff to provide evidence of "an articulable basis for disregarding the FDA's determination that the drug should be available." Id. at 577. In granting summary judgment in favor of the pharmaceutical company, the court emphasized the drug's efficacy for certain classes of patients, notwithstanding its sometimes severely negative side effects:

> No evidence in the record tends to impugn the utility of Tegretol. There is no showing that any [other] drug . . . is effective in treating [plaintiff's disorder]. Tegretol is indicated only for those sufferers of psychomotor and grand mal seizures who do not respond to, or are endangered by, more conventional anticonvulsants which have serious side effects of their own. . . . The consequences of the nonavailability of Tegretol for those patients who suffer seizures, which can be fatal if not controlled, but who cannot take other anticonvulsants, would be grave indeed.

Id. at 578. The decision in *Williams* supports the approach to prescription drug design liability taken in Subsection (c).

Another decision supporting § 6(c)'s position regarding drug design liability is Ortho Pharm. Corp. v. Heath, 722 P.2d 410 (Colo.1986). There, the court adopted a test that, facially, resembles a "reasonableness under all the circumstances" approach. But in describing the manner in which the trial court should instruct the jury on remand, the Supreme Court of Colorado revealed unambiguously that the drug should be found nondefective if the jury concluded that the drug was the drug of choice for at least one class of patients. The general question for the jury was whether the benefits of the defendant's drug, containing 30 milligrams of estrogen more than an alternative drug on the market, did or did not outweigh its risks. In addressing the circumstances under which one or the other conclusion would be warranted, the court concluded:

> Here, the record contained testimony which indicated that the increased risks of adverse reactions occasioned by the extra thirty milligrams of estrogen outweighed any benefits the product might produce. The record also contained evidence that [defendant's drug] was the only available product for patients who experienced breakthrough bleeding *and therefore, produced benefits that outweighed any increased risk.*

Id. at 414 (emphasis added). The emphasized language clearly indicates that, if one class of patients is found to exist for whom defendant's drug is the one of choice, then it is not defective. The Supreme Court of Colorado reaffirmed this risk-benefit analysis, but overruled *Ortho* to the extent that it placed on the manufacturer the burden of proving that the benefits outweighed the risks. Armentrout v. FMC Corp., 842 P.2d 175, 183 (Colo.1992).

Subsection (c) reflects the view that, as long as a given drug or device provides net benefits for some category of patients, it should be available to that group, albeit with adequate warnings and instructions supplied to learned intermediaries. Learned medical intermediaries must be relied upon to direct the appropriate drugs to the appropriate patients. However, when a drug or device provides no net benefits to any ascertainable patient class—when reasonably informed medical providers would not prescribe the drug and no reasonable, informed manufacturer would place it on the market—then the product design is defective and the manufacturer should be liable for the harm caused by selling it.

The proposed rule in § 6(c) best advances the policies and values explicated in Comment *b*. It shows appropriate deference to the regulated market, where the FDA and learned intermediaries select which drugs should be available to the public generally and which drugs should be given to individual patients, respectively. It does not, on the other hand, wholly exempt defendants from liability simply because other institutions have taken steps to improve product safety. Subsection (c) is a significant departure from the general defective design rules espoused in §§ 1 and 2, in recognition of the unique characteristics of prescription drugs and medical devices. Unlike most products, which confer essentially the same benefits to all users, prescription drugs and medical devices have the capacity to do great harm or great good depending on the particular patient. Accordingly, liability will attach only if the design cannot be justified for any class of patients.

For critiques of the position in § 6(c) see Cupp, Rethinking Conscious Design Liability for Prescription Drugs: The Restatement (Third) Standard Versus a Negligence Approach, 63 Geo. Wash. L. Rev. 76 (1994); T. Schwartz, Prescription Products and the Proposed Restatement (Third), 61 Tenn. L. Rev. 1357 (1994). For a Reporter's defense of § 6(c), see Henderson, Prescription Drug Design Liability Under the Proposed Restatement (Third) of Torts: A Reporter's Perspective, 48 Rutgers L. Rev. 471 (1996).

Illustration 1 is based on Tobin v. Astra Pharm. Prods. Inc., 993 F.2d 528 (6th Cir.1993) (applying Kentucky law), cert. denied sub nom. Duphar v. Tobin, 510 U.S. 914, 114 S.Ct. 304, 126 L.Ed.2d 252 (1993).

Although most courts that have faced the issue of drug design review in recent years have opted for some limited form of review, some courts have taken the position that drug design review is inappropriate. See, e.g., Brown v. Superior Court, 751 P.2d 470 (Cal.1988); Artiglio v. Superior Court, 27 Cal.Rptr.2d 589 (Cal.Ct. App.1994) (*Brown* applies to medical devices available only by resort to services of physician); Tansy v. Dacomed Corp., 890 P.2d 881 (Okla. 1994) (Comment *k* bar to design review applies to medical devices); Grundberg v. Upjohn Co., 813 P.2d 89 (Utah 1991).

It should be noted that some cases exempt drugs and medical devices from design review based on a strict liability theory only. They appear to allow plaintiffs to pursue a cause of action for negligence. The rule set forth in § 6(c) would provide the exclusive basis for a cause of action based on objective drug design. As with § 2, the test in § 6 is stated in functional terms. Thus, whether the case is brought under negligence or strict liability a plaintiff would be successful only if it could make out the elements set forth in § 6(c).

Comment g. Foreseeability of risks of harm in prescription drug and medical device cases. For authority supporting the proposition that liability for design and marketing of prescription drugs and medical devices requires that the risk be reasonably foreseeable at the time of sale, see § 2, Comment *m*, Reporters' Notes 1 and 2, supra. See also DeLuryea v. Winthrop Labs., 697 F.2d 222, 228–29 (8th Cir.1983); Lindsay v. Ortho Pharm. Corp., 637 F.2d 87, 91 (2d Cir.1980); Basko v. Sterling Drug, Inc., 416 F.2d 417, 426 (2d Cir.1969); Gaston v. Hunter, 588 P.2d 326, 340 (Ariz.Ct.App.1978); Brown v. Superior Court, 751 P.2d 470, 480 (Cal. 1988); Carlin v. Superior Court, 920 P.2d 1347, 1349 (Cal.1996) ("[W]e have expressly and repeatedly applied a strict liability standard to manufacturers of prescription drugs for failure to warn of known or reasonably scientifically knowable risks."); Woodill v. Parke Davis & Co., 374 N.E.2d 683, 686–87 (Ill.App. Ct.1978); Hahn v. Richter, 673 A.2d 888 (Pa.1996); Ortho Pharm. Corp. v. Chapman, 388 N.E.2d 541, 548 (Ind. Ct.App.1979); Moore v. Vanderloo, 386 N.W.2d 108, 116 (Iowa 1986); Martin v. Hacker, 628 N.E.2d 1308, 1311 (N.Y.1993) ("The manufacturer's duty is to warn of all potential dangers in its prescription drugs that it knew, or, in the exercise of reasonable care, should have known to exist.").

Comment h. Liability of retail seller of prescription drugs and medical devices for defective designs and defects due to inadequate instructions or warnings. Retailers of prescription drugs and medical devices are liable for harm caused by such products only if the retailers are negligent. See, e.g., Elsroth v. Johnson & Johnson, 700 F.Supp. 151 (S.D.N.Y.1988) (applying New York law); Jones v. Irvin, 602 F.Supp. 399 (S.D.Ill.1985) (applying Illinois law); Murphy v. E.R. Squibb & Sons, Inc., 710 P.2d 247 (Cal.1985); Leesley v. West, 518 N.E.2d 758 (Ill.App.Ct.1988); Lemire v. Garrard Drugs, 291 N.W.2d 103 (Mich.Ct.App.1980); Parker v. St. Vincent Hosp., 919 P.2d 1104 (N.M.App.1996) (hospital is analogous to prescription drug retailer, therefore not strictly liable; cites Tentative Draft No. 2, § 8(e) [renumbered § 6(e)] with approval); Batiste v. American Home Prods. Corp., 231 S.E.2d 269 (N.C.Ct.App.1977); Coyle v. Richardson–Merrell, Inc., 584 A.2d

1383 (Pa.1991); Makripodis v. Merrell–Dow Pharms., Inc., 523 A.2d 374 (Pa.Super.Ct.1987); Pittman v. Upjohn Co., 890 S.W.2d 425 (Tenn.1994) (retailer's duty to use reasonable care does not extend to warning patient's grandson). See generally Brushwood and Abood, Strict Liability in Tort: Appropriateness of the Theory for Retail Pharmacists, 42 Food Drug Cosm. L.J. 269 (1987); Travers, Annotation, Druggist's Civil Liability for Injuries Sustained as a Result of Negligence in Incorrectly Filling Drug Prescriptions, 3 A.L.R. 4th 270 (1981).

§ 7. Liability of Commercial Seller or Distributor for Harm Caused by Defective Food Products

One engaged in the business of selling or otherwise distributing food products who sells or distributes a food product that is defective under § 2, § 3, or § 4 is subject to liability for harm to persons or property caused by the defect. Under § 2(a), a harm-causing ingredient of the food product constitutes a defect if a reasonable consumer would not expect the food product to contain that ingredient.

Comment:

a. General applicability of §§ 2, 3, and 4 to food products. Except for the special problems identified in Comment *b*, liability for harm caused by defects in commercially distributed food products are determined under the same rules generally applicable to non-food products. A food product may contain a manufacturing defect under § 2(a), as when a can of peas contains a pebble; may be defectively designed under § 2(b), as when the recipe for potato chips contains a dangerous chemical preservative; or may be sold without adequate warnings under § 2(c), as when the seller fails to inform consumers that the dye applied to the skins of oranges contains a well-known allergen. Section 3 may allow a plaintiff to reach the trier of fact when, unable to identify the specific defect, the plaintiff becomes violently ill immediately after consuming the defendant's food product and other causes are sufficiently eliminated. And § 4 may apply when a commercially distributed food product fails to conform to applicable safety statutes or administrative regulations.

b. The special problem under § 2(a). When a plaintiff suffers harm due to the presence in food of foreign matter clearly not intended by the product seller, such as a pebble in a can of peas or the pre-sale spoilage of a jar of mayonnaise, the claim is readily treated under § 2(a), which deals with harm caused by manufacturing defects. Food product cases, however, sometimes present unique difficulties when it is unclear whether the ingredient that caused the plaintiff's harm is an unanticipated adulteration or is an inherent aspect of the product. For example, is a one-inch chicken bone in a chicken enchilada, or a fish bone in fish chowder, a manufacturing defect or, instead, an inherent aspect of the product? The analytical problem stems from the circumstance that food products in many instances do not have specific product designs that may be used as a basis for determining whether the offending product ingredient constitutes a departure from design, and is thus a manufacturing defect. Food recipes vary over time, within the same restaurant or other commercial food-preparation facility, from facility to facility, and from locale to locale.

Faced with this indeterminacy, some courts have attempted to rely on a distinction between "foreign" and "natural" characteristics of food products to determine liability. Under that distinction, liability attaches only if the alleged adulteration is foreign rather than natural to the product. Most courts have found this approach inadequate, however. Although a one-inch chicken bone may in some sense be "natural" to a chicken enchilada, depending on the context in which consumption takes place, the bone may still be unexpected by the reasonable consumer, who will not be able to avoid injury, thus rendering the product not reasonably safe. The majority view is that, in this circumstance of uncertainty, the issue of whether a food product containing a dangerous but arguably natural component is defective under § 2(a) is to be determined by reference to reasonable consumer expectations within the relevant context of consumption. A consumer expectations test in this context relies upon culturally defined, widely shared standards that food products ought to meet. Although consumer expectations are not adequate to supply a standard for defect in other contexts, assessments of what consumers have a right to expect in various commercial food preparations are sufficiently well-formed that judges and triers of fact can sensibly resolve whether liability should be imposed using this standard.

REPORTERS' NOTE

Comment b. The special problem under § 2(a).

1. A strong majority of courts have applied the "reasonable consumer expectations test" in deciding whether an ingredient that caused the plaintiff's harm is an unanticipated adulteration or is an inherent aspect of the product. See, e.g., Morrison's Cafeteria of Montgomery, Inc. v. Haddox, 431 So.2d 975, 978 (Ala. 1983) (court rejected the foreign-natural test and opted instead for a "reasonable expectations" test, saying, "Under that test, the pivotal issue is what is reasonably expected by the consumer in the food as served, not what might be natural to the ingredients of that food prior to preparation"; applying the reasonable expectations test the court found, as a matter of law, that a one-centimeter

bone in a fish fillet did not disappoint such expectations); see also Clime v. Dewey Beach Enterprises, 831 F.Supp. 341, 348–49 (D.Del.1993) (applying Delaware law) (Plaintiff suffered a disease known as vibrio septicemia after eating raw shellfish at defendant's restaurant. The disease is caused by the ingestion of the bacteria vibrio vulnificus, an organism often contained in raw shellfish. The court rejected the foreign-natural test as the governing standard for food defects, saying, "[t]he distinction is . . . somewhat artificial from a practical perspective. A small, but unforgiving, pearl from an oyster can cause as much damage as a 'foreign' piece of metal when a consumer bites down on it." However, the court held, as a matter of law, that a consumer could not reasonably expect to receive a raw clam free of injurious bacteria.); Yong Cha Hong v. Marriott Corp., 656 F.Supp. 445, 448–49 (D.Md.1987) (applying Maryland law) (Court applied reasonable expectations test, saying that it "had largely displaced the natural/foreign test." In applying the test, the court found that it was a question for the trier of fact whether the presence of a trachea or an aorta in a fast-food fried chicken fell below reasonable consumer expectations.); Hochberg v. O'Donnell's Restaurant, Inc., 272 A.2d 846, 848–49 (D.C.1971); Zabner v. Howard Johnson's Inc., 201 So.2d 824, 826 (Fla.Dist.Ct.App.1967) ("Naturalness of the substance to any ingredients in the food served is important only in determining whether the consumer may reasonably expect to find such substance in the particular type of dish or style of food served"); Jackson v. Nestle–Beich, Inc., 589 N.E.2d 547, 548–49 (Ill.1992) (court adopted reasonable expectation of the consumer test for food products and rejected the foreign-natural test as emblematic of an "outdated and discredited doctrine"); Phillips v. Town of West Springfield, 540 N.E.2d 1331, 1332–33 (Mass. 1989) (court adopted "reasonable expectations" test and rejected foreign-natural dichotomy); Stark v. Chock Full O'Nuts, 356 N.Y.S.2d 403, 404 (N.Y.Sup.App.Term 1974) (reasonable expectations test); Langiulli v. Bumble Bee Seafood, Inc., 604 N.Y.S.2d 1020, 1021 (N.Y.Sup.Ct. 1993) (reasonable expectations test); Goodman v. Wenco Foods Inc., 423 S.E.2d 444, 451 (N.C.1992) (extensive discussion after which court rejected foreign-natural test and adopted a reasonable expectations test); Mathews v. Maysville Seafoods Inc., 602 N.E.2d 764, 765–66 (Ohio Ct.App. 1991) (The court observed that many courts believe that the Ohio rule under Allen v. Grafton, 164 N.E.2d 167 (Ohio 1960), is the foreign-natural test. The court expresses some doubt as to whether that is, in fact, the Ohio rule. On the facts of the case, the court held that under either test, the plaintiff had failed to make out a cause of action since "a consumer must reasonably anticipate and guard against the presence of a fish bone in a fish fillet."); O'Dell v. DeJean's Packing Co., 585 P.2d 399, 401–02 (Okla.Ct.App.1978) (When a deleterious item is found in packaged food, there is a prima facie case that the food is not merchantable. The burden is then shifted to the defendant to prove that the plaintiff should have "reasonably expected to find the item." The "reasonably expected" test is a defense and must be pleaded and proven as such.); Jim Dandy Fast Foods, Inc. v. Carpenter, 535 S.W.2d 786, 790 (Tex.Ct.App.1976) (ordinary consumer expectations test); Ayala v. Bartolome, 940 S.W.2d

727 (Tex.Ct.App.1997) (whether an ordinary consumer would expect raw oysters contaminated by bacteria to be fatal to persons suffering from liver disease is an issue of fact for jury); Gates v. Standard Brands Inc., 719 P.2d 130, 134 (Wash.Ct.App.1986) ("[W]e hold a cause of action for breach of an implied warranty of fitness for human consumption has been succeeded by the 'buyer oriented' consumer expectations test when determining whether food is defective."); Betehia v. Cape Cod Corp., 103 N.W.2d 64, 67–68 (Wis.1960) (early case adopting the reasonable consumer expectations test).

A minority of courts still follow the foreign-natural distinction for strict liability. See, e.g., Title v. Pontchartrain Hotel, 449 So.2d 677, 679–80 (La.Ct.App.1984) (utilized foreign-natural dichotomy to determine whether strict liability applied; held that, if alleged adulteration is natural, defendant is nevertheless liable if it was negligent in failing to remove the harm-causing ingredient); Cohen v. Allendale Coca–Cola Bottling Co., 351 S.E.2d 897, 899 (S.C.Ct.App.1986) (manufacturer owes duty to the consumer of the article to take care that there is no noxious foreign substance in the goods); Harris–Teeter, Inc. v. Burroughs, 399 S.E.2d 801, 802 (Va. 1991) ("[W]here a plaintiff allegedly suffers injury from a deleterious substance in food, the burden is on the plaintiff to show that the food product contained foreign matter at the time the retailer sold and delivered the product to the consumer.").

California, the originator of the foreign-natural test in Mix v. Ingersoll Candy Co., 59 P.2d 144 (Cal.1936), recently has revisited the issue in a lengthy and prolix opinion. In Mexicali Rose v. Superior Court, 822 P.2d 1292 (Cal.1992), the court held that:

> The strict foreign-natural test . . . should be rejected as the exclusive test for determining liability when a substance natural to food injures a restaurant patron. We conclude instead that in deciding the liability of a restaurateur for injuries caused by harmful substances in food, the proper tests to be used by the trier of fact are as follows:
>
> If the injury-producing substance is natural to the preparation of the food served, it can be said that it was reasonably expected by its very nature and the food cannot be determined unfit or defective. A plaintiff in such a case has no cause of action in strict liability or implied warranty. If, however, the presence of the natural substance is due to a restaurateur's failure to exercise due care in food preparation, the injured patron may sue under a negligence theory.
>
> If the injury-causing substance is foreign to the food served then the injured patron may also state a cause of action in implied warranty and strict liability, and the trier of fact will determine whether the substance (i) could be reasonably expected by the average consumer and (ii) rendered the food unfit or defective. (citation and footnote omitted)

Id. at 1303. Dissenting opinions found that the majority was badly out of harmony with the vast majority of authority throughout the country, and that there was no good reason for not simply applying a consumer expectations test to both foreign and natural substances. See id. at 1304–17.

Law review commentators have been unanimous in preferring the "reasonable consumer expectations" test over the "foreign-natural" test for food-related defects. See, e.g., Note, Breach of Implied Warranty: Has the Foreign/Natural Test Lost Its Bite?, 20 Mem. St. U. L. Rev. 377 (1990); Spak, Bone of Contention: The Foreign–Natural Test and the Implied Warranty of Merchantability for Food Products, 12 J.L. & Com. 23 (1992); Eller, Note, Tort Law—Products Liability—Implied Warranties—Foods—Goodman v. Wenco Foods Inc., 333 N.C. 1, 423 S.E.2d 444 (1992), 71 N.C. L. Rev. 2163 (1993).

2. Food defect cases raise difficult proof problems. Very often the plaintiff has suffered the alleged harm while in the privacy of the home and without outside witnesses to verify the occurrence. The defendant seeks to introduce evidence of its quality control for the purpose of establishing the improbability that the food product was contaminated. This argument has cogency, even though the plaintiff is proceeding under a strict liability theory where the issue of whether the defendant's quality control was reasonable is irrelevant. The defendant argues that evidence of quality control goes not to whether its conduct was negligent, but rather whether the product was, in fact, defective when it left its hands. The courts are split on the admissibility of such evidence. Some courts refuse to allow evidence of quality control to disprove defect on the grounds that to do so undermines strict liability. See, e.g., Pulley v. Pacific Coca–Cola Bottling Co., 415 P.2d 636, 640 (Wash.1966) ("The proffered testimony was collateral because it was not directly refutative of the plaintiff's relation of the incident involved. The appellants made no claim as to the infallibility of their particular bottling process. They attempted to demonstrate that it was *highly improbable* that a cigarette could have found its way into a bottle of 'king-size' Coca-Cola in the absence of tampering by a third party.... The ultimate question is whose *inadvertence* or *intentional act* produced the uncontroverted contamination of the bottle of Coca–Cola. As a matter of public policy, the burden of proof in this respect is placed by law upon food manufacturers and retailers and not upon the consumer. The ... evidence [of quality control] of the appellant was properly excluded.").

A significant number of courts, however, allow quality control evidence into the case as circumstantial proof supporting the defendant's contention that the food product was unadulterated at the time of sale. In Brown v. General Foods Corp., 573 P.2d 930, 934 (Ariz.Ct.App.1978), the court said:

> It should be noted that a manufacturer will rarely have available anything other than circumstantial evidence to disprove a plaintiff's claim relating to the discovery and existence of an alleged defect in a product. The circumstantial evidence is admissible, not to show lack of fault or the presence of due care on the manufacturer's part, but rather, as relevant evidence tending to show the improbability of the defect as alleged by the plaintiff. We can hypothesize a fact situation in which, by reason of the intrinsic nature of the defect and the impossibility of its occurrence other than in the manufacturing process, evidence of the manufacturer's quality control procedures would not be relevant and there-

> fore would be inadmissible. However, such is not the case before us. The presence of the banana peel in the cereal box was not a defect of such a nature that it had to have occurred before the product left the possession and control of the defendant-manufacturer. Nor has plaintiff shown that the manufacturer's evidence was unduly prejudicial to him, separate and apart from the prejudice normally inherent in evidence supporting an opponent's position on the legitimate issues of the case. We therefore hold that under the circumstances of this case the defendant-manufacturer's testimony relating to its quality control procedures was properly admitted.

See also Castleberry's Food Co. v. Smith, 424 S.E.2d 33, 35–36 (Ga.Ct.App.1992) (court notes that defendant introduced extensive evidence of its quality control procedures for the purpose of demonstrating the improbability that the product was defective).

In Johnesee v. Stop & Shop Cos., 416 A.2d 956 (N.J. Super. Ct. App. Div. 1980), the trial judge excluded the defendant's evidence of its quality assurance techniques because plaintiff's theory of recovery was implied warranty or strict liability as opposed to negligence, rendering the proof of defendant's exercise of due care irrelevant. In reversing, the appellate court said:

> We disagree with the trial judge's reasoning for excluding the proffered testimony. In a foreign substance case, where it is possible for the substance to enter the food after leaving the manufacturer's hands, evidence that the substance was not present when the food was under defendant's control would be relevant to disprove that necessary element of a products liability claim. However, proof that the soup was made under the most hygienic conditions does not tend to exculpate the maker, since a single can might become contaminated in spite of all reasonable precautions.
>
> Nevertheless, a certain improbability as to the truth of plaintiffs' version exists which defendants should not be foreclosed from establishing. The issue is one of credibility. A manufacturer rarely has available anything more than circumstantial evidence to disprove a plaintiff's claim relating to the discovery and existence of an alleged defect in a product. Evidence such as that proffered here should be admissible, not to show lack of fault or the presence of due care on the manufacturer's part, but rather as relevant evidence tending to show the improbability of the defect as claimed by plaintiffs. While there may be fact situations in which, by reason of the intrinsic nature of the defect and the impossibility of its occurrence other than in the manufacturing process, barring evidence of quality control procedures in manufacture, we do not regard the situation presented here as such. In short, the proffered evidence goes directly toward refuting the credibility of plaintiffs' testimony. We regard the trial judge's exclusion of the offered testimony erroneous for this narrow reason. Of course, the jury should be instructed as to the use of such evidence.

Id. at 960. See also Tardella v. R.J.R. Nabisco, Inc., 576 N.Y.S.2d 965 (N.Y.App.Div.1991).

3. For authority supporting the proposition that the test is that of a reasonable consumer and not a sub-

jective test, see Phillips v. Town of West Springfield, 540 N.E.2d 1331 (Mass.1989).

§ 8. Liability of Commercial Seller or Distributor of Defective Used Products

One engaged in the business of selling or otherwise distributing used products who sells or distributes a defective used product is subject to liability for harm to persons or property caused by the defect if the defect:

(a) arises from the seller's failure to exercise reasonable care; or

(b) is a manufacturing defect under § 2(a) or a defect that may be inferred under § 3 and the seller's marketing of the product would cause a reasonable person in the position of the buyer to expect the used product to present no greater risk of defect than if the product were new; or

(c) is a defect under § 2 or § 3 in a used product remanufactured by the seller or a predecessor in the commercial chain of distribution of the used product; or

(d) arises from a used product's noncompliance under § 4 with a product safety statute or regulation applicable to the used product.

A used product is a product that, prior to the time of sale or other distribution referred to in this Section, is commercially sold or otherwise distributed to a buyer not in the commercial chain of distribution and used for some period of time.

Comment:

a. History. American courts have struggled with the question of whether to hold commercial sellers of used products to the same legal standards of responsibility for defects as commercial sellers of new products. Judicial responses have varied. Some courts hold used-product sellers strictly liable for harm caused by product defects existing at the time of sale. A greater number of courts hold commercial sellers of used products to lesser standards of responsibility. Liability rules applicable to used-product sellers are less stringent than those applicable to new-product sellers due to the wide variations in the type and condition of used products. For example, even in the minority of jurisdictions that generally hold commercial used-product sellers strictly liable for defects, disclaimers of liability may more readily be given effect in connection with sales of used products than in connection with sales of new products. Even in jurisdictions that generally apply more relaxed standards of responsibility for used products, factors that tend to raise a buyer's expectations regarding product quality, such as a seller's advertising a used product as "rebuilt" or "re-conditioned," correspondingly tend to raise the level of the sellers' responsibilities for product defects. The liability rules in this Section seek to accommodate these variations.

b. Rationale. Subsection (a) imposes liability on a commercial used-product seller for harm caused by a used product resulting from the seller's failure to exercise reasonable care. A used-product seller is properly subjected to liability, on both fairness and efficiency grounds, when its negligence causes harm. Even if a buyer does not have the right to expect a used product in obviously used condition to present the same defect-related risks as if the product were new, the buyer at least has the right to expect the used-product seller to exercise reasonable care. Moreover, exposing commercial used-product sellers to liability for harm caused by their negligence creates incentives for them to take reasonable steps to reduce risks of harm. Subsection (a) covers a wide variety of negligent conduct by the used-product seller, including conduct that introduces defects into the product and conduct that allows defects to remain when reasonable care would have eliminated them. Thus, when the requisites of Subsections (b) and (c) imposing strict liability for harm caused by product defects cannot be met, Subsection (a) will, in many instances, provide an appropriate remedy. See Comment *e*.

Subsections (b) and (c) subject commercial sellers of used products to liability without fault only under special circumstances. Consumers of most used products sold in obviously used condition typically do not, and should not, expect those products to perform as safely, with respect to the possibility of mechanical defects, as when those products were new. Many factors affect consumer expectations in this regard. For example, the age and condition of used products and the commensurate lower prices paid for such products alert reasonable buyers to the possibility of defects and the need to monitor the safety aspects of such products over time according to their age and condition. Given the awareness of buyers generally regarding the risks of harm presented by used products in varying stages of physical deterioration, primary responsibility for allocating these risks may, in the absence of fault on the part of the used-product seller or some special circumstance that justifies strict liability, be delegated to commercial markets for used products, in which the terms of sale vary widely depending on the apparent condition of such products at the time of sale.

When a used product is sold commercially under circumstances in which a reasonable buyer would expect the risk of defect to be substantially the same as with a new product, a different judicial response is justified. Thus, under the circumstances described in Subsection (b), many of the same rationales that support strict liability for harm caused by mechanical defects in new products support strict liability for mechanical defects in like-new used products. This section does not adopt the "consumer expectations test" as the governing standard for defining product defect. This Restatement has rejected that test as the sole test for defect in § 2 and does not adopt it in this Section. See § 2, Comment *g*. The question addressed in this Section is under what circumstances a plaintiff may hold the seller of a used product to the liability standard applicable to sellers of new products. When dealing with this more limited question, Subsection (b) takes the position that, when the seller's marketing of the product would lead a reasonable consumer to expect the product to present no greater risk of defect than if the product were new, the law may treat the used-product sale as the functional equivalent of the sale of a new product.

Similarly, when a used product is remanufactured, strict liability under Subsection (c) is justified. The defects referred to in Subsection (c) include manufacturing defects, design defects, and defects based on inadequate instructions and warnings. See Comment *i*. Having undertaken to review and update not only the physical condition but, within limits, the design and marketing of the used product as well, the remanufacturer has taken on a role analogous to that of an original manufacturer with respect to those aspects of the product over which the remanufacturer has chosen to assert control. In that circumstance, Subsection (c) justifiably subjects used-product sellers to liability for harm caused by defects of all types in remanufactured used products.

It will be observed that, in contrast with Subsection (c), Subsection (b) imposes liability without proof of fault only for harm caused by manufacturing defects as defined in § 2(a) and defects whose existence may be inferred under § 3, even in connection with used products sold in such good condition that reasonable buyers would expect the risk of defects to be substantially the same as if the products were new. The factual difference between the circumstances described in Subsection (b) and those described in Subsection (c) is that in the latter the used-product seller (or a predecessor in the chain of distribution of the used product) has somehow introduced or chosen not to eliminate the design defect during remanufacture, whereas under Subsection (b) the design defect originates with the manufacturer in the original, new-product chain of distribution and the used-product seller is in no position to change the design.

Commercial sellers of like-new used products occupy a different position from that occupied by retailers of new products. Retailers of new products are part of the original chain of distribution and in fairness should be liable for harm caused by defects, even design defects, that exist when products are sold new. See § 1, Comment *e*. Retailers of new products have opportunities, as used-product sellers generally do not, to contract with those above them in the chain of distribution regarding who should ultimately bear the costs of defending design claims in court and paying successful claimants. Holding new-product retailers liable for defective designs originating at manufacture encourages them to apply pressure on manufacturers within the distributive chains, directly and indirectly, to produce safe products and to adopt reasonable designs. In contrast, sellers of like-new used products are not, except coincidentally, members of the original distributive chain. Typically they exercise little if any control over original design choices or decisions regarding indemnity for costs of liability.

c. One engaged in the business of selling used products. The rules stated in this Section apply only to commercial sellers engaged in the business of selling used products. They do not apply to noncommercial private owners of used products, such as automobiles or electrical appliances, who sell them to others. Nor do they apply to a commercial establishment that makes an occasional sale of used equipment outside the regular course of its business. See § 1, Comment *c*. Noncommercial and casual used-product sellers may be liable under the general principles of negligence. See Restatement, Second, Torts § 281 et seq. But such sellers are outside the scope of this Restatement. Whether the defendant is a commercial seller or distributor within the meaning of this Section is usually a question of law to be determined by the court.

Illustrations:

1. ABC Car Rental purchases and maintains a fleet of new cars for its business of short-term car leases. At regular intervals it sells these rental cars at public auctions. In connection with these auctions, ABC is in the business of selling used products within the meaning of this Section.

2. ABC Box Co. is in the business of selling cardboard boxes. ABC owns a forklift, manufactured by SRT, that ABC uses for stacking boxes in its warehouse. ABC sells the used forklift to the XYZ Paper Supply Co. and replaces it with a new one. In connection with this sale, ABC is not in the business of selling used products within the meaning of this Section.

d. Definition of used product. To constitute a used product, a product must not only have been used for some period of time prior to the used-product sale transaction referred to in this Section, but that use must have followed its sale to a buyer not in the chain of distribution. Many products are tested, and thus in a sense are "used," within the chain of distribution prior to sale to persons outside the distributive chain. New motor vehicles, for example, are typically delivered to members of the buying public with several miles on their odometers, reflecting predistribution test driving. They are not for that reason used products under this Section. Even a product that is used by a retailer as a demonstration model prior to its first sale to the public does not thereby become a used product. After a new product has been sold or distributed, any use of the product by the buyer or other person not in the chain of distribution, for however short a period of time, transforms the product into a used product. In this connection post-sale use includes post-sale possession by the buyer or other person not in the chain of distribution occurring off the business premises of the seller.

Illustrations:

3. ABC, Inc., a retail dealer selling new and used automobiles, sells a new automobile to Sally, a customer. Sally takes delivery, drives it 300 miles, and then trades it back to ABC on the purchase of a different vehicle. ABC sells the trade-in two weeks later to Fred, another retail customer, at a discounted price. The trade-in automobile is a used product within the definition in this Section at the time of sale by ABC to Fred. (If a defect existing at the time of sale by ABC to Sally causes harm to Fred after the re-sale to him, ABC will be subject to liability to Fred under §§ 1 and 2 as the seller (to Sally) of a defective new product.)

4. ABC, Inc., a retail dealer selling new and used automobiles, offers last year's models for sale at a discounted price. The automobiles have never before been sold to the public and have only a few test miles on their odometers. They are new products at the time of sale by ABC and are not used products within the definition in this Section.

5. ABC, Inc., a retail dealer selling new and used automobiles, offers a demonstration automobile for sale at a discounted price. The demonstrator has been driven over 1,000 miles by ABC's salespersons and prospective buyers. The demonstrator has never before been sold to, or used by, anyone outside the chain of distribution. It is a new product at the time of sale by

ABC and is not a used product within the definition in this Section.

6. XYZ Co. is a discount retailer that buys "seconds" and "overruns" in quantity from various manufacturers and sells them to the public at discounted prices. The products have never been used before sale by XYZ. Whether or not XYZ is considered to be a buyer in the commercial chain of distribution of the products it sells, the products have not been used for any period of time prior to sale by XYZ and therefore are not "used products" within the definition in this Section.

e. Used-product seller's liability for harm caused by seller's failure to exercise reasonable care. A commercial used-product seller who negligently introduces a defect or fails to eliminate a defect in performing such tasks as inspecting, repairing, modifying, rebuilding, redesigning, or reconditioning a used product, or a seller who negligently fails to provide adequate warnings, is subject to liability under Subsection (a) when harm to persons or property results therefrom. Liability under Subsection (a) thus focuses not on a reasonable buyer's expectations of safety but on the reasonableness of the seller's conduct and its causal relation to the defect-related harm suffered by the plaintiff.

Illustrations:

7. ABC Used Machinery Co. repairs used electric generators for commercial resale. In repairing a generator for resale, ABC negligently chooses a grade of electrical wire with inadequate heat resistant properties given the normal uses to which the generator is put. ABC sells the generator to XYZ. Due to the inadequate wiring, the generator causes a fire, resulting in serious harm to XYZ's plant. ABC is subject to liability to XYZ for failure to exercise reasonable care in repairing the used generator.

8. LMN Co. purchases a new punch press from ABC Sales Co. After installing the punch press in its plant, LMN disengages a safety mechanism, the function of which is to shut down the press when an employee's hands get too close to the point of operation. After using the machine for five years, LMN sells it to ABC Machine Co. ABC repairs the used punch press and sells it, with the disengaged safety mechanism, to GHI, Inc. ABC negligently fails to warn GHI that the safety mechanism on the punch press is disengaged. A GHI employee working on the punch press suffers harm due to ABC's failure to warn of the disengaged safety mechanism. ABC is subject to liability for failing to exercise reasonable care with regard to its sale of the used punch press to GHI.

f. Used-product seller's liability for harm caused by manufacturing defects. Section 2(a) defines a manufacturing defect as a departure from a product's intended design. Although designated "manufacturing" defects, such mechanical defects need not originate at time of manufacture. See § 2, Comment *c.* If, at the time of sale or other distribution, the used product departs from its original intended design, a manufacturing defect as defined in § 2(a) exists at the time of the sale of the used product even though the defect arose during use of the product after its first commercial sale as a new product.

This Section subjects used-product sellers to liability for harm caused by manufacturing defects in three sets of circumstances. First, under Subsection (a), even if a reasonable person would expect the used product to present substantially greater risk of defect than if it were new and the product has not been remanufactured, the seller is subject to liability when the seller's negligence results in a manufacturing defect causing harm to persons or property. The seller may negligently fail to discover, repair, or warn about the defect. Second, under Subsection (b) the seller is subject to liability without fault for harm caused by a manufacturing defect when a reasonable person in the buyer's position would expect the used product to present substantially the same risk of defect as if the product were new. And third, under Subsection (c), the seller is subject to liability without fault for harm caused by a manufacturing defect in a remanufactured used product.

Illustrations:

9. XYZ, Inc., a commercial used-product seller, sells a six-month-old used clothes dryer to P. The dryer is in like-new condition. The price reflects the fact that the dryer is used. A manufacturing defect in the dryer causes a fire, harming M. If, at the time of sale by XYZ, a reasonable person in P's position would expect the dryer to present substantially the same risk of defect as if it were new, then XYZ is subject to liability without fault to M under Subsection (b).

10. XYZ, Inc., a commercial used-product seller, sells a used clothes dryer in obviously used condition to P, under circumstances in which a reasonable person in P's position would expect the dryer to present a substantially greater risk of defect than if it were new at the time of sale. XYZ negligently repairs the dryer prior to sale, introducing a manufacturing defect. The defect subsequently causes an accident, harming M. Although XYZ is not subject to liability to M under Subsection (b), XYZ is subject to liability under Subsection (a).

11. XYZ, Inc., a commercial used-product seller, sells a used clothes dryer in obviously used condition to P. XYZ remanufactures the dryer prior to sale to P, nonnegligently introducing a manufacturing defect. The defect subsequently causes an accident, harming M. Although XYZ is not subject to liability to M under Subsection (a) or (b), XYZ is subject to liability under Subsection (c).

g. Used-product seller's liability for harm caused by defects that may be inferred under § 3. Subsections (b) and (c) impose liability on used-product sellers not only for defects as defined in §§ 2(a) and 2, respectively, but also for defects whose existence at the time of sale may be inferred under § 3. Under § 3 an inference of defect may be drawn based on circumstantial evidence.

Illustration:

12. Driver bought a used automobile from Ace Used Cars, Inc. The automobile was in like-new condition, with only 800 miles on the odometer. Shortly after buying the automobile, while driving the automobile nonnegligently on a well-maintained paved road, Driver felt something crack below where the steering column connects with the dashboard. The steering wheel spun to the right and the automobile turned sharply. Before Driver could stop, the automobile crashed into a wall and Driver suffered harm.

Driver brings an action against Ace Used Cars. Driver's qualified expert witness testifies that the accident was caused by a defect in the car's steering mechanism that existed at the time of sale by the defendant. The expert identifies four manufacturing or design defects that could have caused the accident, but is unable to say with reasonable certainty which of the four defects in fact occurred. No evidence of negligence on the part of the defendant is available. The trier of fact could find that a reasonable person in Driver's position would have expected the automobile to present substantially the same risk of defect as if it had been new at the time of sale by Ace Used Cars. The evidence is sufficient to reach the trier of fact with a strict liability claim under Subsection (b), even though it may not be sufficient to support a determination regarding which of the four possible defects caused the accident.

h. Requirement that a reasonable person in the position of the buyer would expect the used product to present substantially the same risk of defect as if the product were new at the time of sale. Reasonable consumer expectations do not constitute the test for defectiveness under Subsection (b) but rather they determine whether or not the used product should be governed by the liability rules applicable to new products, thus imposing strict liability for harm caused by manufacturing defects under § 2(a) and by inferable defects under § 3.

The reasonable expectations test under Subsection (b) is objective, not subjective. The fact that a product has been used prior to sale for even a short period of time necessarily lowers reasonable expectations of safety to some extent. Nevertheless, under Subsection (b) reasonable expectations need only substantially approximate those associated with products in new condition. The comparison is with the actual product in new condition, not with a newer, more advanced design of the product.

The relevant circumstances determining reasonable expectations include but are not limited to: (1) the age and condition of the product unit containing the defect; (2) the price of the product relative to the prices of new and used products of a similar type; (3) the seller's affirmations, if any, that the product is rebuilt or reconditioned; (4) any statements by the seller concerning repairs undertaken with regard to the product; (5) any guarantees or warranties made by the seller with regard to the product, including any limitations accompanying such guarantees or warranties; (6) the presence or absence of contractual disclaimers of liability; and (7) the seller's disclosures of information alerting a reasonable buyer to a higher risk of defect due to prior usage of the product and its condition. The plaintiff ordinarily bears the burden of proving that the circumstances surrounding the sale would lead a reasonable person to expect the used product to present substantially the same risk of defect as if it were new at the time of sale. Whether a reasonable person would so expect may be a question of fact for the jury.

The used-product seller's liability under Subsection (b) for harm caused by a product defect may extend to a specific part of the product or to a specific time period of use. For example, the seller's marketing of the like-new used product may refer to a specific time period during which the product will present substantially the same risk of defect as if it were new. If a defect in the product at the time of sale causes harm during the specified period, then the seller is subject to liability under Subsection (b) for the harm caused by the defect whether or not the seller's marketing could be construed as an enforceable sales warranty.

When a used product contains a new component part and the component contains a manufacturing defect that causes harm, the used-product seller is subject to liability for the harm as a commercial seller of a defective new product component under §§ 1, 2(a), and 3.

Illustrations:

13. XYZ, Inc., a commercial seller of used vacuum cleaners, sells a used vacuum cleaner to P. The vacuum cleaner is three months old and is in like-new condition. A manufacturing defect in the cleaner, existing at the time of sale, causes an accident, harming P's child, C. Without regard to P's subjective expectations, XYZ is subject to liability without fault to C if the trier of fact finds that a reasonable person in P's position would expect the cleaner to present substantially the same risk of defect as if it were new at the time of sale.

14. XYZ, Inc., a commercial used-product seller, sells a used gas stove to P. The stove is five years old and has been subjected to extensive use. XYZ refurbishes the stove prior to sale and asserts to P that it is "rebuilt and in top working condition." The price includes a premium, relative to used stoves generally, reflecting the refurbishing. A manufacturing defect, existing at the time of sale of the used stove, causes an accident that harms M. Whether or not XYZ's assertion is an express warranty, XYZ is subject to liability to M under Subsection (b) if the trier of fact finds that a reasonable person in P's position would expect the refurbished stove to present substantially the same risk of defect as if it were new at the time of sale.

15. XYZ, Inc., a commercial used-product seller, sells a used snowblower to P. The blower is five years old and obviously has been subjected to extensive use. The price is discounted and XYZ asserts to P that the blower is sold "as is and with all defects." A manufacturing defect existing at the time of sale causes an accident, resulting in harm to M. Whether or not XYZ's assertion constitutes a valid disclaimer, in the absence of proof that XYZ's negligence caused the defect XYZ is not subject to liability to M. Regardless of P's subjective beliefs, no reasonable person in P's position would expect that the risk of defect is substantially the same as if the blower were new at the time of sale.

16. Same facts as Illustration 13 except that the used vacuum cleaner at the time of sale contains a new motor, installed by XYZ. Subsequently, a defect in the new motor causes an accident, harming M. XYZ, as a commercial seller of the new motor, is subject to liability without fault to M under §§ 1 and 2.

17. Same facts as Illustration 13 except that XYZ sells the used vacuum cleaner with a representation that "parts and labor are guaranteed for 90 days." A defect existing at the time of sale causes an accident 50 days after the sale, harming M. XYZ is subject to liability without fault to M if the trier of fact finds that

a reasonable person in P's position would expect the vacuum to present substantially the same risk of defect during the 90-day period as if the vacuum were new at the time of sale by XYZ.

i. Remanufacture of the used product. When one undertakes to remanufacture a used product and bring it to market as a product that meets current design and production standards, it is fair to subject the seller of the remanufactured product to liability for harm caused by §§ 2 and 3 defects existing at the time of sale of the remanufactured used product. The fact that the remanufactured product is sold at a discount compared to a new product does not relieve the seller of responsibility for such defects. In part the imposition of liability for §§ 2 and 3 defects arises because of heightened consumer expectations. However, when a used product is remanufactured the plaintiff need not prove that a reasonable buyer would expect the remanufactured product to present no greater risk of defect than if the product were new, as is necessary in establishing a case under Subsection (b). The fact of remanufacture is sufficient to impose liability for § 2 defects. Even when a product is not remanufactured a plaintiff is free to establish liability under Subsections (a) and (b) by proving either that the seller failed to act reasonably with regard to the sale of the used product or that the seller's marketing of the product would cause a reasonable person to expect the used product to present no greater risk of defect than if the product were new.

Illustration:

18. ABC Motor Parts Co. sells both new and remanufactured replacement parts. ABC sold Alice a remanufactured fuel pump for her 1994 Blazer Sedan. XYZ Rebuilders, Inc. remanufactured the fuel pump and sold it to ABC. Alice paid 25 percent less for the remanufactured fuel pump than a new fuel pump would have cost. Shortly after installation of the remanufactured fuel pump Alice's car stalled while making a turn in an intersection. A collision ensued causing serious injury to Alice. Alice's expert presents credible testimony that a bracket in the fuel pump dislodged and blocked the flow of fuel and that the bracket was defectively assembled by XYZ. Both ABC and XYZ are subject to liability without fault for the harm caused by the defect.

j. Short-term product leases. A commercial lessor of new and like-new products is generally subject to the rules governing products liability. See § 20, Comment *c*. In contrast, when the rental units are in obviously used condition, and rented under circumstances in which a reasonable person would not expect the risk of defect to be substantially the same as if the rental units were new, liability of the lessor will depend upon a showing of fault under Subsection (a).

Illustrations:

19. XYZ, Inc., operates a commercial business leasing automobiles to customers on a short-term basis. The average age of its fleet of vehicles is six months; some leased vehicles are new or almost new. XYZ leases a 12–month-old automobile to P for three days. The odometer at the commencement of the lease shows 8,000 miles. XYZ charges P the same rate it charges for new or almost-new automobiles of similar make and model. A defect in the vehicle at the time of commencement of the lease causes an accident, harming M. XYZ is subject to liability to M under §§ 1 and 2 for the harm caused by the defect.

20. ABC Rent-a-Used–Car, Inc., operates a commercial business leasing automobiles in obviously used condition to customers on a short-term basis. The automobiles that ABC leases are at least two years old and many are as old as four years. The odometers range from 35,000 to 75,000 miles. ABC's rates are lower than those charged for the rental of newer automobiles by the leading national car-rental chains. ABC leases a three-year-old automobile to P for one week. The automobile has 40,000 miles on the odometer. A latent manufacturing defect in the brake cylinder causes an accident, harming M. ABC is not liable as a retailer of a new product under §§ 1 and 2. Nor is ABC subject to liability to M under Subsection (b) because a reasonable person in P's position would not expect that the used automobile presents substantially the same risk of defect as if it were new at the time of the lease to P. ABC is subject to liability to P if shown to have been negligent under Subsection (a).

k. Effects of disclaimers on used-product seller's liability. A used-product seller's disclaimer of liability for harm caused by product defects may be given conclusive legal effect under applicable state law, depending on the nature of the harm caused by the defects. See, e.g., § 21, Comment *f*, dealing with recovery of economic loss. Whether a used-product seller's disclaimer of liability for harm to persons is legally conclusive is more problematic, but many courts give such disclaimers conclusive effect. In any event, disclaimer language is relevant in an inquiry into reasonable expectations under Subsection (b). That is, a disclaimer may diminish reasonable expectations as to the safety of a used product. This is especially likely when disclaimer language either reminds the buyer that the product is used or warns the buyer of the increased risk of defect.

l. Relationship between the rule in this Section and the liability of a used-product seller for misrepresentation or breach of express warranty. Subsection (b) imposes liability for manufacturing defects under § 2(a) and for inferable defects under § 3 when a reasonable person in the buyer's position would expect a used product to present substantially the same risk of defect as if the product were new. See Comment *h*. A representation about the product may contribute to such expectations even when the representation does not constitute a misrepresentation under § 9 or an express warranty. However, when the seller's representation is sufficiently explicit to constitute a misrepresentation or an express warranty about the used product, the plaintiff may be entitled to bring an action under § 9 or under Article 2 of the U.C.C.

REPORTERS' NOTE

Comment b. Rationale. Authority on the question of whether strict liability applies to the sale of used products is mixed. This Note canvasses the decisions. Given the varied fact patterns, it is difficult to conclude with any certainty as to the exact degree of support for the rule stated in this Section. The decisions will be set forth and will be commented on where appropriate. See, e.g., Jordan v. Sunnyslope Appliance Propane & Plumbing Supplies Co., 660 P.2d 1236 (Ariz.Ct.App.1983) (strict liability for manufacturing and design defects that existed in used propane tank at the time of original manufacture; court cites with approval the New Jersey decision of Turner v. International Harvester Co., 336 A.2d 62 (N.J.Super.Ct.Law Div.1975), holding that a court may consider the reasonable expectations of the used-product buyer in determining whether a used product, considering its age or condition, is unreasonably dangerous; no indication as to whether disclaimer will be effective to negate liability); Kodiak Elec. Ass'n v. DeLaval Turbine, Inc., 694 P.2d 150, 153 n. 6 (Alaska 1984) (strict liability will apply where the product has undergone extensive repair, inspection, and testing at the hands of the seller prior to resale; this position may be consistent with the rule stated in this Section since, under § 8(b) or (c), a reasonable buyer might expect that a product that had undergone such reconditioning that it would present substantially the same risk of defect as if it were new at time of sale or the used product might be considered to be remanufactured); Petrus Chrysler–Plymouth v. Davis, 671 S.W.2d 749 (Ark.1984) (court applied strict liability to a used car that had an electrical defect that was present at the time of sale by the used-car seller; the relevant part had undergone repair at the buyer's request prior to sale; court applied strict liability and made no mention that strict liability was limited to repaired part).

The California cases are of particular interest. All of the decisions set forth strong policy reasons as to why strict liability should not apply against used-product sellers. On their facts, however, the cases involve "as is" disclaimers. See, e.g., La Rosa v. Superior Court, Santa Clara County, 176 Cal.Rptr. 224 (Cal.Ct.App.1981) (strict liability does not apply to sale of a used punch press when the seller expressly disclaimed any representation as to its condition; strict liability is negated for any defect existing at time of manufacture or one that was introduced into the product subsequent to manufacture but prior to sale); Wilkinson v. Hicks, 179 Cal. Rptr. 5 (Cal.Ct.App.1981) (no strict liability for sale of punch press when defendant purchased the press "as is"); Barrett v. Superior Court, Riverside County, 272 Cal.Rptr. 304 (Cal. Ct.App.1990) (court denied lessor's motion for summary judgment on claim of strict liability for defects in earth mover, given evidence that the lessor had maintained, modified, and repaired the earth mover; court noted that all California cases exempting sellers of used products from strict liability involved sellers who had sold the machinery without making any adjustments, repairs, or modifications to such machinery); Pacific Nat'l Ins. Co. v. Gormsen Appliance Co., 284 Cal.Rptr. 78 (Cal.Ct.App.1991), review denied (Opinion ordered not to be published by the Supreme Court) (lessor who leased a 16–year-old refrigerator "as is" to college students was not liable for the damage to home that was occasioned when the defective refrigerator caused a fire). The only California case in which a court disallowed a strict liability claim against a used-product seller in the absence of a disclaimer is Meyering v. General Motors Corp., 275 Cal. Rptr. 346 (Cal.Ct.App.1990), review granted, 804 P.2d 1301 (Cal.1991), and review dismissed, 819 P.2d 842 (Cal.1991).

In Peterson v. Superior Court, 899 P.2d 905, 914–15 (Cal.1995), the court analogized the liability of a landlord or hotel proprietor for harm caused by defective products on its premises to that of a used-product seller. The court cited at length from earlier decisions holding that a used-product seller was not strictly liable:

> To impose such liability would as a practical matter require all dealers in used goods routinely to dismantle, inspect for latent defects, and repair or recondition their products.... It would in effect render used goods dealers as insurers against defects which came into existence after the original chain of distribution and while the product was under the control of previous consumers. (citation omitted) ...
>
> As to the risk-reduction aspect of strict products liability, the position of the used-goods dealer is normally entirely outside the original chain of distribution of the product. As a consequence, we conclude, any risk reduction which would be accomplished by imposing strict liability on the dealer in used goods would not be significant enough to justify our taking that step. The dealer in used goods generally has no direct relationship with either manufacturers or distributors. Thus, there is no ready channel of communication by which the dealer and the manufacturer can exchange information about possible dangerous defects in particular product lines or about actual and potential liability claims. (citation omitted).

The court did, however, indicate that in the case of a rebuilt or reconditioned product a used-product seller would be strictly liable. Under the rule stated in § 8(b) or (c), the fact that a product was sold as rebuilt or reconditioned would be relevant to whether the consumer would expect the used product to present substantially the same risk of defect as if the product were new or to whether it should be considered to be remanufactured. See Comments *h* and *i*.

See also King v. Damiron Corp., 113 F.3d 93 (7th Cir.1997) (court applying Connecticut law held that strict liability does not apply to sellers of used products); Lecates v. Hertrich Pontiac Buick Co., 515 A.2d 163 (Del.Super.Ct.1986) (court recognized validity of disclaimer of implied warranty of merchantability for seller of used products but denied used-car seller summary judgment because the car was sold with a "guarantee" and the disclaimer of merchantability did not appear conspicuously in the document); Freeman v. Delaware Auto Sales, Inc., 1987 WL 25492 (Del.Super.Ct. Nov.19, 1987) (sale of used vehicles is governed by the U.C.C., which recognizes the validity of disclaimers); Fuquay v. Revels Motors, Inc., 389 So.2d 1238 (Fla.Dist.Ct. App.1980) (strict liability does not apply to the sale of a used car); Keith v. Russell T. Bundy & Assoc., 495 So.2d 1223 (Fla.Dist.Ct.App.1986) (dealer in used bakery equipment who sold a roll-slicing machine in "as-is-running condition" was not strictly liable for design defect in the product).

In Peterson v. Idaho First Nat'l Bank, 791 P.2d 1303 (Idaho 1990), the Idaho court took a strong position against the imposition of strict liability against sellers of used products. It also found such liability precluded under the terms of the Idaho Product Liability Act. Peterson v. Lou Bachrodt Chevrolet Co., 329 N.E.2d 785 (Ill.1975), is an early decision that holds the policies of strict liability inapplicable against the sellers of used products. The court differentiates used-product sellers who are in no position to discover latent product defects from wholesalers and retailers of new products, on the grounds that the latter can exert pressure on the manufacturer to enhance the safety of the product. Also see Timm v. Indian Springs Recreation Ass'n, 543 N.E.2d 538 (Ill.App.Ct.1989) (strict liability does not apply to sale of used golf carts; the golf carts were sold "as is"). In Cruz v. Midland–Ross Corp., 813 F.Supp. 628 (N.D.Ill. 1993), the court held that an "as is" disclaimer would be effective to negate liability for both negligence and strict liability under Illinois law. Also see Zavala–Pizano v. Industrial Handling Equip. Co., 847 F.Supp. 621 (C.D.Ill.1994) (seller of used equipment not subject to strict liability).

The effectiveness of an "as is" disclaimer to negate liability for the implied warranty of merchantability with regard to the sale of a used car was affirmed in DeVoe Chevrolet–Cadillac, Inc. v. Cartwright, 526 N.E.2d 1237 (Ind.Ct.App.1988). In a very limited opinion, the Iowa high court in Grimes v. Axtell Ford Lincoln–Mercury, 403 N.W.2d 781 (Iowa 1987), answering a question certified to it by a federal court, held that strict liability did not apply to a used-goods seller who did not rebuild or recondition the product but merely installed a used axle from a salvage yard into a Ford van. The court specifically left open the question as to whether it might apply strict liability to a used-product seller under other circumstances.

Louisiana law on the subject of strict liability for the sale of used products is not clear. In Buckbee v. United Gas Pipeline Co., 542 So.2d 81, 85 (La.Ct.App.1989), reversed on other grounds, 561 So.2d 76 (La. 1990), the court intimated that any seller who "substantially modifies or materially alters the product after its original manufacture through the use of different components or methods of assembly . . . may be cast in product liability for product modifications that engender injury-causing defects." This would appear to impose liability for a seller who reconditions or rebuilds a used product but only for the changes wrought by the seller. However, the defendant was dismissed from the case since it was not in the business of selling products of the kind that caused the injury. Furthermore, the sale of the defective heater was an "as is" sale.

Maryland appears to take the position that a dealer in used products who does not create the defect is not responsible in strict liability for injuries caused by the defective product. See Harrison v. Bill Cairns Pontiac of Marlow Heights, Inc., 549 A.2d 385 (Md.Ct.Spec.App.1988). Minnesota reached a similar result in Gorath v. Rockwell Int'l, Inc., 441 N.W.2d 128 (Minn.Ct.App.1989), because its statute immunizing nonmanufacturer suppliers from strict liability applies to sellers of used products. The court noted that, if the seller of a used product was more than a mere middleman and had some involvement in altering the condition of the product, strict liability might apply.

In Harber v. Altec Indus., Inc., 812 F.Supp. 954 (W.D.Mo.1993), aff'd, 5 F.3d 339 (8th Cir.), the district court, applying Missouri law, undertook a thorough analysis of the policy implications of applying strict liability to used products. It concluded that, if the used goods were sold "as is" and the seller did not repair, modify, or alter the product, strict liability should not apply.

New York case law is most interesting. In Nutting v. Ford Motor Co., 584 N.Y.S.2d 653 (N.Y.App.Div.1992), the court held that strict liability would apply against a company that purchased several thousand new cars for use by its employees and then sold them to the public as used cars. The court held that many of the goals of strict liability are fostered by applying it against a large purchaser of vehicles since such a purchaser has substantial leverage with the seller of new automobiles and can, through its buying power, affect product safety. Given the reasoning of the court, it remains to be seen whether a regular seller of used cars would be subject to strict liability. In Stiles v. Batavia Atomic Horseshoes, Inc., 579 N.Y.S.2d 790, 792 (N.Y.App.Div. 1992), the court did apply strict liability against a seller of used punch presses. The court drew an inference from Sukljian v. Charles Ross & Son Co., 503 N.E.2d 1358 (N.Y.1986), which held that an occasional seller of a used product is not subject to strict liability because it was not in the business of selling such products. The *Stiles* court reasoned that "[I]mplicit in this holding is that a non-occasional or regular seller of a used product may be strictly liable. . . . " The intermediate appellate court was reversed in Stiles v. Batavia Atomic Horseshoes, Inc., 613 N.E.2d 572 (N.Y. 1993). The Court of Appeals held that "Batavia's business was the manufacture and sale of horseshoes" and that it was not a regular seller of used goods and hence not subject to strict products liability. The court left open the question raised in *Sukljian*, supra, as to whether strict products liability applies to regular sellers of used products.

In Gonzalez v. Rutherford Corp., 881 F.Supp. 829, 842–43 (E.D.N.Y. 1995), the court predicted that New York would adopt strict liability for the sale of used products that contained latent defects. The court acknowledged that case law in New York was indeterminate on this issue and that case law throughout the country was mixed. Nonetheless, the court believed that New York would side with those courts imposing strict liability. It is clear that *Gonzalez* disagrees with the rule stated in this Section.

New Jersey decisions have been influential. Two New Jersey cases are frequently cited. Realmuto v. Straub Motors, Inc., 322 A.2d 440 (N.J.1974), left open the broad question whether strict liability applied to all sellers of used products but held that a used-car dealer is subject to strict liability in tort with respect to a mishap resulting from any defective work, repairs, or replacement performed by the seller on the vehicle. A year later in a landmark case, Turner v. International Harvester Co., 336 A.2d 62 (N.J.Super.Ct.Law Div.1975), the court engaged in an extensive policy analysis and concluded that strict liability should be imposed on a dealer in used goods. The court also held that a simple "as is" disclaimer should not insulate a seller from strict liability when the product is sold to a consumer. The court held that an ordinary consumer does not have the bargaining power and ability to protect its interests. A more recent New Jersey case has, in *dicta*, affirmed the holding in *Turner*. See Santiago v. E.W. Bliss Div., 492 A.2d 1089, 1095 (N.J. Super. Ct. App. Div. 1985).

Perhaps the most oft-cited case on the subject of strict liability for the sale of used products is Tillman v. Vance Equipment Co., 596 P.2d 1299, 1303 (Or.1979). The Oregon court took the position that used-product markets operate

> on the apparent understanding that the seller, even though he is in the business of selling such goods, makes no particular representation about their quality simply by selling them. If a buyer wants some assurance of quality, he typically bargains for it in the specific transaction or seeks out a dealer who routinely offers it.... The flexibility of this kind of market appears to serve the legitimate interests of buyers as well as sellers.

The court thus took the position that the seller of used products "in the absence of some representation of quality beyond the sale itself," should not be held to strict liability. In Crandell v. Larkin & Jones Appliance Co., 334 N.W.2d 31, 34 (S.D.1983), the South Dakota court expressed general agreement with *Tillman* and held that when used products dealers sell goods as reconditioned or rebuilt, strict liability applies and serves to protect the reasonable expectations of consumers. Also see Wynia v. Richard–Ewing Equip. Co., Inc., 17 F.3d 1084 (8th Cir.1994) (holding that *Crandell* is still the governing rule in South Dakota).

An early Texas case, Hovenden v. Tenbush, 529 S.W.2d 302 (Tex.Civ. App.1975), applied strict liability to the seller of used bricks. It appears that the Fifth Circuit believes *Hovenden* represents Texas law. In Galindo v. Precision Am. Corp., 754 F.2d 1212 (5th Cir.1985), reh'g denied, 762 F.2d 1004, the court refused to hold the seller of a used sawmill trimmer strictly liable on the ground that the defendant was not in the business of selling such products. The inference is compelling that, absent the "occasional seller" defense, the seller would have been held strictly liable even though the product was used. Thompson v. Rockford Mach. Tool Co., 744 P.2d 357 (Wash.Ct.App. 1987), review denied, 110 Wash.2d 1007 (1988), applied strict liability to the seller of used products. It should be noted, however, that the action was brought before the effective date of RCW. 7.72.010, which provides that a "product seller" does not include a commercial seller of a used product who resells a product after use by a consumer or other product user provided that, when it is resold, the used product is essentially in the same condition as when it was acquired for resale. It would appear that, even under the statute, strict liability would be imposed on a used-product seller who reconditions or rebuilds a used product.

In Nelson v. Nelson Hardware Inc., 467 N.W.2d 518 (Wis.1991), a hardware store that took a used shotgun in trade and resold it without making any representations concerning the safety mechanism of the gun was liable for an injury caused by a design defect in the shotgun. The court held that a "claim for products liability may be brought under circumstances alleged in this case where the defective condition causing harm to the consumer of the used product arises out of the original manufacturing process and where other elements requisite for liability under Section 402A are present." Id. at 521. The court also reviewed the policy grounds for strict liability and found them relevant to the sale of used goods. The court concluded:

> The general policy reasons for the imposition of strict liability on a seller of goods—new or used—are as set forth in sec. 402A of the Restatement. These policy factors include the ability to compensate the injured party by the seller being able to spread the risk by insurance or indemnity which is inherent in selling products which may cause injury to a purchaser, who has a reasonable expectation that the product is safe for the intended use; and the risk reduction aspect is always present, since imposition of liability may impel a retail seller to purchase only from other sellers or manufacturers who, under threat of liability as a matter of law, will correct or prevent the manufacture of dangerously defective products.

Id. at 525. In a vigorous opinion (concurring on other grounds), Justice Steinmetz argued that many of the policy reasons supporting strict liability for new goods are inapplicable to the sale of used goods. Unlike manufacturers of new goods, the seller of used goods does not create the risk nor is it in a position to avoid distribution of defective used goods. It does not have the capability and expertise to discover and correct latent defects. Furthermore, he observed:

> To the extent trade in used goods continues, it will increasingly tend to take place on a private and individual basis through, for example, the classified advertisements of local newspapers. Indeed, the used goods trade may flourish within such an informal market. Insofar as transactions in this informal market go unreported to the authorities, unfavorable tax revenue consequences are likely to result to state and local units of government. Moreover, it is possible if not likely that the goods that private individuals sell will be more defective, and hence more dangerous, than the used goods that enterprises such as the defendant's formerly sold.

Id. at 529. It should be noted that neither the majority nor the dissent raised the issue of the validity of a disclaimer. The case at bar was not an "as is" sale and there was, therefore, no reason for the court to discuss whether a disclaimer would be valid.

Several law review articles address the issue of liability for the sale of used products. See, e.g., Note, Builders' Liability for Latent Defects in Used Homes, 32 Stan. L. Rev. 607 (1980) (purchasers of used homes should be given the same protection against latent defects as those who purchased the home new; either the implied warranty of quality in new homes should be extended to cover subsequent purchasers, or recovery should be allowed under strict liability); Note, Protecting the Buyer of Used Products: Is Strict Liability for Commercial Sellers Desirable?, 33 Stan. L. Rev. 474 (1981) (strict liability should not apply to commercial sellers of unmodified used products; such liability would raise prices, encouraging buyers to purchase from non-commercial sellers, who would not be subject to the rigors of strict liability and would tend to be less skilled in inspection and risk-reduction, and therefore might result in more frequent harm from used products); Note, The Application of Strict Liability in Tort to the Retailers of Used Products: A Proposal, 16 Okla. City U. L. Rev. 373 (1991) (strict liability for retailers of used products should be imposed on a case-by-case basis; a rebuttable presumption of strict liability should arise once the plaintiff established a prima facie case).

Summary

The rule stated in this Section captures the essence of the vast majority of decisions so that most courts confronted with a used-product case would find that their case law could be accommodated to § 8. The case law in this instance provides a mosaic from which important themes have been synthesized into a clearly articulated and easily understood rule.

This goal is accomplished in this Section by recognizing strict liability for manufacturing defects under § 2(a) or for cases whose facts support an inference of defect under § 3 only when a reasonable person would expect the used product to present substantially the same risk of defect as if the product were new at the time of sale. The buyer and seller are both aware that a used-product seller is in no position to discover many latent defects or to alter the original design of the product. The used-product market is highly elastic and the parties are in a position to adjust price to reflect the relative age and condition of the product. The fact that many courts are willing to recognize "as is" disclaimers is evidence of the fact that they are unwilling to treat the seller of used products as sellers of new products. It is universally recognized that sellers of new products cannot disclaim liability for harm to persons. See § 18. The ubiquitous disclaimer should not be dispositive. The true rationale behind these cases is that the courts are not willing to impose strict liability when the buyer's expectations are that used products present greater risks than new ones. When the used-product seller markets its wares as "reconditioned or rebuilt," whether strict liability should be imposed under this Section should depend on whether a reasonable buyer is led to believe that the product or a component part thereof will present substantially the same risk of defect as if it were new. When this would be the understanding of a reasonable buyer, then strict liability should apply. When it would not, a reasonable buyer should understand that all the used-product seller can do is to exercise reasonable care. Furthermore, liability under § 2 or § 3 should follow when a used product has been remanufactured.

Comment c. One engaged in the business of selling used products. For authority supporting the view that a business entity that sells a used piece of machinery when such a seller is not a merchant in the business of selling goods of the kind is not subject to strict liability, see, e.g., Santiago v. E.W. Bliss Div., 492 A.2d 1089 (N.J. Super. Ct. App. Div. 1985) (defendant who disposed of a punch press after 24 years of use was an occasional seller and thus not subject to strict liability); Timm v. Indian Springs Recreation Ass'n, 543 N.E.2d 538 (Ill.App.Ct.1989) (golf club that sold used golf carts after considerable use was not a seller in the business of selling such items and is not subject to strict liability); Bevard v. Ajax Mfg. Co., 473 F.Supp. 35 (E.D.Mich. 1979) (applying Michigan law) (strict liability did not apply against the owner of a press who sold it as an occasional sale and was not in the business of selling such products); Sukljian v. Charles Ross & Son Co., 503 N.E.2d 1358 (N.Y.1986) (A company that sold a grinding mill as surplus property is an occasional seller and not subject to strict liability.); Galindo v. Precision Am. Corp., 754 F.2d 1212 (5th Cir.1985) (applying Texas law), reh'g denied, 762 F.2d 1004 (strict liability does not apply against a company that sold a sawmill trimmer after it had depreciated and was sold as surplus equipment).

Comments f, g, and h. The authority for the positions taken in these Comments is fully explored in the case law set forth in the Reporters' Note to Comment *a* and need not be repeated. As noted in the summary to this Note, rather than slavishly following the case law of any single jurisdiction, this Section provides rules based on the valid concerns expressed in the case law. Given the varied nature of the decisions and the different approaches taken by the courts, it would be impossible to restate a single majority rule. The rule as stated in this Section comes closest to reflecting a consensus.

Comment j. Short-term product leases. See Reporters' Note, § 20, Comment *c*.

Comment k. Effects of disclaimers on used-product seller's liability. There is little direct case law on disclaimers of negligence by sellers of used products. There is, however, considerable case law dealing with disclaimers of negligence generally. An overwhelming majority of jurisdictions agree that a party may contract out of liability for its own negligence. See, e.g., Continental Airlines, Inc. v. Goodyear Tire & Rubber Co., 819 F.2d 1519 (9th Cir.1987) (applying California law); Cadek v. Great Lakes Dragaway, Inc., 843 F.Supp. 420 (N.D.Ill.1994) (applying Wisconsin law); Robinson Ins. & Real Estate, Inc. v. Southwestern Bell Tel. Co., 366 F.Supp. 307 (W.D.Ark.1973) (applying Arkansas law); Lago v. Krollage, 575 N.E.2d 107 (N.Y.1991); Heil Valley Ranch, Inc. v. Simkin, 784 P.2d 781 (Colo.1989) (en banc); Wagenblast v. Odessa Sch. Dist. No. 105–157–166J, 758 P.2d 968 (Wash.1988) (en banc); Harris v. Walker, 519 N.E.2d 917 (Ill.1988); Corral v. Rollins Protective Servs. Co., 732 P.2d 1260 (Kan.1987); Schutkowski v. Carey, 725 P.2d 1057 (Wyo.1986); Morgan v. South Cent. Bell Tel. Co., 466 So.2d 107 (Ala.1985); Salt River Project Agric. Improvement & Power Dist. v. Westinghouse Elec. Corp.,

694 P.2d 198 (Ariz.1984) (en banc); Skotak v. Vic Tanny International, Inc., 513 N.W.2d 428 (Mich.Ct.App. 1994); DeBoer v. Florida Offroaders Driver's Ass'n, Inc., 622 So.2d 1134 (Fla.Dist.Ct.App.1993). Inherent in such an agreed disclaimer is the creation of tension between "freedom of contract and responsibility for damages caused by one's own negligent acts." This has led the courts to strictly scrutinize such agreements, construing them against the party invoking them, and to require as a condition to validity that the "intention of the parties [be] expressed in clear and unambiguous language." Jones v. Dressel, 623 P.2d 370, 376 (Colo.1981) (en banc). See also O'Brien v. Grumman Corp., 475 F.Supp. 284, 289 (S.D.N.Y.1979) (applying New York law) ("specific and unequivocal"); Buchan v. U.S. Cycling Fed'n, Inc., 277 Cal.Rptr. 887, 894 (Cal.Ct.App.1991) ("clear, unambiguous and explicit"); Sirek v. Fairfield Snowbowl, Inc., 800 P.2d 1291, 1295 (Ariz.Ct.App.1990) ("specific and unequivocal").

Although facially valid, an exculpatory clause or agreement will not be enforced if it is "affected with a public interest"; this exception is narrowly defined by most courts. Tunkl v. Regents of Univ. of California, 383 P.2d 441, 444–45 (Cal.1963) (in banc); accord, *Dressel*, supra, 623 P.2d at 376–77; Banfield v. Louis, 589 So.2d 441, 446 (Fla.Dist.Ct.App.1991); see also Ciofalo v. Vic Tanney Gyms, Inc., 177 N.E.2d 925, 926 (N.Y.1961).

CHAPTER 2

LIABILITY OF COMMERCIAL PRODUCT SELLERS NOT BASED ON PRODUCT DEFECTS AT TIME OF SALE

---

§ 9. Liability of Commercial Product Seller or Distributor for Harm Caused by Misrepresentation

One engaged in the business of selling or otherwise distributing products who, in connection with the sale of a product, makes a fraudulent, negligent, or innocent misrepresentation of material fact concerning the product is subject to liability for harm to persons or property caused by the misrepresentation.

Comment:

a. Liability for fraudulent or negligent misrepresentation. The rules in the Restatement, Second, of Torts, governing liability for fraudulent and negligent misrepresentation, are contained in §§ 310 and 311. Case law has followed these Sections. Although these Sections do not explicitly apply to commercial product sellers, they admit of such application. Given the availability to plaintiffs of the rule under § 402B of the Restatement, Second, of Torts, subjecting product sellers to strict liability even in the absence of fraud or negligence, (see Comment *b*), there can be no doubt that product sellers are subject to liability for fraudulent or negligent misrepresentation. By hypothesis, given the rule stated in § 402B, a plaintiff who proves that the misrepresentation that caused harm was made fraudulently or negligently should have a remedy.

b. Liability for innocent misrepresentation. The rules governing liability for innocent product misrepresentation are stated in the Restatement, Second, of Torts § 402B. Case law has followed that

Section. Section 402B contains two caveats. The first caveat leaves open the question whether a seller should be liable under § 402B for an innocent misrepresentation that is made to an individual and not to the public at large. This question remains open. Case law on the subject of liability for innocent misrepresentation has dealt exclusively with public misrepresentations. The second caveat to § 402B leaves open the question whether a seller should be liable for an innocent misrepresentation that causes harm to the person or property of one who is not a consumer of the product. Case law has not resolved the issue of whether an innocent misrepresentation may, in the absence of a product defect, be a basis of liability to a non-consumer who suffers harm as a result of reliance by an intermediary.

c. The elements of materiality, causation, and contributory fault. It is important to note that § 402B, in Comments *g* and *j*, incorporates by reference §§ 537–548A of the Restatement, Second, of Torts. These Sections define what constitutes a material misrepresentation, see § 538; what is a material fact, see §§ 538–543; the requirement that the misrepresentation be a cause in fact of the harm, see § 546; the requirement that the misrepresentation be a legal cause of the harm, see § 548A; and the role of contributory fault and its relation to justifiable reliance, see § 545A.

d. No requirement of product defect. This Section does not require the plaintiff to show that the product was defective at the time of sale or distribution within the meaning of other Sections of this Restatement Third of Torts: Products Liability.

e. Relationship between the rule stated in this Section and express warranty. The rule stated in this Section provides a remedy in tort in many cases in which a remedy for breach of express warranty or implied warranty of fitness for particular purpose is also available to the plaintiff. Breach of these warranties provides an independent basis of liability under the Uniform Commercial Code and may be combined in the same case with a claim for misrepresentation.

REPORTERS' NOTE

Comment b. Liability for innocent misrepresentation.

1. The history of § 402B is succinctly summarized in American Safety Equipment Corp. v. Winkler, 640 P.2d 216, 219–20 (Colo.1982):

> The theory of recovery for misrepresentation in [S]ection 402B presents an unconventional hybrid between contract and tort law. At common law, an action grounded on breach of warranty sounded in tort rather than in contract. Hansen v. Firestone Tire & Rubber Co., 276 F.2d 254 (6th Cir.1960). See generally Sales, The Innocent Misrepresentation Doctrine: Strict

Tort Liability Under Section 402B, 16 Houston L. Rev. 239, 241 (1979). Characterizing the action as trespass on the case, the English courts permitted recovery for the breach of an express warranty of a material fact, relied upon in the purchase of a chattel, that later proved to be false. *See, e.g.*, Medina v. Stoughton, 1 Lord Raym. 593, 91 Eng. Rep. 1297 (K.B.1700); Cross v. Garnet, 3 Mod. 261, 87 Eng. Rep. 172 (K.B.1689).

By the end of the eighteenth century, however, the tort character of an express warranty action had disappeared in favor of a cause of action based on assumpsit. *See, e.g.*, Stuart v. Wilkins, 1 Dougl. 18, 99 Eng. Rep. 15 (K.B.1778). Thereafter, claims for breach of the express warranty by the manufacturer's representation became the sole cognizable claim for product misrepresentations. Because this contractual cause of action required privity between the parties to the contract of sale, however, suits between the consumer and the manufacturer were uniformly dismissed. *See, e.g.*, Senter v. B.F. Goodrich Co., 127 F.Supp. 705 (D.Colo.1954); Barni v. Kutner, 6 Terry 550, 45 Del. 550, 76 A.2d 801 (1950); Pearl v. William Filene's Sons Co., 317 Mass. 529, 58 N.E.2d 825 (1945); Turner v. Edison Storage Battery Co., 248 N.Y. 73, 161 N.E. 423 (1928).

As the law continued to evolve, the courts increasingly rejected the necessity for a contractual relationship, recognizing that the ultimate consumer, in purchasing a product, often relied heavily upon the manufacturer's express public representations of the qualities and character of the product. In Baxter v. Ford Motor Co., 168 Wash. 456, 12 P.2d 409, on second appeal, 179 Wash. 123, 35 P.2d 1090 (1934), the court used the concept of misrepresentation to conclude that a manufacturer who innocently misrepresented a material fact concerning a product, which was relied upon by the purchaser, was strictly liable for injuries caused by the failure of the product to conform to the represented facts.

. . .

The ultimate result of judicial rejection of the orthodox rule of contractual privity and recognition of a theory of strict tort liability for innocent misrepresentations by a manufacturer was the adoption of § 402B in the Restatement, Second, of Torts by the American Law Institute. Several jurisdictions have since expressly adopted the theory of § 402B. *See, e.g.*, Klages v. General Ordnance Equipment Corp., 240 Pa. Super. Ct. 356, 367 A.2d 304 (1976); Hauter v. Zogarts, 14 Cal.3d 104, 534 P.2d 377, 120 Cal. Rptr. 681 (1975); Crocker v. Winthrop Laboratories, 514 S.W.2d 429 (Tex.1974); Ford Motor Co. v. Lonon, 217 Tenn. 400, 398 S.W.2d 240 (1966). *See generally* W. Prosser, Torts, § 97 (1975).

Section 402B, to which Comment *b* refers, contains the following black letter:

§ 402B. Misrepresentation by Seller of Chattels to Consumer.

One engaged in the business of selling chattels who, by advertising, labels, or otherwise, makes to the public a misrepresentation of a material fact concerning the character or quality of a chattel sold by him is subject to liability for physical harm to a consumer of the chattel caused by justifi-

able reliance upon the misrepresentation, even though

(a) it is not made fraudulently or negligently, and

(b) the consumer has not bought the chattel from or entered into any contractual relation with the seller.

In addition to the cases cited in the excerpt from *American Safety Equipment*, supra, a number of other jurisdictions have recognized § 402B as controlling. See, e.g., Westlye v. Look Sports, Inc., 22 Cal.Rptr.2d 781 (Cal.Ct.App.1993); Gawloski v. Miller Brewing Co., 644 N.E.2d 731 (Ohio App.Ct.1994); Davis v. Berwind Corp., 640 A.2d 1289 (Pa.Super.Ct.1994); Phillips v. Duro–Last Roofing, Inc., 806 P.2d 834 (Wyo. 1991).

For general discussions of the role of misrepresentation and products liability, see Owen, The Highly Blameworthy Manufacturer: Implications on Rules of Liability and Defense in Products Liability Actions, 10 Ind. L. Rev. 769 (1977); Phillips, Product Misrepresentation and the Doctrine of Causation, 2 Hofstra L. Rev. 561 (1974); Shapo, A Representational Theory of Consumer Protection: Doctrine, Function and Legal Liability for Product Disappointment, 60 Va. L. Rev. 1109 (1974).

2. Section 402B requires justifiable reliance on the misrepresentation. It then states:

> The reliance need not necessarily be that of the consumer who is injured. It may be that of the ultimate purchaser of the chattel, who because of such reliance passes it on to the consumer who is in fact injured, but is ignorant of the misrepresentation. Thus a husband who buys an automobile in justifiable reliance upon statements concerning its brakes, and permits his wife to drive the car, supplies the element of reliance, even though the wife in fact never learns of the statements.

Several cases support this position. See, e.g., Westlye v. Look Sports, Inc., 22 Cal.Rptr.2d 781 (Cal.Ct.App. 1993) (manufacturer misrepresented to retailer the safety of ski bindings; retailer rented skis and bindings to plaintiff, who never heard of representation; injured plaintiff was allowed recovery under § 402B); Baughn v. Honda Motor Co., Ltd., 727 P.2d 655 (Wash.1986) (en banc) (reliance by retailer sufficient). In Wechsler v. Hoffman–La Roche Inc., 99 N.Y.S.2d 588, 590 (N.Y.Sup.Ct. 1950), the plaintiff suffered personal injury as a result of an alleged misrepresentation by the drug manufacturer to the plaintiff's physician. The court held that reliance by the plaintiff himself was unnecessary. Admittedly, the court found that the physician was acting as an agent of sorts for the plaintiff. However, before the court made reference to the agency theory, the court said:

> Defendant here claims, however, that its representations were made to physicians and not to the intestate or persons of the class to which intestate belonged and would thus avoid liability in fraud even if the allegations in the complaint are true . . . *But in my view one who misrepresents for his gain and benefit at the expense of human life, should be answerable in fraud for all the reasonable and foreseeable consequences of his deception.* [emphasis added].

Wechsler has been cited with approval in recent cases applying New

York law. See, e.g., Powers v. Ostreicher, 824 F.Supp. 372, 376 (S.D.N.Y.1993); Brown v. Neff, 603 N.Y.S.2d 707 (N.Y.Sup.Ct.1993). In *Brown*, the plaintiff, a passenger in a truck that overturned due to mechanical defects, brought an action for misrepresentation against the defendant, a garage owner, who issued an inspection certificate for the car when the defendant knew that it had not performed the state-mandated inspection. The driver presumably relied on the defendant's misrepresentation, but the passenger did not. In allowing recovery without privity or any reliance by the injured third party, the court said:

> Liability for intentional or negligent misrepresentations which threaten physical harm is grounded upon a duty which is coextensive with foreseeable risk. By contrast, in the separate and distinct sphere of misrepresentations involving the risk of pecuniary loss, the representer's duty is much reduced. Compare §§ 310 and 311 of the Restatement (physical harm) with § 552(2) (pecuniary loss).

Id. at 709.

No cases have been found dealing with the second caveat. Thus, no basis exists to conclude that reliance by an intermediary on an innocent misrepresentation would result in a right to recovery by a non-consumer who was injured.

§ 10. Liability of Commercial Product Seller or Distributor for Harm Caused by Post–Sale Failure to Warn

(a) One engaged in the business of selling or otherwise distributing products is subject to liability for harm to persons or property caused by the seller's failure to provide a warning after the time of sale or distribution of a product if a reasonable person in the seller's position would provide such a warning.

(b) A reasonable person in the seller's position would provide a warning after the time of sale if:

(1) the seller knows or reasonably should know that the product poses a substantial risk of harm to persons or property; and

(2) those to whom a warning might be provided can be identified and can reasonably be assumed to be unaware of the risk of harm; and

(3) a warning can be effectively communicated to and acted on by those to whom a warning might be provided; and

(4) the risk of harm is sufficiently great to justify the burden of providing a warning.

Comment:

a. Rationale. Judicial recognition of the seller's duty to warn of a product-related risk after the time of sale, whether or not the product is defective at the time of original sale within the meaning of other Sections of this Restatement, is relatively new. Nonetheless, a growing body of decisional and statutory law imposes such a duty. Courts recognize that warnings about risks discovered after sale are sometimes necessary to prevent significant harm to persons and property. Nevertheless, an unbounded post-sale duty to warn would impose unacceptable burdens on product sellers. The costs of identifying and communicating with product users years after sale are often daunting. Furthermore, as product designs are developed and improved over time, many risks are reduced or avoided by subsequent design changes. If every post-sale improvement in a product design were to give rise to a duty to warn users of the risks of continuing to use the existing design, the burden on product sellers would be unacceptably great.

As with all rules that raise the question whether a duty exists, courts must make the threshold decisions that, in particular cases, triers of fact could reasonably find that product sellers can practically and effectively discharge such an obligation and that the risks of harm are sufficiently great to justify what is typically a substantial post-sale undertaking. In deciding whether a claim based on breach of a post-sale duty to warn should reach the trier of fact, the court must determine whether the requirements in Subsection (b)(1) through (4) are supported by proof. The legal standard is whether a reasonable person would provide a post-sale warning. In light of the serious potential for overburdening sellers in this regard, the court should carefully examine the circumstances for and against imposing a duty to provide a post-sale warning in a particular case.

b. When a reasonable person in the seller's position would provide a warning. The standard governing the liability of the seller is objective: whether a reasonable person in the seller's position would provide a warning. This is the standard traditionally applied in determining negligence. See Restatement, Second, Torts § 283, Comment *c*. In applying the reasonableness standard to members of the chain of distribution it is possible that one party's conduct may be reasonable and another's unreasonable. For example, a manufacturer may discover information under circumstances satisfying Subsection (b)(1) through (4) and thus be required to provide a post-sale warning. In contrast, a retailer is generally not in a position to know about the risk discovered by the manufacturer after sale and thus is not subject to liability because it neither knows nor should know of the risk. Once the retailer is made aware of the risk, however, whether the retailer is subject to liability for failing to issue a post-sale warning depends on whether a reasonable person in the retailer's position would warn under the criteria set forth in Subsection (b)(1) through (4).

c. Requirement that seller or other distributor knows or should know of the product-related risk. A duty to warn after the time of sale cannot arise unless the product seller or other distributor knows or in the exercise of reasonable care should know of the product-related risk that causes plaintiff's harm. The seller may have known or should have known of the risk at the time of sale, in which case failure to warn will cause the product to be defective under § 2(c). But even if the product is not defective at the time of sale because no reasonable seller would have known of the risk under § 2(c), knowledge of the risk may come after sale and may give rise to a duty to warn at that time.

As a practical matter, most post-sale duties to warn arise when new information is brought to the attention of the seller, after the time of sale, concerning risks accompanying the product's use or consumption. When risks are not actually brought to the attention of sellers, the burden of constantly monitoring product performance in the field is usually too burdensome to support a post-sale duty to warn. However, when reasonable grounds exist for the seller to suspect that a hitherto unknown risk exists, especially when the risk involved is great, the duty of reasonable care may require investigation. With regard to one class of products, prescription drugs and devices, courts traditionally impose a continuing duty of reasonable care to test and monitor after sale to discover product-related risks.

Illustration:

1. ABC manufactures and sells Model 1220 power drills used exclusively in heavy industry. Three years after the Model 1220 is first put on the market, ABC learns that when the drill is used continuously for more than four hours it overheats, causing it to fracture. ABC learns of the overheating problem when the Model 1220 is first used on a new metal alloy that was not previously available, and thus not in use, at the time of first distribution. The new alloy causes the drill to heat well beyond temperatures caused by any other metal for which the Model 1220 has ever been used. No reasonable person could have foreseen the development of the new alloy when any of the drills were sold. Because the risk of overheating was not foreseeable at the time of sale of many of the Model 1220s, those units are not defective within the meaning of § 2. Whether ABC is subject to liability for failing to issue a post-sale warning regarding the risks of overheating is determined based on the factors set forth in Subsection (b)(1) through (4).

d. Requirement that the risk of harm be substantial. For a post-sale duty to arise under this Section, the risk of harm must be at least as great as the level of risk that would require a warning under § 2(c). Because post-sale warnings are invariably costly to provide, and post-sale increases in knowledge of risks are to some extent inevitable, no duty arises after the time of sale to issue warnings regarding product-related accidents that occur infrequently and are not likely to cause substantial harm. If post-sale acquisition of knowledge of adverse outcomes that are both infrequent and insubstantial were to trigger a post-sale duty to warn, sellers would face costly and potentially crushing burdens.

e. Requirement that those to whom a warning might be provided be identifiable. The problem of identifying those to whom product warnings might be provided is especially relevant in the post-sale context. When products are originally sold or distributed, most often the seller accompanies the product, together with its packaging, with whatever warnings are appropriate. When knowledge of product-related risk is available to the seller only after sale, it may be difficult for the seller to determine who, in the general population of product users and consumers, is in a position to respond to warnings effectively. In some instances, customer records may identify the population to whom warnings should be provided. Individual names and addresses are not necessarily required. Records may indicate classes of product users, or geographically limited markets. But when no such records are available, the seller's inability to identify those for whom warnings would be useful may properly prevent a post-sale duty to warn from arising. See Comment *g*.

Illustration:

2. ABC has manufactured and distributed vacuum cleaners commercially to millions of consumers over the course of many years. Only scanty and incomplete sales records have been kept by retailers, and it is practically impossible for ABC to identify who among the consuming public owns and operates its vacuums. Five years after the first commercial distribution of Model 14, ABC discovers a risk when the Model 14 is used to vacuum dust from a chemical carpet cleaner newly introduced to the market. No reasonable person in ABC's position would have foreseen the risk previously, and thus the Model 14 was not defective at time of original sale. The difficulty of ABC's identifying users of its Model 14 vacuum, together with the frequency and severity of the risk, must be weighed by the court in determining whether ABC owes a post-sale duty to warn of the newly discovered risk.

f. The reasonableness of assuming that those to whom a warning might be provided are unaware of the risk. To justify the cost of providing a post-sale warning, it must reasonably appear that those to whom a warning might be provided are unaware of the risk. See § 2, Comment *j*. Similarly, even if knowledge of the risk reasonably becomes available to the seller only after the original sale, if users and consumers are at that time generally aware of the risk a post-sale warning is not required.

g. The seller's ability to communicate the warning effectively to those who are in a position to act to prevent harm. For a post-sale duty to warn to arise, the seller must reasonably be able to communicate the warning to those identified as appropriate recipients. When original customer sales records indicate which individuals are probably using and consuming the product in question, direct communication of a warning may be feasible. When direct communication is not feasible, it may be necessary to utilize the public media to disseminate information regarding risks of substantial harm. As the group to whom warnings might be provided increases in size, costs of communicating warnings may increase and their effectiveness may decrease.

h. Requirement that those to whom a post-sale warning might be provided be able to act effectively to reduce the risk. To justify the potentially high cost of providing a post-sale warning, those to whom such warnings are provided must be in a position to reduce or prevent product-caused harm. Such recipients of warnings need not be original purchasers of the product, so long as they are able to reduce risk effectively.

i. Requirement that the risk of harm be sufficiently great to justify providing a post-sale warning. Compared with the costs of providing warnings attendant upon the original sale of a product, the costs of providing post-sale warnings are typically greater. In the post-sale context, identifying those who should receive a warning and communicating the warning to them can require large expenditures. Courts recognize these burdens and hold that a post-sale warning is required only when the risk of harm is sufficiently great to justify undertaking a post-sale warning program. Subsection (b)(4) requires that, even for a substantial risk, a seller owes a duty to warn after the time of sale only if the risk of harm is sufficiently great to justify the cost of providing a post-sale warning. The test defining unreasonable conduct is that which governs negligence generally. See Restatement, Second, Torts § 291.

j. Distinguishing post-sale failures to warn from defects existing at the time of sale. When a product is defective at the time of sale liability can be established without reference to a post-sale duty to warn. A seller who discovers after sale that its product was defective at the time of sale within the meaning of this Restatement cannot generally absolve itself of liability by issuing a post-sale warning. As long as the original defect is causally related to the harm suffered by the plaintiff, a prima facie case under this Restatement can be established notwithstanding reasonable post-sale efforts to warn. Of course, even when a product is defective at the time of sale a seller may have an independent obligation to issue a post-sale warning based on the rule stated in this Section. Thus, a plaintiff may seek recovery based on both a time-of-sale defect and a post-sale failure to warn.

Illustrations:

3. ABC manufactures and sells Model 1220 power drills used exclusively in heavy industry. ABC sells a Model 1220 drill to XYZ Industries. Six months after the sale to XYZ, ABC learns that when the Model 1220 drill is used continuously for more than four hours it overheats, causing the drill to fracture. ABC should have discovered this problem through reasonable testing before the drill was put on the market. Had ABC done so, it could have adopted a reasonable alternative design that would have avoided the problem. Model 1220 is thus defective within the meaning of § 2(b). After ABC discovers the overheating problem, it sends warning letters to all owners of the Model 1220, including XYZ, that the machine should not be used for more than four hours continuously and that after prolonged use the machine should be turned off for 30 minutes to cool. The post-sale warning states that failure to do so could cause harm. XYZ posts the warning in its plant. Several months thereafter, XYZ's employee, E, is working on the machine during a rush job and the Model 1220 is allowed to run continuously for more than four hours. The machine overheats and the drill shatters, causing harm to E. Notwithstanding ABC's post-sale efforts to warn, ABC is subject to liability for the harm to E caused by the defectively designed Model 1220 under §§ 1 and 2. Whether E's recovery should be reduced because of contributory negligence or comparative fault is governed by § 17. Whether E should be denied recovery due to the absence of proximate causation is governed by § 15.

4. Same facts as Illustration 3 except that ABC fails to issue a post-sale warning after it discovers the overheating problem. E may bring an action based on a § 2 defect and may also assert the failure of ABC to provide a post-sale warning of the overheating problem. Whether it is reasonable also to subject ABC to liability for failure to issue a post-sale warning is determined by applying the factors set forth in Subsection (b)(1) through (4).

REPORTERS' NOTE

Comment *a. Rationale.* A growing number of jurisdictions have taken the position that a post-sale duty to warn is warranted under appropriate circumstances. See, e.g., Fell v. Kewanee Farm Equip. Co., 457 N.W.2d 911, 920–21 (Iowa 1990); La. Rev. Stat. Ann. § 9:2800.57(C) (West 1991); Owens–Illinois, Inc. v. Zenobia, 601 A.2d 633, 645–47 (Md.1992); Comstock v. General Motors Corp., 99 N.W.2d 627 (Mich.1959); Hodder v. Goodyear Tire & Rubber Co., 426 N.W.2d 826 (Minn.1988); Ohio Rev. Code Ann. § 2307.76 (Banks–Baldwin 1988); Patton v. Hutchinson Wil–Rich Mfg. Co., 861 P.2d 1299 (Kan.1993); Dixon v. Jacobsen Mfg. Co., 637 A.2d 915, 922–24 (N.J. Super. Ct. App. Div. 1994); Cover v. Cohen, 461 N.E.2d 864, 871–72 (N.Y.1984); Crowston v. Goodyear Tire & Rubber Co., 521 N.W.2d 401, 406–10 (N.D.1994); Smith v. F.M.C. Corp., 754 F.2d 873, 877 (10th Cir.1985) (applying Oklahoma law); Walton v. Avco Corp., 610 A.2d 454, 459 (Pa.1992) (although product was not defective as originally sold, court recognizes a post-sale duty to warn when defects are brought to its attention); Novak v. Navistar Int'l Transp. Corp., 46 F.3d 844 (8th Cir.1995) (applying South Dakota law); Island Creek Coal Co. v. Lake Shore, Inc., 832 F.2d 274, 280–81 (4th Cir.1987) (applying Virginia law); McAlpin v. Leeds & Northrup Co., 912 F.Supp. 207 (W.D.Va.1996); Wash. Rev. Code § 7.72.030(1)(c) (1992); Kozlowski v. John E. Smith's Sons Co., 275 N.W.2d 915 (Wis.1979).

Commentators have been generally favorable to the imposition of a post-sale duty to warn. See, e.g., V. Schwartz, The Post–Sale Duty to Warn: Two Unfortunate Forks in the Road to a Reasonable Doctrine, 58 N.Y.U. L. Rev. 892, 896 (1983):

> The reasonableness standard is flexible and accommodates society's competing desires to provide product users with complete product information and yet to avoid placing unfair or unjustifiable burdens on manufacturers. Thus, the facts of a particular case, such as the gravity and likelihood of harm, the number of persons affected, and the economic cost and practical problems associated with identifying and contacting current product users, should all be relevant in determining whether a manufacturer has satisfactorily discharged a post-sale duty to warn.

Also see Madden, Products Liability, § 10.13 (2d ed. 1988 and 1994 supp.); Note, The Manufacturer's Duty to Notify of Subsequent Safety Improvements, 33 Stan. L. Rev. 1087, 1098 & n.42 (1981). Model Uniform Products Liability Act, § 104(C)(6) provides that a claim for products liability may arise:

> . . . where a reasonably prudent manufacturer should have learned about a danger connected with the product after it was manufactured. In such a case, the manufacturer is under an obligation to act with regard to the danger as a reasonably prudent manufacturer in the same or similar circumstances. This obligation is satisfied if the manufacturer makes reasonable efforts to inform product users or a person who may be reasonably expected to assure that action is taken to avoid the harm, or that the risk of harm is explained to the actual product user.

Some courts, however, reject the imposition of any post-sale duty to warn if the product was not defective at time of sale. See, e.g., Romero v. International Harvester Co., 979 F.2d 1444 (10th Cir.1992) (applying Colorado law); Carrizales v. Rheem Mfg. Co., 589 N.E.2d 569, 579 (Ill.App.Ct. 1991); Birchler v. Gehl Co., 88 F.3d 518 (7th Cir.1996) (Illinois imposes no general continuing duty to warn); Syrie v. Knoll Int'l, 748 F.2d 304, 311–12 (5th Cir.1984) (applying Texas law); Estate of Kimmel v. Clark Equip. Co., 773 F.Supp. 828, 831 (W.D.Va. 1991). But see McAlpin v. Leeds & Northrup Co., 912 F.Supp. 207 (W.D.Va.1996) (holding that *Kimmel's* refusal to recognize a post-sale duty to warn is limited to cases brought under implied warranty of merchantability but that claims brought for negligent post-sale failure-to-warn are actionable).

Some courts take the position that though there may be a post-sale duty to warn of risks, there is no post-sale duty to inform about safety improvements in the product that would reduce risk. See, e.g., Williams v. Monarch Mach. Tool Co., Inc., 26 F.3d 228, 232 (1st Cir.1994) (applying Massachusetts law). It should be noted that Massachusetts is one of the few states that find liability for failure to warn of risks even though they were not knowable at the time of sale. See Simmons v. Monarch Mach. Tool Co., 596 N.E.2d 318, 320 n. 3 (Mass.1992). This rule was first set forth in Hayes v. Ariens Co., 462 N.E.2d 273, 277 (Mass.1984)

> [T]he adequacy of a warning is measured by the warning that would be given . . . by an ordinarily prudent vendor who, at [time of sale], is fully aware of the risks presented by the product. A defendant vendor is held to that standard regardless of the knowledge of risks that he actually had, or reasonably should have had when the sale took place.

In Massachusetts there is no need for a post-sale duty to warn of risks. All such post-sale knowledge is imputed to the seller and becomes part of its duty to warn. Thus, the distinction between duty to warn of risks and the duty to inform about safety improvements is clearly established.

In Patton v. Hutchinson Wil–Rich Mfg. Co., 861 P.2d 1299, 1311 (Kan. 1993), the court said that "For business reasons, a manufacturer may seek to bring product improvement to the attention of its past customers, and it should be encouraged to do so. . . . " Nonetheless the court held that it would not "impose a requirement that a manufacturer seek out past customers and notify them of changes in the state of the art." The *Patton* court did, however, impose a post-sale duty to warn about risks. Also see Lynch v. McStome & Lincoln Plaza Assocs., 548 A.2d 1276 (Pa.Super.Ct.1988).

This Section does not draw a sharp distinction between failure to warn of risk and failure to inform about safety improvements. If a newly discovered risk imposes risk of serious harm and safety improvements can be practically implemented, there may in certain instances be a duty to inform the buyer of the availability of such safety improvements. See Kozlowski v. John E. Smith's Sons, Co., 275 N.W.2d 915 (Wis.1979). Whether a plaintiff can establish the four factors for imposing liability set forth in § 10 will depend on the facts of each case. It is clear that in most cases it will be difficult to establish each of the four § 10 factors that are a necessary predicate for a post-sale duty to warn if the warning is merely to inform of the availability of a product-safety improvement.

b. When a reasonable person in the seller's position would provide a warning. Factors (1) through (4) are mentioned in many of the post-sale cases. See, e.g., Patton v. Hutchinson Wil–Rich Mfg. Co., 861 P.2d 1299, 1314–15 (Kan.1993); Cover v. Cohen, 461 N.E.2d 864, 872 (N.Y.1984); Crowston v. Goodyear Tire & Rubber Co., 521 N.W.2d 401, 409 (N.D.1994). Also see cases cited in the Reporters' Note to Comment *a*, supra.

c. Requirement that seller or other distributor knows or should know of the product-related risk. In non-drug cases there appears to be no practical post-sale duty to investigate or test a product not defective within the meaning of § 2 unless information comes to the attention of the product seller that there is a problem attendant to its use. An excellent discussion of this aspect of post-sale duty is found in Kociemba v. G.D. Searle Co., 707 F.Supp. 1517, 1528–29 (D.Minn.1989). In discussing the post-sale duty to warn, the court said:

> Minnesota law has traditionally recognized three causes of action based on negligence in products liability cases: negligent design, negligent manufacture and negligent failure to warn. [citation omitted] Plaintiff correctly asserts, and defendant concedes, that a manufacturer has a duty to inspect and test its products. Defendant argues, however, that this duty is subsumed in one of the three causes of action mentioned above.
>
> The Court finds defendant's argument persuasive. The Court elevated the duty to test to an independent cause of action by including an interrogatory on the special verdict form asking whether Searle's negligent failure to test caused plaintiff's injuries.
>
> Presumably, the reason that manufacturers are under a duty to test their products is to discover defects or dangers associated with use of the products. Once the manufacturer has discovered a defect or danger the manufacturer should either change the product's design or manufacturing process, or warn consumers of the danger associated with using the product.
>
> Thus, unless the manufacturer's breach of its duty to test leads the manufacturer to produce a product that is defective in design, manufacture, or warning, no injury can result. If the manufacturer designs the product safely, manufactures the product safely, and provides an adequate warning of dangers inherent in the use of the product, then a failure to test the product cannot, standing alone, cause any injury. The duty to test is a subpart of the other three duties because a breach of the duty to test cannot by itself cause any injury....
>
> ... Minnesota products liability law recognizes a continuing duty to warn of dangers associated with using a product. Hodder v. Goodyear Tire & Rubber Co., 426 N.W.2d 826, 833 (Minn.1988). In *Hodder*, the Minnesota Supreme Court held that a manufacturer is under a continuing post-sale duty to warn in certain "special cases." 426 N.W.2d at 833. The *Hodder* court identified the special circumstances in that case that warranted imposing a continuing duty to warn.

First, the court noted that it had been evident since the late 1950's that there were problems with the Goodyear product at issue. 426 N.W.2d at 833. Further, Goodyear continued to sell the product until 1969, advertised it until 1977, and still sells tires and tubes for use with the product. *Id.* Finally, the court pointed out that Goodyear had undertaken a duty to warn of defects associated with the product (presumably when it was first marketed). *Id.*

This Court has already held that the duty to test is a subpart of the duty to warn. It is logical that a continuing duty to warn would have as a subpart a continuing duty to test. Although Minnesota courts have up until now only recognized a continuing duty to warn, recognizing a continuing duty to test which is subsumed as a part of the continuing duty to warn is a consistent extension of existing law. Therefore, this Court holds that its instruction to the jury concerning a manufacturer's continuing duty to test is not erroneous.

Of course, any continuing duty to test would also be limited to "special cases." *Hodder*, 426 N.W.2d at 833. Courts should only apply a continuing duty to test when the type of special circumstances identified by the *Hodder* court exist: knowledge of a problem with the product, continued sale or advertising of the product, and a pre-existing duty to warn of dangers associated with the product.

Limiting the continuing duty test to cases where the manufacturer has knowledge of problems with a product alleviates defendant's concern that this duty will impose a crushing burden on manufacturers to retest products. If a manufacturer has no information concerning potential dangers associated with a product, it will be under no duty to continually test the product. Conversely, if a manufacturer does obtain sufficient credible information that a product already in use is potentially dangerous, the manufacturer should test that product to determine the extent of any danger, and then issue an appropriate warning or product recall.

In cases involving prescription drugs the courts have imposed a continuous duty to keep abreast of scientific developments touching upon the manufacturer's product and to notify the medical profession of additional side effects discovered from its use. The drug manufacturer's duty to warn is, therefore, commensurate not only with its actual knowledge gained from research and adverse reaction reports, but also with its constructive knowledge as measured by scientific literature and other available means of communication. Wooderson v. Ortho Pharm. Corp., 681 P.2d 1038, 1050–51 (Kan.1984). Also see Schenebeck v. Sterling Drug, Inc., 423 F.2d 919, 922 (8th Cir.1970) (applying Arkansas law); O'Hare v. Merck & Co., 381 F.2d 286 (8th Cir.1967) (applying Minnesota law); Baker v. St. Agnes Hosp., 421 N.Y.S.2d 81, 85 (N.Y.App. Div.1979).

§ 11. Liability of Commercial Product Seller or Distributor for Harm Caused by Post-Sale Failure to Recall Product

One engaged in the business of selling or otherwise distributing products is subject to liability for harm to persons or property caused by the seller's failure to recall a product after the time of sale or distribution if:

(a)(1) a governmental directive issued pursuant to a statute or administrative regulation specifically requires the seller or distributor to recall the product; or

(2) the seller or distributor, in the absence of a recall requirement under Subsection (a)(1), undertakes to recall the product; and

(b) the seller or distributor fails to act as a reasonable person in recalling the product.

Comment:

a. Rationale. Duties to recall products impose significant burdens on manufacturers. Many product lines are periodically redesigned so that they become safer over time. If every improvement in product safety were to trigger a common-law duty to recall, manufacturers would face incalculable costs every time they sought to make their product lines better and safer. Moreover, even when a product is defective within the meaning of § 2, § 3, or § 4, an involuntary duty to recall should be imposed on the seller only by a governmental directive issued pursuant to statute or regulation. Issues relating to product recalls are best evaluated by governmental agencies capable of gathering adequate data regarding the ramifications of such undertakings. The duty to recall or repair should be distinguished from a post-sale duty to warn about product hazards discovered after sale. See §§ 10 and 13.

Illustration:

1. MNO Corp. has manufactured and distributed washing machines for five years. MNO develops an improved model that includes a safety device that reduces the risk of harm to users. The washing machines sold previously conformed to the best technology available at time of sale and were not defective when sold. MNO is under no common-law obligation to recall previously-distributed machines in order to retrofit them with the new safety device.

b. Failure to recall when recall is specifically required by a governmental directive issued pursuant to statute or other governmental regulation. When a product recall is specifically required by a governmental directive issued pursuant to a statute or regulation, failure reasonably to comply with the relevant directive subjects the seller or other distributor to liability for harm caused by such failure. For the product seller or other distributor to be subject to liability under Subsection (a)(1), the directive must specifically require recall. It is not sufficient that an agency has the power to direct product recalls with regard to the product in question if the agency has failed to issue a specific recall directive, nor will it suffice that a general duty to recall is imposed by statute or regulation and the plaintiff alleges that the defendant breached that duty by failing to recall in the absence of a specific directive to do so. When a directive issued pursuant to a statute or regulation specifically requires product recall, the violation by the seller of that requirement constitutes actionable negligence. See § 4, Comment *f.*

To give rise to the duty to recall under this Section, the governmental directive must require the defendant to recall the product during the time period in which the plaintiff claims the defendant breached the duty to recall. For example, if the regulatory scheme calls for a stay of the recall directive pending appeal, no duty to recall arises under this Section until the appeal is decided in a way that makes the recall directive binding on the defendant.

Illustrations:

2. The same facts as Illustration 1, except that a federal agency directs MNO to recall the machines distributed by MNO. Thereafter, MNO unreasonably fails to notify machine owners, whom it can reasonably identify, about the recall. MNO is subject to liability for harm caused by its noncompliance with the governmental directive to recall the machines.

3. The same facts as Illustration 1, except that the agency issues no directive to MNO regarding the washing machines. A plaintiff argues that MNO owed a general tort duty under the statute to recall the washing machine, which the plaintiff claims was defectively designed as defined in § 2(b) and caused the claimant's harm. MNO is not subject to liability under Subsection (a)(1).

c. *When seller or other distributor voluntarily undertakes to recall.* Some courts have held that, when a seller, under no statutory or regulatory obligation to undertake a recall, volunteers to do so, the seller is subject to liability for failing to act reasonably to recall the product. The rationale for this rule lies partly in the general rule that one who undertakes a rescue, and thus induces other would-be rescuers to forbear, must act reasonably in following through. In the context of products liability, courts appear to assume that voluntary recalls are typically undertaken in the anticipation that, if the seller does not recall voluntarily, it will be directed to do so by a governmental regulator. Having presumably forestalled the regulatory recall directive, the seller should be under a common-law duty to follow through on its commitment to recall. In some instances voluntary recalls are subject to regulation by governmental agencies. Whether product sellers are subject to, or protected from, liability for harm caused by noncompliance or compliance with the terms of such regulations is governed by Restatement, Second, of Torts §§ 286–288C. See § 4, Comment *f*.

Illustration:

4. The same facts as Illustration 1, except that MNO voluntarily announces that it will recall and retrofit the washing machines it distributed earlier, and it thereafter unreasonably fails to notify owners whom it can reasonably identify about the recall. MNO is subject to liability under Subsection (a)(2) for harm caused by its failure to act reasonably in undertaking to recall the machines.

d. Distinguishing liability for post-sale failure to recall from liability for the sale or other distribution of defective products. When a product is defective at the time of sale and the defect causes harm to persons or property, the seller is subject to liability whether or not the seller attempts to eliminate the defect by post-sale recall. The fact that one who owns or possesses a product that was defective at time of sale does not respond to a recall notice does not necessarily eliminate the causal connection between the original defect and the plaintiff's harm. See § 15. It may be foreseeable that product owners will fail to respond to recall notices. In a case involving harm caused by an original defect at the time of sale, the plaintiff's failure to act on a recall notice may be taken into account under the rules stated in § 17 governing comparative responsibility. In appropriate cases a plaintiff may seek recovery based on both a claim of original defect and a claim of post-sale failure to recall.

Illustrations:

5. XYZ Motor Co. manufactures and sells the Buster Sedan. XYZ learned that the Buster tends to oversteer dangerously. XYZ should have discovered the problem before the Buster Sedan was put on the market, when it could have adopted a reasonable alternative design. The Buster Sedan was thus defectively designed within the meaning of § 2(b). The National Highway Traffic Safety Administration directed XYZ to recall the Buster to correct the oversteering problem. Sonia Rand, who had purchased a Buster Sedan, received a recall notice. Sonia did not respond to the notice. Six months later, while driving on the highway, Sonia lost control of her car. A trier of fact could find that the oversteering in Sonia's Buster contributed to her loss of control. XYZ is subject to liability under §§ 1 and 2(b) for the injury

caused by the defectively designed Buster Sedan. In her action based on the design defect, Sonia's failure to bring her car in for repair is relevant to the issue of legal causation under § 15 and the issue of comparative responsibility under § 17.

6. Same facts as Illustration 5, except that XYZ failed to undertake the recall directed by the National Highway Traffic Safety Administration. Sonia suffers injury after the time a recall notice should have been issued. XYZ is subject to liability under this Section for failure to recall. XYZ is also subject to liability under § 2(b) based on defective design. Whether XYZ is subject to liability for post-sale failure to warn is governed by the rules stated in § 10.

7. Same facts as Illustration 5, except that the National Highway Traffic Safety Administration refused, after considering the problem, to direct a recall. XYZ is subject to liability to Sonia based on a § 2(b) design defect. XYZ is not subject to liability under this Section for failure to recall. Whether XYZ is subject to liability for post-sale failure to warn is governed by the rules stated in § 10.

e. Causal relationship between failure to recall and plaintiff's harm. For a seller to be subject to liability for post-sale failure to recall, the plaintiff must establish not only that the seller unreasonably failed to recall the product under this Section, but also that the defect that was the subject of recall was a legal cause of the plaintiff's harm. See § 15.

REPORTERS' NOTE

a. Rationale. The most significant recent case supporting the general rule is Gregory v. Cincinnati, Inc., 538 N.W.2d 325 (Mich.1995). See also Romero v. International Harvester Co., 979 F.2d 1444, 1449–50 (10th Cir. 1992) (applying Colorado law) (no duty to recall and retrofit a product that was nondefective under standards existing at the time of manufacture but that could subsequently be made safer by a later-developed safety device or design improvement); Zettle v. Handy Mfg. Co., 837 F.Supp. 222, 224 (E.D.Mich.N.Div. 1992) (if product was nondefective at time of original sale, product manufacturers have no duty to retrofit their products with safety devices that become available after the date of manufacture); Eschenburg v. Navistar Int'l Transp. Corp., 829 F.Supp. 210, 214 (E.D.Mich.S.D.1993) (no duty to recall product even if defective when it left the manufacturer's control); Wallace v. Dorsey Trailers Southeast, Inc., 849 F.2d 341, 344 (8th Cir.1988) (applying Missouri law) (court held that manufacturer was not negligent as a matter of law for failing to retrofit allegedly defective aerial bucket lift); Patton v. Hutchinson Wil–Rich Mfg. Co., 253 Kan. 741, 861 P.2d 1299, 1315 (Kan. 1993) (court recognized a post-sale duty to warn but held that "product recalls are properly the business of administrative agencies as suggested by federal statutes"); Lynch v. McStome & Lincoln Plaza Assocs., 548 A.2d 1276, 1279 (Pa.Super.Ct.1988) (court leaves open the question of whether a manufacturer has a post-sale duty to warn of hazards that present a clear threat to the safety of the users but holds that there is no duty to retrofit or to inform users of new safety improvements). But see Downing v. Overhead Door Corp., 707 P.2d 1027, 1033 (Colo.App.1985) (when product is defective at time of sale, the manufacturer has a duty "either to remedy such defects, or if a complete remedy is not feasible, to give users adequate instructions concerning methods for minimizing danger"); Braniff Airways, Inc. v. Curtiss–Wright Corp., 411 F.2d 451 (2d Cir.1969) (suggesting that a manufacturer has a duty to remedy defects that are not discovered until after the product is sold).

Comment c. When seller or other distributor voluntarily undertakes to recall. Although a seller may be under no statutory or regulatory obligation to recall the product that causes harm, if it volunteers to recall it will be subject to liability for unreasonably failing to do so. See, e.g., Bell Helicopter Co. v. Bradshaw, 594 S.W.2d 519, 532 (Tex.Civ.App.1979) ("Once the duty [to recall and repair] was assumed, Bell had an obligation to complete the remedy by using reasonable means available to it. . . . "); Blossman Gas Co. v. Williams, 375 S.E.2d 117 (Ga.App.1988) (once defendant volunteers, it must use reasonable care to follow through). Also see V. Schwartz, The Post Sale Duty to Warn: Two Unfortunate Forks in the Road to a Reasonable Doctrine, 58 N.Y.U. L. Rev. 892, 897–901 (1983).

Comment d. Distinguishing liability for post-sale failure to recall from liability for the sale or other distribution of defective products. There is a paucity of authority discussing the legal effect of the efforts of a manufacturer to recall its products when such efforts are not successful in avoiding injury due to the fact that either dealers or purchasers do not take advantage of the recall. The little authority there is agrees with the position taken in the Comment that such conduct is relevant to issues of causation and comparative fault. See, e.g., Pan-Alaska Fisheries, Inc. v. Marine Constr. & Design Co., 565 F.2d 1129 (9th Cir.1977); Ford Motor Co. v. Robert J. Poeschl, Inc., 98 Cal.Rptr. 702 (Cal.Ct.App.1971); Anderson v. Whittaker Corp., 692 F.Supp. 734, 758 (W.D.Mich.1987); Brown v. Caterpillar Tractor Co., 741 F.2d 656, 661 (3d Cir.1984) (applying Pennsylvania law); Gracyalny v. Westinghouse Elec. Corp., 723 F.2d 1311, 1322 (7th Cir.1983) (applying Wisconsin law).

CHAPTER 3

LIABILITY OF SUCCESSORS AND APPARENT MANUFACTURERS

---

§ 12. Liability of Successor for Harm Caused by Defective Products Sold Commercially by Predecessor

A successor corporation or other business entity that acquires assets of a predecessor corporation or other business entity is subject to liability for harm to persons or property caused by a defective product sold or otherwise distributed commercially by the predecessor if the acquisition:

(a) is accompanied by an agreement for the successor to assume such liability; or

(b) results from a fraudulent conveyance to escape liability for the debts or liabilities of the predecessor; or

(c) constitutes a consolidation or merger with the predecessor; or

(d) results in the successor becoming a continuation of the predecessor.

Comment:

a. History. The rule that a corporation or other business entity is not, in the absence of the circumstances described in Subsections (a) through (d), subject to liability for harm caused by defective products sold by a corporation from which it purchases productive assets derives from both products liability and corporate law principles. When the alleged successor purchases the assets piecemeal with little or no further continuity of operations between the two corporations or other business entities, the nonliability of the alleged successor derives primarily from the fact that the successor is not within the basic liability rule in § 1 of this Restatement: "one ... *who sells or distributes* a defective product is subject to liability for harm ... caused by the defective product." (Emphasis added.) Thus, when one corporation commercially sells products, some of which are defective, and later transfers its productive assets to another corporation that uses those assets to manufacture products of its own, the purchaser of the assets is not liable for harm caused by a defective product sold earlier by the transferor because the transferee did not "sell or distribute" the defective product that caused the harm. When the alleged successor receives value in the form of the transferor's goodwill and continues to manufacture products of the same sort as manufactured earlier by the predecessor, and thus to some extent constitutes a continuation of the predecessor, the general rule of nonliability derives primarily from the law governing corporations, which favors the free alienability of corporate assets and limits shareholders' exposures to liability in order to facilitate the formation and investment of capital.

When the transferor goes out of business upon, or shortly after, a transfer of productive assets, the rights of plaintiffs injured by defective products sold earlier by the transferor may be adversely affected. For tort plaintiffs who have existing judgments outstanding against the predecessor at the time of transfer and dissolution, the law governing corporations and other business entities provides, within limits, legal protection. Creditors, including tort creditors, who hold existing judgments against a corporation that is in the process of transferring its assets and going out of business may satisfy those claims out of the proceeds from the transfer of assets. Moreover, if the proceeds from the transfer of assets are distributed to shareholders of the transferor corporation in violation of applicable state corporation law or fraudulent transfer law, existing creditors of the corporation may pursue the proceeds in the hands of the transferor's shareholders. These rules, in some states expressed in statutes, are designed to protect, within the limits of practicality, creditors who are identifiable at the time of the transfer of the predecessor's assets to the successor corporation and the transferor's dissolution. The same principles have been applied to the transfer of assets of proprietorships, partnerships, and other business entities.

Tort claimants who, as a result of defective products sold by a predecessor corporation, seek recovery only after transfer of assets to a successor corporation often face difficulties in attempting to bring their claims within the foregoing legal rules. Their claims typically accrue after the predecessor corporation has lawfully distributed to its shareholders the proceeds from the transfer of assets and has ceased to exist. Under these circumstances, tort claimants who were not existing creditors at the time of the transfer of assets ordinarily have no recourse against the predecessor's shareholders. Unless they can pursue their claims against the successor corporation, or can reach other funds provided by existing insurance or by a statute, their only practical remedy lies with retailers and wholesalers in the predecessor's distributive chain, who may not be available as a practical matter. Statutes and judicial precedents governing the rights of creditors after a corporate assets transfer and dissolution generally do not address this problem of post-transfer claims accrual.

Few precedents recognize tort claims against the successor corporation for harm caused by defective products sold by the predecessor unless the transaction by which productive assets are acquired meets criteria established by one of several traditional exceptions. These exceptions apply generally to creditors whose claims accrue after dissolution of the predecessor, and are not limited to products liability claimants. They fall into two basic categories: those in which some conduct of the successor, in addition to acquiring the predecessor's assets, justifies holding the successor responsible (the successor either contractually agrees to be liable or knowingly participates in a fraudulent asset transfer); and those in which the successor itself can be said to have sold or distributed the defective products because the successor constitutes the same juridical entity as the predecessor, perhaps in somewhat different form (the successor merges with, or constitutes a "mere continuation" of, the predecessor). Under this Section, a products liability claimant has a recognized claim against a successor for harm caused by defective products distributed by the predecessor in these circumstances.

A minority of jurisdictions impose liability on a successor corporation based on a broader concept of continuation of the business enterprise, even when there is no continuity of shareholders, officers, or directors. Some courts hold that the continuation of a predecessor's product line by the successor is sufficient to support imposition of successor liability for harm caused by defects in products sold before the assets transfer.

b. Rationale. Limiting the liability of successor corporations to the circumstances described in this Section is supported by fairness and efficiency considerations. An alleged successor that purchases the predecessor's productive assets piecemeal, other than as part of a going concern, cannot, by that fact alone, be said to have either manufactured or sold defective products distributed by the predecessor before the transfer of assets. In the absence of circumstances in which the successor could be said to constitute a continuation of the predecessor, or somehow to have prejudiced subsequent tort plaintiffs by its own pre-acquisition conduct, imposing liability on a business entity that did not make or distribute the defective products that caused harm could be justified only because it increases the amount of money available post-acquisition out of which to satisfy plaintiffs' claims. But that alone cannot be justification for successor liability. Thus, imposing liability on the piecemeal purchase of productive assets would, for no compelling reason, impede the free alienability of corporate assets, thereby discouraging shareholder investment of capital and increasing social costs.

Imposing liability on successor corporations constitutes acceptable public policy when the successor either agrees to be liable or is implicated in the transfer of assets in a way that, without such liability, would unfairly deprive future products liability plaintiffs of the remedies that would otherwise have been available against the predecessor. Subsections (a) through (d) describe the types of corporate asset transfers that have been determined to justify imposing liability on the successor. Subsection (a) recognizes that contractual promises by the successor to pay subsequent tort claims, for which promises the successor has presumably been compensated, should be honored. Subsection (b) provides that when a business entity makes a fraudulent transfer in which the transferee is implicated, successor liability is appropriate for the same reason that liability would be imposed in favor of other creditors. Thus, a predecessor may arrange an asset transfer at an artificially deflated price, accompanied by an agreement by the successor to compensate either the predecessor, its owners, or its managers in ways that escape easy detection; or a successor may knowingly participate in an asset transfer coupled with a liquidating dividend by the predecessor to its shareholders for the purpose of leaving tort plaintiffs without remedy. If those transfers are fraudulent under applicable state law, imposing tort liability on the transferee for having knowingly participated in such transfers is justified.

Subsections (c) and (d) deal with successors that, in a real sense, did produce and distribute the product that caused the harm, though in a somewhat different organizational form. Subsection (c) deals with the transferor corporation that merges by law or in fact into the transferee, typically with no substantial change in corporate management or ownership. Subsection (d) concerns the transfer of corporate assets in the context of a transaction involving only a change in organizational form. In both these situations, liability for harm caused by defective products distributed previously should be imposed on the business entity that emerges from the transaction. In substance, if not in form, the post-transfer entity distributed the defective products and should be held responsible for them. If mere changes in form were allowed to control substance, corporations intending to continue operations could periodically wash themselves clean of potential liability at practically zero cost, in sham transactions, and thereby unreasonably undermine incentives for producers and distributors to invest in product safety and unfairly deny tort plaintiffs adequate remedies when defective products later cause harm.

A small minority of courts have fashioned successor liability rules more advantageous to products liability claimants than the rules stated in this Section. Those minority rules, in effect, extend the "change in form only" exception just described to include circumstances in which the successor continues a product line previously distributed by the predecessor. The minority position is based on the belief that a successor who purchases productive assets should not be allowed to benefit from receiving the goodwill and reputation of the predecessor's business without the burden of responding in tort to claims for harm caused by products sold by the predecessor prior to transfer. An argument advanced to support this minority view is that holding successors liable reduces the price that predecessors receive for transferring assets, thereby helping to strengthen incentives for the managers to invest in care before the transfer of the business.

This reasoning has proven unpersuasive to a substantial majority of courts that have considered the issue. Extending successor liability beyond the exceptions set forth in Subsections (a) through (d) would, in the judgment of most courts, be unfair and socially wasteful. Post-transfer plaintiffs harmed by pre-transfer defects have a right to expect that a transfer of assets will not be allowed to prejudice financially their chances of satisfying a judgment; they have no legitimate claim that the transfer should increase those chances over what they would have been if no transfer had occurred. In the likely event that the successor is financially stronger than the predecessor, imposing a broader liability for pre-transfer product defects would unjustifiably increase the funds available to those injured by such defects compared with what would have been available to them if no transfer had taken place.

As courts have recognized, it would be difficult, and often impossible, to implement and administer a liability rule that attempted to limit post-transfer plaintiffs' rights to an aggregate amount equal to the net value of the predecessor before transfer. Tort judgments are imposed independently of one another, in various jurisdictions; no central authority exists to assure that, in the aggregate, tort judgments do not exceed a predetermined total amount. Thus, the expanded successor liability rules in a minority of states, not limited to time-of-transfer net value, replace one risk of injustice—that the assets transfer may unfairly reduce plaintiffs' recoveries in cases that do not satisfy the traditional exceptions (reflected in Subsections (a) through (d))—with another, possibly greater, injustice: that the transfer may give tort plaintiffs a windfall at the expense of companies who engage in asset transfers and, in turn, at the expense of the consuming public.

Moreover, a majority of courts have concluded that the substantial social costs of a more expansive liability rule would be incurred without actually benefiting very many tort plaintiffs. In most instances, the magnitude of future liability for products distributed pre-transfer is difficult, if not impossible, to assess. As a majority of courts have recognized, the result of imposing successor liability as a general rule would be to depress the prices for transferred assets to the point that piecemeal disposition of assets, which clearly would not subject the buyers to liability, would be a preferable alternative to sale of the assets as part of a going concern. In that event, the products liability claimant harmed by a pre-transfer product defect would still run the risk of ending up with an uncollectible judgment. The benefits to society of preserving the predecessor's assets as a going concern would be sacrificed, with no commensurate benefits to tort claimants.

And even if a more expansive successor liability rule did not invariably lead to piecemeal asset transfers, such a liability rule would depress the prices received for going-concern transfers to an extent that would threaten to undermine the objectives of the law governing corporations. One of the purposes served by the corporate structure is to provide limitation and certainty of risk to shareholders in order to encourage capital formation. Thus, the shareholders' initial risk is limited to the value of their shares of stock and they are able to withdraw from an investment by sale of the stock without incurring future potential liability. A more expansive successor liability rule might threaten shareholders' investments by significantly restraining corporate assets transfers, thereby tending to frustrate corporation law's objective of encouraging shareholder investment.

Some critics of the majority rule argue that, when the successor continues to manufacture the same products as the predecessor, often under the same trademark, consumers have legitimate expectations that the successor will stand behind the predecessor's products. Disappointing these expectations is unfair, according to the critics, quite apart from the effects of successor liability upon the formation of capital. But this argument overlooks the reality that the predecessor's products that cause harm in these cases were distributed prior to the assets transfer, when there could be no reliance by consumers on the financial viability of the successor. One cannot logically rely on post-transfer expectations regarding the successor to justify the imposition of liability on the successor for pre-transfer distributions by the predecessor.

c. Nonliability in the absence of special circumstances. In the absence of the circumstances described in Subsections (a) through (d), a successor company that buys productive assets from another company is not liable for harm caused by a defective product sold or otherwise distributed by the predecessor prior to the successor's acquisition of assets. When the assets are purchased piecemeal, the alleged successor did not "sell or distribute" the product under the liability rule stated in § 1; and attempts to establish continuation of the corporate entity are recognized only under the terms set forth in this Section. The successor is liable under §§ 1–4 for harm caused by defective products it sells after acquisition. In the absence of the circumstances described in this Section, however, the successor is not liable for defective products sold by another prior to that time.

Illustrations:

1. ABC Corp., which manufactures and sells lawn mowers, transfers all its assets to XYZ Corp., a manufacturing corporation with different officers, directors, and shareholders, for cash. ABC then dissolves, distributing the proceeds of the sale to its shareholders. ABC complies with all statutes governing its dissolution, and none of the exceptions in this Section applies. XYZ retains most of ABC's employees and managers and continues to manufacture lawn mowers, some of which are the same as previously manufactured by ABC. A defective lawn mower made and distributed by ABC prior to the transfer of assets to XYZ harms a user three years after the transfer. XYZ is not subject to liability for the harm to the user of the lawn mower.

2. The same facts as Illustration 1, except that a defective lawn mower made and distributed by XYZ after the transfer of assets harms a user three years after the transfer. XYZ is subject to liability for the harm to the user of the lawn mower.

d. Agreement for successor to assume liability. When the successor agrees to assume liabilities for defective products sold by its predecessor, liability is imposed under Subsection (a) in accordance with the terms of the agreement. As a general matter, contract law governs the application of this exception. Courts have interpreted general statements that the successor agrees to assume the liabilities of the predecessor to include products liability claims even though the agreement makes no specific mention of products liability. However, assumption of products liability is not implied by the successor's assumption of specific duties with regard to product service or replacement.

Illustration:

3. The same facts as Illustration 1, except that the transfer-of-assets agreement contains a promise by XYZ to assume all of ABC's liabilities. XYZ is subject to liability for the harm to the user of the lawn mower.

e. Fraudulent transfer in order to avoid debts or liabilities. Subsection (b) incorporates by reference the relevant state law governing fraudulent conveyances and transfers. In contexts other than successor products liability, fraudulent transfers can be set aside on behalf of existing creditors of the transferor. In this context, fraudulent transfers provide a basis for holding successors liable to post-transfer tort plaintiffs. The fact that general creditors are pursuing remedies against the transferee does not prevent tort plaintiffs from pursuing remedies under Subsection (b). What constitutes a fraudulent conveyance or transfer is determined by reference to applicable state law.

Illustration:

4. The same facts as in Illustration 1, except that the transfer of assets by ABC to XYZ is made as part of a plan between ABC and XYZ to leave tort claimants harmed by ABC's defective products without enforceable remedies. If a transaction constitutes a fraudulent transfer under applicable state law, XYZ is subject to liability for harm to the user of the lawn mower.

f. Consolidation or merger. When statutory consolidation or merger of two corporations takes place, products liability devolves on the successor corporation under Subsection (c). A more difficult question is whether, absent statutory merger, a de facto merger has taken place. Local law governing de facto mergers is determinative. Whether a de facto merger under Subsection (c) has occurred generally depends on whether: (1) there is a continuity of management, employees, location, and assets; (2) the successor corporation acquires the assets of the predecessor with shares of its own stock so that shareholders of the transferor corporation become shareholders of the transferee corporation; (3) the predecessor corporation ceases its ordinary business operations immediately or shortly after the transfer of assets; and (4) the successor assumes those liabilities and obligations of the predecessor necessary for the uninterrupted continuation of the normal operations of the predecessor.

Illustrations:

5. The same facts as Illustration 1, except that the transfer of assets is for stock in XYZ and constitutes a statutory merger of

ABC and XYZ under applicable state law. XYZ is subject to liability to the user of the lawn mower.

6. The same facts as Illustration 1, except that the transfer of assets is for stock in XYZ, with which ABC redeems its own stock from its shareholders. ABC then ceases to operate its own business, which XYZ resumes with the same management and employees, at the same location. If it is determined under applicable state law that a de facto merger between ABC and XYZ has occurred, XYZ is subject to liability for harm to the user of the lawn mower.

g. Continuation of the predecessor. The exception recognized in Subsection (d), referred to by many courts as the "mere continuation" exception, applies when there has been a formal redesignation of the predecessor corporate entity but little or no change in underlying substance. The most important indicia of continuation, in addition to the continuation of the predecessor's business activities, are common identities of officers, directors, and shareholders in the predecessor and successor corporations. A minority of jurisdictions recognize a broader exception, referred to as the "continuity of enterprise" exception, that imposes liability on the successor for continuing the business activities of the predecessor even when the corporate form of the successor is different from the predecessor. This Section does not follow that minority position.

Illustration:

7. The same facts as Illustration 1, except that XYZ is a corporation with the same officers, directors, and shareholders as ABC. After the assets transfer, XYZ continues the same manufacturing and distribution operations as ABC did previously. If XYZ is determined to constitute a "mere continuation" of ABC under Subsection (d), XYZ is subject to liability to the user of the lawn mower.

h. Necessity for the predecessor to transfer all of its assets and go out of business. Almost all of the reported decisions applying the bases of successor liability stated in this Section involve predecessors that transfer all of their assets to successors and then dissolve or otherwise cease operations. Indeed, the predecessor's termination is the circumstance that, as a practical matter, most often gives rise to the need for a post-transfer tort plaintiff to look to the successor for recovery. The exceptions set forth in Subsections (c) and (d), merger and continuation, most frequently have significance when the predecessor has transferred all of its assets to the successor and, at least formally, has ceased to exist. But there is no reason that the exceptions set forth in Subsections (c) and (d) might not arise in connection with the transfer of a division of a large company, leaving the company in existence after the transfer. And the exceptions in Subsections (a) and (b) could arise in connection with transfers involving less than all of the predecessor's assets where the predecessor continues in existence after the transfer.

i. Relationship between the rule in this Section and the successor's independent duty to warn. This Section deals with a successor's liability for harm caused by the predecessor's defective products and is not premised on post-transfer wrongdoing by the successor itself. For the rules governing the liability of a successor for its own post-transfer failure to warn its predecessor's customers, see § 13.

REPORTERS' NOTE

Comment b. Rationale. In a much-cited case, Polius v. Clark Equip. Co., 802 F.2d 75 (3d Cir.1986) (applying Virgin Islands law), the court stated that the imposition of successor liability on a company that has merely purchased the assets of a predecessor for cash and does not otherwise fall within the stated exceptions would encourage the dissolution of a financially troubled corporation by piecemeal sale of assets rather than as a going business concern. In this event the plaintiff would not be able to reach the assets when the accident occurred years after dissolution. The end result would be the needless destruction of an ongoing business enterprise with no net advantage to anyone. Other courts have observed that the imposition of successor liability on small corporations could spell financial disaster to them. See, e.g., Bernard v. Kee Mfg. Co. Inc., 409 So.2d 1047 (Fla.1982); DeLapp v. Xtraman Inc., 417 N.W.2d 219, 221 (Iowa 1987); Nissen Corp. v. Miller, 594 A.2d 564, 570 (Md.1991); Niccum v. Hydra Tool Corp., 438 N.W.2d 96, 100 (Minn.1989). These courts have concluded that the imposition of strict liability on successor corporations is inconsistent with the principle of products liability law that imposes responsibility on the party who created the risk and was in a position to prevent its occurrence. See also Johnston v. Amsted Indus., Inc., 830 P.2d 1141 (Colo.Ct.App.1992); Downtowner v. Acrometal Prods., Inc., 347 N.W.2d 118 (N.D.1984); Fish v. Amsted Indus., Inc., 376 N.W.2d 820, 827 (Wis. 1985).

Corporate successor liability has been the subject of considerable law review commentary. See, e.g., Phillips, Product Continuity and Successor Corporation Liability, 58 N.Y.U. L. Rev. 906 (1983) (the article contains an exhaustive listing of law review literature; author supports the "product line" exception); Green, Successor Liability: The Superiority of Statutory Reform to Protect Product Liability Claimants, 72 Cornell L. Rev. 17 (1986) (criticizing the rationale offered by courts and commentators in support of the liability based on "product line" or "continuity of business enterprise" and suggesting a statutory solution to the problem by requiring dissolving corporations to provide products liability plaintiffs with adequate protection); Note, A Policy Analysis of a Successor Corporation's Liability for Its Predecessor's

Defective Products When the Successor Has Acquired the Predecessor's Assets for Cash, 71 Marq. L. Rev. 815 (1982) (author criticizes the rationale offered to support expansive rules imposing liability on successor corporations and suggests expansion of independent duty to warn and fraudulent transfer category when the successor had actual or constructive knowledge of product defects); Rogala, Nontraditional Successor Product Liability: Should Society Be Forced to Pay the Cost?, 68 U. Det. L. J. 37 (1990) (economic analysis supports the retention of the four basic exceptions and the rejection of "product line" and "continuity of enterprise" theories); Comment, Successor Liability: The Debate Over the Continuity of Enterprise Exception in Ohio Is Really No Debate at All, 21 Ohio N.L. Rev. 297 (author criticizes both "product line" and "continuity of enterprise" exceptions and predicts that Ohio will follow four traditional exceptions). Much of the law review commentary supports liberalizing the rules imposing liability on corporate successors. The articles acknowledge, however, the overwhelming judicial rejection of the liberalizing rules. It is interesting that, after an early spurt of cases in the late 1970s and early 1980s arguing for more expansive liability, courts have refused to impose liability unless the plaintiff is able to come within the four traditional exceptions. See Green, Successors and CERCLA: The Imperfect Analogy to Products Liability and an Alternative Proposal, 87 Nw. U. L. Rev. 897, 909–10 (1993); Henderson and Eisenberg, The Quiet Revolution in Products Liability: An Empirical Study of Legal Change, 37 UCLA L. Rev. 479, 492 and n.64 (1990).

Several courts and commentators have recognized that the problems set forth in this Comment can best be addressed by legislation. For an insightful analysis and recommendation, see Green, Successor Liability: The Superiority of Statutory Reform to Protect Product Liability Claimants, 72 Cornell L. Rev. 17 (1986) (criticizing the rationale offered by courts and commentators in support of liability based on "product line" or "continuity of business enterprise" and suggesting a statutory solution to the problem by requiring dissolving corporations to provide products-liability plaintiffs with adequate protection). Courts have repeatedly espoused the same view. See, e.g., Fish v. Amsted Indus., Inc., 376 N.W.2d 820, 829 (Wis.1985):

> We conclude that the legislature is in a better position to make broad public policy decisions in actions based on products liability law. [Citation omitted]. The questions concerning the effect on the manufacturing business, the potential size and economic strength of successor corporations, the availability of commercial insurance and the cost of such insurance are all questions that . . . the legislature is in a better position to ascertain.

A similar sentiment was expressed in Leannais v. Cincinnati, Inc., 565 F.2d 437, 441 (7th Cir.1977):

> In recent years, for a variety of reasons, many have thought it necessary to turn to the courts in search of solutions to social problems. Courts are ill-equipped, however, to balance equities among future plaintiffs and defendants. . . . [S]uch broad public policy issues are best handled by legislatures with their comprehensive machinery for public input and debate.

See also Myers v. Putzmeister, Inc., 596 N.E.2d 754 (Ill.App.1992); Welco Indus. v. Applied Co., 617 N.E.2d 1129 (Ohio 1993); Nguyen v. Johnson Mach. & Press Corp., 433 N.E.2d 1104 (Ill.App.Ct.1982); Holifield v. Setco Indus., Inc., 168 N.W.2d 177 (Wis.1969), overruled on other grounds, Hansen v. A.H. Robins, Inc., 335 N.W.2d 578 (Wis.1983).

One possible statutory approach might be to require that whenever a product manufacturer transfers a business or a product line as a going concern, some form of bond or other security must be posted by the predecessor manufacturer in an amount not to exceed the net value of the predecessor at time of transfer. The value of the bond or other security would be available to future tort plaintiffs to satisfy claims for harm caused by previously distributed defective products. The posting of such a security would, under terms of the statute, protect the successor from future liability for previously distributed products in excess of the value of the security. Presumably, obligations on the bond would be limited in time. Future plaintiffs injured by products previously distributed by the predecessor would be no worse off financially than if the transfer of assets had not occurred. The limit based on the value of the predecessor at the time of transfer, with an appropriate time limit, would render more calculable the amount of the security required, in contrast to the difficulty of calculating future liabilities without such limits under the more expansive successor liability rules applied in a minority of jurisdictions. The value of the predecessor's product line as a going concern, whenever that value exceeds the cost of the security against future liability, would be preserved without allowing the transfer of assets to prejudice tort plaintiffs' chances of recovery.

Comment c. Nonliability in the absence of special circumstances. The following jurisdictions have limited the liability of successor corporations to the four exceptions set forth in § 12 and would reject both the "continuity of enterprise" approach (Turner v. Bituminous Cas. Co., 244 N.W.2d 873 (Mich.1976)) and the "product line" exception (Ray v. Alad Corp., 560 P.2d 3 (Cal.1977)). See, e.g., Arkansas (Swayze v. A.O. Smith Corp., 694 F.Supp. 619, 623 (E.D.Ark. 1988); Reed v. Armstrong Cork Co., 577 F.Supp. 246, 247–48 (E.D.Ark. 1983)); Colorado (Florom v. Elliott Mfg., 867 F.2d 570 (10th Cir.1989) (applying Colorado law); Johnston v. Amsted Indus., Inc., 830 P.2d 1141 (Colo.Ct.App.1992)); Florida (Bernard v. Kee Mfg. Co., 409 So.2d 1047 (Fla. 1982)); Georgia (Bullington v. Union Tool Corp., 328 S.E.2d 726 (Ga.1985)); Illinois (Gonzalez v. Rock Wool Eng'g & Equip. Co., 453 N.E.2d 792 (Ill. App.Ct.1983); Domine v. Fulton Iron Works, 395 N.E.2d 19 (Ill.App.Ct. 1979)); Iowa (Pancratz v. Monsanto Co., 547 N.W.2d 198 (Iowa 1996)); Kentucky (Conn v. Fales Div. of Mathewson Corp., 835 F.2d 145 (6th Cir. 1987) (applying Kentucky law)); Maryland (Nissen Corp. v. Miller, 594 A.2d 564 (Md.Ct.Spec.App.1991)); Massachusetts (Guzman v. MRM/Elgin, 567 N.E.2d 929 (Mass.1991)); Minnesota (Costello v. Unipress Corp., No. C6–95–2341, 1996 WL 106215 (Minn.Ct.App., Mar. 12, 1996); Cooper v. Lakewood Engineering & Mfg. Co., 45 F.3d 243 (8th Cir.1995) (applying Minnesota law)); Missouri (Bozell v. H & R 1871, Inc., 916 F.Supp. 951 (E.D.Mo.1996); Wallace v. Dorsey Trailers Southeast, Inc.,

849 F.2d 341, 343 (8th Cir.1988) (applying Missouri law)); Nebraska (Jones v. Johnson Mach. & Press Co., 320 N.W.2d 481 (Neb.1982)); North Carolina (Budd Tire Corp. v. Pierce Tire Co., Inc., 370 S.E.2d 267 (N.C.Ct.App.1988); Comment, Beyond Budd Tire: Examining Corporate Successor Liability in North Carolina, 30 Wake Forest L. Rev. 889 (Winter 1995)); North Dakota (Downtowner Inc. v. Acrometal Prods., Inc., 347 N.W.2d 118 (N.D.1984)); Ohio (Welco Indus., Inc. v. Applied Co., 617 N.E.2d 1129 (Ohio 1993)); Oklahoma (Goucher v. Parmac, Inc., 694 P.2d 953 (Okla.Ct.App.1984)); South Dakota (Hamaker v. Kenwel–Jackson Mach., Inc., 387 N.W.2d 515 (S.D. 1986)); Texas (Griggs v. Capitol Mach. Works, Inc., 690 S.W.2d 287 (Tex.Ct.App.1985); Mudgett v. Paxson Mach. Co., 709 S.W.2d 755 (Tex. Ct.App.1986)); Vermont (Ostrowski v. Hydra–Tool Corp., 479 A.2d 126 (Vt. 1984)); Virginia (Harris v. T.I., Inc., 413 S.E.2d 605 (Va.1992)); West Virginia (Jordan v. Ravenswood Aluminum Corp., 455 S.E.2d 561 (W.Va. 1995) (per curiam)); Wisconsin (Fish v. Amsted Indus., Inc., 376 N.W.2d 820 (Wis.1985)); District of Columbia (LeSane v. Hillenbrand Indus., 791 F.Supp. 871, 873–74 (D.D.C.1992) (applying District of Columbia law)); Virgin Islands (Polius v. Clark Equip. Co., 802 F.2d 75 (3d Cir.1986, V. I.)). Only a few states appear to have adopted liability based on the successor corporation's continuation of the predecessor's line of products: California (Ray v. Alad Corp., 560 P.2d 3 (Cal.1977)); New Jersey (Ramirez v. Amsted Indus., 431 A.2d 811 (N.J. 1981); (but see possible limit to "product line" exception recognized in dicta in Leo v. Kerr–McGee Chem. Corp., 37 F.3d 96, 100–01 (3d Cir.1994) (applying New Jersey law) ("It seems apparent that, except perhaps in design defect cases, a defect in a product when the manufacturer distributed the product is likely to manifest itself and cause injury within a reasonable time after the product is manufactured. Accordingly, as a practical matter, successor liability under *Ramirez* is likely to be imposed in most cases, if at all, for a limited period.")); New Mexico (Garcia v. Coe Manufacturing Co., 933 P.2d 243 (N.M.1997)); Pennsylvania (Dawejko v. Jorgensen Steel Co., 434 A.2d 106 (Pa.Super.Ct.1981)); Bogart v. Phase II Pasta Machs., Inc., 817 F.Supp. 547 (E.D.Pa.1993)); Washington (Martin v. Abbott Labs., 689 P.2d 368 (Wash.1984); Fox v. Sunmaster Prods., Inc., 821 P.2d 502 (Wash.Ct. App.1991) (the continued product line must be the one that harms the plaintiff)). Although the product line exception is still theoretically viable in Pennsylvania, if a plaintiff has a possible remedy against the predecessor, a recent opinion held the exception could not be invoked. LaFountain v. Webb Indus. Corp., 951 F.2d 544 (3d Cir.1991).

In an earlier draft of these Reporters' Notes, New Jersey was categorized as a jurisdiction that employs a very liberal test for corporate successor liability, a test premised on maximizing recovery rather than on evidence of express agreement to be liable or substantial deprivation of remedies for plaintiffs against the predecessor corporation. In support of this position Pacius v. Thermtroll Corp., 611 A.2d 153 (N.J.Super.Ct.Law Div.1992), was cited. In that case, the court held that *any* transfer of assets or use of the predecessor's goodwill entailed a de facto merger that, in turn, triggered successor liability. Id. at 157. Elaborating on the policy underlying this holding, the Pacius court quoted Rawlings v. DM Oliver Inc., 159 Cal.Rptr. 119, 124 (1979) for the following proposition:

> Fundamental fairness has been sought through a balancing of the rights of the injured party against the rights of those engaged in business, including the latter's reasonable commercial expectations. Placing the economic burden on those *best able to pay* for those costs, while permitting the transfer to those most culpable is consistent with the equitable considerations inherent in the resolution of the difficult problems which have been judicially posed. The thrust from our high court as a matter of first priority has been to *maximize recovery for the victim.*

Id. at 157 (emphasis added).

Recently, however, New Jersey has reigned in the "deep pocket" approach set forth above by the *Pacius* court. In Saez v. S & S Corrugated Paper Machinery Co., 695 A.2d 740 (N.J.Super.App.Div.1997), the court expressed disagreement both with the decision of the *Pacius* court and with this Restatement's earlier characterization of New Jersey law. The court first noted that, in contrast to the holding in *Pacius*, in order for a successor corporation to be liable under New Jersey law, the corporation must not only benefit from the predecessor's goodwill but must also continue to manufacture the predecessor's product. Id at 16. Moreover, the court stated that the question to answer in determining whether successor liability has been triggered is "not whether there was 'any benefit that the successor obtain[ed] from the acquisition of the assets of its predecessor' or if the successor eliminated a competitor [since] [s]o broad a test would be no test at all." Id.

Several other jurisdictions have imposed liability based on a continuation of the predecessor's business even when there was no stock transfer or a common identity of corporate directors. See, e.g., Andrews v. John E. Smith's Sons, Co., 369 So.2d 781, 785 (Ala.1979); Turner v. Bituminous Cas. Co., 244 N.W.2d 873 (Mich.1976); MacCleery v. T.S.S. Retail Corp., 882 F.Supp. 13 (D.N.H.1994).

Comment d. Agreement for successor to assume liability.

1. For general authority that agreements to assume liability will be enforced in favor of plaintiffs with products liability claims, see cases cited in the Reporters' Note to Comment *a*.

2. General assumption of a predecessor's liability, even without specific mention of products liability, will be interpreted to include liability for products liability claims. See, e.g., Bouton v. Litton Indus., Inc., 423 F.2d 643 (3d Cir.1970) (applying New York law); Grugan v. BBC Brown Boveri, Inc., 729 F.Supp. 1080 (E.D.Pa.1990). If the contractual obligation as to the successor's assumption of products liability is subject to conflicting interpretations, the issue is for the trier of fact. See, e.g., Gee v. Tenneco, Inc., 615 F.2d 857, 862–63 (9th Cir.1980) (applying California law); Florom v. Elliott Mfg., 867 F.2d 570, 574–76 (10th Cir.1989) (applying Colorado law); Davis v. Loopco Indus., Inc., 609 N.E.2d 144 (Ohio 1993).

3. Contractual agreements by the successor to repair or service a product sold by the predecessor do not amount to an agreement to assume products liability for injuries caused

by the predecessor's defective products. See, e.g., Schwartz v. McGraw–Edison Co., 92 Cal.Rptr. 776 (Cal.Ct.App.1971) (disapproved on other grounds in Ray v. Alad Corp., 560 P.2d 3 (Cal.1977)); Shane v. Hobam, Inc., 332 F.Supp. 526 (E.D.Pa.1971) (applying New York law). Whether agreements to service a predecessor's products may create an independent duty to warn about defects is discussed in connection with § 13.

Comment e. Fraudulent transfer in order to avoid debts or liabilities. For the reason set forth in the Comment, this exception has rarely been used to impose successor liability for products liability claims. However, in Schmoll v. AC & S, Inc., 703 F.Supp. 868 (D.C.Or.1988), the court found that a complex corporate restructuring was undertaken to avoid both pending and future liability to persons who were certain to suffer asbestos-related illness and was thus the functional equivalent of a fraudulent transfer. See also Morgan v. Cavalier Acquisition Corp., 432 S.E.2d 915 (N.C.Ct.App.1993) (reversing summary judgment when plaintiff's evidence raised a question of fact as to whether the defendant had purchased assets from the predecessor corporation in order to avoid creditors' claims); Budd Tire Corp. v. Pierce Tire Co., 370 S.E.2d 267 (N.C.Ct.App.1988); Mullen v. Alarmguard of Delmarva, Inc., No. CIV. A. 90C–11–40–1–CV, 1993 WL 258696 (Del.Super.Ct., Jun.16, 1993).

A much closer question is whether a successor corporation's actual or constructive knowledge that the predecessor's products are defective and likely to cause injury in the future is sufficient to render the transaction sufficiently tainted so as to come within the umbrella of this exception. There is little authority on the issue. In Nissen Corp. v. Miller, 594 A.2d 564, 569 n. 2 (Md.1991), the court noted that either knowledge of pending claims or knowledge of product defects might be sufficient to expose a successor liability since either would put in question the bona fides of the transaction.

Comment f. Consolidation or merger. For a discussion of what constitutes a "de facto merger," see Fletcher, Cyclopedia Corporations, § 7124.20; American Law of Products Liability § 7:10; Frumer and Friedman, Products Liability § 7.04[5]; Comment, Successor Liability: The Debate Over the Continuity of Enterprise Exception in Ohio Is Really No Debate at All, 21 Ohio N.L. Rev. 297, 313 nn.136–137 (1994) (describing de facto merger and "mere continuation" doctrines). When the successor purchases the assets of the predecessor for cash, a de facto merger will not be found to have occurred. See, e.g., Travis v. Harris Corp., 565 F.2d 443, 447 (7th Cir.1977) (applying Indiana law); Jordan v. Hawker Dayton Corp., 62 F.3d 29 (1st Cir.1995) (applying Maine law); Niccum v. Hydra Tool Corp., 438 N.W.2d 96 (Minn. 1989); Hamaker v. Kenwel–Jackson Mach., Inc., 387 N.W.2d 515, 518 (S.D.1986); Leannais v. Cincinnati, Inc., 565 F.2d 437, 439–40 (7th Cir. 1977) (applying Wisconsin law). Only courts applying the "continuity of enterprise" exception will impose liability when the successor corporation purchased the assets of the predecessor for cash and there is evidence of continuity of the original business. See Reporters' Note to Comment *c*.

Comment g. Continuation of the predecessor. For a discussion of the "mere continuation" exception, see Fletcher, Cyclopedia Corporations

§ 7124.10; American Law of Products Liability § 7:14; Frumer and Friedman § 7.04[4]. Also see Winch v. Yates Am. Mach. Co., Inc., 613 N.Y.S.2d 980 (N.Y.App.Div.1994); Swayze v. A.O. Smith Corp., 694 F.Supp. 619 (E.D.Ark.1988); Florom v. Elliott Mfg., 867 F.2d 570, 578 n. 3 (10th Cir.1989) (applying Colorado law); Johnston v. Amsted Indus., Inc., 830 P.2d 1141, 1146 (Colo.Ct.App. 1992); Nissen Corp. v. Miller, 594 A.2d 564, 567 (Md.1991); Tucker v. Paxson Mach. Co., 645 F.2d 620 (8th Cir.1981) (applying Missouri law); Chemical Design, Inc. v. American Standard, Inc., 847 S.W.2d 488 (Mo. Ct.App.1993); U.S. v. Atlas Minerals & Chem., Inc., 824 F.Supp. 46 (E.D.Pa.1993); Hamaker v. Kenwel–Jackson Mach., Inc., 387 N.W.2d 515, 518 (S.D.1986).

In analyzing continuation questions, some courts require purchase of stock or other benchmarks in order to establish the requisite continuity. See, e.g., Gehin–Scott v. Newson, Inc., 848 F.Supp. 585 (E.D.Pa.1994); Pancratz v. Monsanto Co., 547 N.W.2d 198, 201 (Iowa 1996) ("[t]he exception has no application without proof of continuity of management and ownership between the predecessor and successor corporations"); Harris v. T.I., Inc., 413 S.E.2d 605 (Va.1992) (also requiring a common identity of officers, directors, and stockholders). Other courts deny a merger if no transfer of assets has taken place, as in Carreiro v. Rhodes Gill & Co., 68 F.3d 1443 (1st Cir. 1995). Contra, Jordan v. Hawker Dayton Corp., 62 F.3d 29 (1st Cir. 1995) (applying Maine law) (holding that purchase of assets is not sufficient to warrant a finding of a de facto merger); Lemelle v. Universal Mfg. Corp., 18 F.3d 1268 (5th Cir. 1994) (applying Louisiana law). But several other states have imposed liability based on a continuation of the predecessor's business even when there was no stock transfer or common identity of corporate directors. See, e.g., Andrews v. John E. Smith's Sons, Co., 369 So.2d 781, 785 (Ala. 1979); Turner v. Bituminous Cas. Co., 244 N.W.2d 873 (Mich.1976); MacCleery v. T.S.S. Retail Corp., 882 F.Supp. 13 (D. N.H. 1994). See generally Sweatland v. Park Corp., 587 N.Y.S.2d 54 (N.Y.App.Div.1992).

§ 13. Liability of Successor for Harm Caused by Successor's Own Post–Sale Failure to Warn

(a) A successor corporation or other business entity that acquires assets of a predecessor corporation or other business entity, whether or not liable under the rule stated in § 12, is subject to liability for harm to persons or property caused by the successor's failure to warn of a risk created by a product sold or distributed by the predecessor if:

(1) the successor undertakes or agrees to provide services for maintenance or repair of the product or enters into a similar relationship with purchasers of the predecessor's products giving rise to actual or potential economic advantage to the successor, and

(2) a reasonable person in the position of the successor would provide a warning.

(b) A reasonable person in the position of the successor would provide a warning if:

(1) the successor knows or reasonably should know that the product poses a substantial risk of harm to persons or property; and

(2) those to whom a warning might be provided can be identified and can reasonably be assumed to be unaware of the risk of harm; and

(3) a warning can be effectively communicated to and acted on by those to whom a warning might be provided; and

(4) the risk of harm is sufficiently great to justify the burden of providing a warning.

Comment:

a. Rationale. Corporations that acquire assets from other corporations are liable for harm caused by defective products sold by predecessors only in limited circumstances. See § 12. This Section subjects a successor to liability for its own failure to warn after acquiring the predecessor's assets when certain conditions are satisfied and when a reasonable person in the successor's position would provide a warning. Liability under this Section is similar to liability under § 10, in which a seller is liable for harm caused by breach of a post-sale duty to warn even if the product was not defective at the time of original sale. Unlike product sellers in § 10, the successor governed by this Section did not manufacture or sell the defective product. However, by virtue of succeeding to the predecessor's interests, the successor is often in a good position to learn of problems arising from use of the predecessor's product and to prevent harm to persons or property. When the relationship between the successor and pre-transfer purchasers of the predecessor's products gives rise to actual or potential economic benefit to the successor, it is both fair and efficient to require the successor to act reasonably to prevent such harm.

b. Relationship between the successor and the predecessor's customers. Absent some additional circumstance besides having become a successor, the successor remains a pure volunteer upon whom the law usually imposes no duty to act or to warn. Many courts have recognized four elements as being significant in determining the existence of a duty to warn: (1) succession to a predecessor's service contracts; (2) coverage of the defective product under a service contract made directly with the successor; (3) actual service of the defective product by the successor; and (4) the successor's knowledge of the existence of defects and the identities of the predecessor's customers who own the defective product. However, these factors are not exhaustive and the inquiry should be whether the successor's relationships with the predecessor's customers give rise to actual or potential economic advantage.

In most instances, in the absence of service contracts governing the predecessor's products or actual service of the defective product by the successor, it will be difficult to establish that the successor's relationships with the predecessor's customers give rise to actual or potential economic benefit to the successor. Furthermore, in the absence of service contracts, it may be difficult to establish under Subsection (b)(1) through (4) that a reasonable person in the position of the successor would provide a warning. Thus, when the successor has established no systematic relationships with the predecessor's customers through service contracts, usually the successor has no practical method of identifying those customers and communicating effectively with them. The successor who has no continuing contacts with a predecessor's customers may also be unable to discover risks that should be addressed through warnings. Similarly, when a successor has discontinued both the sale of a predecessor's product line and the provision of services to the predecessor's customers, it may not be in a position reasonably to discover risks about the discontinued line or to determine the persons to whom a warning should be addressed.

Notwithstanding the importance of service contracts in the application of this Section, a contract is not the only method of establishing a relationship with a predecessor's customers. For example, a successor may sell or offer to sell spare parts to the predecessor's customers for machinery sold by the predecessor when the successor knows or should know the machinery is defective. Such conduct should be considered by courts in deciding whether sufficient actual or potential economic advantage has accrued to the successor to warrant the imposition of a duty to warn the predecessor's customers.

c. Factors in determining whether a reasonable successor would provide a warning. Whether a reasonable person in the successor's position would provide a warning is governed by the same requirements that determine whether a reasonable seller should provide a post-sale warning under § 10. Subsection (b)(1) through (4) are identical to the requirements set forth in Subsection (b)(1) through (4) of § 10 and are explained in the Comments to § 10.

Illustrations:

1. ABC Corp., which manufactures and sells plastic molding machines, transfers all its assets to XYZ Corp. for cash and then dissolves. There is no continuity of shareholders, officers, or directors from ABC to XYZ. Thus, XYZ is not liable as a successor corporation for defective products previously sold by ABC under the rule stated in § 12. Marks Plastics Co. purchased five Model 1010 molding machines from ABC one year before ABC's transfer of assets to XYZ. At that time Marks entered into a three-year service contract with ABC. After acquiring ABC's assets, XYZ continues to service ABC's customers and periodically sends its service people to the Marks plant. The ongoing service contracts between XYZ and Marks constitute relationships that give rise to actual economic advantage to XYZ. Two years after acquiring ABC's assets, XYZ begins to receive reports from the field that, after completing one cycle, the Model 1010 machine sometimes recycles unexpectedly. XYZ does not inform Marks about the problem. Subsequently, Marks's employee, E, is injured when the Model 1010 recycles unexpectedly. XYZ owes a duty to E to act as a reasonable person in warning Marks about the dangers attendant to the use of Model 1010. Whether XYZ breached its duty is to be determined based on the factors set forth in Subsection (b)(1) through (4).

2. Same facts as Illustration 1, except that XYZ does not succeed to any service contracts from ABC nor does it enter into any service contracts of its own with Marks Plastic Co. However, after XYZ becomes aware of the recycling problem with the Model 1010 machine it enters into negotiations with Marks to sell replacement parts for the Model 1010. Before the sale is completed, Mark's employee, E, is injured when the Model 1010 unexpectedly recycles. The offer to sell replacement parts for Model 1010 constitutes a relationship that gives rise to potential economic advantages to XYZ. XYZ owes a duty to act as a reasonable person in providing a warning. Whether XYZ breached its duty to E to warn Marks about the dangers attendant to the use of the Model 1010 is to be determined upon the basis of the factors set forth in Subsection (b)(1) through (4).

3. Same facts as Illustration 1, except that, upon purchasing the assets of ABC, XYZ discontinues the manufacture and sale of molding machines and thereafter manufactures only drill presses. XYZ also discontinues all service contracts with ABC's customers, including Marks, and is not otherwise in contact with them. XYZ is not subject to liability for failure to warn. There is no relationship between XYZ and Marks that would give rise to actual or

potential benefit to XYZ. XYZ has no duty to warn Marks about the dangers attendant to the use of the Model 1010.

REPORTERS' NOTE

Comment a. Rationale. A significant body of case law supports the proposition that a successor corporation has an independent duty to warn when it has a substantial continuing relationship with the customer of the predecessor corporation. See, e.g., Gee v. Tenneco, Inc., 615 F.2d 857, 866 (9th Cir.1980) (applying California law); Florom v. Elliott Mfg., 867 F.2d 570, 577 (10th Cir.1989) (applying Colorado law); Gonzalez v. Rock Wool Eng'g & Equip., 453 N.E.2d 792 (Ill.App.Ct.1983); Travis v. Harris Corp., 565 F.2d 443, 449 (7th Cir. 1977) (applying Indiana law); Stratton v. Garvey Int'l, Inc., 676 P.2d 1290 (Kan.Ct.App.1984); Patton v. TIC United Corp., 77 F.3d 1235 (10th Cir. 1996) (applying Kansas law); Pelc v. Bendix Mach. Tool Corp., 314 N.W.2d 614, 621 (Mich.Ct.App.1981); Mozingo v. Correct Mfg. Corp., 752 F.2d 168, 177 (5th Cir.1985) (applying Mississippi law); Tucker v. Paxson Mach. Co., 645 F.2d 620 (8th Cir.1981) (applying Missouri law); Wilson v. Fare Well Corp., 356 A.2d 458 (N.J.Super.Ct.Law Div.1976); Schumacher v. Richards Shear Co., 451 N.E.2d 195 (N.Y.1983); Downtowner, Inc. v. Acrometal Prods. Inc., 347 N.W.2d 118, 125 (N.D.1984); Flaugher v. Cone Automatic Mach. Co., 507 N.E.2d 331, 337–38 (Ohio 1987); Shane v. Hobam, Inc., 332 F.Supp. 526 (E.D.Pa.1971); Tracey by Tracey v. Winchester Repeating Arms Co., 745 F.Supp. 1099 (E.D.Pa.1990) (applying New York law); Ostrowski v. Hydra–Tool Corp., 479 A.2d 126, 127–28 (Vt.1984); Polius v. Clark Equip. Co., 802 F.2d 75, 84 (3d Cir.1986) (applying Virgin Islands law); Leannais v. Cincinnati, Inc., 565 F.2d 437, 441–42 (7th Cir.1977) (applying Wisconsin law).

In a recent case, Sherlock v. Quality Control Equipment Co., 79 F.3d 731 (8th Cir.1996) (applying Missouri law), the court affirmed a jury verdict for the plaintiff against a successor corporation that sold replacement parts for a machine sold to the predecessor's customer and rejected the defendant's argument that it had no post-sale duty to warn the predecessor's customers of dangers it had learned about concerning the machinery after succeeding to the interests of the predecessor. The court said:

> In determining the existence of a relationship sufficient to justify foisting a duty to warn of known dangers on the successor corporation, the courts have often cited four factors as being significant. *See, e.g., Tucker*, 645 F.2d at 626. These elements include: "(1) succession to a predecessor's service contracts; (2) coverage of the particular machine under the contract; (3) service of that machine by the purchaser-corporation; and (4) the purchaser-corporation's knowledge of defects and of the location or owner of that machine." *Id. While these factors are indisputably important, and in many cases dispositive, we remain mindful that they are merely useful tools which provide evidence in resolving the ultimate inquiry: whether there is an adequate nexus between the successor and the predecessor's customers. See* Downtowner, Inc. v.

Acrometal Prods., Inc., 347 N.W.2d 118, 125 (N.D.1984) ("This listing [of factors] cannot be said to be exhaustive."). As explained in one of the foremost authorities on corporate law:

> The critical element required for the imposition of the duty is a continuing relationship between the successor and the predecessor's customers for the benefit of the successor. Hence, rather than relying only on the four specific factors above, which are not exhaustive in establishing a nexus between the successor and its predecessor's customers sufficient to justly impose an independent duty to warn upon notice of dangers or potential dangers, the courts also employ a risk/benefit analysis. Thus, the focus in deciding whether the relationship between the successor corporation and the preexisting customer is sufficient to create a duty to warn has been upon the actual or potential economic advantage to the successor corporation.

15 William M. Fletcher, Fletcher Cyclopedia of the Law of Private Corporations § 7123.08 (perm. ed. rev. vol. 1990).

Id. at 734 (emphasis added).

The court reviewed the evidence and found that a sufficient nexus was made out to support an independent post-sale duty to warn:

> Relying on testimony from Quality's own officers and employees, the jury could reasonably have inferred that in 1983 Quality was probably the sole remaining manufacturer in the world of chitterling cleaning machines. Further, it appeared that Quality was by far the most easily accessible, if not the only, supplier of replacement parts for the Strickler chitterling cleaning machine. Indeed, this state of affairs contributed to Quality's decision to purchase the rights to assemble the machine, as Quality's president testified that an "attractive" feature of the transaction was the fact that Strickler was going out of business and Quality would thus be able to "step into [Strickler's] shoes" vis a vis the predecessor corporation's customers. Consequently, one could justifiably conclude that Quality perceived it to be economically advantageous to foster relationships with Strickler's customers; for, through these associations, Quality would have the opportunity not only to peddle replacement parts, but to one day possibly benefit from the sale of new machines to a clientele with apparently no other viable source for a needed product. To be sure, Quality did benefit in the instant case, having sold replacement parts to Monfort on twenty-four separate occasions.

79 F.3d at 735.

For a comprehensive and thoughtful analysis of this subject, see Victoria A. Kommer, The Successor Corporation's Continuing Duty to Warn, 23 Prod. Safety & Liab. Rep. (BNA) No. 36, p. 990 et seq. (1995). The author notes that the cases speak of a "special relationship" necessary to trigger a duty to warn but fail to give content to that term.

As the Comment indicates, many courts place heavy emphasis on whether the successor had ongoing service contracts with the customer of the predecessor corporation. See, e.g., Florom v. Elliott Mfg. Co., 867 F.2d 570 (10th Cir.1989) (applying

Colorado law); Stratton v. Garvey Int'l, Inc., 676 P.2d 1290 (Kan.App. 1984); Mozingo v. Correct Mfg. Corp., 752 F.2d 168 (5th Cir.1985) (applying Mississippi law); Tucker v. Paxson Mach. Co., 645 F.2d 620 (8th Cir. 1981) (applying Missouri law); Polius v. Clark Equip. Co., 802 F.2d 75 (3d Cir. 1986) (applying Virgin Islands law). But see Schumacher v. Richards Shear Co., 451 N.E.2d 195 (N.Y. 1983). This Section does not make the existence of a service contract a *sine qua non* for the imposition of a duty to warn on a successor corporation. Other similar relationships with purchasers of the predecessor's products giving rise to actual or potential economic advantage to the successor may suffice to create a duty to act reasonably and provide warnings.

Comment c. Factors in determining whether a reasonable successor would provide a warning. Although some courts list actual or constructive knowledge of defect as a "factor" to be considered in determining whether a successor corporation owes a duty to warn others require actual knowledge as a necessary condition for the imposition of liability on the successor corporation. See, e.g., Gee v. Tenneco, Inc., 615 F.2d 857, 865–66 (9th Cir. 1980); Flaugher v. Cone Automatic Mach. Co., 507 N.E.2d 331, 337–38 (Ohio 1987); Downtowner v. Acrometal Prods., Inc., 347 N.W.2d 118, 125 (N.D.1984); Polius v. Clark Equip. Co., 802 F.2d 75, 84 (3d Cir.1986) (applying Virgin Islands law).

This Section does not require actual knowledge of the risk as a condition for imposing liability. This is true both with regard to a seller's post-sale duty to warn and to a successor's independent duty to warn. As a practical matter it may be very difficult to establish that a seller or a successor could reasonably be saddled with the duty to investigate product performance. But the law should not establish an absolute barrier to recovery if constructive knowledge can be established. Otherwise one would encourage sellers or successors to close their eyes so that they not be tinged with "actual knowledge" that would impose duty upon them. As noted, drug manufacturers quite routinely have a duty to keep up with scientific research and to investigate when information of risk is brought to their attention. Other products may involve very significant risk and may require similar investigation. Thus, the duty to go out and "discover" risk may most often impose too onerous a burden. However, when the facts justify investigation and it can be practically accomplished, this Section sets up no artificial barrier against recovery.

§ 14. Selling or Distributing as One's Own a Product Manufactured by Another

One engaged in the business of selling or otherwise distributing products who sells or distributes as its own a product manufactured by another is subject to the same liability as though the seller or distributor were the product's manufacturer.

Comment:

a. History. The rule stated in this Section derives from § 400 of the Restatement, Second, of Torts, promulgated in 1965. Section 400 incorporates by reference §§ 394–398, setting forth the rules governing the liability of manufacturers of chattels. These rules establish a regime of fault-based manufacturers' liability and treat product manufacturers differently than other actors, including nonmanufacturer product sellers. After inclusion of § 402A in the Restatement, Second, imposing strict liability on all commercial sellers of defective products for harm caused by product defects, it was questionable whether § 400 remained relevant in the context of products liability. Once § 402A imposed strict liability on all product sellers it made little, if any, difference whether the seller of a defective product was a retailer or a manufacturer. Compare Comment *b.*

b. Relevance of this Section when all commercial product sellers are held to the same standards of liability under §§ 1–4. To the extent that nonmanufacturers in the chain of distribution are held to the same standards as manufacturers, the rule stated in this Section is of little practical significance. However, many jurisdictions by statute treat nonmanufacturers more leniently. See § 1, Comment *e.* To the extent that a statute specifies responsibilities, the statutory terms control. But to the extent that a statute does not, the rule in this Section states the common-law rule.

c. Representing oneself as the manufacturer or one for whom the product has been specially manufactured. When a commercial seller sells a product manufactured by another under its own trademark or logo, the seller is liable as though it were the manufacturer of the product. This rule applies even if the seller discloses that the product was produced by an identified manufacturer specifically for the seller. In this circumstance, the seller is presumed to cause the product to be used or consumed, in part at least, in reliance on the seller. The seller's reputation is an implied assurance of the quality of the product, and the seller should be estopped from denying that it stands behind that assurance.

Illustrations:

1. M manufactures and sells washing machines to R, a large retailer. R places its own name on the machines and sells and promotes them as made by R. R is subject to the same liability as though R were the manufacturer. M is also subject to liability as a manufacturer.

2. The same facts as Illustration 1, except that, in addition to R placing its own logo on the machines, R adds the words "Made especially for R by M." R is subject to the same liability as though R were the manufacturer. M is also subject to liability as a manufacturer.

d. Liability of trademark licensors. The rule stated in this Section does not, by its terms, apply to the owner of a trademark who licenses a manufacturer to place the licensor's trademark or logo on the manufacturer's product and distribute it as though manufactured by the licensor. In such a case, even if purchasers of the product might assume that the trademark owner was the manufacturer, the licensor does not "sell or distribute as its own a product manufactured by another." Thus, the manufacturer may be liable under §§ 1–4, but the licensor, who does not sell or otherwise distribute products, is not liable under this Section of this Restatement.

Trademark licensors are liable for harm caused by defective products distributed under the licensor's trademark or logo when they participate substantially in the design, manufacture, or distribution of the licensee's products. In these circumstances they are treated as sellers of the products bearing their trademarks.

Illustrations:

3. MD owns a popular, well-known logo for sports equipment. RS is a manufacturer of sports equipment. MD licenses RS to place MD's logo on RS's equipment, but plays no other role in RS's operations. MD is not subject to liability for harm caused by defective products manufactured and distributed by RS. RS is subject to liability as a manufacturer.

4. The same facts as Illustration 3 except that MD participates substantially in, and exerts control over, RS's operations. MD is subject to liability as a manufacturer for harm caused by defective products distributed by RS. RS is also subject to liability as a manufacturer.

REPORTERS' NOTE

Section 400 of the Restatement, Second, of Torts, the predecessor of the rule stated in this Section, reads as follows:

§ 400. Selling as Own Product Chattel Made by Another

One who puts out as his own product a chattel manufactured by another is subject to the same liability as though he were its manufacturer.

A clear majority of jurisdictions recognize the rule stated in this Section. See, e.g., Mello v. K–Mart Corp., 604 F.Supp. 769 (D.Mass.1985); Hebel v. Sherman Equip., 442 N.E.2d 199 (Ill.1982); Haymore v. Thew Shovel Co., 446 S.E.2d 865 (N.C.Ct.App. 1994); Lopez v. Chicago Bridge & Iron Co., 546 So.2d 291 (La.Ct.App. 1989); Sears, Roebuck & Co. v. Black, 708 S.W.2d 925 (Tex.App.1986).

The rule stated in this Section does not generally apply to trademark licensors. Such licensors are liable as sellers for harm caused by product defects only when they participate in the design, manufacture, or distribution of the products in question. See, e.g., Nelson v. International Paint Co., Inc., 734 F.2d 1084 (5th Cir.1984) (licensor not liable); Hebel v. Sherman Equip., 442 N.E.2d 199 (Ill.1982) (licensor not liable); Jackson v. Coldspring Terrace Property Owners Assn., 939 S.W.2d 762 (Tex.Ct.App. 1997) (licensor not liable). When licensors do participate, they are strictly liable as sellers. See, e.g., Torres v. Goodyear Tire & Rubber Co., 786 P.2d 939 (Ariz.1990) (licensor liable); City of Hartford v. Associated Constr. Co., 384 A.2d 390 (Conn.Sup. Ct.1978) (licensor liable).

The observation in Comment *a*, to the effect that promulgation of § 402A left arguably little for the rule in this Section to accomplish, has been recognized by some courts. See, e.g., Hebel v. Sherman Equip., 442 N.E.2d 199, 202 (Ill.1982) ("The function of the apparent-manufacturer doctrine, as it were, has been absorbed by the theory of seller's strict liability in tort."). See also Seasword v. Hilti, Inc., 537 N.W.2d 221 (Mich. 1995) (court holds that Michigan will not adopt apparent-manufacturer doctrine because nonmanufacturing sellers are strictly liable in any event).

CHAPTER 4

PROVISIONS OF GENERAL APPLICABILITY

TOPIC 1. CAUSATION

§ 15. General Rule Governing Causal Connection Between Product Defect and Harm

Whether a product defect caused harm to persons or property is determined by the prevailing rules and principles governing causation in tort.

Comment:

a. Requirement of causal connection between defect and harm. Sections 1, 5, 6, 7, and 8 require that the defect of which the plaintiff complains cause harm to person or property. The rules that govern causation in tort law generally are, subject to § 16, also applicable in products liability cases.

b. Misuse, alteration, and modification. When the plaintiff establishes product defect under the rules stated in Chapter 1, a question can arise whether the misuse, alteration, or modification of the product by the user or a third party contributed to the plaintiff's harm in such a way as to absolve the defendant from liability, in whole or in part. Such a question is to be resolved under the prevailing rules and principles governing causation or the prevailing rules and principles governing comparative responsibility, as the case may be. See § 17.

Illustrations:

1. XYZ Co. manufactures and sells automobiles. Sam purchased a new XYZ Model 300 and drove it around town for several days. Unknown to Sam, the lug nuts that hold the right front wheel to the axle were too large, allowing them to loosen and present a serious risk of eventual failure. On Sam's fifth day of ownership, a large truck rear-ended the XYZ automobile while Sam was driving it. Both Sam and the automobile suffer harm. XYZ Co. is not liable to Sam. Although the automobile was defective when Sam purchased it, and although the automobile was a cause of Sam's injuries, the defect was not a substantial factor in causing the injuries, which would have occurred even if the defect had not been present.

2. XYZ Co. manufactures and sells automobiles. Sam purchased a new XYZ Model 300 and drove it around town for several days. On one trip Sam felt the right front wheel wobbling. Upon examination Sam discovered that the five lug nuts holding the wheel to the axle were too large, causing them to loosen. Had Sam not stopped when he did, the wheel would have fallen off. Sam removed the five over-sized lug nuts, borrowed two correct-sized nuts from the right rear wheel, and reattached the right front wheel with them. Sam did nothing more about the wheels for more than a month, whereupon he loaned the automobile to a friend, saying nothing about the wheels. The friend inadvertently drove into a large pothole, causing the two nuts on the right front wheel to break. The wheel came off and both the automobile and Sam's friend suffered harm. Had five proper-sized lug nuts been on the wheel instead of just two, they would not have broken and the accident would not have occurred. XYZ Co. is not liable to Sam or Sam's friend. Although the XYZ automobile was defective when sold, and although the defect was a necessary condition to the occurrence of the accident, Sam's modification and subsequent failure to effect adequate repair were sufficiently unforeseeable that the defect was not a substantial factor in causing the friend's injury.

c. Causation and proportional liability. In certain cases involving generic toxic substances, the plaintiffs may be unable to identify which among a number of manufacturers produced the particular product that caused a particular plaintiff's harm. In this context, especially with respect to the drug diethylstilbestrol (DES), some courts have relieved the plaintiff of responsibility to identify the causal producer, and allow recovery instead against each producer named by the plaintiff in proportion to each defendant's market share. Other courts have refused to effect such a basic change in traditional rules of causation.

In deciding whether to adopt a rule of proportional liability, courts have considered the following factors: (1) the generic nature of the product; (2) the long latency period of the harm; (3) the inability of plaintiffs to discover which defendant's product caused plaintiff's harm, even after exhaustive discovery; (4) the clarity of the causal connection between the defective product and the harm suffered by plaintiffs; (5) the absence of other medical or environmental factors that could have caused or materially contributed to the harm; and (6) the availability of sufficient "market share" data to support a reasonable apportionment of liability. The Institute leaves to developing law the question of whether, given the appropriate factors, a rule of proportional liability should be adopted.

However, if a court does adopt some form of proportional liability, the liability of each defendant is properly limited to the individual defendant's share of the market. The rules of joint and several liability are incompatible with a market-share approach to causation. Unlike the case of concurrent tortfeasors, in which several parties contribute to a single plaintiff's entire harm, it is not established in the market-share context that all the defendants contributed to the plaintiff's injury. Instead, each defendant should pay for harm in proportion to the risk that it caused in the market at large. Joint and several liability would impose liability on each defendant for the entirety of the harm based on its presence in the market with other defendants. In the absence of some concerted conduct among the defendants, such liability is inappropriate.

REPORTERS' NOTE

Comment a. Requirement of causal connection between defect and harm. The basic rules governing causation in products liability litigation are the same as those governing tort law generally. It is unnecessary, therefore, to draft a set of causation standards limited in application to products liability; the prevailing rules and principles of causation may be applied in products litigation. Defect-related increases in harm are sufficiently unique to the products liability field to warrant separate, special treatment. See § 16(c). Otherwise, the general rules governing causation in tort law should suffice.

Comment b. Misuse, alteration, and modification. This Comment refers to the way in which product misuse, alteration, and modification may be treated as an aspect of causation. In Hughes v. Magic Chef, Inc., 288 N.W.2d 542 (Iowa 1980), the plaintiff suffered injuries when a propane stove exploded in a mobile home. The propane tank had run dry and was subsequently refilled. Two pilot lights were relighted but a third was overlooked. At trial, the court instructed the jury regarding the plaintiff's theory of defective design and the defendant's theory of misuse as an affirmative defense. On appeal the Supreme Court reversed, concluding:

> Misuse of the product is no longer to be considered an affirmative defense in products liability actions but is rather to be treated in connection with the plaintiff's burden of proving an unreasonably dangerous condition and legal cause. Regardless of whether a defendant does or does not plead misuse of the product the burden is on the plaintiff to prove that the legal cause of the injury was a product defect which rendered the product unreasonably dangerous.

288 N.W.2d at 546.

As one might expect, courts react differently to misuse/proximate cause cases. Because the facts differ from case to case, reconciling the decisions is difficult. Most courts send the misuse/proximate cause issue to the jury. See, e.g., Kavanaugh v. Kavanaugh, 641 P.2d 258 (Ariz.Ct.App.1981); Hilliard v. A. H. Robins, 196 Cal.Rptr. 117 (Cal.Ct.App.1983); Sipari v. Villa Olivia Country Club, 380 N.E.2d 819 (Ill.App.Ct.1978). Although technically the burden of persuasion is on the plaintiff, more often than not as a practical matter the defendant must raise the issue of causation and argue that even if the design had been different the same harm would have occurred anyway. See generally Prosser and Keeton, the Law of Torts 270 (5th ed. 1984). Occasionally courts hold that the misuse is so unforeseeable that there is no proximate cause as a matter of law. See, e.g., Dugan v. Sears Roebuck & Co., 454 N.E.2d 64 (Ill.App.Ct.1983); Genteman v. Saunders Archery Co., 355 N.E.2d 647 (Ill.App.Ct.1976); Winnett v. Winnett, 310 N.E.2d 1 (Ill.1974); Hegwood v. General Motors Corp., 286 N.W.2d 29 (Iowa 1979).

Comment c. Causation and proportional liability. American courts are divided regarding whether, and on what basis, group (or "alternative") liability should be imposed in DES cases. The leading case approving such liability is Sindell v. Abbott Labs., 607 P.2d 924 (Cal.1980) (drug companies liable in proportion to their shares of relevant DES market). See also McCormack v. Abbott Labs., 617 F.Supp. 1521 (D.Mass. 1985) (applying Massachusetts law); McElhaney v. Eli Lilly & Co., 564 F.Supp. 265 (D.S.D.1983) (applying South Dakota law); Hardy v. Johns–Manville Sales, Corp., 509 F.Supp. 1353 (E.D.Tex.1981) (applying Texas law), rev'd in part, 681 F.2d 334 (5th Cir.1982); Conley v. Boyle Drug Co., 570 So.2d 275 (Fla.1990); Smith v. Cutter Biological, Inc., 823 P.2d 717 (Haw.1991); Abel v. Eli Lilly & Co., 343 N.W.2d 164 (Mich.1984), cert. denied, 469 U.S. 833, 105 S.Ct. 123, 83 L.Ed.2d 65 (1984) (joint and several liability if plaintiff joins all DES manufacturers in Michigan market); Hymowitz v. Eli Lilly Co., 539 N.E.2d 1069 (N.Y.1989) (market share based on national market); Shackil v. Lederle Labs., 530 A.2d 1287 (N.J. Super. Ct. App. Div. 1987) (suggesting risk-modified market-share theory), rev'd, 561 A.2d 511 (1989); (court's reversal was on the limited point that market-share theory should not apply to vaccines for which a separate federal remedy was available); Collins v. Eli Lilly Co., 342 N.W.2d 37 (Wis.1984), cert. denied sub nom. E. R. Squibb & Sons, Inc. v. Collins, 469 U.S. 826, 105 S.Ct. 107, 83 L.Ed.2d 51 (1984) (risk share apportionment); Martin v. Abbott Labs., 102 Wash. 2d 581, 689 P.2d 368 (Wash. 1984). For favorable commentary, see Note, Market Share Liability: A New Method of Recovery for D.E.S. Litigants, 30 Cath. U. L. Rev. 551 (1981); Note, Market Share Liability: An Answer to the DES Causation Problem, 94 Harv. L. Rev. 668 (1981).

A substantial number of courts have rejected the market-share approach. See, e.g., Jackson v. Anchor Packing Co., 994 F.2d 1295 (8th Cir. 1993) (applying Arkansas law); Jefferson v. Lead Industries Assn., Inc., 106 F.3d 1245 (5th Cir.1997) (applying Louisiana law); Tidler v. Eli Lilly & Co., Inc., 851 F.2d 418 (D.C.Cir. 1988) (applying D.C. and Maryland law); Ryan v. Eli Lilly & Co., 514 F.Supp. 1004 (D.S.C.1981) (applying South Carolina law); Mizell v. Eli Lilly & Co., 526 F.Supp. 589 (D.S.C. 1981) (applying South Carolina law); Smith v. Eli Lilly & Co., Inc., 560 N.E.2d 324 (Ill.1990); Mulcahy v. Eli Lilly & Co., 386 N.W.2d 67 (Iowa 1986); Zafft v. Eli Lilly & Co., 676 S.W.2d 241 (Mo.1984) (en banc); Kurczi v. Eli Lilly & Co., 113 F.3d 1426 (6th Cir.1997) (applying Ohio law); Gorman v. Abbott Labs., 599 A.2d 1364 (R.I.1991). The attempt to apply market share to the asbestos litigation has met with hostility. See Celotex Corp. v. Copeland, 471 So.2d 533 (Fla.1985), for a full listing of the cases; see also Bateman v. Johns-Manville Sales Corp., 781 F.2d 1132 (5th Cir.1986) (applying Louisiana law). Some courts also have refused to apply market share to the lead-paint industry. See Santiago v. Sherwin Williams Co., 3 F.3d 546 (1st Cir.1993) (applying Massachusetts law); Skipworth v. Lead Industries, Inc., 690 A.2d 169 (Pa.1997). But see Jackson v. Glidden Co., 647 N.E.2d 879 (Ohio Ct.App.1995). For negative commentary on market share, see Fischer, Products Liability—An Analysis of Market Share Liability, 34 Vand. L. Rev. 1623 (1981); Note, Market Share Liability—The California Roulette of Causation Eliminating the Identification Requirement, 11 Seton Hall L. Rev. 610 (1981). For a sharply critical view of the application of market-share theory to blood products, see Klein, Beyond DES: Rejecting the Application of Market Share Liability in Blood Products Litigation, 68 Tul. L. Rev. 883 (1994).

Several decisions have held that joint and several liability is incompatible with market-share theory. See, e.g., Brown v. Superior Court, 751 P.2d 470 (Cal.1988); Hymowitz v. Eli Lilly Co., 539 N.E.2d 1069 (N.Y. 1989).

§ 16. Increased Harm Due to Product Defect

(a) When a product is defective at the time of commercial sale or other distribution and the defect is a substantial factor in increasing the plaintiff's harm beyond that which would have resulted from other causes, the product seller is subject to liability for the increased harm.

(b) If proof supports a determination of the harm that would have resulted from other causes in the absence of the product defect, the product seller's liability is limited to the increased harm attributable solely to the product defect.

(c) If proof does not support a determination under Subsection (b) of the harm that would have resulted in the absence of the product defect, the product seller is liable for all of the plaintiff's harm attributable to the defect and other causes.

(d) A seller of a defective product that is held liable for part of the harm suffered by the plaintiff under Subsection (b), or all of the harm suffered by the plaintiff under Subsection (c), is jointly and severally liable or severally liable with other parties who bear legal responsibility for causing the harm, determined by applicable rules of joint and several liability.

Comment:

a. Liability for increased harm. This Section deals with the problem of increased harm, often referred to as the issue of "enhancement" of harm. Liability for increased harm arises most frequently in automobile crashworthiness cases, but can also arise in connection with other products. Typically, the plaintiff is involved in an automobile accident caused by conduct or circumstances other than a product defect. The plaintiff would have suffered some injury as a result of the accident even in the absence of the claimed product defect. However, the plaintiff contends that the injuries were aggravated by the vehicle's failure reasonably to protect occupants in the event of an accident.

In the early era of product design litigation, controversy arose over whether a manufacturer owed any obligation to design its product so that injuries would be reasonably minimized in the event of an accident. That controversy is now settled. Although accidents are not intended uses of products, they are generally foreseeable. A manufacturer has a duty to design and manufacture its product so as reasonably to reduce the foreseeable harm that may occur in an accident brought about by causes other than a product defect. See Comment *b*. Since the product seller is responsible only for the increased harm, and not for the harm that would have occurred even in the absence of the product defect, basic principles of causation limit the damages to those resulting from the increased harm caused by the defect. The plaintiff must establish that the defect was a substantial factor in increasing the harm beyond that which would have resulted from other causes. Once the plaintiff establishes such increased harm, Subsection (b) or (c) applies. If proof supports a determination of what harm would have occurred without a defect, then liability is limited to the increased harm. If proof does not support such a determination, then the product seller is liable for all of the plaintiff's harm from both the defect and other causes.

Illustrations:

1. Bob negligently lost control of his car and collided with Ann's car, causing Ann to suffer harm from being thrown against her car's steering wheel. Ann was driving a car manufactured by XYZ Motor Co. In addition to suing Bob for his negligence, Ann sues XYZ. Expert testimony establishes that a reasonable alternative design of the steering mechanism was available that would have cushioned the impact between Ann and the steering column and that its omission rendered the car not reasonably safe. Further expert testimony describes the extent to which the omission of the alternative design increased the harm. Defendant XYZ is liable for harm that the trier of fact concludes the plaintiff suffered beyond the harm that would have been suffered had the car been equipped with the reasonable alternative design.

2. While Arthur was driving a snowmobile manufactured by ABC Co., the snowmobile hit a snow-covered rock. On impact, Arthur fell off the snowmobile and his face struck a brake bracket on the side of the snowmobile. Two sharp metal protrusions on the bracket caused serious facial injury. Competent testimony establishes that the brake bracket could have been covered by a safety guard that would have prevented such serious injury and that omission of the guard rendered the product not reasonably safe. Competent testimony also indicates the extent to which absence of the guard increased Arthur's harm. ABC is subject to liability for the harm that the trier of fact finds would have been prevented by a safety guard.

b. Establishing defect in increased-harm cases. To establish liability for increased harm, the plaintiff must prove that a product defect caused the harm under the rules stated in §§ 1–4. When the plaintiff alleges that a manufacturing defect caused increased harm, the plaintiff must establish a defect as set forth in § 2(a). When the plaintiff alleges that a design defect or a defect due to inadequate instructions or warnings caused increased harm, the plaintiff must establish that a reasonable alternative design could have been adopted, or that reasonable instructions or warnings could have been provided, as set forth in §§ 2(b) and 2(c).

In connection with a design defect claim in the context of increased harm, the plaintiff must establish that a reasonable alternative design would have reduced the plaintiff's harm. The factors enumerated in § 2, Comment *f*, for determining the reasonableness of an alternative design and the reasonable safety of the product are fully applicable to establishing defect in an increased-harm case. Furthermore, the alternative to the product design must increase the overall safety of the product. It is not sufficient that the alternative design would have reduced or prevented the harm the plaintiff suffered if the alternative would introduce into the product other dangers of equal or greater magnitude.

Proof of defect does not, of itself, establish a case of increased harm. The plaintiff must also establish that the defect was a substantial factor in increasing the plaintiff's harm beyond the harm that would have occurred from other causes. Subsection (c) provides that, when proof does not support a determination of increased harm, the product seller is liable for all harm suffered by the victim. However, the rule stated in Subsection (c) does not take effect until the plaintiff establishes under Subsection (a), by competent testimony, that the plaintiff's harm was increased as a result of the product defect.

Illustrations:

3. George was a passenger in a van manufactured by the XYZ Motor Co. The van was driven by a co-worker, Alice, who was proceeding non-negligently along a highway at 50 mph. To avoid a dog that unexpectedly ran across the highway, Alice swerved and lost control of the van, which struck an abutment. The force and angle of the collision caused the van to fly in the air and travel 75 feet before coming to rest upside down. During or after the initial collision, the roof panel separated from the van. George was thrown through the roof area and landed 50 feet from the van. Competent testimony by George's expert establishes that the welds meant to hold the roof to the body of the van were defective and did not meet the XYZ design standards. George's expert evidence also supports a determination that, had the roof been properly welded, it would not have come off as a result of the collision, that George would have remained in the van, and that the harm he suffered as a result of being thrown from the van was more serious than it would have been if the roof had kept George inside the van. Expert testimony also supports a determination of the extent to which George would have been harmed if he had stayed in the van, and thus the extent to which George's harm was increased by the failure of the roof to remain attached to the van. XYZ is liable for George's harm above that which the

trier of fact determines George would have suffered in the absence of the defective welds.

4. Alice was operating a tractor manufactured by XYZ Farm Equipment. The tractor was designed for use on hills and sharp inclines. The tractor struck a large rock protruding from the ground, causing the tractor to roll over down a slope. Alice was thrown from the tractor and pinned beneath it. Alice's expert testifies that, had the tractor been designed with a rollover protection system, Alice would not have been thrown from the tractor and that the omission of the rollover protection system rendered the product not reasonably safe. This testimony supports a finding of defective design. Expert testimony also describes the extent to which Alice's harm was increased by the omission of the rollover protection system. Defendant XYZ is subject to liability for Alice's harm beyond that which the trier of fact finds she would have suffered had the tractor been equipped with the rollover protection system.

5. Richard suffered harm as a result of an automobile accident that occurred when he lost control of his car on a rain-soaked highway. The car slid off the highway and collided sideways with a steel pole. As a result of the force of the collision, the pole ripped through the body of the car and crushed Richard between the front seat and the area of the roof just above the windshield. Richard brings suit against the XYZ Motor Co., the manufacturer of the car, alleging that the car was defective in design in that it did not have a continuous steel frame extending through the door panels. Richard's experts assert that, had the vehicle been so designed, it would have bounced off the pole, preventing penetration by the pole into the passenger space. XYZ's experts assert that a continuous steel frame would also reduce front-to-back deformation of the body of the vehicle in a head-on crash. Deformation is desirable in head-on crashes because it absorbs the impact of the crash and decreases risk of harm to the occupants of the vehicle. Richard's experts admit on cross-examination that, for head-on automobile accidents, the alternative design offered by Richard would decrease safety. Even if the design alternative offered by Richard would have reduced his harm, if the trier of fact finds that Richard's proposed alternative would have decreased the overall safety of the vehicle, it should return a verdict for XYZ.

c. Determination of what harm would have resulted in the absence of the product defect. The task of determining what harm would have resulted had the product not been defective under Subsection (b) is often difficult. Outright guesswork is not permitted, but neither should anything approaching certainty be required. When an expert offers a rational explanation derived from a causal analysis, the testimony should, subject to the normal discretion of the trial court, be admitted for consideration by the trier of fact.

d. Extent of liability for increased harm when proof does not support determination of what harm would have resulted in the absence of the product defect. Subsection (c) provides that when the plaintiff has proved defect-caused increased harm, the product seller is subject to liability for all harm suffered by the plaintiff if proof does not support a determination of what harm would have resulted if the product had not been defective. The defendant, a wrongdoer who in fact has caused harm to the plaintiff, should not escape liability because the nature of the harm makes such a determination impossible. Compare § 433B(2) of the Restatement, Second, of Torts.

Illustration:

6. The same facts as Illustration 3, in that George proves that the defect was a substantial factor in increasing the harm beyond that which he would have suffered if the roof had kept him inside the van, but George is unable to quantify the extent of the increased harm. Neither party introduces proof that supports the apportionment of liability. XYZ is liable for all of George's harm.

e. Joint and several liability for increased harm. When the plaintiff proves defect-caused increased harm, and the seller of the defective product is held liable for part of the harm suffered by the plaintiff under Subsection (b) or all of the harm suffered by the plaintiff under Subsection (c), liability of the seller and other tortfeasors is joint and several. In a case under Subsection (b), the manufacturer is jointly and severally liable only for the increased harm; in a case under Subsection (c), for the entire harm. Joint and several liability is imposed because there is no practical method of apportioning responsibility that would reflect the separate causal contributions of those tortfeasors who caused the increased harm. The general rules governing joint and several liability determine the liability of the parties to the injured plaintiff. In those jurisdictions that retain the common-law rule, all parties bear full responsibility for the entirety of the harm. In many jurisdictions, the common-law rules of joint and several liability have undergone significant legislative modification limiting liability to the percentage of fault allocated to each party.

Illustrations:

7. Same facts as Illustration 6, except that Alice's negligent driving caused her to lose control of her van. The XYZ Motor Co. is liable under Subsection (c) for all of George's harm. The case is

governed by the law of State A, which follows the common-law rule of joint and several liability. George may recover all of his damages from either Alice or XYZ.

8. Same facts as Illustration 7. The XYZ Motor Co. is liable under Subsection (c) for all of George's harm. The case is governed by the law of State B, whose statute limits the liability of joint tortfeasors to the percentage of responsibility allocated to each party. The trier of fact allocates 40 percent of the responsibility to Alice and 60 percent of the responsibility to XYZ. XYZ's liability is limited to 60 percent of the total damages.

9. Same facts as Illustration 7. The XYZ Motor Co. is liable under Subsection (c) for all of George's harm. The case is governed by the law of State C, whose statute retains the common-law rule of joint and several liability for economic loss but limits the liability of joint tortfeasors for noneconomic loss to the percentage of responsibility allocated to each party. The trier of fact has allocated 40 percent of the responsibility to Alice and 60 percent to XYZ. George may recover all of his economic loss damages from either Alice or XYZ. His recovery from XYZ for noneconomic damages is limited to 60 percent.

f. Plaintiff's fault in cases of increased harm. Section 17 sets forth the general rules governing plaintiff's fault in products liability litigation. It provides that plaintiff's fault is relevant in apportioning liability between the plaintiff and the product seller. The seriousness of the plaintiff's fault and the nature of the product defect are relevant in apportioning the appropriate percentages of responsibility between the plaintiff and the product seller. See § 17, Comment *d*. Accordingly, the contributory fault of the plaintiff in causing an accident that results in defect-related increased harm is relevant in apportioning responsibility between or among the parties, according to applicable apportionment law. In apportioning responsibility in such cases, it may be important that requiring a product to be designed reasonably to prevent increased harm aims to protect persons in circumstances in which they are unable to protect themselves.

REPORTERS' NOTE

Comment a. Liability for increased harm. Increased-harm liability problems have also arisen with regard to products other than motor vehicles. See, e.g., McGee v. Cessna Aircraft Co., 188 Cal.Rptr. 542 (Cal.Ct.App. 1983) (airplane); Camacho v. Honda Motor Co. Ltd., 741 P.2d 1240 (Colo. 1987), cert. denied, 485 U.S. 901, 108 S.Ct. 1067, 99 L.Ed.2d 229 (1988) (motorcycle); Tafoya v. Sears, Roebuck & Co., 884 F.2d 1330 (10th Cir. 1989) (applying enhanced injury doctrine to riding lawnmower under Colorado law); Rubin v. Brutus Corp., 487 So.2d 360 (Fla.Dist.Ct.App.1986), review denied, 500 So.2d 543 (1986) (pleasure boat); Hillrichs v. Avco Corp., 478 N.W.2d 70 (Iowa 1991) (grain harvester); Miller v. Todd, 551 N.E.2d 1139 (Ind.1990) (motorcycle); Masterman v. Veldman's Equip., Inc., 530 N.E.2d 312 (Ind.Ct.App.1988) (snowplow mount); Smith v. Ariens Co., 377 N.E.2d 954 (Mass.1978) (snowmobile); Valk Mfg. Co. v. Rangaswamy, 537 A.2d 622 (Md.Ct. Spec.App.1988) (snowplow hitch), rev'd, Montgomery County v. Valk Mfg. Co., 562 A.2d 1246 (Md.1989); Pree v. Brunswick Corp., 983 F.2d 863 (8th Cir.1993) (applying Missouri law), cert. denied, 510 U.S. 815, 114 S.Ct. 65, 126 L.Ed.2d 35 (1993) (motorboat propeller); Roe v. Deere & Co., Inc., 855 F.2d 151 (3d Cir.1988) (applying Pennsylvania law) (agricultural tractor); Farrell v. John Deere Co., 443 N.W.2d 50 (Wis.App.1989) (corn picker).

In the early years of tort liability for defective product design, some courts refused to recognize a duty on the part of an auto manufacturer to design a reasonably crashworthy vehicle. See, e.g., Evans v. General Motors Corp., 359 F.2d 822 (7th Cir. 1966), cert. denied, 385 U.S. 836, 87 S.Ct. 83, 17 L.Ed.2d 70 (1966). The overwhelming majority, however, followed the view of Larsen v. General Motors Corp., 391 F.2d 495 (8th Cir. 1968), which held that collisions are foreseeable and that manufacturers must design cars so that they are reasonably crashworthy. The *Larsen* rule appears now to be the unanimous position of American courts. In Blankenship v. General Motors Corp., 406 S.E.2d 781 (W.Va.1991), the court reviewed the authority and found no support for *Evans*, which itself was overruled in Huff v. White Motor Corp., 565 F.2d 104, 110 (7th Cir. 1977). The Reporters are unaware of any jurisdiction that espouses *Evans*. For an exhaustive listing of the cases following *Larsen*, see Levenstam and Lapp, Plaintiff's Burden of Proving Enhanced Injury in Crashworthiness Cases: A Clash Worthy of Analysis, 38 De Paul L. Rev. 55, 61 n.33 (1989).

Illustration 1 is based on Larsen v. General Motors Corp., 391 F.2d 495 (8th Cir.1968). Illustration 2 is based on Smith v. Ariens Co., 377 N.E.2d 954 (Mass.1978).

Comment b. Establishing defect in increased-harm cases. When a plaintiff alleges that the product should have been designed more safely, or been accompanied by instructions or warnings so as to avoid enhanced injuries, a plaintiff must establish that a reasonable alternative design could have been adopted or reasonable instructions or warnings could have been provided. See, e.g., General Motors Corp. v. Edwards, 482 So.2d 1176, 1188 (Ala.1985), overruled on other grounds by Schwartz v. Volvo North Am. Corp., 554 So.2d 927 (Ala. 1989). (" ... proof of defectiveness [in an enhanced harm case] also requires proof that a safer practical, alternative design was available to the manufacturer"); Hillrichs v. Avco Corp., 478 N.W.2d 70, 75 (Iowa 1991) (one of the elements of a prima facie claim for enhanced injury is " ... proof of an alternative safer design, practicable under the circumstances"); Reed v. Chrysler Corp., 494 N.W.2d 224, 226 (Iowa 1992); Miller v. Todd, 551 N.E.2d 1139, 1143 (Ind.1990) ("A claimant should be able to demonstrate that a feasible, safer, more practicable product design would have afforded better protection."); Page v. Gilbert, 598 So.2d

1110, 1114 (La.Ct.App.1992). For cases arising after the passage of La. Rev. Stat. § 9:2800.56 the plaintiff in a crashworthiness case must establish (1) the availability of an alternative design that would have reduced the plaintiff's harm; and "(2) the likelihood that the product's design would cause the claimant's damage and the gravity of that damage outweighed the burden on the manufacturer of adopting such alternative design and the adverse effect, if any, of such alternative design on the utility of the product." See Toliver v. General Motors Corp., 482 So.2d 213, 218 (Miss. 1985) ("To prove his case [crashworthiness based on defective design], the plaintiff may introduce evidence of industry standards, to show deviation therefrom, or an alternate design, to show the feasibility thereof."); Huddell v. Levin, 537 F.2d 726, 737–38 (3d Cir.1976) (applying New Jersey law); Crispin v. Volkswagenwerk AG, 591 A.2d 966, 976–78 (N.J.Super.Ct.App.Div.1991), cert. denied, 599 A.2d 162 (1991) (given the tendency of the VW seat to yield upon impact, VW had a duty to warn about the necessity to wear seat belts to protect occupants from injury in the case of collision. *Crispin* is a crashworthiness case in which the failure-to-warn issue was presented as relevant to increased harm). Contra, e.g., Rahmig v. Mosley Mach. Co., Inc., 412 N.W.2d 56, 81–82 (Neb.1987) (plaintiff does not have to prove alternative safer design); Couch v. Mine Safety Appliances Co., 728 P.2d 585 (Wash.1986).

Illustration 3 is based on Lahocki v. Contee Sand & Gravel Co., Inc., 398 A.2d 490 (Md.Ct.Spec.App.1979). Illustration 4 is based on Roe v. Deere & Co., Inc., 855 F.2d 151 (3d Cir.1988). Illustration 5 is based on Dawson v. Chrysler Corp., 630 F.2d 950 (3d Cir.1980).

Comment c. Determination of what harm would have resulted in the absence of the product defect. Numerous courts have recognized that the task of allocating causal responsibility in enhanced injury cases is a difficult one and certainty in apportionment often is not attainable. Rather, courts must rely on reasonable estimations by experts to accomplish apportionment. See, e.g., May v. Portland Jeep, Inc., 509 P.2d 24 (Or.1973); Hillrichs v. Avco Corp., 478 N.W.2d 70 (Iowa 1991); Reed v. Chrysler Corp., 494 N.W.2d 224 (Iowa 1992).

Comment d. Extent of liability for increased harm when proof does not support determination of what harm would have resulted in the absence of the product defect. A strong majority of courts that have considered the question have adopted a rule that supports § 16(c). Thus, if a plaintiff establishes that a product defect was a substantial factor in increasing the harm suffered by the plaintiff beyond that which would have resulted from other causes, and if proof adduced at trial does not support apportionment of liability, then the product seller is liable for all the harm suffered by the plaintiff from both the defect and the other causes.

The rule in § 16(c) is similar to that set forth in § 433B(2) of the Restatement, Second, of Torts. Section 433B(2) provides that when the tortious conduct of two or more actors combines to bring about harm to a plaintiff, and one of the actors seeks to limit liability claiming that the harm is apportionable, the burden of proof concerning apportionment is upon that actor. As Comment *d* to § 433B(2) explains, the reason for shifting the burden of apportionment to the defendant is the injustice of allowing a proved wrongdoer, who has in fact caused harm to the plaintiff, to escape liability because another wrongdoer or causal agent also was involved and the nature of the harm makes apportionment impossible. Illustration 8 to § 433B(2) is parallel to a case of product-defect-caused increase in harm. In that Illustration, two automobiles collide and an occupant of one of the cars suffers harm to his shoulder caused by the negligence of the other. Immediately thereafter a car negligently driven by a third party drives into the wreckage and inflicts further harm to the occupant's shoulder. As a result of one impact or the other, or both, the occupant's arm becomes paralyzed. The burden is upon the third driver, who drove into the wreckage, to prove that the additional injury inflicted by that driver's conduct did not cause the paralysis.

Section 16(c) does not formally shift any burden of proof to the defendant. Its effect is that, if the plaintiff has established that the product defect increased the harm over and above that which the plaintiff would have suffered had the product been nondefective, and if, at the close of the case, proof does not support a determination of the harm that would have resulted in the absence of the product defect, then the defendant is liable for all the harm suffered by the plaintiff.

The majority view will be referred to as the *Fox-Mitchell* approach, named after two early cases that espoused the position. The opposing, minority view, which will be referred to as the *Huddell* approach, insists that the plaintiff must prove the extent of the increased harm. If the plaintiff is unable to quantify the increased harm, even if the plaintiff can establish that some increased harm was caused by the defendant, the plaintiff is unable to recover.

The Fox–Mitchell approach. This discussion sets forth the case law that supports the *Fox-Mitchell* approach. It includes those states whose law either supports, or is strongly leaning toward, the majority view. The following states are in the *Fox-Mitchell* camp: Alabama, Alaska, Arizona, California, Florida, Georgia, Idaho, Illinois, Indiana, Louisiana, Maryland, Minnesota, Missouri, Nebraska, New Jersey, Ohio, Oklahoma, Oregon, Rhode Island, Texas, West Virginia, Wisconsin, and Wyoming. Thus, a total of 23 states favor the position taken in § 16(c). In addition, cases in Arkansas and Colorado offer good reason to believe that they would adopt the *Fox-Mitchell* approach when next that issue comes before them. In the ensuing discussion the cases that support the *Fox-Mitchell* position are listed without commentary. When some explanation is necessary for concluding that a state would adopt the *Fox-Mitchell* approach, it is set forth.

General Motors Corp. v. Edwards, 482 So.2d 1176, 1189 (Ala.1985), overruled on other grounds by Schwartz v. Volvo North Am. Corp., 554 So.2d 927 (Ala.1989), clearly supports the majority view. The Alabama court held:

> Consequently, the only proof of damages that will limit the manufacturer's liability in crashworthiness cases is proof that, regardless of the design used, the identical injuries were inevitable. In such a case, the manufacturer's liability is not only limited, it is completely eliminated, because plaintiff has failed to prove 'cause in fact,' a

> fundamental element necessary to prove proximate cause between the defective condition and his injuries.... If, on the other hand, the proof shows that an alternative design would have eliminated plaintiff's injuries totally or would have reduced them, proximate cause between the defect and the injury is proven, and the manufacturer is jointly and severally liable along with the striking driver (assuming that he is found liable) for the entire amount of the injuries suffered. Thus, the manufacturer faces an all or nothing proposition; either he is liable for all the damages or he is liable for none, depending upon whether an alternative design would have prevented or reduced plaintiff's injuries.

See also Czarnecki v. Volkswagen of Am., 837 P.2d 1143, 1148 (Ariz.Ct. App.1991) ("[I]n a crashworthiness case with an indivisible injury, the plaintiff fulfills his burden of proof by showing that the defective design caused him to sustain injuries over and above those that otherwise would have occurred in the first collision. Once the plaintiff has [proven some enhancement], the burden shifts to the defendant to show that the damages that arose from the enhanced injury are apportionable."); McLeod v. American Motors Corp., 723 F.2d 830, 834–35 (11th Cir.1984) (applying Florida law, drawing analogy from successive collision cases in which plaintiff is able to recover from either defendant if damages cannot be apportioned); Polston v. Boomershine Pontiac–GMC Truck, Inc., 423 S.E.2d 659 (Ga.1992); Fouche v. Chrysler Motors Corp., 692 P.2d 345 (Idaho 1984).

Buehler v. Whalen, 374 N.E.2d 460 (Ill.1977), has been cited in support of the rule that in a crashworthiness case the tortfeasor who caused the accident and the auto manufacturer whose design was responsible for the increased harm should be treated as joint tortfeasors. There is language in *Buehler* that supports such a reading. 374 N.E.2d at 465. However, on its facts, it is clear that the design defect alleged by the plaintiffs was responsible for all the enhanced injury. The parties had stipulated that the harm suffered by the plaintiffs was entirely caused by burns. The burns resulted when the car in which the plaintiffs were riding was rear-ended. The design defect was inadequate fire protection between the trunk and the passenger compartment that permitted the fire to spread before the occupants could exit the vehicle. Thus, the auto manufacturer could not claim that it was being held liable for injuries which it did not, in fact, cause. However, in Oakes v. General Motors Corp., 628 N.E.2d 341 (Ill.App.Ct. 1993), leave to appeal denied, 633 N.E.2d 4 (1994), an intermediate appellate court reviewed *Buehler*, supra and other Illinois cases and found that Illinois law rejects *Huddell* and would follow the *Fox-Mitchell* majority view. In rejecting *Huddell* the *Oakes* court noted:

> This formulation of the enhanced injury doctrine would require a plaintiff who sustains injuries as a result of the defective design of an automobile to separate those injuries sustained as a result of the defect from those injuries which he would have sustained in the occurrence absent the defect. As plaintiff points out, under this rule, he would be required to establish what injuries he might have received even though he did not receive them. In other words, plaintiff

> would have to prove a negative based on a hypothetical set of facts. We consider this to be a nearly insurmountable burden, particularly here where plaintiff's injury is incapable of being logically or reasonably divided. In *Larsen*, the defendant, General Motors, concurred in this view. Ostensibly arguing against the enhanced injury doctrine in that case, General Motors contended that the enhanced injury arising from a design defect would be "difficult to assess." (*Larsen*, 391 F.2d at 503). It is ironic that here, notwithstanding the indivisible nature of plaintiff's injury, the determination of the enhanced injury, in General Motors's view, is an easy feat.

628 N.E.2d at 348.

The *Oakes* court then went on to adopt the *Mitchell* approach to crashworthiness and noted that under *Mitchell*:

> The plaintiff must show only that the design defect was a "substantial factor" in producing damages over and above those which were probably caused as a result of the original impact or collision. The [*Mitchell*] court went on to hold that if the manufacturer's negligence is found to be a substantial factor in causing an indivisible injury such as paraplegia or death, then "absent a reasonable basis to determine which wrongdoer actually caused the harm, the defendants should be treated as joint and several tortfeasors. . . . "

Id. 628 N.E.2d at 349. See also DePaepe v. General Motors Corp., 33 F.3d 737 (7th Cir.1994) (adopting *Oakes* as the governing law in Illinois).

In Masterman v. Veldman's Equip., Inc., 530 N.E.2d 312 (Ind.Ct.App. 1988), the court placed the burden of proving the amount of increased harm on the plaintiff. However, in Jackson v. Warrum, 535 N.E.2d 1207, 1220 (Ind.Ct.App.1989), the court held that a plaintiff can establish proximate cause in a crashworthiness case by "establishing that the defectively designed product was a substantial factor in producing damages over and above those which were probably caused as a result of the original impact or collision. Once the plaintiff establishes the foregoing, the burden shifts to the defendant to establish and prove that the damages that arose from the enhanced injury are apportionable." The *Jackson* case contains a thorough analysis of Indiana law on the issue and more likely reflects what Indiana law on the subject ultimately will be.

See also Page v. Gilbert, 598 So.2d 1110 (La.Ct.App.1992). *Page* does not speak directly to the burden of proof issue raised in § 16(c). However, it indirectly supports the position that the manufacturer responsible for second-collision injuries is treated as a joint tortfeasor. In *Page*, the driver of the car who caused the collision and the manufacturer of the automobile in which the plaintiff was a passenger were each held to be 50 percent at fault. It is clear from the decision that no causal apportionment based on how much increased harm was caused by the design defect in the automobile was undertaken. Armstrong v. Lorino, 580 So.2d 528 (La. Ct.App.1991), is erroneously cited in Polston v. Boomershine Pontiac–GMC Truck, Inc., 423 S.E.2d 659, 661 n. 1 (1992), as supportive of the *Huddell* position. In *Armstrong*, the appellate court upheld the trial court's grant of a directed verdict on the grounds that the plaintiff failed to establish either defect or any enhancement whatsoever. Thus, *Armstrong*, often cited in support of *Huddell*, does not support that position in any fashion.

Lahocki v. Contee Sand & Gravel Co., Inc., 398 A.2d 490, 498 (Md.Ct. Spec.App.1979), rev'd on other grounds, General Motors Corp. v. Lahocki, 410 A.2d 1039 (Md.1980); Valk Mfg. Co. v. Rangaswamy, 537 A.2d 622, 633 (Md.Ct.Spec.App.1988), rev'd on other grounds, Montgomery County v. Valk Mfg. Co., 562 A.2d 1246 (Md.1989); Mitchell v. Volkswagenwerk, AG, 669 F.2d 1199 (8th Cir. 1982) (applying Minnesota law); Richardson v. Volkswagenwerk, A.G., 552 F.Supp. 73, 82–83 (W.D.Mo.1982) (applying Missouri law) and McDowell v. Kawasaki Motors Corp. U.S.A., 799 S.W.2d 854, 867 (Mo.Ct.App.1990) (rejecting *Huddell* and holding that "a plaintiff meets his burden of proof on causation if the evidence shows that the product was a substantial factor in causing injuries in excess of those caused by the first collision"). Kudlacek v. Fiat S.p.A., 509 N.W.2d 603, 611 (Neb.1994) (adopting *Fox-Mitchell*).

Even New Jersey, the state in which the rule contrary to *Fox-Mitchell* was spawned, may wind up adopting *Fox-Mitchell*. Huddell v. Levin, 537 F.2d 726 (3d Cir. 1976) (applying New Jersey law), is the leading case requiring the plaintiff to prove the extent of enhanced damages as a predicate for recovery. But in Crispin v. Volkswagenwerk AG, 591 A.2d 966, 980 n. 1 (N.J.Super.Ct.App.Div.1991), the court noted that the New Jersey Supreme Court had not as yet decided whether plaintiff or defendant has the burden of apportionment in a crashworthiness case. It then noted, "[a] rule placing upon the defendant the burden of proof with respect to the apportionment of damages, may be more in line with our Supreme Court's recent decision in Scafidi v. Seiler, . . . 574 A.2d 398 (N.J.1990). See also Fosgate v. Corona, . . . 330 A.2d 355 (N.J. 1974). . . . " But see McLaughlin v. Nissan Motor Corp., 630 A.2d 857 (N.J.Super.Ct.Law Div.1993) and Thornton v. General Motors Corp., 655 A.2d 107 (N.J.Super.Ct.Law Div. 1994) (disagreeing with *McLaughlin* and applying *Fox-Mitchell* in a New Jersey crashworthiness case).

See also Warren v. Colombo, 377 S.E.2d 249 (N.C.Ct.App.1989) (adopting crashworthiness theory). The court acknowledged that courts would be faced with difficult apportionment problems. But see opinion of Green, J., concurring, in which he applies Restatement, Second, Torts § 433(B)(2) to a crashworthiness case. In Seese v. Volkswagenwerk A.G., 648 F.2d 833 (3d Cir.1981), cert. denied, 454 U.S. 867, 102 S.Ct. 330, 70 L.Ed.2d 168 (1981), the court predicted that North Carolina would adopt *Huddell*. This position was refuted by the Fourth Circuit in a series of cases. See Erwin v. Jeep Corp., 812 F.2d 172 (4th Cir.1987). The authority of *Seese* as a predictor of North Carolina law on the subject of apportionment is weak. *Seese* did not undertake any analysis of North Carolina law on the subject of who should bear the burden of proof on apportionment. It simply applied the *Huddell* criteria unquestioningly. Pang v. Minch, 559 N.E.2d 1313, 1324 (Ohio 1990) (successive collision case holding that when "a single indivisible injury is proximately caused by the successive tortious acts of multiple defendants," § 433B(2) of the Restatement, Second, of Torts, applies, and the plaintiff is entitled to treat the successive tortfeasors as jointly and severally liable). *Pang* cites with approval Richardson v. Volkswagenwerk, A.G., supra, a crashworthiness case that treats the manufacturer and the tortfeasor as joint tortfeasors; see also Ault v. Navistar Int'l Transp. Corp., 880 F.2d 414 (6th Cir.1989) (unpublished disposition) (Sixth Circuit refuses to apply *Huddell* standard in a crashworthiness wrongful death case). *Pang* almost certainly places Ohio among the states that would adopt the rule stated in Subsection (c).

See also Lee v. Volkswagen of Am., Inc., 688 P.2d 1283, 1287–88 (Okla. 1984) (Plaintiff has the burden of proving that the product defect was the cause of enhanced injuries. If the court finds that the injury is single and indivisible, the parties are treated as concurrent tortfeasors and are jointly and severally liable. At that point the burden shifts to the defendant to prove apportionment of the enhanced injuries, if possible.); May v. Portland Jeep, Inc., 509 P.2d 24, 26–27 (Or.1973) (*May* predates the *Huddell-Mitchell* controversy; however, in allowing plaintiff to reach the trier of fact with an increased harm claim, the court said:

> There is no way of determining, of course, what the exact extent of plaintiff's injuries would have been had the roll bar not collapsed. However, we allow juries to make somewhat similar inexact determinations such as the extent of pain and suffering and its value in money. We do because we believe such pain and suffering should be compensable, and there is no way of determining its extent and value other than to allow the jury to use its best judgment. The only alternative in this case is to say that plaintiff probably was additionally injured by the collapse of the bar, but that because we cannot determine exactly what his injuries would have been if it had not collapsed, he cannot recover at all. This is not an acceptable alternative....).

It is likely that if apportionment is not possible, the Oregon court would reject *Huddell.*

McInnis v. A.M.F. Inc., 765 F.2d 240, 249 (1st Cir.1985) (applying Rhode Island law), is an enhanced injury case that deals with the admissibility of a release from the tortfeasor who caused the accident in the case against the product manufacturer who was alleged to be responsible for the increased harm. Rule 408 of the Federal Rules prohibits the introduction of the release when used to prove "liability for or the invalidity of the claim." The defendant-manufacturer that was defending against the enhanced injury claim argued that "because there were two separate accidents involved in the case—the collision with the ... car and the crashing of the motorcycle—each party is liable only for the alleged divisible portion of the plaintiff's injury that their respective acts immediately caused." 765 F.2d at 249. In rejecting the defendant's argument, the court said that under Rhode Island law "the parties are both jointly and severally liable if they are both the legal cause of the harm that cannot be apportioned, *whether the conduct is concurring or consecutive.*" Id. (emphasis added). Engberg v. Ford Motor Co., 205 N.W.2d 104 (S.D.1973), has been cited in support of the rule stated in Subsection (c). See, e.g.,

Polston v. Boomershine Pontiac–GMC Truck, Inc., 423 S.E.2d 659, n. 1 (Ga.1992). *Engberg* predates the *Mitchell-Huddell* controversy and does not speak to the issue of burden of apportionment once increased harm has been established. The court merely pointed out that the expert testimony that supported a finding of increased harm was adequate and could not be disregarded merely because the defendant had suggested other causes for the increased harm.

See also Shipp v. General Motors Corp., 750 F.2d 418 (5th Cir.1985) (applying Texas law); Blankenship v. General Motors Corp., 406 S.E.2d 781 (W.Va.1991); Sumnicht v. Toyota Motor Sales, U.S.A., Inc., 360 N.W.2d 2, 11 (Wis.1984) ("once the plaintiff has proven that the defect was a cause of his injuries, he need not prove what portion of indivisible harm is attributable solely to the manufacturer"). A Wisconsin court has specifically rejected *Huddell*. In Maskrey v. Volkswagenwerk, A.G., 370 N.W.2d 815, 822 (Wis.Ct.App.1985), the court, relying on *Sumnicht*, applied the rule stated in this Subsection: "The trial court properly placed the initial burden on Maskrey to prove that Szuta's negligence and VW's defective product were substantial factors in causing the harm for which he claimed damages. Once such evidence was adduced, the trial court also properly placed the burden on VW to apportion the damages." Fox v. Ford Motor Co., 575 F.2d 774 (10th Cir.1978) (applying Wyoming law); Chrysler Corp. v. Todorovich, 580 P.2d 1123 (Wyo.1978); Harvey by Harvey v. General Motors Corp., 873 F.2d 1343 (10th Cir.1989) (The holding of *Todorovich* clearly rejects *Huddell*. 580 P.2d at 1131. The court said, "The [enhanced] injuries sustained by [the plaintiff] are incapable of any logical, reasonable, or practical division. Since the conduct of Chrysler and that of Rummell each constituted a legal cause of the injuries sustained by [the plaintiff], they stand jointly and severally liable for the full extent of his injuries." Id.).

The statement by the court in Harvey by Harvey v. General Motors Corp., 873 F.2d at 1349, that "[u]nder Wyoming law, an enhancement instruction should not even be given unless the injuries are capable of logical, reasonable, or practical division" cannot be read to contradict the holding of *Todorovich*. The court seems to be saying that apportionment cannot be attempted unless there is adequate evidence to support it. The plaintiff apparently based his claim on the hypothesis that the harm he suffered was divisible and was ultimately unable to establish what kind of harm he would have suffered had the auto design not been defective. Furthermore, there is a very real question whether there was any enhancement whatsoever. Admittedly, the question how a finding of no damages by the jury can be reconciled with the finding that the design defect was a proximate cause of the plaintiff's injuries is difficult. Nonetheless, *Harvey* cannot be read flatly to contradict the direct holding of *Todorovich*, which is a clear pronouncement by the Wyoming Supreme Court of governing law within the state.

The statement in *Harvey* that the court reads its opinion in Fox v. Ford Motor Co. in a "different light" than did the Fifth Circuit in Shipp v. General Motors Corp., 750 F.2d 418 (5th Cir.1985), is somewhat enigmatic. As noted earlier, the more pressing question is *Todorovich*, not *Fox*, since the former is the last word from the Wyoming Supreme Court.

In addition to direct authority supporting the rule stated in this subsection, there is authority in some jurisdictions dealing with successive collisions in which the courts hold the second tortfeasor who causes increased harm jointly and severally liable. See, e.g., Woodward v. Blythe, 462 S.W.2d 205, 209 (Ark.1971) ("[W]here the concurrent or successive negligent acts or omissions of two or more persons, although acting independently of each other, are, in combination, the direct and proximate cause of a single injury to a third person, and it is impossible to determine in what proportion each contributed to the injury, either is responsible for the whole injury . . ." quoting 38 Am. Jur., Negligence, § 257); Romero v. Parker, 619 P.2d 89 (Colo.Ct.App.1980) (in personal injury action arising out of successive automobile collisions, the party who negligently caused the second collision is liable for entire award to injured person if the negligence of each defendant proximately caused injury to the plaintiff and the injuries cannot be apportioned).

Furthermore, in some jurisdictions courts have taken positions with regard to the burden of proof issue that militate strongly in favor of the majority view. See, e.g., Caterpillar Tractor Co. v. Beck, 593 P.2d 871 (Alaska 1979) and Barker v. Lull Eng'g Co., 573 P.2d 443 (Cal.1978). Both *Beck* and *Barker* take the position that, once plaintiff proves that a product design proximately caused the plaintiff's injury, the burden of proof shifts to the defendant to prove that the product met risk-utility norms. If the court is willing to accomplish burden shifting on the basic issue of defect, it is unlikely that, if the plaintiff proves a causal relationship between defect and enhanced injury, the court would not shift the burden of apportioning damages to the defendant.

Two California intermediate appellate court cases tend to support the proposition that California would follow the rule stated in Subsection (c). See McGee v. Cessna Aircraft Co., 188 Cal.Rptr. 542 (Cal.Ct.App.1983) (discussion of burden of proof in airplane crashworthiness case); Doupnik v. General Motors Corp., 275 Cal. Rptr. 715, 719 (Cal.Ct.App.1990). The court held that as long as the defect is a substantial factor in bringing about the enhanced injury, liability attaches. The case does not specifically address the shifting burden of proof issue, but the inference is strong that a plaintiff who establishes enhancement has fulfilled his burden of proof. Recently, the Georgia high court in Polston v. Boomershine Pontiac–GMC Truck, Inc., 423 S.E.2d 659, 661 n. 1 (Ga.1992), cited *Doupnik* as authority for the proposition that once the plaintiff establishes enhancement the burden of apportionment shifts to the defendant.

The Huddell approach. Only six states are clearly in the *Huddell* camp: Michigan, New Mexico, New York, Pennsylvania, South Carolina, and Virginia. A recent Iowa opinion follows the formal structure of *Huddell*, but one may reasonably doubt whether, if forced to make a choice, the Iowa court would follow *Huddell*.

For cases supporting the minority position, see Sumner v. General Motors Corp., 538 N.W.2d 112 (Mich.Ct. App.1995); Huddell v. Levin, 537 F.2d 726 (3d Cir.1976) (applying New Jersey law) (See discussion supra as to whether *Huddell* is still good authority in New Jersey); Duran v. General Motors Corp., 688 P.2d 779 (N.M.Ct. App.1983), overruled on other grounds by Brooks v. Beech Aircraft Corp., 902 P.2d 54 (N.M.1995); Caiazzo v. Volkswagenwerk, A.G., 647 F.2d 241 (2d Cir.1981) (applying New York law; cited with approval in Held v. Ball, 507 N.Y.S.2d 98 (N.Y.App.Div. 1986); Garcia v. Rivera, 553 N.Y.S.2d 378 (N.Y.App.Div.1990), appeal denied, 567 N.E.2d 980, 566 N.Y.S.2d 586 (1991)); Craigie v. General Motors Corp., 740 F.Supp. 353 (E.D.Pa. 1990); Kupetz v. Deere & Co., 644 A.2d 1213 (Pa.Super.Ct.1994); Stonehocker v. General Motors Corp., 587 F.2d 151, 157 (4th Cir.1978) (applying South Carolina law); Chretien v. General Motors Corp., 959 F.2d 231 (4th Cir.1992) (unpublished disposition). Applying Virginia law in *Chretien*, the court held that expert testimony that the plaintiff's injuries were enhanced by defect was not sufficient and that the plaintiff had the burden of proving the extent of the injuries. The court cited *Huddell* in support of this proposition.

Thus, not only does the weight of the authority support the rule stated in § 16(c), but it also reflects the more recent developments. It is significant that most of the authority cited as supporting the position that the plaintiff has the burden of establishing the extent of the enhanced injury damages is from older cases. See, e.g., Wernimont v. International Harvester Corp., 309 N.W.2d 137 (Iowa.Ct.App.1981). *Wernimont* is sometimes cited in support of the *Huddell* position. The court does cite *Huddell* for the elements of the crashworthiness cause of action. However, as to whether the burden should shift to the defendant once the plaintiff has established some enhancement, the court is silent. In fact, the court notes that the Iowa Supreme Court has yet to address the problem. 309 N.W.2d at 140 n.2.

The most recent Iowa Supreme Court cases dealing with crashworthiness, Hillrichs v. Avco Corp., 478 N.W.2d 70 (Iowa 1991), and Reed v. Chrysler Corp., 494 N.W.2d 224 (Iowa 1992), do not confront the question directly. In *Hillrichs*, the court found that there was adequate evidence from which a jury could calculate the extent of the enhanced injury. The court did, however, say that "Damages, may be awarded, ... when the only dispute is the amount of damages and the evidence affords a reasonable basis for estimating the loss." 478 N.W.2d at 75. In *Reed*, the court found that some reasonable estimation of add-on damages was, in fact, possible. The court said, "[w]here some damages appear, recovery should not be denied merely because of difficulty in fixing an exact amount." 494 N.W.2d at 228. One cannot be certain whether, if the Iowa court were faced with a case in which apportionment could not be reasonably determined, even by a relaxed standard of proof, the court would deny recovery. The language of *Hillrichs* would seem to imply that some reasonable apportionment is necessary. However, the Iowa court appears determined not to turn a plaintiff away because of the difficulties in proving the extent of the increased harm.

One final point concerning the sources of authority on the issue of increased harm. Much of the authority stems from federal courts making *Erie* guesses about how state courts would hold. However, of the state courts that have spoken, the following states have taken a position consistent with the rule stated in § 16(c): Alabama (1985), Arizona (1991) (intermediate appellate court, and review denied by supreme court), Georgia (1992), Idaho (1984), Illinois (1993) (intermediate appellate court), Maryland (1988), Missouri (1990) (intermediate appellate court), Nebraska (1994), Ohio (1990), Oklahoma (1984), West Virginia (1991), Wisconsin (1984), and Wyoming (1978). Only three states that have spoken support the rule that a plaintiff who is unable to establish the extent of apportionment fails to make out a cause of action: Michigan (1995) (intermediate appellate court), New Mexico (1983), and New York (1986), intermediate appellate court, and (1990) (intermediate appellate court).

The Legal Commentators—Some Reflections

An early law review Note was influential in the development of the *Fox-Mitchell* position. See Note, Apportionment of Damages in the "Second Collision" Case, 63 Va. L. Rev. 475 (1977). In general, the writers continue to support the rule as stated in this Section. See, e.g., Beck, Enhanced Injury: A Direction for Washington, 61 Wash. L. Rev. 571 (1986); Tietz, Bushman and Podraza, Crashworthiness and Erie: Determining State Law Regarding the Burden of Proving and Apportioning Damages, 62 Temp. L.Rev. 587 (1989).

The *Huddell* view, however, has its supporters. See, e.g., Hoenig, Resolution of "Crashworthiness" Design Claims, 55 St. Johns L. Rev. 633, 699–706 (1981); Levenstam and Lapp, Plaintiff's Burden of Proving Enhanced Injury in Crashworthiness Cases: A Clash Worthy of Analysis, 38 De Paul L. Rev. 55 (1989); Shad, Warren v. Colombo: North Carolina Recognizes Claim for Enhanced Injury, 68 N.C. L. Rev. 1330 (1990).

In formulating the rule stated in § 16(c), careful consideration was given to the view of those who support the *Huddell* position. Two points are worthy of special consideration. First, the cases that have specifically confronted the burden of proof problem strongly support the position taken in § 16(c). There is considerable language in many of the decisions that a defendant in a crashworthiness case is only liable for the increased harm caused by the inadequate design that made it non-crashworthy. As a general proposition, these statements are true and fully consistent with the rule set forth in § 16(c). For the most part, those cases do not address the problem of what a court should do when a plaintiff establishes that the inadequate design was responsible for some increase in harm but cannot establish with any specificity the amount of the increase.

Second, several commentators argue that, by absolving the plaintiff of the responsibility for proving the degree of increase in harm, no basis exists for determining that an increase in harm has occurred since in a second-collision case proof of causation and proof of increased harm are one and the same. They also argue that reliance on Restatement, Second, Torts § 433B(2) is erroneous because that section deals with apportionment of harm among defendants. The standards as set forth in §§ 2 and 16, however, demand that the plaintiff establish that a reasonable alternative design could have been adopted and that failure to adopt such a safer design was a substantial factor in causing increased harm. Furthermore, the position taken herein is fully consistent with that set forth in

§ 433(B)(2). An excellent discussion of this point is found in Tietz, Bushman and Podraza, Crashworthiness and Erie, supra, 62 Temp. L. Rev. at 619 n.270. The authors set forth Illustration 8 of § 433B(2) and then analyze it in relation to *Huddell*:

> . . . Two automobiles negligently driven by A and B collide, and in the collision C, a passenger in A's car, suffers an injury to his right shoulder. Almost immediately afterward a car negligently driven by D drives into the wreckage, and in this second collision C's shoulder is further injured. As a result of one injury or the other, or both, C's arm becomes paralyzed. The burden is upon D to prove that the injury inflicted by him did not cause the paralysis. . . . § 433B Comment *d*, Illustration 8.

If one superimposes the *Huddell* court's reasoning on the above scenario, it is easily discernible that the *Huddell* court's conclusion that the plaintiff must prove the extent of injury caused by the manufacturer's defective product in the "second collision" is in direct conflict with the *Restatement*. *See Huddell*, 537 F.2d at 737–38 (plaintiff must establish extent of enhanced injuries attributable to defective design). For clarity, assume that A and C represent Dr. Huddell; B represents Levin; and D represents General Motors' defective head restraint causing some injury in the second collision. The *Huddell* court reasoned that B, who set this above scenario into motion, is responsible for all the resulting harm to A/C, including the harm subsequently caused by D's conduct. The *Restatement* would agree with the *Huddell* court's conclusion as to B's liability. See Restatement, Second, of Torts § 433A Comment *c*, [I]llustration 2 (successive injuries). The *Huddell* court also concluded that D's liability for A/C's aggregate harm would be for that amount over and above that caused by B's conduct. The *Restatement* would also agree with this premise, as a general rule. . . .

The *Restatement* and the *Huddell* decision substantially diverge, however, on the issue of which party in the action commenced by A/C against B and D would have to prove the extent of A/C's harm caused by B's and D's conduct. *Huddell* places this burden on A/C, the injured plaintiff. *See Huddell*, 537 F.2d at 737–38 (plaintiff's burden of proof). The *Restatement*, however, follows traditional principles of apportionment by placing the burden of apportioning A/C's harm on D, the tortfeasor who is graced theoretically with limited liability, reasoning that it is unfair to permit a "proved wrongdoer who has in fact caused harm to the plaintiff to escape liability merely because the harm which he has inflicted has combined with similar harm inflicted by other wrongdoers, and the nature of the harm itself has made it necessary that evidence be produced before it can be apportioned." Restatement, Second, of Torts § 433B comment *d* (1965).

The majority of courts that have addressed the issue find the analogy compelling. The Reporters agree.

Comment e. Joint and several liability for increased harm. A plethora of authorities support § 16(d). See, e.g., Mitchell v. Volkswagenwerk, A.G., 669 F.2d 1199 (8th Cir.1982) (applying Michigan law); General Motors Corp. v. Edwards, 482 So.2d

1176 (Ala.1985), overruled on other grounds by Schwartz v. Volvo North Am. Corp., 554 So.2d 927 (Ala.1989); McDowell v. Kawasaki Motors Corp., USA, 799 S.W.2d 854 (Mo.Ct.App. 1990); Oakes v. General Motors Corp., 628 N.E.2d 341 (Ill.App.Ct. 1993).

Comment f. Plaintiff fault in cases of increased harm.

The issue of reduction of damages for a plaintiff's negligent failure to wear a seat belt is covered by statute in most jurisdictions. The statutes break down into four categories:

(1) *Failure to wear a seat belt may not be used to mitigate damages.* Illinois specifically provides that "failure to wear a seat belt shall not be considered evidence of negligence, shall not limit the liability of an insurer, and shall not diminish any recovery for damages arising out of . . . operation of a motor vehicle." 625 Ill. Comp. Stat. § 5/13–603.1 (1996). Similar statutes have been enacted in Alabama, Connecticut, Delaware, Georgia, Idaho, Kentucky, Kansas, Louisiana, Maine, Maryland, Massachusetts, Minnesota, Mississippi, Montana, Nevada, New Mexico, North Carolina, Ohio, Oklahoma, Pennsylvania, Rhode Island, South Carolina, South Dakota, Texas, Utah, Vermont, Virginia, Washington, West Virginia, Wyoming, and the District of Columbia.

(2) *Failure to wear a seat belt may be used to mitigate damages.* The New York statute provides that failure to wear a seat belt may be introduced into evidence in mitigation of damages. N.Y. Veh. & Traf. Law 1229–c (McKinney 1991). Similar statutes have been enacted in Arkansas, California, Colorado, Florida, Indiana, and Tennessee. In California, while non-use of a safety belt is inadmissible as negligence per se, the statute does not preclude a jury's consideration of a failure to ensure passengers are fastened in seat belts in determining the reasonableness of the conduct in question. In Colorado, mitigation is limited to awards for pain and suffering and is not used to limit recovery of economic loss and medical payments. In Florida, mitigation is not allowed but non-use of a seat belt is admissible as evidence of comparative negligence.

(3) *Mitigation is permitted, with a cap on reduction.* Iowa, Michigan, Missouri, Nebraska, Oregon, and Wisconsin allow for reduction in damages based on the failure to wear a seat belt, but cap the reduction.

(4) *Issue of mitigation is left to the developing case law.* The New Jersey and Hawaii statutes appear to punt the question of mitigation of damages for failure to wear a seat belt over to the courts since they provide that their respective seat-belt laws shall not be deemed "to change existing laws, rules, or procedures pertaining to a trial of a civil action for damages or personal injuries. . . . " N.J. Stat. Ann. § 39:3–76.2 (West Supp. 1988); Haw. Rev. Stat. § 291–11.6 (1985).

See generally Victor E. Schwartz, Comparative Negligence § 4–6(b) (3d ed. 1994); Arthur Best, Comparative Negligence: Law and Practice § 4.40(1) (rep. vol. 1996).

In the absence of a statute, Restatement Third, Torts: Apportionment of Liability § 3, Proposed Final Draft (1998) (Illustration 3) takes the position that failure to wear a seat belt is relevant in determining whether the plaintiff was negligent and, if so, the extent to which damages should be reduced under the principle of comparative responsibility.

The more difficult issue is whether the plaintiff's negligent conduct leading to the underlying accident should be a subject of comparative fault in determining liability for increased harm. The courts are sharply split on this issue. Several courts have taken the position that a plaintiff's negligent conduct should not be considered. See, e.g., Cota v. Harley Davidson, 684 P.2d 888 (Ariz.Ct.App. 1984) (holding evidence of plaintiff's intoxication at the time of accident is irrelevant and inadmissible in an enhanced-injury case); Andrews v. Harley Davidson, Inc., 796 P.2d 1092, 1095 (1990):

> Contributory negligence is not a defense in a strict liability case where the issue is whether the design of a vehicle is crashworthy.... A major policy behind holding manufacturers strictly liable for failing to produce crashworthy vehicles is to encourage them to do all they reasonably can do to design a vehicle which will protect a driver in an accident. Hence, the jury in such a case should focus on whether the manufacturer produced a defective product, not on the consumer's negligence.

See also Pree v. Brunswick Corp., 983 F.2d 863, 866 n. 3 (8th Cir.1993) (applying Missouri law) (" ... we conclude that evidence of intoxication is irrelevant in a strict tort liability action for enhancement of injury."); Harris, Enhanced Injury Theory: An Analytic Framework, 62 N.C. L. Rev. 643, 673–74 (1984):

> In enhanced injury cases, unlike ordinary products liability cases, a claimant's fault in causing the accident is not a basis for reducing his recovery. Undoubtedly, many accidents are the result of the injured party's negligence. Nevertheless, a manufacturer's duty is that of minimizing the injurious effects of contact however caused. The inevitability of both operator negligence and injury-producing contact was a primary reason for the judicial recognition of the duty to protect against enhanced injuries. The cause of the contact has no bearing on the issue of whether an object's response to the contact was a reasonable one. The trier of fact's analysis must be limited to the nature and severity of the contact and the object's response. A negligent operator is entitled to the same protection against unnecessary injury as the careful user of the same product is entitled.

A majority of courts, however, allows the introduction of plaintiff's conduct as comparative fault in a crashworthiness context. See, e.g., Keltner v. Ford Motor Co., 748 F.2d 1265 (8th Cir.1984) (applying Arkansas law; comparative fault applies in a crashworthiness case and jury properly considered the plaintiff's intoxication in assessing fault); Daly v. General Motors Corp., 575 P.2d 1162, 1174 (Cal.1978) (Evidence of plaintiff's intoxication and failure to use seat belts and door locks was admissible on the issue of comparative fault. The case was reversed because the trial judge did not limit the admissibility to comparative fault, but also allowed the evidence in as grounds for totally barring the plaintiff's claim because of product misuse.); see also Dahl v. Bayerische Motoren Werke, 748 P.2d 77 (Or.1987) (all of plaintiff's conduct that contributed to injuries, including failure to wear a seat belt, may be considered in a comparative fault reduction); Trust Corp. of Montana v. Piper Aircraft Corp., 506 F.Supp. 1093 (D.Mont.1981) (applying Montana law) (negligent conduct of pilot must be considered in a crashworthiness claim against the aircraft manufacturer); Hinkamp v. American Motors Corp., 735 F.Supp. 176 (E.D.N.C.1989) (plaintiff's intoxication is contributory negligence which may be taken into account in a crashworthiness case); Day v. General Motors Corp., 345 N.W.2d 349 (N.D.1984). In *Day*, plaintiff's fault in causing the injury and plaintiff's fault in enhancing the injury were included in assessing the percentage of fault attributed to the plaintiff. Thus, plaintiff's negligence in falling asleep at the wheel and plaintiff's failure to wear a seat and harness belt were both considered in reducing plaintiff's recovery under comparative fault. See also Duncan v. Cessna Aircraft Co., 665 S.W.2d 414 (Tex.1984) (in an airplane crashworthiness case comparative fault principles apply against the negligent pilot of the airplane); Harvey v. General Motors Corp., 873 F.2d 1343 (10th Cir.1989) (applying Wyoming law, in a crashworthiness case, evidence of plaintiff's drinking and reckless driving is relevant as to the reasonableness of plaintiff's conduct).

TOPIC 2. AFFIRMATIVE DEFENSES

§ 17. Apportionment of Responsibility Between or Among Plaintiff, Sellers and Distributors of Defective Products, and Others

(a) A plaintiff's recovery of damages for harm caused by a product defect may be reduced if the conduct of the plaintiff combines with the product defect to cause the harm and the plaintiff's conduct fails to conform to generally applicable rules establishing appropriate standards of care.

(b) The manner and extent of the reduction under Subsection (a) and the apportionment of plaintiff's recovery among multiple defendants are governed by generally applicable rules apportioning responsibility.

Comment:

a. History. The rule stated in this Section recognizes that the fault of the plaintiff is relevant in assessing liability for product-caused harm. Section 402A of the Restatement, Second, of Torts, recognizing strict liability for harm caused by defective products, was adopted in 1964 when the overwhelming majority rule treated contributory negligence as a total bar to recovery. Understandably, the Institute was reluctant to bar a plaintiff's products liability claim in tort based on conduct that was not egregious. Thus, § 402A, Comment *n*, altered the general tort defenses by narrowing the applicability of contributory negligence and emphasizing assumption of risk as the primary defense. Since then, comparative fault has swept the country. Only a tiny minority of states retain contributory fault as a total bar.

A strong majority of jurisdictions apply the comparative responsibility doctrine to products liability actions. Courts today do not limit the relevance of plaintiff's fault as did the Restatement, Second, of Torts to conduct characterized as voluntary assumption of the risk. See Comment *d.*

Certain forms of consumer behavior—product misuse and product alteration or modification—have been the subject of much confusion and misunderstanding. Early decisions treated product misuse, alteration, and modification, whether by the plaintiff or a third party, as a total bar to recovery against a product seller. Today misuse, alteration, and modification relate to one of three issues in a products liability action. In some cases, misuse, alteration, and modification are important in determining whether the product is defective. In others, they are relevant to the issue of legal cause. Finally, when the plaintiff misuses, alters, or modifies the product, such conduct may constitute contributory fault and reduce the plaintiff's recovery under the rules of comparative responsibility. See Comment *c.*

b. Conduct of the plaintiff. The applicable rules of apportionment of responsibility vary among jurisdictions. Some states have adopted "pure" comparative fault, which allocates responsibility to each actor purely in proportion to the actor's percentage of total fault. Others follow some variant of "modified" comparative fault, in which actors' responsibilities are adjusted according to predetermined thresholds of responsibility. For example, in many modified jurisdictions the plaintiff is totally barred if found more than 50 percent at fault. The apportionment of responsibility principles as they have developed in each jurisdiction should be applied to products liability cases. With respect to whether special exceptions should be made in products liability cases for certain categories of plaintiff conduct, see Comment *d.*

Illustration:

1. Roger was driving his car, manufactured by the ABC Motor Co., when he noticed the temperature light flashing. The instruction manual warned drivers that when the temperature light flashes it is a sign that the car is seriously overheating and that the car should be brought to a stop and the motor shut off. The overheating in this instance was caused by a hose, leaking coolant, that was defective at the time of sale by ABC. Roger had not read the instruction manual and paid no attention to the flashing temperature light. He continued driving for 30 minutes.

The overheating of the car was so intense that it started an electrical fire in the car causing Roger serious harm. Roger's conduct in failing to read the manual and failing to pay attention to the flashing temperature light may be considered by the trier of fact to be negligent conduct warranting a reduction of Roger's recovery against ABC based on the percentage of fault attributed to him.

c. Misuse, alteration, and modification. Product misuse, alteration, and modification, whether by a third party or the plaintiff, are not discrete doctrines within products liability law. Instead such conduct is relevant to the determination of the issues of defect, causation, and comparative responsibility. See § 2, Comment *p*.

Jurisdictions differ on the question of who bears the burden of proof regarding conduct that constitutes misuse, modification, and alteration. The allocation of burdens in this regard is not addressed in this Restatement and is left to local law.

Illustration:

2. ABC Machine Tools, Inc. manufactures and sells pelletizer machines, which draw strands of plastic into position to be cut into very small pellets. The pelletizer comes equipped with a removable guard. It is necessary periodically to remove the guard so that the inside of the machine can be cleaned. Fred, an employee of a plastics company, removed the guard on an ABC pelletizer to perform the cleaning but neglected to reinstall it. Fred resumed operation of the machine without the guard. Shortly thereafter a strand of plastic caught his hand and pulled it into the rollers of the machine, causing harm. Fred alleges that the pelletizer should have been equipped with an interlock mechanism that would have prevented the machine from operating without the safety guard in place. A trier of fact may conclude that the pelletizer was defectively designed and also that Fred's failure to replace the safety guard was a foreseeable alteration of the machine. The trier of fact may further find that Fred's conduct in failing to reinstall the safety guard and operating the machine without the guard constitutes negligent conduct on his part that should reduce his recovery proportionate to his fault.

d. Particular forms or categories of plaintiff's conduct. Some courts accord different treatment to special categories of plaintiff conduct. For example, some decisions hold that when the plaintiff's negligence is the failure to discover a product defect, reduction of damages on the basis of apportionment of responsibility is improper, reasoning that a consumer has a right to expect a defect-free product and should not be burdened with a duty to inspect for defects. Other decisions hold that apportionment of responsibility is improper when the product lacked a safety feature that would protect against the risk that resulted in the injury in question, reasoning that the defendant's responsibility should not be diminished when the plaintiff engages in the very conduct that the product design should have prevented. On the other hand, some decisions hold that a plaintiff's assumption of the risk is a complete defense to a products liability action, not merely a basis for apportionment of responsibility. Product misuse, alteration, and modification have been treated by some courts as an absolute bar to recovery and by others as a form of plaintiff fault that should be compared with that of other parties to reduce recovery. The majority position is that all forms of plaintiff's failure to conform to applicable standards of care are to be considered for the purpose of apportioning responsibility between the plaintiff and the product seller or distributor.

Before the court will allow any apportionment of responsibility, the defendant must introduce sufficient evidence to support a finding of fault on the part of the plaintiff. Thus, for example, when the defendant claims that the plaintiff failed to discover a defect, there must be evidence that the plaintiff's conduct in failing to discover a defect did, in fact, fail to meet a standard of reasonable care. In general, a plaintiff has no reason to expect that a new product contains a defect and would have little reason to be on guard to discover it. Or when a plaintiff is injured due to inattention to a danger that should have been eliminated by a safety feature, there must be evidence supporting the conclusion that the plaintiff's momentary inattention or inadvertence in a workplace setting constitutes failure to exercise reasonable care. In the absence of such evidence courts refuse to submit the plaintiff's conduct to the trier of fact for apportionment based on the principles of comparative responsibility. When evidence of plaintiff fault is established, how much responsibility to attribute to a plaintiff will vary with the circumstances. The seriousness of the plaintiff's fault and the nature of the product defect are relevant in apportioning the appropriate percentages of responsibility between the plaintiff and the product seller.

REPORTERS' NOTE

Comment a. History. For authority supporting the proposition that the majority of courts utilize comparative fault to reduce the recoveries of products liability plaintiffs, see, e.g., Butaud v. Suburban Marine & Sporting Goods, Inc., 555 P.2d 42 (Alaska 1976); Ark. Code Ann. § 16–64–122 (Michie 1987); Daly v. General Motors Corp., 575 P.2d 1162 (Cal.1978); Colo. Rev. Stat. § 13–21–406 (1987); Huffman v. Caterpillar Tractor Co., 908 F.2d 1470 (10th Cir.1990) (holding that the Colorado comparative fault statute covered all forms of culpable conduct); Champagne v. Raybestos–Manhattan, Inc., 562 A.2d 1100 (Conn.1989); Kaneko v. Hilo Coast Processing, 654 P.2d 343 (Haw. 1982); Armstrong v. Cione, 738 P.2d 79 (Haw.1987) (holding that, in a case based on strict tort liability, Hawaii would apply pure comparative negligence rather than modified comparative negligence mandated by statute for negligence actions); West v. Caterpillar Tractor Co., 336 So.2d 80 (Fla.1976); Idaho Code § 6–1304 (1990); Coney v. J.L.G. Indus., Inc., 454 N.E.2d 197 (Ill.1983); Kennedy v. City of Sawyer, 4 Kan.App.2d 545, 608 P.2d 1379, rev'd on other grounds, 618 P.2d 788 (Kan.1980); Mich. Comp. Laws Ann. § 600.2959 (West Supp. 1997); Minn. Stat. Ann. § 604.01 (West Supp. 1993); Omnetics, Inc. v. Radiant Tech. Corp., 440 N.W.2d 177 (Minn.Ct.App.1989); Miss. Code Ann. § 11–7–15 (1972); Edwards v. Sears, Roebuck & Co., 512 F.2d 276 (5th Cir.1975) (applying Mississippi law); 1992 Neb Laws L.B. 262 (§ 1 applies comparative negligence regardless of the theory of liability against the defendant); Thibault v. Sears, Roebuck & Co., 395 A.2d 843 (N.H.1978); Marchese v. Warner Communications, Inc., 670 P.2d 113, 117 (N.M.Ct.App.), cert. denied, 669 P.2d 735 (1983); N.Y.C.P.L.R. § 1411 (McKinney 1976); Bell v. Jet Wheel Blast, Div. of Ervin Indus., 462 So.2d 166 (La.1985); N.D. Cent. Code § 32–03.2–03 (1996); Sandford v. Chevrolet Div. of General Motors, 642 P.2d 624 (Or.1982); Fiske v. MacGregor, Div. of Brunswick, 464 A.2d 719 (R.I. 1983); Star Furniture Co. v. Pulaski Furniture Co., 297 S.E.2d 854 (W.Va. 1982); Tex. Civ. Prac. & Rem. Code Ann. § 33.001(b) (West Supp. 1993); Utah Code Ann. § 78–27–37 to 78–27–43 (1986); Webb v. Navistar Int'l, 692 A.2d 343 (Vt.1996) (Vermont adopts comparative fault in products liability cases); and Murray v. Fairbanks Morse, 610 F.2d 149 (3d Cir. 1979) (applying Virgin Islands law); Wash. Rev. Code Ann. § 4.22.005 et seq. (West 1988); Lundberg v. All–Pure Chem. Co., 55 Wash.App. 181, 777 P.2d 15 (Ct.App.1989); Dippel v. Sciano, 155 N.W.2d 55 (Wis.1967).

A minority of courts either refuse to recognize the doctrine of comparative fault as a defense to strict products liability or limit its application to cases in which the plaintiff has voluntarily and unreasonably assumed a known risk. See, e.g., Lippard v. Houdaille Indus., Inc., 715 S.W.2d 491 (Mo.1986) (en banc); Bowling v. Heil Co., 511 N.E.2d 373 (Ohio 1987); Zahrte v. Sturm, Ruger & Co., 661 P.2d 17 (Mont.1983) (only voluntary and unreasonable assumption of risk provides grounds for application of Montana's comparative negligence statute to a strict products liability case); Young's Mach. Co. v. Long, 692 P.2d 24 (Nev.1984) (only assumption of risk and misuse are defense to a strict products liability action); Cartel Capital Corp. v. Fireco of New Jersey, 410 A.2d 674 (N.J.1980) (only voluntary and unreasonable assumption of a known risk provides grounds for application of New Jersey's comparative negligence statute to a strict products liability case); Suter v. San Angelo Foundry & Mach. Co., 406 A.2d 140 (N.J.1979) (comparative fault will not reduce plaintiff's recovery when plaintiff was injured by machinery in an industrial setting even for conduct which constitutes assumption of risk); Kimco Dev. Corp. v. Michael D's Carpet Outlets, 637 A.2d 603 (Pa.1993) (rejecting comparative fault to reduce damages in strict products liability); Phillips v. Duro–Last Roofing, Inc., 806 P.2d 834 (Wyo.1991) (comparative negligence statute does not apply to claims brought under strict liability).

For a discussion of the policy arguments against recognizing comparative fault as a defense to strict products liability, see, e.g., Butaud v. Suburban Marine and Sporting Goods, Inc., 555 P.2d 42, 47 (Alaska 1976) (Burke, J., dissenting); Daly v. General Motors Corp., 575 P.2d 1162, 1167–69 (Cal.1978) (excellent discussion of the policy arguments for and against the application of comparative fault to strict products liability); Bowling v. Heil Co., 511 N.E.2d 373, 379 (Ohio 1987) ("strict liability is at odds with traditional notions of due care").

Many courts have noted that comparing plaintiff's fault with a product defect is no easy task. See, e.g., Butaud v. Suburban Marine & Sporting Goods, Inc., 555 P.2d 42, 43 (Alaska 1976) ("we are mindful of the theoretical argument that the strict liability of the defendant is difficult to compare with the contributory negligence of the plaintiff"); Huffman v. Caterpillar Tractor Co., 908 F.2d 1470, 1475 (10th Cir.1990) (Applying Colorado law, the court said: " ... the doctrinal tension between strict products liability and comparative fault or comparative negligence becomes clear: Strict liability reflects the effort to remove the issue of negligence or fault from product liability analysis ... Comparative negligence or comparative fault rules, as applied to product liability actions, inject a culpability inquiry into the process of apportioning damages.") (footnote omitted); Sandford v. Chevrolet Div. of General Motors, 642 P.2d 624, 628–36 (Or.1982) (extensive review of case law and literature on the various methods for comparing fault and product defect); Star Furniture Co. v. Pulaski Furniture Co., 297 S.E.2d 854, 861 (W.Va.1982) ("Application of comparative negligence principles ... to strict liability in tort presents conceptual hurdles."); Dippel v. Sciano, 155 N.W.2d 55, 64 (Wis.1967).

Courts that have opted for damages reduction based on comparative fault in strict products liability have argued that it is unwise to relieve users and consumers of all responsibility for safe product use and consumption. See, e.g., Daly v. General Motors Corp., 575 P.2d 1162, 1172 (Cal.1978); Duncan v. Cessna Aircraft Co., 665 S.W.2d 414, 425 (Tex.1984) ("Unfairness ... is not the only serious flaw of virtually ignoring plaintiff and third party misconduct in strict products liability actions. The failure to allocate costs in proportion to the parties' relative abilities to prevent or reduce those costs is economically inefficient..."), rev'd on other grounds, Smithson v. Cessna Aircraft Co., 665 S.W.2d 439 (Tex.1984); Smith v. Goodyear Tire & Rubber Co., 600 F.Supp. 1561, 1568 (D.Vt.1985) (predicting that Vermont would adopt comparative fault in a strict products liability case: "[I]t ... does not seem fair to allow a negligent plaintiff, who may have contributed as much as fifty percent of his injuries, to pay for none of them and to recover as much as a plaintiff who had taken all precautions reasonable under the circumstances.").

See generally Madden, Products Liability §§ 13.14–13.19 (2d ed. 1988); Davis, Individual and Institutional Responsibility: A Vision for Comparative Fault in Products Liability, 39 Vill. L. Rev. 281 (1994); Fischer, Products Liability—Applicability of

Comparative Negligence, 43 Mo. L. Rev. 431 (1978); Wade, Products Liability and Plaintiff's Fault: The Uniform Comparative Fault Act, 29 Mercer L. Rev. 373 (1978); Levine, Strict Products Liability and Comparative Negligence: The Collision of Fault and No–Fault, 14 San Diego L. Rev. 337 (1977); Brewster, Comparative Negligence in Strict Liability Cases, 42 J. Air L. & Com. 107 (1976); Feinberg, The Applicability of a Comparative Negligence Defense in a Strict Liability Suit Based on Section 402A of the Restatement of Torts, 2d, 42 Ins. Couns. J. 39 (1975).

Comment b. Conduct of the plaintiff. Of the states that have adopted comparative fault, approximately one-third have opted for pure comparative fault. Approximately two-thirds follow some variant of modified comparative fault. See V. Schwartz, Comparative Negligence §§ 3.2 and 3.3 (2d ed. 1986 and 1990 Supp.); Woods, Comparative Fault §§ 4.2 and 4.3 (2d ed. 1987 and 1992 Supp.).

Comment c. Misuse, alteration, and modification. Most courts take the position that even when a plaintiff has established a prima facie case, if the plaintiff was negligent in misusing, modifying, or altering a product, and such negligence combined with the product defect to bring about harm, the plaintiff's conduct should result in the diminution of damages under comparative fault principles. See, e.g., States v. R.D. Werner Co., 799 P.2d 427, 430 (Colo.Ct.App.1990) (if plaintiff has established defect and causation, then plaintiff's contributory fault is used to diminish damages); West v. Caterpillar Tractor, 336 So.2d 80, 90 (Fla.1976); Idaho Code § 6–1305(3)(b) (1992); Coney v. J.L.G. Indus. Inc., 454 N.E.2d 197, 204 (Ill. 1983) ("Once defendant's liability is established, and where both the defective product and the plaintiff's misconduct contribute to cause the damages, the comparative fault principle will operate to reduce plaintiff's recovery by that amount which the trier of fact finds him at fault."); Minn. Stat. § 604.01.1a (1988); Thibault v. Sears, Roebuck & Co., 395 A.2d 843, 849 (N.H.1978); Utah Code Ann. § 78–27–37 (1992); Wash. Rev. Code Ann. § 4.22.015 (West 1988) (product misuse is a form of fault for comparison purposes); Duncan v. Cessna Aircraft Co., 665 S.W.2d 414, 428 (Tex. 1984); Schuh v. Fox River Tractor Co., 218 N.W.2d 279 (Wis.1974) (unforeseeable misuse or alteration of a product is a total bar, but foreseeable misuse by plaintiff is contributory fault and is governed by comparative negligence). But see Corbridge v. Clark Equip. Co., 730 P.2d 1005 (Idaho 1986).

Illustration 2 is based on Cepeda v. Cumberland Engineering Co., 386 A.2d 816 (N.J.1978).

Comment d. Particular forms or categories of plaintiff's conduct. A number of courts take the position that when the plaintiff's negligence consists solely in the failure to discover the defect in the product, no reduction of damages is warranted. See, e.g., Murray v. Fairbanks Morse, 610 F.2d 149, 161 n. 14 (3d Cir.1979) (applying Virgin Islands law); Star Furniture Co. v. Pulaski Furniture Co., 297 S.E.2d 854, 863 (W.Va.1982) ("comparative negligence is available as an affirmative defense in a cause of action founded on strict liability so long as the complained of conduct is not a failure to discover a defect or guard against it"); West v. Caterpillar Tractor Co., 336 So.2d 80, 92 (Fla. 1976) ("comparative negligence is a defense in a strict liability action if based upon grounds other than the failure of the user to discover the defect or to guard against the possibility of its existence"); Idaho Code § 6–1305(1)(a) (1990); Coney v. J.L.G. Indus., Inc., 454 N.E.2d 197, 204 (Ill. 1983) ("We believe that a consumer's unobservant, inattentive, ignorant, or awkward failure to discover or guard against a defect should not be compared as a damage-reducing factor."); Simpson v. General Motors Corp., 483 N.E.2d 1 (Ill.1985) (excellent discussion in dissent against creating separate categories of plaintiff conduct that are exempt from comparative fault); Busch v. Busch Constr., Inc., 262 N.W.2d 377, 393–94 (Minn. 1977); Sandford v. Chevrolet Div. of General Motors, 642 P.2d 624 (Or. 1982); Duncan v. Cessna Aircraft Co., 665 S.W.2d 414, 432 (Tex.1984). But see Minn. Stat. Ann. § 604.01.1a (West 1988).

Some states engraft an exception to comparative fault when the defendant's duty was to provide a safety feature to protect users from the risks associated with product use. See, e.g., Caterpillar Tractor Co. v. Beck, 593 P.2d 871, 891 (Alaska 1979) ("If the focus is on the nature of the product as defective, and the jury has found the lack of a safety device to render the product defective, it is inconsistent to turn around and reduce the user's recovery merely because he bought and used the product as marketed."); Bell v. Jet Wheel Blast, Div. of Ervin Indus., 462 So.2d 166 (La.1985); Suter v. San Angelo Foundry & Mach. Co., 406 A.2d 140, 148 (N.J.1979); Bexiga v. Havir Mfg. Corp., 290 A.2d 281, 286 (N.J.1972) (The court reasoned: "It would be anomalous to hold that defendant has a duty to install safety devices but a breach of that duty results in no liability for the very injury the duty was meant to protect against.").

Some courts take the position that classic assumption of the risk is a total bar to a products liability action. See, e.g., Tafoya v. Sears, Roebuck & Co., 884 F.2d 1330 (10th Cir.1989) (applying Colorado law); Conn. Gen. Stat. Ann. § 52–572 (West 1991); Young v. Up–Right Scaffolds, Inc., 637 F.2d 810, 814 (D.C.Cir.1980); Ind. Code Ann. § 33–3–1.5–4 (1992) (voluntary and unreasonable assumption of a known risk is a complete bar); Bowling v. Heil Co., 511 N.E.2d 373 (Ohio 1987); Fiske v. MacGregor Div. of Brunswick et. al., 464 A.2d 719, 728–29 (R.I.1983).

A fair number of states hold that assumption of the risk should be subject to fault apportionment. See, e.g., Bonds v. Snapper Power Equip. Co., 935 F.2d 985, 987 (8th Cir.1991) (applying Arkansas law; assumption of risk is an element of fault, not a complete bar to recovery); Daly v. General Motors Corp., 575 P.2d 1162, 1172 (Cal.1978); Coney v. J.L.G. Indus., Inc., 454 N.E.2d 197, 204 (Ill. 1983); Zahrte v. Sturm, Ruger & Co., 661 P.2d 17 (Mont.1983); Sandford v. Chevrolet Div. of General Motors, 642 P.2d 624, 628 (Or.1982); Wash. Rev. Code § 4.22.015 (1991); Utah Code Ann. § 78–27–37 (1986); South v. A.B. Chance Co., 635 P.2d 728 (Wash.1981) (assumption of risk operates as a damage-reducing factor rather than complete bar to plaintiff in strict liability cause of action); King v. Kayak Mfg. Corp., 387 S.E.2d 511, 517 (W.Va.1989) ("comparative assumption of risk . . . is applicable to a product liability case based on strict liability in tort . . ."); Dippel v. Sciano, 155 N.W.2d 55, 63 (Wis.1967).

Some states have abolished implied assumption of the risk as a separate defense from comparative fault. See, e.g., Li v. Yellow Cab Co., 532 P.2d 1226 (Cal.1975); Blackburn v. Dorta, 348 So.2d 287, 292–93 (Fla.1977); Parker v. Redden, 421 S.W.2d 586 (Ky. 1967); Minn. Stat. Ann. § 604.01.1a (West 1988); Or. Rev. Stat. § 18.475(2) (1995); Utah Code Ann. § 78–27–37 (1992); King v. Kayak Mfg. Corp., 387 S.E.2d 511, 512 (W.Va.1989) (Elements of assumption of the risk are different from contributory negligence but " . . . plaintiff is not barred from recovery by the doctrine of assumption of risk unless his degree of fault arising therefrom equals or exceeds the combined fault of the other parties to the accident."); McConville v. State Farm Mut. Auto. Ins. Co., 113 N.W.2d 14 (Wis.1962).

§ 18. Disclaimers, Limitations, Waivers, and Other Contractual Exculpations as Defenses to Products Liability Claims for Harm to Persons

Disclaimers and limitations of remedies by product sellers or other distributors, waivers by product purchasers, and other similar contractual exculpations, oral or written, do not bar or reduce otherwise valid products liability claims against sellers or other distributors of new products for harm to persons.

Comment:

a. Effects of contract defenses on products liability tort claims for harm to persons. A commercial seller or other distributor of a new product is not permitted to avoid liability for harm to persons through limiting terms in a contract governing the sale of a product. It is presumed that the ordinary product user or consumer lacks sufficient information and bargaining power to execute a fair contractual limitation of rights to recover. For a limited exception to this general rule, see Comment *d*. The rule in this Section applies only to "sellers or other distributors of new products." For rules governing commercial sellers of used products, including whether they may rely on disclaimers, waivers, and other contractual defenses, see § 8. Nothing in this Section is intended to constrain parties within the commercial chain of distribution from contracting inter se for indemnity agreements or save-harmless clauses.

b. Distinguishing disclaimers from warnings. This Section invalidates disclaimers and contractual exculpations of liability by sellers of new products when they are interjected to bar or limit claims by plaintiffs for harm to persons. Disclaimers should be distinguished from warnings. Warnings convey information to the buyer about avoiding risk in using the product. In some cases warnings inform the consumer of risks that cannot be avoided. Both types of warnings provide consumers with valuable information concerning the risks attendant to using the product. A product sold with reasonable instructions or warnings may be nondefective. See § 2, Comments *i*, *j*, *k*, and *l*. Disclaimers attempt contractually to avoid liability for defective products. For the reasons set forth in Comment *a*, courts refuse to enforce disclaimers that purport to deny recovery for harm to persons caused by new products that were defective at the time of sale.

c. Effects of disclaimers on claims for harm to property or for economic loss. For the effect of disclaimers on tort claims for defect-caused harm to property or for economic loss, see § 21, Comment *f*.

d. Waiver of rights in contractual settings in which product purchasers possess both adequate knowledge and sufficient economic power. The rule in this Section applies to cases in which commercial product sellers attempt unfairly to disclaim or otherwise limit their liability to the majority of users and consumers who are presumed to lack information and bargaining power adequate to protect their interests. This Section does not address whether consumers, especially when represented by informed and economically powerful consumer groups or intermediaries, with full information and sufficient bargaining power, may contract with product sellers to accept curtailment of liability in exchange for concomitant benefits, or whether such consumers might be allowed to agree to substitute alternative dispute resolution mechanisms in place of traditional adjudication. When such contracts are accompanied by alternative nontort remedies that serve as an adequate quid pro quo for reducing or eliminating rights to recover in tort, arguments may support giving effect to such agreements. Such contractual arrangements raise policy questions different from those raised by this Section and require careful consideration by the courts.

REPORTERS' NOTE

Comment a. Effects of contract defenses on products liability tort claims for harm to persons. When a product defect causes harm to persons, courts generally refuse, in tort actions brought by individual plaintiffs to recover for such harm, to give effect to disclaimers, waivers, or other contract-based defenses.

The leading decision denying effect to a disclaimer in a personal-injury case is Henningsen v. Bloomfield Motors, Inc., 161 A.2d 69, 94–95 (N.J. 1960) (The court declared that the legislators who passed the Uniform Sales Act "did not authorize the automobile manufacturer to use its grossly disproportionate bargaining power to relieve itself from liability and to impose on the ordinary buyer, who in effect has no real freedom of choice, the grave danger of injury to himself and others that attends the sale of such a dangerous instrumentality as a defectively made automobile."). Comment *m* to § 402A of the Restatement, Second, of Torts adopts the same position: "The consumer's cause of action [in tort] . . . is not affected by any disclaimer or other agreement. . . . "; see also Sipari v. Villa Olivia Country Club, 380 N.E.2d 819 (Ill.App.Ct.1978); Fontenot v. F. Hollier & Sons, 478 So.2d 1379 (La.Ct. App.1985); Webster v. Empiregas, Inc., 648 S.W.2d 198 (Mo.Ct.App. 1983).

A clear majority of courts follow this approach. See, e.g., Anderson v. Fairchild Hiller Corp., 358 F.Supp. 976 (D.Alaska 1973) (applying Alaska law) (in case involving personal injuries from helicopter blade, court noted that sellers of defective products are strictly liable, without regard to disclaimers, for personal injuries caused by the defect); Greeno v. Clark Equip. Co., 237 F.Supp. 427, 429 (N.D.Ind.1965) (applying Indiana law) (in defective forklift case, court stated, the "seller cannot disclaim . . . a duty which the law would impose upon him"); Sipari v. Villa Olivia Country Club, 380 N.E.2d 819 (Ill. App.Ct.1978) (exculpation clause in rental ticket did not preclude imposition of strict liability on lessor of golf cart for injuries sustained by lessee); Meiman v. Rehabilitation Ctr., Inc., 444 S.W.2d 78 (Ky.1969) (exculpatory contract invalid as being against public policy and thus cannot be relied on as defense to action for fractured hip in course of therapeutic treatment); Webster v. Empiregas, Inc., 648 S.W.2d 198 (Mo.Ct.App.1983) (in case involving defective space heater, court held that marketing of unreasonably dangerous product eliminates manufacturer's or seller's right to disclaim liability); Collins v. Uniroyal, Inc., 315 A.2d 16 (N.J.1974) (in tire blow-out case, court recognized statute prohibiting contractual limitation of damages in the case of consumer goods when the claim is for personal injury).

The effectiveness of disclaimers in connection with the commercial sale of used products has considerable judicial support. The cases very often raise the issue of the "as is" used-product sale in conjunction with the question of the applicability of strict liability to used-product sales. In any event, the cases demonstrate a solicitude to disclaimers that does not exist in sales of new products. See, e.g., Wilkinson v. Hicks, 179 Cal.Rptr. 5 (Cal.Ct.App.1981) (seller of used punch press, sold "as is" without reconditioning, not strictly liable for injuries sustained when press crushed plaintiff's hand); LaRosa v. Superior Court, 176 Cal.Rptr. 224 (Cal.Ct.App. 1981) (strict liability inapplicable against seller of used punch press sold "as is" when press malfunctioned and caused personal injuries to plaintiff); DeVoe Chevrolet–Cadillac, Inc. v. Cartwright, 526 N.E.2d 1237 (Ind. Ct.App.1988) ("as is" disclaimer adequately disclaims an implied warranty); Harber v. Altec Indus., 812 F.Supp. 954 (W.D.Mo.1993) (applying Missouri law) (strict liability does not extend to sellers of used goods who perform no maintenance, modification, or repair on the used product, and who successfully disclaim all warranties of title), aff'd, 5 F.3d 339 (8th Cir.1993); Turner v. International Harvester Co., 336 A.2d 62 (N.J.Super.Law Div.1975) (ordinary "as is" disclaimers are ineffective in a claim of strict liability involving a used vehicle; however, evidence may be shown to prove that the "as is" language was the intentional relinquishment of a known right); Sukljian v. Charles Ross & Son, Co., 503 N.E.2d 1358 (N.Y.1986) (in holding that strict liability did not apply to the sale of used equipment by a seller not regularly engaged in the business of selling the equipment in issue, the court found it important that the machinery was sold on an "as is" basis with an invitation to inspect); Tillman v. Vance Equip. Co., 286 Or. 747, 596 P.2d 1299 (Or. 1979) (court held strict liability inapplicable in personal injury action against seller of used crane sold "as is" when defect existed at time of manufacture).

Comment d. Waiver of rights in contractual settings in which product purchasers possess both adequate knowledge and sufficient economic power. See, e.g., O'Connell, Elective No–Fault Liability by Contract: With or Without an Enabling Statute, 1975 U. Ill. L. F. 59, 65–71; Offers That Can't Be Refused: Foreclosure of Personal Injury Claims by Defendants' Prompt Tender of Claimants' Net Economic Losses, 77 Nw. U. L. Rev. 589 (1982). Also see Vol. II, The American Law Institute, Reporters' Study: Enterprise Responsibility for Personal Injury 517–536 (1991); The National Childhood Vaccine Injury Act of 1986, 42 U.S.C.A. § 300 et seq.; Schwartz and Mahshigian, National Childhood Vaccine Injury Act of 1986: An Ad Hoc Remedy or a Window for the Future?, 48 Ohio St. L.J. 387 (1987). This Section does not address the wisdom of such proposals. It speaks only to traditional disclaimers that function *unfairly* to deny or limit liability to persons who lack either information or bargaining power to protect their interests.

TOPIC 3. DEFINITIONS

§ 19. Definition of "Product"

For purposes of this Restatement:

(a) A product is tangible personal property distributed commercially for use or consumption. Other items, such as real property and electricity, are products when the context of their distribution and use is sufficiently analogous to the distribution and use of tangible personal property that it is appropriate to apply the rules stated in this Restatement.

(b) Services, even when provided commercially, are not products.

(c) Human blood and human tissue, even when provided commercially, are not subject to the rules of this Restatement.

Comment:

a. History. The question of whether something distributed in commerce is a product for purposes of tort liability is important in this Restatement, but relatively less so than it was in the period from the early 1960s to the early 1980s. Before 1960, American courts had not yet recognized strict liability in tort for harm caused by defective products, particularly if there was no privity of contract between plaintiff and defendant. Thus, prior to that time, plaintiffs claiming in tort against product sellers were required to prove causal negligence; if they could prove negligence they could usually recover in tort whether or not a product was involved. Once the era of strict products liability in tort arrived in the early 1960s, liability turned primarily on whether what the defendant distributed was, or was not, a product. Most of the focus during this period was on liability for harm caused by manufacturing defects, in connection with which strict liability had a distinctive character. See § 2(a).

By the early 1980s, the emphasis of products liability litigation had shifted from manufacturing defects to defective designs and defects due to inadequate instructions and warnings. Thereafter, design and warning cases came to dominate. Given that design and warning cases turn on essentially risk-utility evaluations, see § 2, Comment *d*, the practical importance of whether something is, or is not, a product has diminished somewhat. Nevertheless, that issue remains important in the modern era to the extent that the concept of strict liability retains functional meaning. See § 1, Comment *a*. Statutes enacted to reform products liability law, many of which impose nontraditional conditions and limitations on product-related liability, tend to enhance the importance of classifying something as a product.

Apart from statutes that define "product" for purposes of determining products liability, in every instance it is for the court to determine as a matter of law whether something is, or is not, a product.

b. Tangible personal property: in general. For purposes of this Restatement, most but not necessarily all products are tangible personal property. In certain situations, however, intangible personal property (see Comment *d*) and real property (see Comment *e*) may be products. Component parts are products, whether sold or distributed separately or assembled with other component parts. An assemblage of component parts is also, itself, a product. Raw materials are products, whether manufactured, such as sheet metal; processed, such as lumber; or gathered and sold or distributed in raw condition, such as unwashed gravel and farm produce. For treatment of the special problems presented when plaintiffs join sellers of component parts and raw materials in actions against those who subsequently combined those materials to create defective products, see § 10.

Courts are divided regarding whether living animals, such as pets or livestock, should be considered to be products for the purpose of determining a commercial seller's liability in tort. Frequently, as when diseased livestock are sold and subsequently must be destroyed, the claim to recover for their value involves a claim for harm to the product itself and thus represents a claim for pure economic loss not permitted by this Restatement. See § 21. But when a living animal is sold commercially in a diseased condition and causes harm to other property or to persons, the animal constitutes a product for purposes of this Restatement.

c. Tangible personal property: human blood and human tissue. Although human blood and human tissue meet the formal requisites of Subsection (a), they are specifically excluded from the coverage of this Restatement. Almost all the litigation regarding such products has dealt with contamination of human blood and blood-related products by the hepatitis virus or the HIV virus. Absent a special rule dealing with human blood and tissue, such contamination presumably would be subject to the rules of §§ 1 and 2(a). Those Sections impose strict liability when a product departs from its intended design even though all possible care was exercised in the preparation and marketing of the product. However, legislation in almost all jurisdictions limits the liability of sellers of human blood and human tissue to the failure to exercise reasonable care, often by providing that human blood and human tissue are not "products" or that their provision is a "service." Where legislation has not addressed the problem, courts have concluded that strict liability is inappropriate for harm caused by such product contamination.

What constitutes reasonable care for those engaged in providing professional services is defined in § 299A of the Restatement, Second, of Torts.

d. Intangible personal property. Two basic types of intangible personal property are involved. The first consists of information in media such as books, maps, and navigational charts. Plaintiffs allege that the information delivered was false and misleading, causing harm when actors relied on it. They seek to recover against publishers in strict liability in tort based on product defect, rather than on negligence or some form of misrepresentation. Although a tangible medium such as a book, itself clearly a product, delivers the information, the plaintiff's grievance in such cases is with the information, not with the tangible medium. Most courts, expressing concern that imposing strict liability for the dissemination of false and defective information would significantly impinge on free speech have, appropriately, refused to impose strict products liability in these cases. One area in which some courts have imposed strict products liability involves false information contained in maps and navigational charts. In that context the falsity of the factual information is unambiguous and more akin to a classic product defect. However, the better view is that false information in such documents constitutes a misrepresentation that the user may properly rely upon.

The second major category of intangible, harm-causing products involves the transmission of intangible forces such as electricity and X rays. With respect to transmission of electricity, a majority of courts have held that electricity becomes a product only when it passes through the customer's meter and enters the customer's premises. Until then, the system of high-voltage transmission provides, not a product, but a service; before passing the meter and entering the plaintiff's premises, so it is said, the electricity has not entered the stream of commerce. Some courts employ this analysis to conclude that, while electricity is a "product" prior to delivery, it has not yet been "sold or otherwise distributed." Whether or not these rationales are cogent, the distinction drawn between pre-and post-delivery is reasonable. Plaintiffs in the post-delivery cases typically complain of unexpected drops or surges in voltage, resulting in personal injury or property damage. Those claims seem better governed by principles of strict liability for physical deviations from intended design. Plaintiffs in the pre-delivery, high-voltage cases complain of the inherent dangers that unavoidably accompany the transmission of high-voltage electricity. Courts have refused to impose strict liability on electric utilities for high voltage-related accidents either on a strict products liability basis or under the abnormally dangerous activities doctrine set out in § 520 of the Restatement, Second, of Torts. This Restatement does not alter that approach.

The cases involving harm caused by X-rays and radiation treatments rest not on assertions that the X-rays themselves were defective, but rather on assertions that they were improperly administered by medical technicians. Courts have refused to impose liability in the absence of a showing by plaintiff either that the X-rays or other forms of radiation treatment were defective or that the medical technicians acted negligently. These cases may also reflect courts' traditional refusal to impose strict liability on providers of medical care.

e. Real property. Traditionally, courts have been reluctant to impose products liability on sellers of improved real property in that such property does not constitute goods or personalty. A housing contractor, building and selling one house at a time, does not fit the pattern of a mass producer of manufactured products, nor is such a builder perceived to be more capable than are purchasers of controlling or insuring against risks presented by weather conditions or earth movements. More recently, courts have treated sellers of improved real property as product sellers in a number of contexts. When a building contractor sells a building that contains a variety of appliances or other manufactured equipment, the builder, together with the equipment manufacturer and other distributors, are held as product sellers with respect to such equipment notwithstanding the fact that the built-in equipment may have become, for other legal purposes, attachments to and thus part of the underlying real property. Moreover, the builder may be treated as a product seller even with respect to the building itself when the building has been prefabricated—and thus manufactured—and later assembled on-or off-site. Finally, courts impose strict liability for defects in construction when dwellings are built, even if on-site, on a major scale, as in a large housing project.

f. The distinction between services and products. Services, even when provided commercially, are not products for purposes of this Restatement. Thus, apart from the sale of a product incidental to the service, one who agrees for a monetary fee to mow the lawn of another is the provider of a service even if the provider is a large firm engaged commercially in lawn care. Moreover, it is irrelevant that the service provided relates directly to products commercially distributed. For example, one who contracts to inspect, repair, and maintain machinery owned and operated by another is the provider of a product-related service rather than the provider of a product. If a product repairer replaces a worn-out component part with a new part, the replacement constitutes a sale of the part; but the repair itself constitutes a service. For consideration of commercial transactions combining elements of both sale and service, see § 20(c).

REPORTERS' NOTE

Comment a. History. This Section establishes the boundaries of the subject matter affected by strict products liability in tort. Cases that do not satisfy this Section may support liability under negligence, misrepresentation, or some other liability theory. But only when the complained-of injury was allegedly caused by a defect in something within this Section's definition of "product" should the defendant manufacturer or seller be strictly liable for the harm caused. Strict liability is especially relevant when the case involves a manufacturing defect, or when a nonmanufacturer seller (wholesaler, retailer, or the like) is the defendant.

A number of state statutes have been enacted in recent years, codifying or changing the rules applicable to products liability actions. Many of these statutes define the term "product." For example, the Maryland statute defines the term as "[a] tangible article, including attachments, accessories, and component parts, and accompanying labels, warnings, instructions, and packaging." Md. Code. Ann., Cts. & Jud. Proc. § 5–115 (Supp. 1993). The Ohio statute defines a product as "any object, substance, mixture or raw material that constitutes tangible personal property and that satisfies all of the following: (1) . . . capable of delivery itself . . .; (2) produced, manufactured, or supplied for introduction into trade or commerce; and (3) intended for sale or lease to persons for commercial or personal use." Ohio Rev. Code Ann. § 2307.71 (Anderson 1991). In sharp contrast, the Tennessee statute contains a very broad definition: "any tangible object or goods produced." Tenn. Code Ann. § 29–28–102 (1980). The Model Uniform Product Liability Act defines "product" as "any object possessing intrinsic value, capable of delivery either as an assembled whole or as a component part or parts, and produced for introduction into trade or commerce. Human tissue or organs, including human blood and its components, are excluded from this term." MUPLA § 102(C), 44 Fed. Reg. 62714 (1979).

Courts have defined the term "product" in a variety of ways. See, e.g., Wyrulec Co. v. Schutt, 866 P.2d 756, 760 (Wyo.1993) ("a 'product' is anything made by human industry or art"); Pierson v. Sharp Memorial Hosp., 264 Cal.Rptr. 673, 675 (Cal.Ct. App.1989) ("[a product is] a physical article which results from a manufacturing process and is ultimately delivered to a consumer"); Hines v. JMJ Constr. Co., No. CV92–506329, 1993 WL 7269 (Conn.Super.Ct. Jan.11, 1993) (adopts U.C.C. definition of "goods" in § 2–215(1): "goods . . . [are] [a]ll things . . . which are movable at time of identification"); Olympic S.S. Co. v. Centennial Ins. Co., 789 P.2d 309, 313 (Wash.Ct.App.1990) ("[products are] goods which are processed or assembled in the ordinary channels of commerce"); Alexander v. Beech Aircraft Corp., 952 F.2d 1215, 1220 (10th Cir.1991) ("We note that the Indiana Products Liability Act (IPLA) contains a definition that 'product' means any item or good that is personalty at the time it is conveyed by the seller to another party . . . Ind. Code Ann. § 34–4–20A–2A–Z (Burns 1986))."

When the applicable definition fails to provide an unequivocal answer, decisions regarding whether a "product" is involved are reached in light of the public policies behind the imposition of strict liability in tort. Some of the policy considerations include: (1) the public interest in life and health; (2) the invitations and solicitations of the manufacturer to purchase the product; (3) the justice of imposing the loss on the manufacturer who created the risk and reaped the profit; (4) the superior ability of the commercial enterprise to distribute the risk of injury as a cost of doing business; (5) the disparity in position and bargaining power that forces the consumer to depend entirely on the manufacturer; (6) the difficulty in requiring the injured party to trace back along the channel of trade to the source of the defect in order to prove negligence; and (7) whether the product is in the stream of commerce. See Trent v. Brasch Mfg. Co., 477 N.E.2d 1312, 1315 (Ill.App.Ct.1985); see also Bastian v. Wausau Homes Inc., 620 F.Supp. 947, 949 (N.D.Ill.1985) (applying Illinois law); Firkin v. United States Polychemical Corp., 835 F.Supp. 1048, 1051 (N.D.Ill.1993) (applying Illinois law); Jackson v. City of Franklin, 554 N.E.2d 932 (Ohio Ct. App.1988) (courts should determine whether something is a product only in light of the relevant public policies; a one-of-a-kind swimming pool, built by the defendant contractor, was not a "product" because the opportunity for cost spreading via mass-marketed products was nonexistent); Board of Educ. v. W.R. Grace Corp., 609 A.2d 92, 106 (N.J.Super.Ct.Law Div.1992) (Quoting from an earlier opinion, "[t]hus, we believe that strict liability did not evolve simply because something was a product. The policy reasons brought it into being and continued to expand. It is those reasons then that should determine what is a product and not that it was simply something resulting from production, or 'produced naturally or as a result of a natural process,' the dictionary definition.... "); see also Prosser and Keeton, The Law of Torts §§ 98, 99 (5th ed. 1988 Supp.).

The issue of what is, or is not, a product for the purposes of strict products liability is an issue of law for the court to decide. See, e.g., Johnson v. Murph Metals, Inc., 562 F.Supp. 246 (N.D.Tex.1983) (applying Texas law); Kaneko v. Hilo Coast Processing, 654 P.2d 343 (Haw.1982).

The courts' treatment of this issue is well documented in the academic literature. See generally Cantu, The Illusive Meaning of the Term "Product" Under Section 402A of the Restatement (Second) of Torts, 44 Okla. L. Rev. 635 (1991); Wunsh, The Definition of a Product for the Purposes of Section 402A, Ins. Couns. J. 344 (1983); Buser, Strict Products Liability Litigation in Review, 70 Ill. B.J. 148, 150–52 (1981); Note, What Is or Is Not a Product Within the Meaning of Section 402A, 57 Marq. L. Rev. 625, 648 (1974). For application to more specific areas, see, e.g., William and German, The Liability of Raw Material Manufacturers: It's Time to Restate the Restatement, 43 Fed. of Ins. & Corp. Counsel 26 (1992); Note, Read at Your Own Risk: Publisher Liability for Defective How–To Books, 44 Ark. L. Rev. 699 (1991).

Comment b. Tangible personal property: in general. The majority of strict products liability cases involve tangible personal property that unequivocally falls into the category of products. See, e.g., Greenman v. Yuba Power Prods., Inc., 377 P.2d 897 (Cal.1963) (power lathe); Barker v. Lull Eng'g Co., 573 P.2d 443 (Cal. 1978) (high-lift loader); Camacho v. Honda Motor Co., 741 P.2d 1240 (Colo.1987), cert. denied, 485 U.S. 901, 108 S.Ct. 1067, 99 L.Ed.2d 229 (1988) (motorcycle); Back v. Wickes Corp., 378 N.E.2d 964 (Mass.1978) (motor home); Prentis v. Yale Mfg. Co., 365 N.W.2d 176 (Mich.1984) (forklift); Glover v. BIC Corp., 6 F.3d 1318 (9th Cir.1993) (applying Oregon law) (cigarette lighter); Stanley v. Schiavi Mobile Homes, Inc., 462 A.2d 1144 (Me.1983) (mobile home); Colt Inds. Operating Corp. v. Frank W. Murphy Mfr., Inc., 822 P.2d 925 (Alaska 1991) (sandblaster); Cramer v. Toledo Scale Co., Inc., 158 A.D.2d 966 (N.Y.App.Div.1990) (meat grinder); Dunham v. Vaughan & Bushnell Mfg. Co., 247 N.E.2d 401 (Ill.1969) (hammer).

Although the drafters of the Restatement, Second, of Torts, attached a caveat to § 402A in which they expressed no opinion as to whether § 402A applied to a seller of a component part of a product to be assembled later, the courts are in agreement that component parts should be considered products for the purposes of strict products liability. Thus, when a defective component is incorporated into something larger, the supplier or manufacturer of the component may be held strictly liable in tort for any damages proximately caused by the defect. See, e.g., Estate of Carey v. Hy–Temp Mfg., Inc., 702 F.Supp. 666 (N.D.Ill.1988) (applying Illinois law) (a component maker can be held liable if its component is defective for a known use); Jones v. Aero–Chem Corp., 680 F.Supp. 338 (D.Mont.1987) (applying Montana law) (tear gas canister valve); Burbage v. Boiler Eng'g & Supply Co., 249 A.2d 563 (Pa.1969) (boiler valve); Roy v. Star Chopper Co., 584 F.2d 1124, 1134 (1st Cir. 1978) (applying Rhode Island law) (Citing Prosser: "There is no dispute that strict liability applies to the manufacturer of the product, including the maker of a component part.... "), cert. denied, 440 U.S. 916, 99 S.Ct. 1234, 59 L.Ed.2d 466 (1979); Alvarez v. Felker Mfg. Co., 41 Cal.Rptr. 514 (Cal.Ct.App.1964) (manufacturer of defective blade was strictly liable when blade was incorporated into a concrete cutting machine); Bradford v. Bendix-Westinghouse Automotive Air Brake Co., 517 P.2d 406 (Colo.Ct.App.1973) (truck brake pedal assembly); Kaneko v. Hilo Coast Processing, 654 P.2d 343 (Haw.1982) (service platform).

The mere fact that the component part is shipped in a separate state and that it must be later assembled by the manufacturer or the end-user of the larger product, does not relieve the component maker of strict liability. See, e.g., Pust v. Union Supply Co., 561 P.2d 355, 361 (Colo.Ct.App. 1976) ("It would be anomalous, indeed, to adopt 402A, and yet permit a manufacturer to insulate itself from liability by categorizing the sale of its products as components simply because they have to be assembled.... "), aff'd in part and rev'd in part on other grounds, 572 P.2d 148 (Colo.1977), aff'd, 583 P.2d 276 (Colo. 1978); Komanekin v. Inland Truck Parts, 819 F.Supp. 802, 810 (E.D.Wis. 1993) (applying Wisconsin law) ("The mere fact that the [component] was supplied unassembled ... does not relieve its suppliers of liability.").

Furthermore, even a significant subsequent alteration of a component will not relieve a component part manufacturer of strict liability unless the change itself creates the defect that constitutes the proximate cause of injury. See, e.g., Michalko v. Cooke Color and Chem. Corp., 451 A.2d 179, 186 (N.J.1982) ("[I]f the defect which, singly or in combination, caused the injury existed before, as well as after, the change, the manufacturer is not relieved of liability, regardless of how much the product has been changed."); Dennis v. Ford Motor Co., 332 F.Supp. 901 (W.D.Pa.1971) (applying Pennsylvania law) (for substantial change in the product to relieve manufacturer of liability, the change must be causally connected to the accident). These decisions suggest that the "substantial change" issue is, in essence, another way of presenting the issue of "defect at time of sale."

When nondefective component parts are combined with other nondefective components, the manufacturers or suppliers of the components are not generally held strictly liable for injuries arising from defects in the final product. See § 5 and Reporters' Note.

Most courts treat raw materials as products for the purposes of strict products liability in tort, provided that the injury resulted from an identifiable defect in the raw material. In recent years, the bulk of litigation concerning a defective raw material has dealt with processed asbestos. See, e.g., Menna v. Johns–Manville Corp., 585 F.Supp. 1178, 1183 (D.N.J. 1984) (applying New Jersey Law) (asbestos is "[considered] a product for purposes of strict liability," because "pathological consequences [can occur] whether the dust emanates from processed or unprocessed asbestos"); Hammond v. North Am. Asbestos Corp., 435 N.E.2d 540, 544 (Ill.App. Ct.1982) ("Although raw asbestos is processed before it is ultimately sold to consumers, raw asbestos and not some manufactured article caused the harm in this case. There is no change in the condition of the asbestos from the time it was sold until it reached the 'ultimate user.' "). For an extensive discussion of asbestos litigation, see generally 9 Am. Law Prod. Liab. 3d §§ 113.1–113.46 (1987).

Processed lumber also is treated as a product for purposes of strict products liability. See, e.g., Housman v. C. A. Dawson & Co., 245 N.E.2d 886 (Ill.App.Ct.1969) (court held that processed lumber was a product for purposes of strict liability); Velez v. Craine & Clark Lumber Corp., 305 N.E.2d 750 (N.Y.1973) (lumber planks); Zehring v. Wick Agri–Buildings, 590 F.Supp. 138 (N.D.Ohio 1984) (applying Ohio law) (purlin board).

Courts have held manufacturers of such raw materials as sheet metal or plastics strictly liable for any defects therein. See, e.g., Hastings v. Dis. Tran. Prods., Inc., 389 F.Supp. 1352 (W.D.La.1975) (applying Louisiana law) (metal strap); Davis v. Wells Aluminum Southeast, Inc., 323 S.E.2d 215 (Ga.Ct.App.1984) (aluminum); Seegers Grain Co. v. United States Steel Corp., 577 N.E.2d 1364 (Ill.App. Ct.1991) (steel plates); Prather v. Upjohn Co., 797 F.2d 923 (11th Cir.1986) (applying Florida law; polyurethane); Smith v. Borg–Warner Corp., 626 F.2d 384 (5th Cir.1980) (applying Texas law) (thermoplastic powder).

Whether live animals are products presents an interesting question. In a handful of cases, American courts have addressed the issue of whether a household pet constitutes a product for the purposes of strict liability in tort. If the pet is diseased at the time of sale, courts have considered the pet a product, and have extended strict liability to any harm caused by the disease. Beyer v. Aquarium Supply Co., 404 N.Y.S.2d 778, 779 (N.Y.Sup.Ct.1977) ("[T]here is no reason why a breeder, distributor or vendor who places a diseased animal in the stream of commerce should be less accountable for his actions than one who markets a defective manufactured product."); Sease v. Taylor's Pets, Inc., 700 P.2d 1054, 1058 (Or.Ct. App.1985), review denied, 704 P.2d 514 (1985) (the court dismissed the view that live animals "may not be deemed products because of their mutability," and held that a rabid pet skunk constitutes product); Worrell v. Sachs, 563 A.2d 1387 (Conn.Super.Ct.1989) (a parasite-carrying puppy constitutes a product for purposes of strict liability because the animal was diseased).

By contrast, if the challenged condition or characteristic is inherent in the nature of the animal or is subject to change over time, such as friskiness or the tendency to bite, courts have refused to hold the suppliers of live animals strictly liable. See Kaplan v. C Lazy U Ranch, 615 F.Supp. 234 (D.Colo.1985) (applying Colorado law) (the court rejected a claim by a ranch guest, who had fallen from a horse, that a saddled horse constitutes a product; the horse allegedly expanded its chest when being saddled and then later relaxed, resulting in a loose saddle); Whitmer v. Schneble, 331 N.E.2d 115 (Ill.App.Ct.1975) (a Doberman dog that bit a child after giving birth could not be considered a product because its nature was not fixed when it left the seller's control several years earlier); Latham v. Wal–Mart Stores, Inc., 818 S.W.2d 673, 676 (Mo.Ct.App.1991) ("[D]ue to their mutability and their tendency to be affected by the purchaser, animals should not be products under § 402A as a matter of law."). However, even if the court refuses to treat an animal as a product, the animal's condition might support liability in negligence against the seller or the owner.

One of the few cases to address the issue whether livestock are products for purposes of strict products liability is Anderson v. Farmers Hybrid Cos., 408 N.E.2d 1194 (Ill.App.Ct. 1980). In that case, the court refused to extend strict liability when allegedly diseased gilts infected other pigs, which then had to be destroyed. The court held that gilts could not be considered products because their nature had not been fixed at the time they left the control of their suppliers. When a court is faced with this issue, it may draw support from the Uniform Commercial Code. Under the Code livestock are considered goods, and the injured buyer may recover damages. See, e.g., Vince v. Broome, 443 So.2d 23 (Miss.1983) (cattle); Claxton v. Boothe, 790 P.2d 1201 (Or.Ct.App.1990) (horse); Trad Inds., Ltd. v. Brogan, 805 P.2d 54 (Mont.1991) (elk).

Comment c. Tangible personal property: human blood and human tissue. Human blood and human tissue are specifically excluded from the coverage of this Restatement. Human blood and human tissue both satisfy the formal requisites of § 19(a), and have been regarded as products for the purposes of strict liability in the past. See, e.g., Rostocki v. Southwest Florida Blood Bank, Inc., 276 So.2d 475 (Fla.1973) (court held that, when the action arose before the passage of [the blood shield law], the sale of blood constituted the sale of a product, and defendant blood bank was subject to strict liability). In recent years, however, legislatures and courts alike have concluded that public policy concerns behind the availability of both human blood and tissue outweigh the risks inherent in their supply. Thus, in almost all states, liability of human blood and tissue suppliers is limited through legislation. See, e.g., La. Rev. Stat. Ann. § 9:2800.53(3) (West 1988) ("'Product' does not mean blood, blood components, human organs, human tissue.... "); Ala. Code § 7–2–314(4) (1975) ("Procuring, furnishing, donating, processing, distributing, or using human whole blood, plasma, blood products, blood derivatives, and other human tissues ... is declared for all purposes to be the rendition of a service ... and whether any remuneration is paid therefor is declared not to be a sale of such whole blood, plasma, blood products, blood derivatives, and other human tissues."); Cal. Health and Safety Code § 1606 (West 1963) ("The procurement, processing, distribution, or use of whole blood, plasma, blood products, and blood derivatives ... shall be construed to be, and is declared to be, for all purposes whatsoever, the rendition of a service ..."); see also 745 Ill. Comp. Stat. 40/1 (West 1993); Mich. Comp. Laws. Ann. § 333.9121(2) (West 1992); N.Y. Pub. Health Law § 580(4) (McKinney 1971); 42 Pa. Cons. Stat. Ann. § 8333(a) (West 1982).

In states where legislation does not address the problem directly, courts have refused to extend strict liability in tort to harm caused from adulterated human blood or tissue. See, e.g., Kirkendall v. Harbor Ins. Co., 887 F.2d 857 (8th Cir.1989) (applying Arkansas law) (court held that human blood is not a product for purposes of strict liability in tort); Gibson v. Methodist Hosp., 822 S.W.2d 95 (Tex. Ct.App.1991) (court held that blood was not a product for purposes of strict liability and products liability claims against hospital); see 1992 WL 140842 (application for writ of error denied; original opinion withdrawn).

Although human blood and human tissue providers may not be held strictly liable in tort for any harm caused by defective products, they may be held liable in negligence for failing to use reasonable care in handling and administering the product. For what constitutes reasonable care for those involved in providing medical services, see § 299A of the Restatement, Second, of Torts.

Comment d. Intangible personal property. A leading case involving the issue of whether information in a published book constitutes a product is Winter v. G.P. Putnam's Sons, 938 F.2d 1033 (9th Cir.1991) (applying California law). In that case, mushroom enthusiasts became severely ill from picking and eating mushrooms after relying on information in "The Encyclopedia of Mushrooms," a book published by the defendant. The plaintiff sued the publisher and sought damages for harm caused by a defective product. Summary judgment for the defendant was affirmed on appeal. The court reasoned that the information in the book constituted ideas, rather than a product, and explained the distinction between tangible and intangible aspects of a publication as follows:

> A book containing Shakespeare's sonnets consists of two parts, the material and the print therein, and the ideas and expression thereof. The first may be a product, but the second is not. The latter, were Shakespeare alive, would be governed by copyright laws; the laws of libel, to the extent consistent with the First Amendment; and the laws of misrepresentation, negligent misrepresentation, negligence, and mistake. These doctrines applicable to the second part are aimed at the delicate issues that arise with respect to intangibles such as ideas and expression. Products liability law is geared to the tangible world.

Id. at 1034; see also Way v. Boy Scouts of Am., 856 S.W.2d 230 (Tex. Ct.App.1993) (boy died after reading shooting-sports supplement in boy's magazine; court held that the ideas are "intangible characteristics not tangible properties," and do not constitute a product); Birmingham v. Fodor's Travel Pubs., Inc., 833 P.2d 70 (Haw.1992) (swimmer injured by rocks while body surfing at beach brought action against the publisher of a travel guide that advised that beach was safe; court held the travel guide was not a product for purposes of products liability law); Jones v. J.B. Lippincott Co., 694 F.Supp. 1216, 1217–18 (D.Md.1988) (nursing student injured treating self with constipation remedy listed in nursing textbook; court held that Restatement § 402A does not extend to dissemination of an idea or knowledge); Herceg v. Hustler Magazine, Inc., 565 F.Supp. 802, 803–04 (S.D.Tex. 1983) (person died after imitating "autoerotic asphyxiation" described in magazine article; court held that contents of magazines are not within meaning of Restatement § 402A); Walter v. Bauer, 439 N.Y.S.2d 821, 822–23 (N.Y.Sup.Ct.1981) (student injured doing science project described in textbook; court held that the book was not a defective product for purposes of products liability law because the intended use of a book is reading and the plaintiff was not injured by reading), aff'd in part & rev'd in part on other grounds, 451 N.Y.S.2d 533 (N.Y.App.Div.1982); Smith v. Linn, 563 A.2d 123, 126 (Pa.Super.Ct.1989) (reader of Last Chance Diet book died from diet complications; court held that book is not a product under Restatement § 402A), aff'd, 587 A.2d 309 (1991).

In Appleby v. Miller, 554 N.E.2d 773 (Ill.App.Ct.1990), the appellate court refused to extend strict liability in tort to standardized medical history intake forms, which aid doctors in making a diagnosis. In that case, the plaintiff claimed that her dentist's reliance on allegedly defective medical history forms supplied by the defendant resulted in improper treatment. In granting the publisher's motion to dismiss the claim, the court reasoned that the history intake forms represented a service provided to the dentist, rather than a product subjecting the publisher to strict liability in tort.

One state high court has held that a ticket to see a hockey game is not a product for purposes of strict products liability in tort. In Kennedy v. Providence Hockey Club, Inc., a spectator at a hockey game brought a claim against the hockey club for injuries received when a hockey puck struck her in the eye. 376 A.2d 329 (R.I.1977). In order to invoke strict products liability against the club, the plaintiff seized upon the tangible nature of the admissions ticket, and argued that it constituted a defective product. Summary judgment in favor of the club was affirmed on appeal. The Supreme Court of Rhode Island concluded: "[Plaintiff's] purchase of a ticket . . . is neither a transaction in goods . . . nor a 'product' within the meaning of products liability." Id. at 333.

The Ninth Circuit suggested in dictum that computer software might be considered a product for purposes of strict products liability in tort. Winter v. G.P. Putnam's Sons, 938 F.2d 1033, 1035 (9th Cir.1991) (applying California law). Although there are no cases on point on their facts, numerous commentators have discussed the issue and urged that software should be treated as a product. See, e.g., Gemignani, Product Liability and Software, 8 Rutgers Computer & Tech. L.J. 173, 196–99 (1981) (arguing that the same policies that gave rise to strict liability apply as well to software); Note, Strict Products Liability and Computer Software: Caveat Vendor, 4 Computer/ L.J. 373 (1983) (predicting that mass-marketed, off-the-shelf software will be subject to strict products liability); Note, Negligence: Liability for Defective Software, 33 Okla. L. Rev. 848, 855 (1980) ("In terms of software, [analysis of public policy considerations] . . . means that when software is distributed to the public through mass merchandising, strict liability in tort should be an available theory for a consumer who is injured because of a defect in the software."); Note, Computer Software and Strict Products Liability, 20 San Diego L. Rev. 439 (1983) (arguing that strict products liability should be extended to the computer industry); see also Note, Easing Plaintiffs' Burden of Proving Negligence for Computer Malfunction, 69 Iowa L. Rev. 241 (1983).

When a court will have to decide whether to extend strict liability to computer software, it may draw an analogy between the treatment of software under the Uniform Commercial Code and under products liability law. Under the Code, software that is mass-marketed is considered a good. See, e.g., Systems Design v. Kansas City Post Office, 788 P.2d 878 (Kan.Ct.App.1990); Advent Sys. Ltd. v. Unisys Corp., 925 F.2d 670 (3d Cir.1991) (applying Pennsylvania law); RRX Indus., Inc. v. Lab–Con, Inc., 772 F.2d 543 (9th Cir.1985) (applying California law). However, software that was developed specifically for the customer is a service. See, e.g., Data Processing Servs., Inc. v. L.H. Smith Oil Corp., 492 N.E.2d 314 (Ind.Ct.App.1986); Micro–Managers, Inc. v. Gregory, 434 N.W.2d 97 (Wis. Ct.App.1988); see also Note, Computer Software as a Good Under the Uniform Commercial Code: Taking a Byte Out of the Intangibility Myth, 65 B.U. L. Rev. 129 (1985); Comment, The Warranty of Merchantability and Computer Software Contracts: A Square Peg Won't Fit in a Round Hole, 59 Wash. L. Rev. 511 (1984).

One area in which courts have imposed strict products liability involves false information in maps and navigational charts. In these cases, the courts emphasized that navigational charts are used for their physical characteristics rather than for the ideas contained in them. Aetna Cas. & Sur. Co. v. Jeppesen & Co., 642 F.2d 339, 341–42 (9th Cir.1981) ("The [landing] specifications prescribed are set forth by the FAA in tabular form. Jeppesen acquires this FAA form and portrays the information therein on a graphic approach chart. This is Jeppesen's 'product.' "); Brocklesby v. United States, 767 F.2d 1288, 1298 (9th Cir.1985), cert. denied, 474 U.S. 1101, 106 S.Ct. 882, 88 L.Ed.2d 918 (1986) ("Jeppesen's charts are more than just a republication of the text of the government's [landing] procedure. Jeppesen converts a government procedure from text into graphic form and represents that the chart contains all necessary information."). The courts also noted that the total reliance placed by pilots on navigational charts directly links the charts to the accidents. In differentiating navigational charts from a magazine supplement, the Texas Appellate Court, in Way v. Boy Scouts of America, observed in dictum: "In those cases, the charts were physically used in the operation of the aircraft at the time of the accident. The inaccurate data directly caused or was alleged to have caused the accidents in question in the same manner in which a broken compass or an inaccurate altimeter would have caused a plane to crash." 856 S.W.2d 230, 238–39 (Tex.Ct.App.1993); see also Fluor Corp. v. Jeppesen & Co., 216 Cal.Rptr. 68, 71–72 (Cal.Ct.App. 1985) ("[A]lthough a sheet of paper might not be dangerous, per se, it would be difficult indeed to conceive of a salable commodity with more inherent lethal potential than an aid to aircraft navigation that, contrary to its own design standards, fails to list the highest land mass immediately surrounding a landing site."); Saloomey v. Jeppesen & Co., 707 F.2d 671 (2d Cir.1983) (applying Colorado law).

The weight of authority supports extending strict liability to electrical utilities. Once the electricity passes through the customer's meter, it is considered a product in the stream of commerce, and is subject to strict liability. See, e.g., Pierce v. Pacific Gas & Elec. Co., 212 Cal.Rptr. 283 (Cal.Ct.App.1985) (the court rejected the argument that electricity by its intrinsic nature cannot be a product within the meaning of strict products liability); see also Ransome v. Wisconsin Elec. Power Co., 275 N.W.2d 641 (Wis.1979); Williams v. Detroit Edison Co., 234 N.W.2d 702 (Mich.Ct. App.1975); Aversa v. Public Serv. Elec. & Gas Co., 451 A.2d 976 (N.J.Super.Ct.Law Div.1982); Elgin Airport Inn, Inc., v. Commonwealth Edison Co., 410 N.E.2d 620 (Ill.App. Ct.1980); Carbone v. Conn. Light &

Power Co., 482 A.2d 722 (Conn.Super.Ct.1984).

Before the electricity reaches the meter, however, and is made available to the customer, courts have held that it is not a product in the stream of commerce. Most of these cases refusing to extend strict liability involve injuries from accidental contact with a power line. See, e.g., Smith v. Home Light and Power Co., 734 P.2d 1051, 1055 (Colo.1987) (plaintiff injured when he pulled a portable grain auger into a power line; the court held "that at least until the electricity reaches a point where it is made available for consumer use, it is not a 'product' that has been sold or otherwise 'placed in the stream of commerce' for the purposes of strict products liability"); Hedges v. Public Serv. Co., 396 N.E.2d 933 (Ind.Ct.App.1979) (plaintiff injured when ladder he was carrying came in contact with power line); Petroski v. Northern Ind. Pub. Serv. Co., 354 N.E.2d 736 (Ind.Ct.App.1976) (minor injured when he grabbed a power line in a tree); Fuller v. Central Me. Power Co., 598 A.2d 457 (Me.1991) (deceased electrocuted when ladder he was carrying touched a power line); Priest v. Brown, 396 S.E.2d 638 (S.C.App.1990) (deceased electrocuted when he tried to move downed power line).

Some courts have held that high-voltage electrical power is a "product," but that it has not been "sold" until it has passed through a customer's meter. See, e.g., Monroe v. Savannah Elec. & Power Co., 471 S.E.2d 854 (Ga.1996) (a boat-in-tow struck a high power line; no strict liability).

A small number of courts have held strict liability inapplicable to electricity regardless of whether the harm was caused before or after the electricity passed through the customer's meter. See Wyrulec Co. v. Schutt, 866 P.2d 756 (Wyo.1993) (electricity is a service and not a product); Bowen v. Niagara Mohawk Power Corp., 590 N.Y.S.2d 628 (N.Y.App.Div.1992); Wood v. Public Serv. Co., 317 A.2d 576 (N.H.1974); Rodgers v. Chimney Rock Pub. Power Dist., 345 N.W.2d 12 (Neb.1984).

The courts are split on the issue of whether stray voltage should be treated as a product. For cases holding utilities strictly liable for harm caused by stray voltage, see, e.g., Public Serv. Ind., Inc. v. Nichols, 494 N.E.2d 349, 355 (Ind.Ct.App.1986) ("[T]he stray electricity had been reduced to consumption level and passed through the customers' meters. Therefore it had been introduced into the stream of commerce.... The [damage was done] by stray voltage or the end product electricity."); Schriner v. Pennsylvania Power & Light Co., 501 A.2d 1128 (Pa.Super.Ct.1985) (tacitly acknowledging stray voltage to be a product). The better position, however, is that stray voltage is a natural byproduct which is not introduced into the stream of commerce. See, e.g., Kolpin v. Pioneer Power & Light Co., 453 N.W.2d 214 (Wis.App.1990) (holding that for purposes of strict liability, stray voltage, which is a natural, low-voltage byproduct of the transmission of electric power and is not sold to or even used by the consumer, is not a product); Otte v. Dayton Power & Light Co., 523 N.E.2d 835, 838 (Ohio 1988) ("[N]atural-to-earth voltage, the purported 'product' in this case, has no benefit to the consumer, is clearly not the subject of a 'sale' to a consumer, and is indisputably not 'defective' ... [even] after it passed through the [customer's] meter."); G

& K Dairy v. Princeton Elec. Plant Bd., 781 F.Supp. 485 (W.D.Ky.1991) (applying Kentucky law). High-voltage electricity generated by lightning is not a product. Mancuso v. Southern Cal. Edison Co., 283 Cal.Rptr. 300, 308 (Cal.Ct.App.1991) ("[T]he conclusion that lightning-generated electricity cannot be a 'product' flows from the fact that it has not been marketed nor placed in the 'stream of commerce' by any act of [the utility]."); see also Pierce v. Pacific Gas & Elec. Co., 212 Cal.Rptr. 283, n. 10 (Cal.Ct. App.1985).

X-rays used during medical therapy are treated as a service and do not support strict products liability in tort. See Dubin v. Michael Reese Hosp., 415 N.E.2d 350 (Ill.1980) (radiation is a service because "the true object of [the complaint] is the alleged error in professional judgment and not . . . the nature of X-radiation itself."); see also Greenberg v. Michael Reese Hosp., 415 N.E.2d 390 (Ill.1980); Pitler v. Michael Reese Hosp., 415 N.E.2d 1255 (Ill.App.Ct. 1980). The same rule applies also to other forms of radiation therapy. See, e.g., Nevauex v. Park Place Hosp., Inc., 656 S.W.2d 923 (Tex.Ct.App. 1983) (radiation burns from cobalt therapy).

Comment e. Real property. One area that has prompted significant judicial and academic commentary involves improvements to real property. Traditionally, courts were reluctant to impose strict liability upon sellers of improvements to real property because such improvements were not goods or personalty. A number of states continue to hold this position. See, e.g., Lowrie v. City of Evanston, 365 N.E.2d 923 (Ill.App.Ct. 1977) (open-air parking garage); Jackson v. L.A.W. Contracting Corp., 481 So.2d 1290 (Fla.App.1986) (road resurface); McClanahan v. American Gilsonite, 494 F.Supp. 1334 (D.Colo. 1980) (applying Colorado law) (oil refinery building); Easterday v. Masiello, 518 So.2d 260 (Fla.1988) (jail); Messier v. Ass'n of Apartment Owners, 735 P.2d 939 (Haw.Ct.App.1987) (condominium apartment building); Papp v. Rocky Mountain Oil & Minerals, Inc., 769 P.2d 1249 (Mont.1989) (oil treating facility); Pennington v. Cecil N. Brown Co., 371 S.E.2d 106 (Ga.Ct.App.1988) (church parking lot); McMichael v. United States, 856 F.2d 1026 (8th Cir.1988) (applying Arkansas law; building); Charlton v. Day Island Marina, Inc., 732 P.2d 1008 (Wash.Ct.App.1987) (boat house); Holifield v. Pitts Swabbing Co., 533 So.2d 1112 (Miss.1988) (oil well).

The landmark case breaking from the tradition is Schipper v. Levitt & Sons, Inc., 207 A.2d 314 (N.J.1965). In that case, the plaintiff brought an action to recover for injuries resulting from a design defect in a water distribution system that allowed excessively hot water into a bathroom faucet. The New Jersey Supreme Court, arguing that a mass-builder is in a better position to bear the risks associated with any construction defects, found "that there is no meaningful distinction between [the builder's] mass production and sale of homes and the mass production and sale of automobiles and that pertinent overriding policy considerations are the same." Id. at 325; accord, Kriegler v. Eichler Homes, Inc., 74 Cal. Rptr. 749 (Cal.Ct.App.1969) (strict liability extended to a builder of mass-produced tract homes for damages resulting from a defectively installed radiant heating system); Oliver v. Superior Court, 259 Cal.Rptr. 160, 161

(Cal.Ct.App.1989) ("[T]he doctrine of strict liability has been applied to defendants who were characterized as mass-producers ... not to occasional or isolated construction."); La Jolla Village Homeowners' Ass'n v. Superior Court, 261 Cal.Rptr. 146 (Cal.Ct. App.1989); see also Model Uniform Product Liability Act § 102(A)(1), 44 Fed. Reg. 62, 714, 62, 717–19 (1979) (builder-vendor strictly liable only if it is a mass producer and seller of standardized dwellings, including modular homes).

The arguments used to justify imposing strict liability on mass-builders also support the extension of strict liability to unsafe design or manufacturing defects in prefabricated homes or structures. See, e.g., Kaneko v. Hilo Coast Processing, 654 P.2d 343 (Haw.1982) (iron worker injured when temporary weld in prefabricated building collapsed underneath him; court cited extensively from Schipper v. Levitt & Sons, Inc.); Bastian v. Wausau Homes, Inc., 620 F.Supp. 947 (N.D.Ill.1985) (applying Illinois law) (defective baseboard heater); see also Products Liability: Prefabricated Buildings, 4 A.L.R.5th 667.

A number of courts extended the reasoning to defects in less standardized structures. See, e.g., Patitucci v. Drelich, 379 A.2d 297, 298 (N.J.Super.Ct. Law Div.1977) ("Strict liability extends to a professional builder-vendor because the buyer of a home from a builder vendor can no more dig up the ground to inspect the sewage system than the buyer of an automobile can cause the car to be disassembled and tested."); Salka v. Dean Homes of Beverly Hills, Inc., 864 P.2d 1037 (Cal.1993) (one family home); Blagg v. Fred Hunt Co., 612 S.W.2d 321, 324 (Ark.1981) ("[I]n construing the Arkansas strict liability statute, we hold that the word product is as applicable to a house as to an automobile."); Hyman v. Gordon, 111 Cal.Rptr. 262 (Cal.Ct.App.1973) (residential building); Towers Tenant Ass'n. v. Towers Ltd. Partnership, 563 F.Supp. 566 (D.D.C.1983) (applying D.C. law) (converted condominiums). See generally Bearman, Caveat Emptor in Sales of Reality—Recent Assaults Upon the Rule, 14 Vand. L. Rev. 541 (1961); Haskell, The Case for an Implied Warranty of Quality in Sales of Real Property, 53 Geo. L.J. 633 (1965); Roberts, The Case of the Unwary Home Buyer: The Housing Merchant Did It, 52 Cornell L.Q. 835 (1967); Morgan, When the Walls Come Tumbling Down—Theories of Recovery for Defective Housing, 56 St. John's L. Rev. 670 (1982) (arguing that policy considerations justify recovery in strict liability for a defect in a house).

In California, a land developer may be held strictly liable for injuries and damages resulting from defects in the land itself, as in the case of soil erosion or subsidence. See Avner v. Longridge Estates, 77 Cal.Rptr. 633, 639 (Cal.Ct.App.1969) (soil subsidence; "[W]e conclude that the manufacturer of a lot may be held strictly liable in tort for damages suffered by the owner as a proximate result of any defects in the manufacturing process."); GEM Devs. v. Hallcraft Homes of San Diego, Inc., 261 Cal. Rptr. 626, 633 (Cal.Ct.App.1989) (soil subsidence; "It is settled law in California that a developer who mass grades land into finished lots for sale to the public for residential housing has produced a product and is strictly liable to the consumer for any defects in the design or manufacture of the lots."); Del Mar Beach Club Owners

Ass'n. v. Imperial Contracting Co., 176 Cal.Rptr. 886 (Cal.Ct.App.1981) (erosion).

The majority of courts hold that a defective product that is incorporated into an improvement to realty does not lose its identity as a product, and that a manufacturer or a contractor may be strictly liable for any damages proximately caused by the defect. See, e.g., Pamperin v. Interlake Cos., Inc., 634 So.2d 1137 (Fla.Dist. Ct.App.1994) (storage rack system); Berman v. Watergate West, Inc., 391 A.2d 1351 (D.C.1978) (air-conditioning system); O'Laughlin v. Minnesota Natural Gas Co., 253 N.W.2d 826 (Minn.1977) (grate of gas floor furnace); Trustees of Columbia Univ. v. Exposaic Indus., Inc., 505 N.Y.S.2d 882 (N.Y.App.Div.1986) (concrete panels); Worrell v. Barnes, 484 P.2d 573 (Nev.1971) (fitting in water heater); Halpryn v. Highland Ins. Co., 426 So.2d 1050 (Fla.Dist.Ct.App.1983) (paint on driveway); Smith v. Fluor Corp., 514 So.2d 1227 (Miss.1987) (heat exchanger); Trent v. Brasch Mfg. Co., 477 N.E.2d 1312 (Ill.App. Ct.1985) (heating, ventilating, and air-conditioning system); Brokenshire v. Rivas and Rivas, Ltd., 922 P.2d 696 (Or.Ct.App.1996) (defendant who installed acrylic floor in bakery was strictly liable for supplying sale-service "hybrid"). Some courts have reached this conclusion by reasoning that such products may be detached from the real property and resold. See, e.g., Pamperin v. Interlake Cos., Inc., 634 So.2d 1137 (Fla.Dist.Ct.App. 1994) (storage rack system is a product because it can be disassembled and resold and is not a permanent fixture). Other jurisdictions have rejected the alienability distinction and based their decisions on an analysis of the policy considerations supporting the imposition of strict liability. See Trent v. Brasch Mfg. Co., 477 N.E.2d 1312 (Ill.App.Ct.1985) (determination whether heating, ventilating, and air-conditioning system is a product is to be based on analysis of policy considerations supporting imposition of strict liability, not whether article is "attached" to real estate). But see Moore v. Jesco, Inc., 531 So.2d 815 (Miss.1988) (components of chicken houses constituted improvements to real property and were not products); Edward M. Chadbourne, Inc. v. Vaughn, 491 So.2d 551 (Fla. 1986) (paving materials not a product).

Comment f. The distinction between services and products. Courts are unanimous in refusing to categorize commercially-provided services as products for the purposes of strict products liability in tort. Thus, strict products liability does not extend to professionally-provided services, such as medical or legal help. See, e.g., Estate of Hannis v. Ashland State Gen. Hosp., 554 A.2d 574 (Pa.Cmwlth. Ct.1989) (medical services); Micciche v. Eastern Elevator Co., 645 A.2d 278 (Pa.Super.Ct.1994) (elevator maintenance company provided a service); Hoven v. Kelble, 256 N.W.2d 379 (Wis.1977) (medical services); Lucas v. Hamm, 364 P.2d 685 (Cal.1961) (attorney not strictly liable for allegedly defective work product); Denzer v. Rouse, 180 N.W.2d 521 (Wis.1970) overruled on other grounds by Hansen v. A.H. Robins, Inc., 335 N.W.2d 578 (Wis.1983) (attorney not strictly liable in tort). Similarly, a wide range of other service-providers are insulated from strict products liability in tort. Saddler v. Alaska Marine Lines, Inc., 856 P.2d 784 (Alaska 1993) (common carrier who filled barrels with asphalt and shipped them not strictly liable); Snyder v. ISC Alloys, Ltd., 772 F.Supp. 244 (W.D.Pa.1991) (architect not strictly liable for alleged defect in package of designs, technical drawings, and professional advice); Pena v. Sita World Travel, Inc., 152 Cal.Rptr. 17 (Cal.Ct.App.1978) (travel agency that prepared packaged tour not strictly liable to plaintiff injured on a bus); Ferrari v. Grand Canyon Dories, 38 Cal.Rptr.2d 65 (Cal.Ct.App.1995) (white-water rafting trip not a product); Coleman v. Charlesworth, 608 N.E.2d 464 (Ill. App.Ct.1992) (balloon-ride provider not strictly liable for plaintiff's injuries when hot-air balloon struck power lines); Lally v. Printing Mach. Sales & Serv. Co., 572 A.2d 1187 (N.J.Super.App.Div.1990) (strict liability does not apply against one who does routine maintenance and service on a machine).

Even when the service relates directly to a product that is commercially distributed, as in the case of installation or repair, the courts do not extend strict liability to the service provided. See Watts v. Rubber Tree, Inc., 853 P.2d 1365 (Or.Ct.App. 1993) (tire recapper); Ramos v. Silent Hoist & Crane Co., 607 A.2d 667 (N.J.Super.Ct.App.Div.1992) (installer of electrical components). The Supreme Court of Ohio held that a company that altered fire-fighting coats provided a product for the purposes of strict products liability. Jackson v. Alert Fire & Safety Equip., 567 N.E.2d 1027 (Ohio 1991). The court emphasized that the alterations entailed adding additional material to the coats and that it was that material that was alleged to be defective. See generally William Powers, Distinguishing Between Products and Services in Strict Liability, 62 N.C. L. Rev. 415 (1984).

§ 20. Definition of "One Who Sells or Otherwise Distributes"

For purposes of this Restatement:

(a) One sells a product when, in a commercial context, one transfers ownership thereto either for use or consumption or for resale leading to ultimate use or consumption. Commercial product sellers include, but are not limited to, manufacturers, wholesalers, and retailers.

(b) One otherwise distributes a product when, in a commercial transaction other than a sale, one provides the product to another either for use or consumption or as a preliminary step leading to ultimate use or consumption. Commercial nonsale product distributors include, but are not limited to, lessors, bailors, and those who provide products to others as a means of promoting either the use or consumption of such products or some other commercial activity.

(c) One also sells or otherwise distributes a product when, in a commercial transaction, one provides a combination of products and services and either the transaction taken as a whole, or the product component thereof, satisfies the criteria in Subsection (a) or (b).

Comment:

a. History. Until the mid–1960s, the only transactions that gave rise to what today is known as "products liability" were commercial product sales, as defined in Subsection (a). In large part this limitation reflects the origins of liability without fault in the law of warranty, which has traditionally focused on sales transactions. During the formative years in the development of strict products liability, courts extended liability to some nonsale transactions, but always by assimilating such transactions to sales. Section 402A of the Restatement, Second, of Torts, approved in 1964, limited itself to "one who *sells* a product in a defective condition. . . . " (Emphasis added). After the promulgation of § 402A, courts began to extend strict liability for harm caused by product defects to some nonsale commercial transactions involving the distribution of products. Rather than stretching to call these transactions "sales," courts simply declared that the same policy objectives that supported strict liability in the sales context supported strict liability in other contexts. The first significant extension involved commercial product lessors. Although title does not pass in lease transactions, courts have reasoned that the same policy objectives that are served by holding commercial product sellers strictly liable also apply to commercial product lessors. Over time, courts have extended strict products liability to a wide range of nonsale, nonlease transactions.

b. Product sales and giveaways. Sales occur at all levels in the distributive chain including manufacturer sellers, wholesale sellers, and retail sellers. Food served in a restaurant is sold to the customer, as are products given away free of separate charge in the context of a commercial sales promotion. Thus, businesses are liable for defects in free samples or defects in products given away for other promotional purposes. Even if the final transaction through which a defective product reaches the plaintiff is not a commercial sales transaction, with the result that products liability is not imposed on the final transferor—as when one buys a soft drink at a store and then gives it to a friend—a plaintiff may recover in tort for resulting harm against all commercial sellers who sold the product in a defective condition.

c. Commercial product leases. A commercial lessor of new and like-new products is generally subject to the rules governing new product sellers. When an individual rents a new or an almost-new used product on a short-term basis, with the lessee having no opportunity to inspect the product or adequately to assess its condition, and the product unit is drawn from a pool of rental units that includes new and almost-new used units with no attempt by the leasing agent to distinguish among units on the basis of age and condition, the lessor is subject to liability as if it were the retail seller of a new product. When the rental units are in obviously used condition, liability of the lessor depends on the rules stated in § 8.

d. Sales-service combinations. When the same person provides both products and services in a commercial transaction, whether a product has been sold may be difficult to determine. When the product and service components are kept separate by the parties to the transaction, as when a lawn-care firm bills separately for fertilizer applied to a customer's lawn or when a machinery repairer replaces a component part and bills separately for it, the firm will be held to be the seller of the product. This is especially true when the parties to the transaction explicitly characterize the property aspect as a sale.

When the parties do not clearly separate the product and service components, courts differ in their treatment of these so-called "sale-service hybrid transactions." These transactions tend to fall into two categories. In the first, the product component is consumed in the course of providing the service, as when a hair dye is used in treating a customer's hair in a salon. Even when the service provider does not charge the customer separately for the dye, the transaction ordinarily is treated as a sale of the material that is consumed in providing the service. When the product component in the sale-service transaction is not consumed or permanently transferred to the customer—as when defective scissors are used in the hair salon—the transaction ordinarily is treated as one not involving a sale of the product to the customer. But while the salon is not a seller, all commercial sellers in the chain of distribution of the scissors, from the manufacturer through the retailer who sold them to the salon, are clearly sellers of the scissors and are subject to liability to the salon customer under the rules of this Restatement. It should be noted that, in a strong majority of jurisdictions, hospitals are held not to be sellers of products they supply in connection with the provision of medical care, regardless of the circumstances.

e. Other means of commercial distribution: finance leases. A finance lessor, as distinct from a commercial lessor under Comment *c*, is not subject to the rule of this Section in the absence of active participation in the underlying commercial product distribution.

f. Other means of commercial distribution: product bailments. Bailments typically involve short-term transfers of possession. Several categories of cases are fairly clear. When the defendant is in the business of selling the same type of product as is the subject of the bailment, the seller/bailor is subject to strict liability for harm caused by defects. Thus, an automobile dealer who allows a prospective customer to test-drive a demonstrator will be treated the same as a seller of the demonstrator car. Even when sale of a product is not contemplated, the commercial bailor is subject to strict liability if a charge is imposed as a condition of the bailment. Thus, a laundromat is subject to strict liability for a defective clothes dryer, and a roller rink that rents skates is treated similarly. When products are made available as a convenience to customers who are on the defendant's premises primarily for different, although related purposes, and no separate charge is made, strict liability is not imposed. Thus, bowling alleys that supply bowling balls for customer use and markets that supply shopping carts are not subject to strict products liability for harm caused by defects in those items. Similarly, doctors who use medical devices while treating patients are not considered distributors of those products.

g. Other means of commercial distribution: product distribution facilitators. Persons assisting or providing services to product distributors, while indirectly facilitating the commercial distribution of products, are not subject to liability under the rules of this Restatement. Thus, commercial firms engaged in advertising products are outside the rules of this Restatement, as are firms engaged exclusively in the financing of product sale or lease transactions. Sales personnel and commercial auctioneers are also outside the rules of this Restatement.

REPORTERS' NOTE

a. History. Cases involving actual sale include Hiigel v. General Motors Corp., 544 P.2d 983 (Colo.1975) (manufacturer); Seattle–First Nat'l Bank v. Volkswagen of Am., Inc., 525 P.2d 286 (Wash.Ct.App.1974) (importer/wholesaler); Webb v. Zern, 220 A.2d 853 (Pa.1966) (distributor); Vandermark v. Ford Motor Co., 391 P.2d 168 (Cal.1964) (retailer). Sales may occur independently of the provision of services; and they may also occur in the context of so-called "sales-service combination." See § 20(c).

When confronted with nonsale situations to which the logic of strict products liability applied, historically courts tended to stretch the word "sell" to cover new situations. This Restatement, acknowledging that strict products liability applies to these nonsale methods of distribution, designates them with the phrase "otherwise distributes." In these areas into which strict products liability is expanding, courts frequently consider public policy in making their decisions. See, e.g., Newmark v. Gimbel's Inc. (infra, under *Sales-service combinations*) and Peterson v. Superior Court (infra, under *Commercial product leases*).

b. Product sales and giveaways. Once something has been deemed to be a "product," it remains to be determined whether the product was "sold" or "otherwise distributed" by the defendant. Thus, a commercial entity is subject to strict liability for products it distributes free of charge, since title has passed to the consumer. See, e.g., McKisson v. Sales Affiliates, Inc., 416 S.W.2d 787 (Tex.1967) (free sample); Perfection Paint & Color Co. v. Konduris, 258 N.E.2d 681 (Ind.Ct.App.1970) (free lacquer thinner supplied following sale of lacquer that did not bond properly); Levondosky v. Marina Assocs., 731 F.Supp. 1210 (D.N.J.1990) (defective glass in which free drink was served by casino). Plaintiffs also have been able to recover for harm caused by defective products prior to actual purchase. See, e.g., Barker v. Allied Supermarket, 596 P.2d 870 (Okla.1979) (implied warranty of merchantability in self-service store); Gillispie v. Great Atl. & Pac. Tea Co., 187 S.E.2d 441 (N.C.Ct.App.1972) (jury question on sale and implied warranty of bottle that exploded in self-service store before customer had paid for it). Although these cases were tried under the Uniform Commercial Code, they support the idea that the seller is liable when the product has been placed into the stream of commerce even though the customer has not yet paid for it. The same reasoning would apply under strict products liability.

c. Commercial product leases. The most significant extension of the boundaries of strict products liability is the inclusion of commercial product lessors in the category of suppliers held strictly liable for product defects. See, e.g., Samuel Friedland Family Enterprises v. Amoroso, 630 So.2d 1067 (Fla.1994); Kemp v. Miller, 453 N.W.2d 872 (Wis.1990).

In a landmark decision, the Supreme Court of New Jersey held the commercial lessor of a truck fleet strictly liable for injuries to the driver-employee of the lessee. See Cintrone v. Hertz Truck Leasing & Rental Serv., 212 A.2d 769 (N.J.1965). Relying doctrinally upon implied warranty concepts, the court concluded that "the relationship between the parties fairly calls for implied warranty of fitness of use, at least equal to that assumed by a new car manufacturer." Commentators have praised this decision as consistent with the policy objectives of strict products liability. See, e.g., Comment, Strict Liability of the Bailor, Lessor and Licensor, 57 Marq. L. Rev. 111 (1973); Comment, Products Liability—Liability of the Bailor for Hire for Personal Injuries Caused by Defective Goods, 51 N.C. L. Rev. 786 (1973); Annotation, Application of Strict Liability in Tort Doctrine to Lessor of Personal Property, 52 A.L.R.3d 121 (1973).

Courts have imposed strict liability on commercial lessors of a broad range of products, including motor vehicles (see, e.g., Stewart v. Budget Rent-a-Car Corp., 470 P.2d 240 (Haw. 1970); Galluccio v. Hertz Corp., 274 N.E.2d 178 (Ill.App.Ct.1971), superseded by statute; Stang v. Hertz Corp., 497 P.2d 732 (N.M.1972)); aircraft (see, e.g., George v. Tonjes, 414 F.Supp. 1199 (W.D.Wis.1976) (applying Wisconsin law); Bachner v. Pearson, 479 P.2d 319 (Alaska 1970); Rudisaile v. Hawk Aviation, Inc., 592 P.2d 175 (N.M.1979)); tools (see, e.g., McClaflin v. Bayshore Equip. Rental, 79 Cal.Rptr. 337 (Cal.Ct.App.1969)); and sailboats (see, e.g., Samuel Friedland Family Enterprises v. Amoroso, 630 So.2d 1067 (Fla.1994)).

By contrast with commercial lessors, financial lessors are not held strictly liable in the absence of active participation in the underlying commercial product distribution. See, e.g., Brescia v. Great Road Realty Trust, 373 A.2d 1310 (N.H.1977); Nath v. Nat'l Equip. Leasing Corp.,

439 A.2d 633 (Pa.1981) ("[A] finance lessor is not in the business of selling or marketing merchandise. A finance lessor is in the business of circulating funds. Such an activity cannot possibly produce reasonable reliance upon the safety of the merchandise."); Cole v. Elliott Equip. Co., 653 F.2d 1031 (5th Cir.1981) (applying Texas law); Abco Metals Corp. v. Equico Lessors, Inc., 721 F.2d 583 (7th Cir.1983) (applying Illinois law); Wright v. Newman, 735 F.2d 1073 (8th Cir.1984) (applying Missouri law); Bickram v. Case I.H., 712 F.Supp. 18 (E.D.N.Y. 1989) (applying New York law); Dominguez Mojica v. Citibank, N.A., 830 F.Supp. 668 (D.P.R.1993) (applying Puerto Rico law).

One category of leases, those involving real property, present special problems. Traditionally landlords were not held strictly liable for latent defects in the premises. Although that may still be the majority rule, some jurisdictions hold landlords strictly liable for defects in the premises. See, e.g., Kaplan v. Coulston, 381 N.Y.S.2d 634, 638 (N.Y.Civ.Ct. 1976) ("a landlord is in a similar position to a seller . . . and a tenant is in a similar position to a purchaser"). Other jurisdictions limit landlord liability to nonstructural items. See, e.g., Armstrong v. Cione, 738 P.2d 79, 85 (Haw.1987) (strict liability does not apply because "the shower and its door were an integral part of the structure of the apartment building and there is no evidence that [the landlord] installed the shower"); Boudreau v. General Elec. Co., 625 P.2d 384 (Haw.App.1981) (landlord can be held strictly liable for explosion in washer/dryer unit that he installed). Other jurisdictions do not hold the landlord strictly liable at all. See, e.g., Dwyer v. Skyline Apartments, Inc., 123 N.J.Super. 48, 56, 301 A.2d 463, 467 (N.J.Sup.Ct.App.Div.1973), aff'd., 311 A.2d 1 (N.J.1973) ("to apply the broad brush of strict liability to the landlord-tenant relationship in a dwelling house would impose an unusual and unjust burden on property owners"); Old Town Dev. Co. v. Langford, 349 N.E.2d 744 (Ind.Ct. App.1976) (defective heating system caused fire resulting in injury and deaths).

Hotel operators, however, generally are not held strictly liable for inherent defects in fixtures or furnishings. See, e.g., Wagner v. Coronet Hotel, 458 P.2d 390 (Ariz.App.1969) (hotel-guest relationship is that of inviter-invitee); Peterson v. Superior Court, 899 P.2d 905 (Cal.1995) (hotel not strictly liable to guest who slipped in allegedly defective shower; overruling Becker v. IRM Corp., 698 P.2d 116 (Cal.1985)); Ranalli v. Edro Motel Corp., 690 A.2d 137 (N.J.Super.1997) (motel owner not strictly liable for defective frying pan supplied to a guest); Livingston v. Begay, 652 P.2d 734 (N.M.1982) (asphyxiation by carbon dioxide from disconnected exhaust pipe).

d. Sales-service combinations. No unifying test has been devised to determine whether strict liability applies in any given sales-service combination.

Hybrid cases often arise in the medical context, as when a surgeon uses defective forceps during an operation. Most jurisdictions hold that hospitals and doctors provide a service—medical treatment—and immunize them from strict liability for harm from defective products used in medical treatment, whether the product is implanted in the patient, loaned to the patient, or merely used as a tool. See, e.g., Vergott v. Deseret

Pharm. Co., Inc., 463 F.2d 12 (5th Cir.1972) (applying Texas law) (hospital not strictly liable for catheter that broke, necessitating open-heart surgery); Magrine v. Krasnica, 227 A.2d 539 (N.J.Co.Ct.1967) (dentist not strictly liable for hypodermic needle which broke, leaving portion in patient's jaw); Silverhart v. Mount Zion Hosp., 98 Cal.Rptr. 187 (Cal.Ct.App. 1971) (hospital not strictly liable for surgical needle that broke during operation); Hector v. Cedars–Sinai Med. Ctr., 225 Cal.Rptr. 595 (Cal.Ct.App. 1986) (hospital not strictly liable for defective pacemaker implanted in patient); Porter v. Rosenberg, 650 So.2d 79 (Fla.App.1995) (physician who supplied patient with prosthesis in breast implant procedure not strictly liable; see n.1, collecting authorities); Goldfarb v. Teitelbaum, 540 N.Y.S.2d 263 (N.Y.App.Div.1989) (dentist not strictly liable for defective mandibular prosthesis placed in patient's mouth); Podrat v. Codman–Shurtleff, Inc., 558 A.2d 895 (Pa.Super.Ct.1989) (hospital not strictly liable for forcep, the tip of which broke off and lodged in patient's spine); Johnson v. Mountainside Hosp., 571 A.2d 318 (N.J.Super.Ct.App.Div.1990) (hospital not strictly liable for defective respirator loaned to patient); Cafazzo v. Central Med. Health Serv., Inc., 635 A.2d 151 (Pa.Super.Ct.1993) (neither doctor nor hospital strictly liable for defective prosthesis implanted in patient's jaw). Public policy supports this immunity. See, e.g., Newmark v. Gimbel's Inc., 258 A.2d 697, 703 (N.J. 1969) ("[T]he nature of the [medical] services, the utility of and the need for them, involving as they do, the health and even survival of many people, are so important to the general welfare as to outweigh in the policy scale any need for the imposition on dentists and doctors of the rules of strict liability in tort."). But see Bell v. Poplar Bluff Physicians Group, 879 S.W.2d 618 (Mo.Ct.App.1994) (holding the hospital as a seller of a surgical implant); Parker v. St. Vincent Hosp., 919 P.2d 1104 (N.M.Ct.App.1996) (limiting immunity of hospital from strict liability to claims of design defects in medical products chosen by the treating physician).

Interesting questions arise in the medical context when the product is not integrally associated with the medical treatment. One court refused to hold a hospital strictly liable for latent defects in the premises. This court reasoned that the provision of a hospital room was "an integral part of its delivery of professional medical service." Pierson v. Sharp Mem. Hosp., Inc., 264 Cal.Rptr. 673 (Cal.Ct. App.1989). Other courts have held that a hospital is strictly liable for harm caused by defective products not immediately related to medical treatment. See, e.g., Thomas v. St. Joseph Hosp., 618 S.W.2d 791 (Tex. Civ.App.1981) (patient's hospital gown caught fire from match); Johnson v. Sears, Roebuck & Co., 355 F.Supp. 1065 (E.D.Wis.1973) (hospital can be held strictly liable for "mechanical and administrative services").

Courts are likely to apply strict liability in nonmedical sales-service combinations in which the product is used up or consumed. See, e.g., Newmark v. Gimbel's Inc., 258 A.2d 697 (N.J.1969) (beauty parlor held strictly liable for permanent wave solution); Villari v. Terminix Int'l, Inc., 692 F.Supp. 568 (E.D.Pa.1988) (applying Pennsylvania law) (pest control company strictly liable for product used in termite control). Similarly, a contractor/remodeler was held to have "manufactured" and "sold" a propane gas piping system that leaked, resulting in a fire. See Worrell v. Barnes, 484 P.2d 573 (Nev.1971). If the product is not used up or consumed, the transaction is usually not treated as a sale of the product, but rather as a service. See, e.g., Coleman v. Charlesworth, 608 N.E.2d 464 (Ill.App.Ct. 1992) (sightseeing balloon ride is a service); Siciliano v. Capitol City Shows, Inc., 475 A.2d 19 (N.H.1984) (amusement ride is a service, not a product); Allen v. Nicole, Inc., 412 A.2d 824 (N.J.Super.Ct.Law Div. 1980) (amusement ride operator is more a consumer of the equipment than a seller).

f. Other means of commercial distribution: product bailments. Distributors of demonstration models have been held strictly liable for harm caused by defects. See, e.g., First Nat'l Bank of Mobile v. Cessna Aircraft Co., 365 So.2d 966 (Ala.1978) (strict liability is applicable when a product is placed in the stream of commerce by demonstration); Robert F. Bullock, Inc. v. Thorpe, 353 S.E.2d 340 (Ga.1987) (deep-fat fryer placed in restaurant kitchen on trial basis); Delaney v. Towmotor Corp., 339 F.2d 4 (2d Cir.1964) (applying New York law) (demonstrator fork-lift truck).

When a sale is not contemplated, but a separate charge is imposed as a condition of the bailment, the bailor typically is held strictly liable for harm caused by the defective bailed product. See, e.g., Garcia v. Halsett, 82 Cal.Rptr. 420, 423 (Cal.Ct.App. 1970) (laundromat customer "is actually in a worse position than a retail buyer or member of the buyer's family"); Golt v. Sports Complex, Inc., 644 A.2d 989 (Del.Super.Ct.1994) (go-cart track operator was strictly liable for defective go-cart rented to plaintiff); Wilson v. Dover Skating Ctr., Ltd., 566 A.2d 1020, 1024 (Del.Super.Ct.1989) (rental of roller skates is "an integral and essential part of defendant's profit-oriented operation"). Anomalously, a municipal golf course was not held strictly liable for harm caused by a defective rental golf cart. Katz v. Slade, 460 S.W.2d 608 (Mo. 1970). Amusement ride operators, however, are considered to provide a service, not a product, and thus are not held strictly liable. See, e.g., Siciliano v. Capitol City Shows, Inc., 475 A.2d 19 (N.H.1984) (amusement ride is more of a service than a product); Allen v. Nicole, Inc., 412 A.2d 824 (N.J.Super.Ct.Law Div.1980) (amusement ride operator is more a consumer of the equipment than a seller).

Bailors who furnish products that are an integral part of their sales or marketing operation are held strictly liable for harm caused by defective bailed products, even if a separate charge is not imposed. See Bainter v. Lamoine LP Gas Co., 321 N.E.2d 744, 746 (Ill.App.Ct.1974) (propane tank loaned to farmer by propane gas company was "a necessary incident of periodic sales of gas"); Fulbright v. Klamath Gas Co., 533 P.2d 316, 321 (Or.1975) ("sale of propane gas cannot logically be separated from the loan of the vine burner"); Gabbard v. Stephenson's Orchard, Inc., 565 S.W.2d 753 (Mo.Ct.App.1978) (orchard strictly liable for defective ladder furnished to "you-pick" customers). Thus, restaurants are held strictly liable for injuries from defects in their dishware. See, e.g., Shaffer v. Victoria Station, Inc., 588 P.2d 233 (Wash.1978) (wine glass broke, injuring customer's hand); Levondosky v. Marina Assocs., 731 F.Supp. 1210 (D.N.J.1990) (applying New Jersey law) (defective glass in which free drink was served).

Commercial bailors, who furnish products as a convenience for use by their customers on the bailors' business premises, but who do not charge separately for the product's use, typically are excluded from strict liability rules. See, e.g., Keen v. Dominick's Finer Foods, Inc., 364 N.E.2d 502, 505 (Ill.App.Ct.1977) ("The store, like its customer, is merely a user of the shopping cart."); Dixon v. Four Seasons, 424 A.2d 428 (N.J.Super.Ct.App.Div.1980) (bowling alley not strictly liable for defect in bowling ball); Gilliland v. Rothermel, 403 N.E.2d 759, 761 (Ill.App.Ct.1980) (tire gauge loaned to customer "was neither a necessary incident of the products which the defendant offered for sale nor an integral part of defendant's marketing operation"). Neither is the bailor held strictly liable when the product is furnished as a convenience and is used on the customer's business premises: Jones v. McCook Drum & Barrel Co., Inc., 595 N.E.2d 670 (Ill.App.Ct.1992) (defective semitrailer full of purchased drums was left in customer company's yard for customer's convenience).

g. Other means of commercial distribution: product distribution facilitators. Sales personnel, sales representatives, and other sales facilitators are not subject to strict products liability. See, e.g., Dillard Dep't Stores, Inc. v. Associated Merchandising Corp., 782 P.2d 1187 (Ariz.App.1989) (non-profit merchandising organization is essentially providing a service); Alvarez v. Koby Mach. Co., Ltd., 516 N.E.2d 930 (Ill.App.Ct.1987) (sales facilitator); Lyons v. Premo Pharm. Labs, Inc., 406 A.2d 185 (N.J.Super.Ct.App.Div.1979) (broker never had control over product, and his passive role prevents holding him strictly liable); Memphis Bank & Trust Co. v. Water Serv., Inc., 758 S.W.2d 525 (Tenn.1988) (sales representative not subject to strict liability). But exclusive sales representatives or exclusive agents have been held strictly liable for harm caused by defective products. See, e.g., Bittler v. White & Co., Inc., 560 N.E.2d 979 (Ill.App.Ct.1990) (participatory connection with the defective product was sufficient to subject the exclusive sales representative to strict products liability); Brumbaugh v. CEJJ, Inc., 547 N.Y.S.2d 699, 701 (N.Y.App.Div.1989) (exclusive marketing agent was "a mandatory link in this distributive chain").

The relationship of auctioneers to products is similar to that of sales personnel; thus auctioneers also are not held strictly liable. See, e.g., Musser v. Vilsmeier Auction Co., Inc., 562 A.2d 279, 283 (Pa.1989) ("[An] auctioneer is . . . an ad hoc salesman of the goods of another. . . . He bears no relationship to the manufacturer or the goods, beyond their immediate sale."); Tauber–Arons Auctioneers Co., Inc. v. Superior Court, 161 Cal. Rptr. 789 (Cal.Ct.App.1980) (treating auctioneer as dealer in used machinery).

Similarly, licensors of trademarks are not held strictly liable when they do not participate in the design, manufacture, or distribution of the licensee's product. See, e.g., Nelson v. International Paint Co., Inc., 734 F.2d 1084 (5th Cir.1984) (licensor not liable); Hebel v. Sherman Equip., 442 N.E.2d 199 (Ill.1982) (licensor not liable). When licensors do participate, they are strictly liable as sellers. See, e.g., Torres v. Goodyear Tire & Rubber Co., 786 P.2d 939 (Ariz.1990) (licensor liable); City of Hartford v. Associated Constr. Co., 384 A.2d 390 (Conn.Super.1978) (licensor liable).

§ 21. Definition of "Harm to Persons or Property": Recovery for Economic Loss

For purposes of this Restatement, harm to persons or property includes economic loss if caused by harm to:

(a) the plaintiff's person; or

(b) the person of another when harm to the other interferes with an interest of the plaintiff protected by tort law; or

(c) the plaintiff's property other than the defective product itself.

Comment:

a. Rationale. This Section limits the kinds of harm for which recovery is available under this Restatement. Two major constraints on tort recovery give content to this Section. First, products liability law lies at the boundary between tort and contract. Some categories of loss, including those often referred to as "pure economic loss," are more appropriately assigned to contract law and the remedies set forth in Articles 2 and 2A of the Uniform Commercial Code. When the Code governs a claim, its provisions regarding such issues as statutes of limitation, privity, notice of claim, and disclaimer ordinarily govern the litigation. Second, some forms of economic loss have traditionally been excluded from the realm of tort law even when the plaintiff has no contractual remedy for a claim.

b. Economic loss resulting from harm to plaintiff's person. Loss of earnings and reductions in earning capacity are common forms of economic loss resulting from harm to the plaintiff's person and are included in Subsection (a). Other forms of economic loss resulting from harm to the plaintiff's person are recoverable if they are within the general principles of legal cause. See Restatement, Second, Torts §§ 430–461.

c. When harm to another interferes with an interest of the plaintiff protected by tort law. When tort law recognizes the right of a plaintiff to recover for economic loss arising from harm to another's person, that right is included within the rules of this Restatement Third, Torts: Products Liability. Thus, for example, actions under local common law and statutes for loss of consortium or wrongful death on behalf of next of kin, although not direct harms to the plaintiff's person, are included in Subsection (b). Other examples of such rights may be recognized under local law, but the categories included in Subsection (b) have traditionally been limited in number.

Illustrations:

1. A machine that is used to anesthetize dental patients was delivered to Dr. Smith with the labels for nitrous oxide and oxygen reversed. Dr. Smith, believing she was administering oxygen to a patient, mistakenly administered nitrous oxide, which caused the patient to die. Due to the adverse publicity arising from accurate media reporting of the case, Dr. Smith suffered a sharp drop in her practice and substantial economic loss. Dr. Smith's interest in her professional reputation is an interest protected by tort law against economic loss arising from harm to a patient in her care. Thus, Dr. Smith's damages for economic loss are recoverable in tort from the seller of the machine under Subsection (b).

2. Robert, a skilled electrical engineer, was employed by ABC Contractors, Inc. Robert was killed in an automobile accident caused by a defect in an automobile manufactured by XYZ. ABC suffered substantial economic loss as a result of Robert's death because ABC was unable to complete a building contract in a timely fashion. ABC cannot recover its economic loss from XYZ because an employer does not have a tort cause of action against a third party for deprivation of the services of an employee arising from personal injury to the employee.

d. Harm to the defective product itself. When a product defect results in harm to the product itself, the law governing commercial transactions sets forth a comprehensive scheme governing the rights of the buyer and seller. Harm to the product itself takes two forms. A product defect may render the product ineffective so that repair or replacement is necessary. Such a defect may also result in consequential loss to the buyer. For example, a machine that becomes inoperative may cause the assembly line in which it is being used to break down and may lead to a wide range of consequential economic losses to the business that owns the machine. These losses are not recoverable in tort under the rules of this Restatement. A somewhat more difficult question is presented when the defect in the product renders it unreasonably dangerous, but the product does not cause harm to persons or property. In these situations the danger either (1) never eventuates in harm because the product defect is discovered before it causes harm, or (2) eventuates in harm to the product itself but not in harm to persons or other property. A plausible argument can be made that products that are dangerous, rather than merely ineffectual, should be governed by the rules governing products liability law.

However, a majority of courts have concluded that the remedies provided under the Uniform Commercial Code—repair and replacement costs and, in appropriate circumstances, consequential economic loss—are sufficient. Thus, the rules of this Restatement do not apply in such situations.

A second category of economic loss excluded from the coverage of this Restatement includes losses suffered by a plaintiff but not as a direct result of harm to the plaintiff's person or property. For example, a defective product may destroy a commercial business establishment, whose employees patronize a particular restaurant, resulting in economic loss to the restaurant. The loss suffered by the restaurant generally is not recoverable in tort and in any event is not cognizable under products liability law.

Illustration:

3. ABC Rubber Company sells a conveyor belt to XYZ Automobile Company. XYZ installs the belt in its engine assembly line. A defect in the conveyor belt causes it to break, damaging the assembly line. Until the assembly belt is repaired, no engines can be assembled. Because no engines are available, the production lines for automobiles shut down as well. XYZ loses many days of production at a critical time when its best-selling new model has just appeared in the showroom. Expert witnesses testify and the trier of fact finds that as a consequence of this shutdown, XYZ not only lost the sales of the automobiles that would have been produced but for the shutdown, but also lost the crucial race to be the first in the market with its new model, thereby losing additional millions of dollars of sales to its arch rival MNO Motor Cars, which introduced its new model a week ahead of XYZ instead of a week behind it. Under Subsection (c), XYZ's losses were caused by harm to the defective product itself. XYZ may not recover those losses from ABC under the rules in this Restatement.

e. Harm to the plaintiff's property other than the defective product itself. A defective product that causes harm to property other than the defective product itself is governed by the rules of this Restatement. What constitutes harm to other property rather than harm to the product itself may be difficult to determine. A product that nondangerously fails to function due to a product defect has clearly caused harm only to itself. A product that fails to function and causes harm to surrounding property has clearly caused harm to other property. However, when a component part of a machine or a system destroys the rest of the machine or system, the characterization process becomes more difficult. When the product or system is deemed to be an integrated whole, courts treat such damage as harm to the product itself. When so characterized, the damage is excluded from the coverage of this Restatement. A contrary holding would require a finding of property damage in virtually every case in which a product harms itself and would prevent contractual rules from serving their legitimate function in governing commercial transactions.

The characterization of a claim as harm to other property may trigger liability not only for the harm to physical property but also for incidental economic loss. The extent to which incidental economic loss is recoverable in tort is governed by general principles of legal cause. See Restatement, Second, Torts §§ 430–461.

One category of claims stands apart. In the case of asbestos contamination in buildings, most courts have taken the position that the contamination constitutes harm to the building as other property. The serious health threat caused by asbestos contamination has led the courts to this conclusion. Thus, actions seeking recovery for the costs of asbestos removal have been held to be within the purview of products liability law rather than commercial law.

Illustration:

4. Same facts as Illustration 3, except that the breakdown in the assembly line occurred when a defective steering mechanism in a forklift driven by an XYZ employee caused the forklift to go out of control and collide with the assembly line, breaking the conveyor belt. The forklift was manufactured by Liftco. In a tort action by XYZ against Liftco the conveyor constitutes other property and is within the coverage of this Restatement. The extent of the economic loss recoverable by XYZ is to be determined by the application of the general principles of legal cause set forth in Restatement, Second, Torts §§ 430–461.

f. Harm to other property: disclaimers and limitations of remedies. Although recovery for harm to property other than the defective product itself is governed by this Restatement, the Institute leaves to developing case law the questions of whether and under what circumstances contracting parties may disclaim or limit remedies for harm to other property. Of course, such contractual limitations would be effective only between the parties themselves. When a defective product causes harm to property owned by third persons, the contractual arrangements between the contracting parties should not shield the seller from liability to the third party. However, contractual limitations on tort liability for harm to property, when fairly bargained for, may provide an effective way for the contracting parties efficiently to allocate risks of such harm between themselves.

REPORTERS' NOTE

Comment d. Harm to the defective product itself. Section 21(c) sets forth the limitations that courts have placed on the application of products liability law to various forms of economic loss. A strong majority of courts have taken the position that the key to whether products liability law or commercial law principles should govern depends on the nature of the loss suffered by the plaintiff. If the plaintiff has suffered loss because the defective product simply malfunctioned or self-destructed, the loss is deemed economic loss within the purview of the Uniform Commercial Code (U.C.C.). Similarly, if a plaintiff suffers economic loss not caused by damage to the plaintiff's person or other property, that type of loss is to be governed by the U.C.C.

The leading decision espousing the position that the nature of the loss should be the determining factor is East River Steamship Corp. v. Transamerica Delaval, Inc., 476 U.S. 858, 106 S.Ct. 2295, 90 L.Ed.2d 865 (1986). In that case, the plaintiff contracted with the defendant for the construction of four supertankers. Upon taking possession of the tankers, the plaintiff discovered that they had defective turbines. The plaintiff brought a products liability suit in admiralty against the manufacturer of the turbines for the cost of repair and for income lost while the tankers were out of service. Affirming summary judgment for the defendant, the Court held that the plaintiff could not recover in tort on the grounds that plaintiff was in a commercial relationship with the defendant, who was under no duty to prevent its product from injuring itself. The Court refused to characterize the losses alleged as harm to "other property," reasoning that the turbines that propelled the tanker were part of a single integrated system, and thus one product.

The Court advanced a number of reasons for denying recovery in tort for harm to the product itself. To begin with, the Court believed that the deterrence value of tort liability is reduced when the damage is to the product itself. Also, such damage is merely a failure of the product to meet the customer's expectations. Furthermore, the Court saw no restriction on tort liability for economic loss and feared that manufacturers might be liable for vast sums. The Court believed that unrestricted liability would make it difficult for the manufacturer to take into account the expectations of buyers down the stream of commerce. Last, the Court noted that the parties had the opportunity to allocate risk through negotiation and insurance.

The Court considered and rejected the position of some courts that products liability law should govern if the product was dangerous or failed in a sudden and calamitous manner. If the nature of the loss is to the product itself or consequential economic loss alone, the Court insisted that contract norms govern the case.

Recently, in Saratoga Fishing Co. v. J.M. Martinac & Co., ___ U.S. ___, 117 S.Ct. 1783, 138 L.Ed.2d 76 (1997), the Supreme Court clarified just what exactly constitutes the product itself under *East River*, as well as how recovery would be affected if the party seeking damages was not the initial purchaser of the product. In that case, an individual purchased a boat from the defendant-manufacturer and subsequently added certain equipment to the boat. The individual then sold the boat to the plaintiff. Sometime thereafter the boat sank due to an engine-room fire that resulted from a defectively designed hydraulic system supplied to the defendant-manufacturer by a component supplier. The Supreme Court held that the plaintiff could recover for the physical damage to the equipment added by the initial purchaser, as this constituted "other property" and not the "product itself."

In concluding that the term "other property" encompassed the equipment added by the initial purchaser, the Supreme Court explained:

> When a Manufacturer places an item in the stream of commerce by selling it to an Initial User, that item is the "product itself" under *East River*. Items added to the product by the Initial User are therefore "other property," and the Initial User's sale of the product to a Subsequent User does not change these characterizations.

Id. at 1786.

The Court asserted several grounds as justification for this holding. For one, the Court reasoned that to hold the manufacturer liable for damage to the equipment added by the initial purchaser only when the initial purchaser still possessed the product "makes the scope of a manufacturer's liability turn on what seems . . . a fortuity." Id. at 1787. Moreover, the Court noted that subsequent purchasers are not in a position to contract for appropriate sharing of the risks of harm with the manufacturer as are the initial purchasers, and it is likely more difficult for the initial purchaser (a consumer) to offer the appropriate warranty to the subsequent purchaser on used products. Id. In addition, the Court also found unconvincing the respondents' argument that "if a Subsequent User can recover for damage a defective manufactured product causes to property added by the Initial User, then a user might recover damage a defective component causes the manufactured product, other than the component itself." Id. at 1788. Finally, the court did not agree with the respondents' contention that its holding would expose manufacturers to too great a potential of tort liability. The Court explained that "a host of other tort principles, such as foreseeability, proximate cause, and the 'economic loss' doctrine already do . . . limit liability in important ways." Id. In fact, earlier in the opinion the Court stated that preventing subsequent purchasers from recovering for damage to equipment added by initial purchasers would create a "tort damage immunity beyond that set by any relevant precedent." Id. at 1787.

A strong majority of courts follow the *East River* rule (some of the cases cited preceded *East River* and were relied upon by the *East River* court), and it is likely that these courts will follow *Saratoga* as well.

For cases consistent with *East River*, see, e.g., Wellcraft Marine Div. of Genmar Indus. v. Zarzour, 577 So.2d 414, 416, 418 (Ala.1990) (purchaser of a motor boat that had a manufacturing defect that caused serious damage to the boat when it struck a submerged object did not have a cause of action in products liability, since the damage was to the boat itself; plaintiff was relegated to remedies under the U.C.C. and was barred by the U.C.C. from suing the manufacturer since there was no privity between the purchaser and the manufacturer); Seely v. White Motor Co.,

403 P.2d 145 (Cal.1965). *Seely* is the leading state court case taking the position that damage to the product itself is economic loss and remedies for such losses are to be decided under the U.C.C. It was heavily relied upon by the Court in *East River*.

In *Seely*, the plaintiff purchased a truck from defendant for use in plaintiff's business of heavy hauling. After the plaintiff took possession, the truck bounced violently; shortly thereafter, it overturned. A defective brake system caused the accident. The plaintiff brought a products action seeking damages for the repair of the truck, for the money already paid for the truck, and for lost profits relating to the loss of use of the truck. *Seely*, 403 P.2d at 147–48. The court refused to allow the plaintiff to proceed under a products liability theory on the grounds that it was a commercial purchaser that could only resort to the law of warranty to recover for what the court considered to be economic losses. Id. at 150–51.

In reaching its decision, the *Seely* court noted several reasons for denying recovery under strict products liability. First, the court characterized the harm as a business loss caused by the failure of the truck to meet specific business needs; the court believed that the product failure was merely the inability of the truck to haul heavy loads. The court reasoned that recovery for a loss that amounted to a product's failure to meet economic expectations would be an unwise extension of tort law, and concluded that a defendant should not be liable for the level of performance of products in the consumer's business unless the defendant agreed that the product was designed to meet the consumer's demands. The court reasoned further that the law of warranty functions well when losses are sustained in a commercial setting. Id. at 151–52; Sacramento Reg'l Transit Dist. v. Flxible, 204 Cal.Rptr. 736 (Cal.Ct. App.1984) (the U.C.C., not products liability law, governs a cause of action for repair and replacement of cracked fuel tank supports on a fleet of buses purchased by the plaintiff); Lewinter v. Genmar Indus., 26 Cal. App.4th 1214 (Cal.Ct.App.1994) (reviewing summary judgment, doctrine adopted to preclude recovery for damage caused by catastrophic hull failure on yacht).

In Danforth v. Acorn Structures, Inc., 608 A.2d 1194 (Del.1992), the court strongly endorsed the *East River* rule and held that damages for inadequate value, costs of repair, and replacement of defective product, or consequential claims without any claim of personal injury or damage to other property, constitute economic loss covered under the U.C.C. and not products liability law. A two-year limited warranty barred plaintiff's claim in contract. *Danforth*, 608 A.2d at 1198–99; Airport Rent–A–Car, Inc. v. Prevost Car, Inc., 788 F.Supp. 1203, 1205–06 (S.D.Fla.1992) (applying Florida law) (when damage was to product itself, recovery for economic loss under tort law was disallowed even though the product failed in a sudden and calamitous manner); Exxon Shipping Co. v. Pacific Resources, Inc., 835 F.Supp. 1195 (D.Haw.1993) (doctrine adopted to preclude recovery for damage to bus caused by fire); Prairie Prod., Inc. v. Agchem Div.–Pennwalt Corp., 514 N.E.2d 1299 (Ind.App.Ct.1987) (reviewing summary judgment, court adopted doctrine to preclude recovery for lost profits arising out of manufacturer's negligent manufacture, sale, distribution, and labeling of pesticide); Nelson v. Todd's Ltd., 426 N.W.2d 120 (Iowa 1988) (doctrine applied to preclude butcher's recovery for spoiled meat caused by defective meat curing agent); Elite Prof'ls, Inc. v. Carrier Corp., 827 P.2d 1195, 1202 (Kan.Ct.App.1992) (damages for inadequate value, costs of repair, replacement of defective product, and consequential loss of profits are economic losses, but damage caused by a defective refrigeration unit was damage to other property, which is subject to products liability law); Bowling Green Mun. Utils. v. Thomasson Lumber Co., 902 F.Supp. 134 (W.D.Ky.1995) (applying Kentucky law) (doctrine adopted to bar recovery for damage caused to utility poles); ERA Helicopters, Inc. v. Bell Helicopter Textron, Inc., 696 F.Supp. 1096 (E.D.La.1987) (applying Louisiana law) (doctrine applied to preclude recovery for damage resulting from helicopter's defective engine component); Oceanside at Pine Point Condominium Owners Ass'n v. Peachtree Doors, Inc., 659 A.2d 267 (Me.1995) (court applied doctrine to preclude recovery for water damage to building caused by allegedly defective manufacture of windows); Bay State–Spray & Provincetown Steamship, Inc. v. Caterpillar Tractor Co., 533 N.E.2d 1350, 1352 (Mass.1989) (steamship engines malfunctioned causing plaintiff to incur repair costs and loss of profits; court held that such losses were governed by the U.C.C. sales provisions and were barred by the U.C.C. statute of limitations and not the products liability statute of limitations, which runs from the date of injury); FMR Corp. v. Boston Edison Co., 613 N.E.2d 902 (Mass.1993) (court adopted doctrine to preclude recovery when power outages caused economic losses).

Minnesota has dealt with the issue of economic loss by statute:

> **Sec. 604.10.** Economic loss arising from the sale of goods.
>
> (a) Economic loss that arises from a sale of goods that is due to damage to tangible property other than the goods sold may be recovered in tort as well as in contract, but economic loss that arises from a sale of goods between parties who are each merchants in goods of the kind is not recoverable in tort.
>
> (b) Economic loss that arises from the sale of goods, between merchants, that is not due to damage to tangible property other than the goods sold may not be recovered in tort.
>
> (c) The economic loss recoverable in tort under this section does not include economic loss due to damage to the goods themselves.
>
> (d) The economic loss recoverable in tort under this section does not include economic loss incurred by a manufacturer of goods arising from damage to the manufactured goods and caused by a component of the goods.

Minn. Stat. Ann. § 604.10 (West 1994). It should be noted that Minnesota limits the exemption from products liability law to a sale between "merchants." Also note that in a sale between merchants, damage to other property is not recoverable in tort. See, e.g., Lloyd F. Smith Co. v. Den–Tal–Ez Inc., 491 N.W.2d 11, 16 (Minn.1992) (defective motorized dental chair caused fire and damage both to itself and other property; the sale was not between merchants and thus tort law applied). Note, however, that under § 604.10(c), even if a tort action is allowed, damage to the product itself is excluded from a tort recovery; this subsection makes no distinction between merchants and non-merchants.

In East Miss. Elec. Power Ass'n v. Porcelain Prods. Co., 729 F.Supp. 512 (S.D.Miss.1990) (applying Mississippi law), the federal court predicted that Mississippi would embrace *East River* and would reject the view that a product that was dangerous rather than merely ineffective should come under the umbrella of products liability law. In Sharp Bros. Contracting Co. v. American Hoist & Derrick Co., 703 S.W.2d 901 (Mo.1986), the counterweight of a crane broke from its place and crushed the crane's cab. The court held that when damage was to the product itself, even if the damage occurred as a result of a "sudden and calamitous" event, there was no recovery under strict liability in tort. Id. at 903; see also National Union Fire Ins. Co. of Pittsburgh, Pa. v. Pratt & Whitney Canada, 815 P.2d 601, 604 (Nev.1991) (adopting *East River* and holding that damages resulting from an airplane engine that failed and destroyed the entire airplane accrued from harm to the product itself and were thus merely economic losses not recoverable in tort); Lempke v. Dagenais, 547 A.2d 290, 291–93 (N.H.1988) (subsequent purchasers of a garage could not sue in tort for economic loss, but court reexamined whether privity was necessary for a contract cause of action and decided that, under the facts of the case, privity was not a bar).

In Spring Motors Distributors v. Ford Motor Co., 489 A.2d 660 (N.J. 1985), the New Jersey Supreme Court determined that, in an action for damages based on economic loss involving commercial parties of comparable bargaining power, the plaintiff must bring the action under the U.C.C. and not in tort. Recently, in Alloway v. General Marine Industries, 695 A.2d 264 (N.J.1997), the Supreme Court of New Jersey was confronted with an economic loss case in which both parties were not commercial entities. The plaintiff, an ordinary consumer, sought to recover damages sustained to the boat he purchased from the defendant. Apparently, the boat, due to a manufacturing defect, sank overnight while fastened to a dock. No one was aboard the boat at the time it sank, and the only harm was to the boat itself. The court held that the plaintiff could not maintain an action for economic loss in tort reasoning that "a tort cause of action for economic loss duplicating the one provided by the U.C.C. is superfluous and counterproductive." Id. at 275.

In Utah Int'l, Inc. v. Caterpillar Tractor Co., 775 P.2d 741, 744 (N.M.Ct.App.1989), cert. denied, 772 P.2d 884 (1989), the court adopted *East River* and specifically rejected the plaintiff's argument that it ought to distinguish between products that are merely disappointing to the buyer and products that are dangerous to persons and property. The court applied the *East River* rule to commercial transactions and left open the question whether the same rule should apply to non-commercial consumers. Id. In Bellevue S. Assocs. v. HRH Constr. Corp., 579 N.E.2d 195, 199–200 (N.Y.1991), the court carefully reviewed *East River* and noted that it has significant influence. However, the court left open the question whether it would apply *East River* when the product was hazardous and bound to cause a catastrophic accident. The New York court has now addressed the issue it left open in the

Bellevue case. In Bocre Leasing Corp. v. General Motors Corp., 645 N.E.2d 1195 (N.Y.1995), the Court of Appeals adopted the bright-line rule of *East River Steamship Co.*, supra. The court concluded that:

> Tort recovery in strict products liability and negligence against a manufacturer should not be available to a downstream purchaser where the claimed losses flow from damage to the property that is the subject of the contract. Transforming manufacturers into insurers, with the empty promise that they can guarantee perpetual and total public safety, by making them liable in tort for all commercial setbacks and adversities is not prudent or sound tort public policy. In such instances, no directly related or commensurate public interest is served or protected by holding manufacturers liable. Tort law should not be bent so far out of its traditional progressive path and discipline by allowing tort law suits where the claims at issue are, fundamentally and in all relevant respects, essentially contractual, product-failure controversies. Tort law is not the answer for this kind of loss of commercial bargain.

Id. at 1199. The North Dakota Supreme Court clearly has cast its lot with *East River* in Cooperative Power Ass'n v. Westinghouse Elec. Corp., 493 N.W.2d 661 (N.D.1992). In that case, an electrical arc in a bushing contaminated transformer coils, causing serious damage to the transformer. The court rejected the view that, if a product creates a risk of harm, tort law should apply, but was careful to limit the holding of *East River* to commercial transactions. Id. at 663–66.

After an exhaustive review of existing authority, the Ohio Supreme Court adopted *East River*, stating that it represents the overwhelming majority view. In Chemtrol Adhesives, Inc. v. American Mfrs. Mut. Ins. Co., 537 N.E.2d 624 (Ohio 1989), serious internal damage was caused to the product itself as a result of a defective component. In applying *East River*, the court said:

> We find the above analysis of economic losses applies equally to Chemtrol's consequential business expenses and to the damage sustained by the arch dryer itself. As to the latter, some courts have held that where the defect poses an unreasonable danger to persons or to other property of the buyer, recovery in strict liability is available despite the "fortuity" that only the defective product was damaged. However, we agree that "where the loss to a defective product alone occurs in such a way as to pose no unreasonable danger of harm to person or other property, then U.C.C. remedies will generally be appropriate and exclusive for recovery of the damage to the defective product itself.

537 N.E.2d at 635 (citations omitted); see also Waggoner v. Town & Country Mobile Homes, Inc., 808 P.2d 649, 652 (Okla.1990) (adopting *East River* when damage was to the property itself, but not discussing the question of whether tort liability would apply if the product was dangerously defective but caused only economic loss); Oklahoma Gas & Elec. Co. v. McGraw–Edison Co., 834 P.2d 980 (Okla.1992) (adopted doctrine to preclude recovery for damage to exploding transformer and subsequent economic harm).

Pennsylvania's law on this subject shows the strong influence of *East River*. An influential and oft-cited case from the Third Circuit, Pennsylvania Glass Sand Corp. v. Caterpillar Tractor Co., 652 F.2d 1165 (3d Cir. 1981), took the position that, when economic loss was occasioned by a defectively dangerous product, products liability law rather than contract principles would govern. However, in REM Coal Co. v. Clark Equip. Co., 563 A.2d 128 (Pa.Super.Ct.1989), the court reviewed Pennsylvania case law and concluded that the Third Circuit's *Erie* prognostication was incorrect. The court held that if the damage was to the product itself, it made no difference whether "the defect posed a risk of other damage or injury or manifested itself in a sudden and calamitous occurrence." Id. at 132. Once again, the holding was limited to products liability actions between commercial enterprises. Id. at 131–33; accord, Aloe Coal v. Clark Equip., 816 F.2d 110, 117–19 (3d Cir. 1987) (on similar facts to *Pennsylvania Glass Sand*, Third Circuit specifically disapproved that earlier opinion's prediction of the Pennsylvania law, due to the persuasiveness of the analysis in *East River*), cert. denied, 484 U.S. 853, 108 S.Ct. 156, 98 L.Ed.2d 111 (1987); Boston Inv. Property v. E.W. Burman, Inc., 658 A.2d 515 (R.I.1995) (doctrine applied to bar building purchaser's recovery for economic damage caused by general contractor); 2000 Watermark Ass'n v. Celotex Corp., 784 F.2d 1183 (4th Cir.1986) (applying South Carolina law) (citing South Carolina cases holding that a negligent act is not actionable unless it results in actual physical damage to the plaintiff); Carolina Winds Owners' Ass'n v. Joe Harden Builder, Inc., 383 S.E.2d 463 (S.C.Ct.App.1988) (applied doctrine to preclude recovery for damage to building caused by defective construction); City of Lennox v. Mitek Indus., Inc., 519 N.W.2d 330 (S.D.1994) (applied doctrine to preclude recovery for losses caused by defective building trusses). In Mid-Continent Aircraft Corp. v. Curry County Spraying Serv., Inc., 572 S.W.2d 308 (Tex. 1978), a defective crankshaft forced an airplane to land on a rough country road, causing substantial damage to its fuselage and wings. The court held that even though the product was unreasonably dangerous there was no liability in tort; the parties were relegated to their contractual remedies. The court observed: "In transactions between a commercial seller and commercial buyer, when no physical injury has occurred to persons or other property, injury to the defective product itself is an economic loss governed by the Uniform Commercial Code." Id. at 313; Klo–Zik Co. v. General Motors Corp., 677 F.Supp. 499 (E.D.Tex.1987) (applying Texas law) (doctrine adopted to preclude recovery for pure economic loss caused by engine breakdown); Maack v. Resource Design & Constr., 875 P.2d 570 (Utah.Ct.App.1994) (reviewing summary judgment, doctrine applied to preclude recovery for damage to residence caused by water leakage); Sensenbrenner v. Rust, Orling & Neale, Architects, Inc., 374 S.E.2d 55 (Va.1988) (adopted doctrine to preclude recovery for damage to foundation of house caused by leaking swimming pool); Sunnyslope Grading, Inc. v. Miller, Bradford & Risberg, Inc., 437 N.W.2d 213 (Wis.1989) (applied doctrine to preclude recovery for damage caused by defective piece of construction equipment). But see Northridge Co. v. W.R. Grace & Co., 471 N.W.2d 179 (Wis.1991) (applied doctrine to permit recovery for damage to building caused by defective fireproofing material containing asbestos); Continental Ins. v. Page Eng'g Co., 783 P.2d 641, 647–48 (Wyo.1989) (adopting *East River* and rejecting the view that products liability law should govern when the product is unreasonably dangerous and fails in a sudden and catastrophic manner).

A view labelled by courts as the "intermediate rule" would relegate parties to their remedies under the Uniform Commercial Code when the product was ineffective and failed to work properly. However, if the product was dangerous in that it presented risks of harm to persons or other property, then products liability law would govern; additionally, some courts engraft a requirement that the product must have failed in a sudden and calamitous manner as a prerequisite to recovery. See, e.g., Kodiak Elec. Ass'n v. DeLaval Turbine, Inc., 694 P.2d 150, 153 (Alaska 1984) (when defective product creates a situation potentially dangerous to persons or other property, strict liability applies even though the damage is confined to the product itself); Salt River Project Agric. Improvement and Power Dist. v. Westinghouse Elec. Corp., 694 P.2d 198, 206 (Ariz.1984) (whether products liability law or commercial-law principles govern is determined by examining the nature of the defect, the manner in which the loss occurred, and the type of loss or damage); Berkeley Pump Co. v. Reed–Joseph Land Co., 653 S.W.2d 128, 131–32 (Ark.1983) (recovery under products liability law denied because product was simply deficient, not unreasonably dangerous); Vulcan Materials Co. v. Driltech, Inc., 306 S.E.2d 253, 257 (Ga.1983) (tort recovery is allowed for the defective product itself if it fails in a sudden and calamitous manner); American Xyrofin, Inc. v. Allis–Chalmers Corp., 595 N.E.2d 650, 656 (Ill.App.Ct.1992) (the demarcation between tort recovery for physical harm and economic loss depends on nature of defect and manner in which harm occurred), cert. denied, 602 N.E.2d 445 (Ill.1992); see also Ind. Code Ann. § 33–1–1.5–5 (West 1994) ("Physical harm" means "sudden, major damage to property."); Morris v. Osmose Wood Preserving, 667 A.2d 624 (Md.Ct.App. 1995) (although ordinary tort claims for purely economic losses are not permissible, when coupled with serious risk of death or personal injury resulting from a dangerous condition there is a tort remedy); Hilt Truck Line, Inc. v. Pullman, Inc., 382 N.W.2d 310 (Neb.1986) (in order to recover in strict liability for the cost of repairs of a product, the damage must have resulted from a sudden, violent event that either aggravated the inherent defect or caused it to manifest itself; in order to recover under negligence, there is no requirement that damages result from sudden, violent event); Russell v. Ford Motor Co., 575 P.2d 1383, 1387 (Or. 1978) (damage to the product itself is recoverable under products liability law when the product defect was unreasonably dangerous); Corporate Air Fleet of Tenn., Inc. v. Gates Learjet, Inc., 589 F.Supp. 1076, 1082 (M.D.Tenn.1984) (applying Tennessee law) (If "a product is unreasonably dangerous and the only property damage is to the product itself, a plaintiff may pursue recovery under a theory of strict liability."); Washington Water Power Co. v. Graybar Elec. Co., 774 P.2d 1199 (Wash.1989) (in a case involving faulty insulators, the court declined to follow *East River*, and embraced the risk of harm analysis finding that damage to property alone may afford a basis for a tort claim); Star Furniture Co. v. Pulaski Furniture Co., 297 S.E.2d 854, 859 (W.Va.1982) (products liability law applies to a defect that causes injury to the product itself); Kaiser Aluminum & Chem. Corp. v. Westinghouse Elec. Corp., 981 F.2d 136 (4th Cir.1992) (applying West Virginia law) (court held that because damage was not the result of a "calamitous event," recovery in strict liability was not permissible).

Santor v. A & M Karagheusian, Inc., 207 A.2d 305 (N.J.1965), was the leading case allowing a products liability action when a product did not create an unreasonable risk of harm but merely caused economic loss when it failed to meet performance expectations. *Santor* attracted very few adherents. See, e.g., Cova v. Harley Davidson Motor Co., 182 N.W.2d 800, 804 (Mich.App.1970); City of La Crosse v. Schubert, Schroeder Assoc., 240 N.W.2d 124 (Wis.1976). In a recent decision, Alloway v. General Marine Industries, 695 A.2d 264 (N.J. 1997), the New Jersey Supreme Court overruled *Santor*, holding that, if a product created no unreasonable risk of harm to persons or property, the U.C.C. rather than tort law should control whether economic loss is to be recovered. The case thoroughly reviews the authority and the position set forth in a draft of this Restatement and supports its view that *Santor* was out of line with the overwhelming majority of courts.

The subject of liability for economic loss has engaged the attention of legal commentators. See, e.g., Franklin, When Worlds Collide: Liability Theories and Disclaimers in Defective–Product Cases, 18 Stan. L. Rev. 974 (1966); Rabin, Tort Recovery for Negligently Inflicted Economic Loss: A Reassessment, 37 Stan. L. Rev. 1513 (1985); Speidel, Products Liability, Economic Loss and the U.C.C., 40 Tenn. L. Rev. 309 (1973); Speidel, Warranty Theory, Economic Loss and the Privity Requirement: Once More Into the Void, 67 B.U. L. Rev. 9 (1987); Way, The Problem of Economic Damages: Reconceptualizing the Moorman Doctrine, 1991 U. Ill. L. Rev. 1169 (1991); Note, Economic Loss in Products Liability Jurisprudence, 66 Colum. L. Rev. 917 (1966).

Comment e. Harm to the plaintiff's property other than the defective product itself: asbestos abatement. When plaintiffs seek to recover from asbestos sellers for the costs of abating asbestos insulation from buildings, it could be argued that the buildings have not been harmed, but rather the insulation itself has failed to provide safe heat-retention qualities. Notwithstanding this argument, courts generally allow recovery in such cases, treating the buildings as "other property." See Northridge Co. v. W.R. Grace and Co., 471 N.W.2d 179, 185 (Wis.1991) (Court assessed the character of plaintiffs' tort claims in light of traditional purposes of contract/warranty and tort law. "Plaintiffs do not appear to assert in their tort counts . . . that the Monokote itself was inferior in quality or did not work for its intended purpose, the essence of a claim for economic loss. . . . [Instead] the essence of the plaintiff's claim is that . . . their property has been physically altered by the defendant's product, whether or not such alteration is outwardly visible."); see also Tioga Pub. Sch. Dist. #15 of Williams County, State of N.D. v. United States Gypsum Co., 984 F.2d 915, 918 (8th Cir.1993) (applying North Dakota law) (Court held that injury was not merely damage to the buildings themselves, but "the contamination of the Tioga school buildings by asbestos and the consequent health risk to the buildings' occupants. USG should not be allowed to escape liability by arguing that its product is merely a component of a larger product and that any damages are to the school buildings."); 80 S. Eighth St. L.P. v. Carey–Canada, Inc., 486 N.W.2d 393, 397 (Minn.1992), amended 492 N.W.2d 256 (Minn.1992) ("The claim here is not that the fireproofing failed to perform satisfactorily as fireproofing.... In seeking the costs of maintenance, removal and replacement, 80 South Eighth seeks the costs of eliminating the risks of injury and of making the building safe for all those who use and occupy this property," not "enforcement of the benefit of their bargain."); Independent Sch. Dist. No. 622 v. Keene Corp., 495 N.W.2d 244, 247–48 (Minn.Ct.App.1993), affirmed in part, reversed in part 511 N.W.2d 728 (Minn.1994); Kershaw County Bd. of Educ. v. United States Gypsum Co., 396 S.E.2d 369, 371 (S.C.1990) (school held to be "other property" cognizable in tort); Board of Educ. of City of Chicago v. A, C, & S, Inc., 546 N.E.2d 580, 588 (Ill.1989) ("[I]t would be incongruous to argue there is no damage to other property when a harmful element exists throughout a building or an area of a building which by law must be corrected and at trial may be proven to exist at unacceptably dangerous levels."); Detroit Bd. of Educ. v. Celotex Corp., 493 N.W.2d 513, 518–19 (Mich. Ct.App.1992), appeal denied, 512 N.W.2d 318 (Mich.1993); School Dist. of City of Independence, Mo., No. 30 v. United States Gypsum Co., 750 S.W.2d 442, 457 (Mo.Ct.App.1988) ("The School District does not allege that Audicote failed to perform its function as plaster but that it contaminated the school buildings and posed a serious risk of personal injury to those in contact with it. The risk here is not the type of risk that is normally allocated between the parties to a contract by agreement such as that contemplated by *East River*. The product in this case did not require replacement or repair in order to function as it was intended."); Clayton Ctr. Assoc. v. W.R. Grace & Co., 861 S.W.2d 686, 689 (Mo.Ct.App.1993) (whether fireproofing product that contained asbestos was "unreasonably dangerous" was held to be a question of fact for a jury). But see Banc One Bldg. Mgmt. Corp. v. W.R. Grace and Co.-Conn., 461 N.W.2d 448 (Wis.Ct.App.1990) (unreported case) (Economic loss doctrine held to preclude plaintiff's claim in tort. Court accepted defendant's arguments that asbestos had been in place for 28 years without physical harm to any building occupants, and that damage alleged was consequential in that it was related to removal of the asbestos. The court reasoned that, "even though asbestos is considered dangerous, steps can be taken to avoid any physical injury to those occupying the building, and therefore, that leaves only economic loss as the subject of damages.").

For an excellent review of the case law, see Richard C. Ausness, Tort Liability for Asbestos Removal Costs, 73 Or. L. Rev. 505 (1994).

TABLE OF CASES

A

B

TABLE OF CASES

C

D

G

H

I

J

K

L

M

N

O

P

R

S

TABLE OF CASES

T

U

V

TABLE OF CASES

W

Y

Z

*

TABLE OF STATUTES

UNITED STATES

UNITED STATES CODE ANNOTATED

7 U.S.C.A.—Agriculture

Sec.	This Work Sec.
136 et seq.	2, RN, p. 69

42 U.S.C.A.—The Public Health and Welfare

Sec.	This Work Sec.
300 et seq.	17, RN, p. 267

STATE STATUTES

ALABAMA CODE

Sec.	This Work Sec.
7–2–314(4)	19, RN, p. 276

ARKANSAS CODE ANNOTATED

Sec.	This Work Sec.
16–64–122	17, RN, p. 259
16–116–104(a)(1)	2, RN, p. 82

WEST'S ANNOTATED CALIFORNIA CIVIL CODE

Sec.	This Work Sec.
1714.4	2, RN, p. 89

WEST'S ANNOTATED CALIFORNIA HEALTH AND SAFETY CODE

Sec.	This Work Sec.
1606	19, RN, p. 276

WEST'S COLORADO REVISED STATUTES ANNOTATED

Sec.	This Work Sec.
13–21–403(1)(a)	2, RN, p. 82
13–21–406	17, RN, p. 259
13–21–501	2, RN, p. 89

CONNECTICUT GENERAL STATUTES ANNOTATED

Sec.	This Work Sec.
52–572	17, RN, p. 263

DELAWARE CODE

Tit.	This Work Sec.
18, § 7001	1, RN, p. 13

GEORGIA CODE

Sec.	This Work Sec.
51–11.1	1, RN, p. 13

HAWAII REVISED STATUTES

Sec.	This Work Sec.
291–11.6	16, RN, p. 254

IDAHO CODE

Sec.	This Work Sec.
6–1304	17, RN, p. 260
6–1305(1)(a)	17, RN, p. 263

IDAHO CODE

Sec.	This Work Sec.
6–1305(3)(b)	17, RN, p. 262
6–1407	1, RN, p. 13
6–1410	2, RN, p. 89

ILLINOIS COMPILED STATUTES

Ch.	This Work Sec.
735 ILCS 5/2–621(a)—(c)	1, RN, p. 13
735 ILCS 5/2–2104	2, RN, p. 48
745 ILCS 40/1	19, RN, p. 276

WEST'S ANNOTATED INDIANA CODE

Sec.	This Work Sec.
33–1–1.5–2.5	2, RN, p. 49
33–1–1.5–4(b)(4)	2, RN, p. 82
	2, RN, p. 83
33–1–1.5–5	21, RN, p. 304
33–3–1.5–4	17, RN, p. 263
34–4–20A–2A–Z	17, RN, p. 272

IOWA CODE ANNOTATED

Sec.	This Work Sec.
613.18	1, RN, p. 13
668.12	2, RN, p. 83

KANSAS STATUTES ANNOTATED

Sec.	This Work Sec.
60–3306	1, RN, p. 13

KENTUCKY REVISED STATUTES

Sec.	This Work Sec.
411.310(2)	2, RN, p. 82

KENTUCKY REVISED STATUTES

Sec.	This Work Sec.
411.340	1, RN, p. 13

LOUISIANA STATUTES ANNOTATED—REVISED STATUTES

Sec.	This Work Sec.
9:2800.53(3)	19, RN, p. 276
9:2800.55	2, RN, p. 43
9:2800.55—9:2800.57	1, RN, p. 10
9:2800.56	2, RN, p. 50
	2, RN, p. 82
	10, RN, p. 243
9:2800.56(1)	2, RN, p. 89
9:2800.57	2, RN, p. 105
9:2800.57(C)	10, RN, p. 197
9:2800.59	2, RN, p. 82

MARYLAND CODE, COURTS AND JUDICIAL PROCEEDINGS

Sec.	This Work Sec.
5–115	17, RN, p. 271
5–311	1, RN, p. 13

MARYLAND CODE, CRIMINAL LAW

Sec.	This Work Sec.
27, § 36–I	2, RN, p. 89

MICHIGAN COMPILED LAWS ANNOTATED

Sec.	This Work Sec.
333.9121(2)	19, RN, p. 276

TABLE OF STATUTES

TABLE OF STATUTES

NEW YORK, MCKINNEY'S PUBLIC HEALTH LAW

Sec.	This Work Sec.
580(4)	19, RN, p. 276

NORTH CAROLINA GENERAL STATUTES

Sec.	This Work Sec.
99B–1.1	2, RN, p. 65
99B–2	1, RN, p. 13
99B–6	2, RN, p. 64

NORTH DAKOTA CENTURY CODE

Sec.	This Work Sec.
28–01.1–06.1	1, RN, p. 13
32–03.2–03	17, RN, p. 260

OHIO REVISED CODE

Sec.	This Work Sec.
2307.71	17, RN, p. 271
2307.74	2, RN, p. 44
2307.74—2304.76	1, RN, p. 10
2307.75(A)—(F)	2, RN, p. 65
2307.75(F)	2, RN, p. 83
	2, RN, p. 91
2307.76	10, RN, p. 197
2307.76(A)(1)(a)	2, RN, p. 105
2307.76(A)(1)(b)	2, RN, p. 105
2307.78	1, RN, p. 13

OREGON REVISED STATUTES

Sec.	This Work Sec.
18.475(2)	17, RN, p. 264

OREGON REVISED STATUTES

Sec.	This Work Sec.
30.900	1, RN, p. 10

PENNSYLVANIA CONSOLIDATED STATUTES ANNOTATED

Tit.	This Work Sec.
42, § 8333(a)	19, RN, p. 276

SOUTH DAKOTA CODIFIED LAWS

Sec.	This Work Sec.
20–9–9	1, RN, p. 13

TENNESSEE CODE ANNOTATED

Sec.	This Work Sec.
29–28–102	17, RN, p. 272
29–28–106	1, RN, p. 13

V.T.C.A., CIVIL PRACTICE & REMEDIES CODE

Sec.	This Work Sec.
33.001(b)	17, RN, p. 260
82.005	1, RN, p. 10
	2, RN, p. 59
	2, RN, p. 83
82.006	2, RN, p. 89

UTAH CODE ANNOTATED

Sec.	This Work Sec.
78–27–37	17, RN, p. 262
	17, RN, p. 263
	17, RN, p. 264
78–27–37 to 78–27–43	17, RN, p. 260

TABLE OF STATUTES

WEST'S REVISED CODE OF WASHINGTON ANNOTATED

Sec.	This Work Sec.
4.22.005 et seq.	17, RN, p. 260
	17, RN, p. 262
	17, RN, p. 263
7.72.010	8, RN, p. 183
7.72.030	1, RN, p. 11
7.72.030(1)(c)	10, RN, p. 197
7.72.030(2)(a)	2, RN, p. 44
7.72.040	1, RN, p. 13

UNIFORM CODES AND ACTS

UNIFORM COMMERCIAL CODE

Sec.	This Work Sec.
Art. 2	8, Com. *l*, p. 178
2–215(1)	17, RN, p. 272
2–314(c)	2, RN, p. 54

MODEL UNIFORM PRODUCT LIABILITY ACT

Sec.	This Work Sec.
102(A)(1)	19, RN, p. 282
102(C)	17, RN, p. 272
104	1, RN, p. 11
104(A)	2, RN, p. 44
104(C)(6)	10, RN, p. 197

*

TABLE OF CROSS REFERENCES TO DIGEST SYSTEM KEY NUMBERS AND ALR ANNOTATIONS*

CHAPTER 1. LIABILITY OF COMMERCIAL PRODUCT SELLERS BASED ON PRODUCT DEFECTS AT TIME OF SALE

TOPIC 1. LIABILITY RULES APPLICABLE TO PRODUCTS GENERALLY

Section 1. Liability of Commercial Seller or Distributor for Harm Caused by Defective Products

1. Digest System Key Numbers

Products Liability ⚷23.1, 25.

2. A.L.R. Annotations

Causes of action governed by limitations period in UCC sec. 2–725. 49 ALR5th 1.

Products liability of endorser, trade association, certifier, or similar party who expresses approval of product. 1 ALR5th 431.

Trademark licensor's liability for injury or death allegedly due to defect in licensed product. 90 ALR4th 981.

Liability of auctioneer under doctrine of strict products liability. 83 ALR4th 1188.

Exterminator's tort liability for personal injury or death directly resulting from operations. 29 ALR4th 987.

Products liability: application of strict liability in tort doctrine to agency merely financing sale or lease-purchase of personal property. 28 ALR4th 326.

Application of rule of strict liability in tort to person or entity rendering medical services. 100 ALR3d 1205.

When is person "engaged in the business" for purposes of doctrine of strict tort liability. 99 ALR3d 671.

Who is "merchant" under UCC sec. 2–314(1) dealing with implied warranties of merchantability. 91 ALR3d 876.

Products liability: proof, under strict tort liability doctrine, that defect was present when product left hands of defendant. 54 ALR3d 1079.

Products liability: application of strict liability in tort doctrine to lessor of personal property. 52 ALR3d 121.

---

* Prepared by West Group.

Products liability: necessity and sufficiency of identification of defendant as manufacturer or seller of product alleged to have caused injury. 51 ALR3d 1344.

Liability of product indorser or certifier for product-caused injury. 39 ALR3d 181.

Products liability: extension of strict liability in tort to permit recovery by a third person who was neither a purchaser nor user of product. 33 ALR3d 415.

Application of rule of strict liability in tort to person rendering services. 29 ALR3d 1425.

Privity of contract as essential in action against remote manufacturer or distributor for defects in goods not causing injury to person or to other property. 16 ALR3d 683.

Products liability: strict liability in tort. 13 ALR3d 1057.

Privity of contract as essential to recovery in action based on theory other than negligence, against manufacturer or seller of product alleged to have caused injury. 75 ALR2d 39.

Privity of contract as essential to recovery in negligence action against manufacturer or seller of product alleged to have caused injury. 74 ALR2d 1111.

Intervening purchaser's knowledge of defects in or danger of article, or failure to inspect therefor, as affecting liability of manufacturer or dealer for personal injury or property damage to subsequent purchaser or other third person. 164 ALR 371.

Liability of bailor for personal injuries or death due to defects in subject of bailment. 131 ALR 845.

Liability of manufacturer or packer of defective article for injury to person or property of ultimate consumer, who purchased from a middleman. 17 ALR 672, Supp. 39 ALR 992, 63 ALR 340, 88 ALR 527, 105 ALR 1502, 111 ALR 1239, 140 ALR 191, 142 ALR 1490.

Liability of seller of article not inherently dangerous for personal injuries to the buyer, due to the defective or dangerous condition of the article. 13 ALR 1176, Supp. 74 ALR 343, 168 ALR 1054.

Admiralty products liability: recovery against remote manufacturer or distributor for economic or commercial loss caused by defect in product. 81 ALR Fed 181.

Section 2. Categories of Product Defect

1. Digest System Key Numbers

Products Liability ⚿11–14.

2. A.L.R. Annotations

Causes of action governed by limitations period in UCC sec. 2–725. 49 ALR5th 1.

Presumption of inference, in products liability action based on failure to warn, that user of product would have heeded an adequate warning had one been given. 38 ALR5th 683.

Burden of proving feasibility of alternative safe design in products liability action based on defective design. 78 ALR4th 154.

Products liability: what is an "unavoidably unsafe" product. 70 ALR4th 16.

Validity and construction of products liability statute precluding or limiting recovery where product has been altered or modified after leaving hands of manufacturer or seller. 41 ALR4th 47.

Products liability: modern status of rule that there is no liability for patent or obvious dangers. 35 ALR4th 861.

Strict products liability: liability for failure to warn as dependent on defendant's knowledge of danger. 33 ALR4th 368.

Products liability: admissibility of expert or opinion evidence as to adequacy of warning provided to user of product. 26 ALR4th 377.

Products liability: admissibility of expert or opinion evidence that product is or is not defective, dangerous, or unreasonably dangerous. 4 ALR4th 651.

Products liability: manufacturer's or seller's obligation to supply or recommend available safety accessories in connection with industrial machinery or equipment. 99 ALR3d 693.

Products liability: modern cases determining whether product is defectively designed. 96 ALR3d 22.

Products liability: duty of manufacturer to equip product with safety device to protect against patent or obvious danger. 95 ALR3d 1066.

Liability of manufacturer or seller for injury or death allegedly caused by failure to warn regarding danger in use of vaccine or prescription drug. 94 ALR3d 748.

Products liability: product as unreasonably dangerous or unsafe under doctrine of strict liability in tort. 54 ALR3d 352.

Failure to warn as basis of liability under doctrine of strict liability in tort. 53 ALR3d 239.

Necessity and propriety of instructing on alternative theories of negligence or breach of warranty, where instruction on strict liability in tort is given in products liability case. 52 ALR3d 101.

Products liability: proof of defect under doctrine of strict liability in tort. 51 ALR3d 8.

Products liability: contributory negligence or assumption of risk as defense under doctrine of strict liability in tort. 46 ALR3d 240.

Products liability: alteration of product after it leaves hands of manufacturer or seller as affecting liability for product-caused harm. 41 ALR3d 1251.

Manufacturer's duty to test or inspect as affecting his liability for product-caused injury. 6 ALR3d 91.

Seller's duty to test or inspect as affecting his liability for product-caused injury. 6 ALR3d 12.

Manufacturer's or seller's duty to give warning regarding product as affecting his liability for product-caused injury. 76 ALR2d 9.

Intervening purchaser's knowledge of defects in or danger of article, or failure to inspect therefor, as affecting liability of manufacturer or dealer for personal injury or property damage to subsequent purchaser or other third person. 164 ALR 371.

Manufacturer's liability for injury or damage as affected by his test, or by his failure to test, for defects. 156 ALR 479.

Section 3. Circumstantial Evidence Supporting Inference of Product Defect

1. Digest System Key Numbers

Products Liability ⚷75.1–80.

2. A.L.R. Annotations

Products liability: sudden or unexpected acceleration of motor vehicle. 66 ALR4th 20.

Strict products liability: product malfunction or occurrence of accident as evidence of defect. 65 ALR4th 346.

Products liability: admissibility of experimental or test evidence to disprove defect in motor vehicle. 64 ALR4th 125.

Products liability: modern cases on explosion or breakage of beverage bottles. 36 ALR4th 419.

Products liability: proof of defect under doctrine of strict liability in tort. 51 ALR3d 8.

Products liability: admissibility of evidence of other accidents to prove hazardous nature of product. 42 ALR3d 780.

Infected or tainted condition of milk or other food, or contamination in water, and its causation of the sickness of the consumer, as inferable from such sickness. 130 ALR 616.

Liability for injuries by breaking or bursting of container in which goods are sold. 4 ALR 1094.

Section 4. Noncompliance and Compliance with Product Safety Statutes or Regulations

1. Digest System Key Numbers

Products Liability ⟹3, 11, 14, 75.1–80.

2. A.L.R. Annotations

Products liability: equipment and devices directly relating to passengers' standing or seating safety in land carriers. 35 ALR4th 1050.

Admissibility in evidence, on issue of negligence, of codes or standards of safety issued or sponsored by governmental body or by voluntary association. 58 ALR3d 148.

Products liability: proof of defect under doctrine of strict liability in tort. 51 ALR3d 8.

Comment Note—Effect of violation of safety equipment statute as establishing negligence in automobile accident litigation. 38 ALR3d 530.

When is product safety standard "reasonably necessary to eliminate or reduce an unreasonable risk of injury" under sec. 9(c)(2)(A) of Consumer Product Safety Act (15 USCS sec. 2058(c)(2)(A)). 47 ALR Fed 371.

Liability of United States, under Federal Tort Claims Act (28 USCS secs. 1346, 2671–2680), for damages caused by ingestion or administration of drugs, vaccines, and the like, approved as safe for use by government agency. 24 ALR Fed 467.

TOPIC 2. LIABILITY RULES APPLICABLE TO SPECIAL PRODUCTS OR PRODUCT MARKETS

Section 5. Liability of Commercial Seller or Distributor of Product Components for Harm Caused by Products Into Which Components Are Integrated

1. Digest System Key Numbers

Products Liability ⟹8, 15, 16.

2. A.L.R. Annotations

Products liability: personal jurisdiction over nonresident manufacturer of component incorporated in another product. 69 ALR4th 14.

Products liability: mechanical or chain saw or components thereof. 22 ALR4th 206.

Products liability: industrial accidents involving conveyor belts or systems. 2 ALR4th 262.

Products liability: personal injury or death allegedly caused by defect in motorcycle or its parts, supplies, or equipment. 98 ALR3d 317.

Products liability: personal injury or death allegedly caused by defect in aircraft or its parts, supplies, or equipment. 97 ALR3d 627.

Products liability: liability for injury or death allegedly caused by defective tires. 81 ALR3d 318.

Liability of builder or subcontractor for insufficiency of building resulting from latent defects in materials used. 61 ALR3d 792.

Products liability: manufacturer's responsibility for defective component supplied by another and incorporated in product. 3 ALR3d 1016.

Section 6. Liability of Seller or Other Distributor for Harm Caused by Defective Prescription Drugs and Medical Devices

1. Digest System Key Numbers

Drugs and Narcotics ⚷19; Products Liability ⚷46.

2. A.L.R. Annotations

Liability of manufacturer of oral live polio (Sabin) vaccine for injury or death from its administration. 66 ALR4th 83.

Products liability: sufficiency of evidence to support product misuse defense in actions concerning food, drugs, and other products intended for ingestion. 58 ALR4th 7.

Products liability: pertussis vaccine manufacturers. 57 ALR4th 911.

Liability of blood supplier or donor for injury or death resulting from blood transfusion. 24 ALR4th 508.

Liability of hospital, physician, or other individual medical practitioner for injury or death resulting from blood transfusion. 20 ALR4th 136.

Druggist's civil liability for injuries sustained as result of negligence in incorrectly filling drug prescriptions. 3 ALR4th 270.

Products liability in connection with prosthesis or other products designed to be surgically implanted in patient's body. 1 ALR4th 921.

Promotional efforts directed toward prescribing physician as affecting prescription drug manufacturer's liability for product-caused injury. 94 ALR3d 1080.

Liability of manufacturer or seller for injury or death allegedly caused by failure to warn regarding danger in use of vaccine or prescription drug. 94 ALR3d 748.

Liability of manufacturer or seller for injury or death allegedly caused by use of contraceptive. 70 ALR3d 315.

Liability of hospital or medical practitioner under doctrine of strict liability in tort, or breach of warranty, for harm caused by drug, medical instrument, or similar device used in treating patient. 54 ALR3d 258.

Liability of manufacturer or seller for injury caused by medical and health supplies, appliances, and equipment. 79 ALR2d 401.

Liability of manufacturer or seller for injury caused by drug or medicine sold. 79 ALR2d 301.

Federal pre-emption of state common-law products liability claims pertaining to drugs, medical devices, and other health-related items. 98 ALR Fed 124.

Exemption from provision of sec. 502(f) of the Federal Food, Drug, and Cosmetic Act (21 USCS sec. 352(f)) that drug or device is misbranded unless its label bears "adequate directions for use". 65 ALR Fed 725.

Section 7. Liability of Commercial Seller or Distributor for Harm Caused by Defective Food Products

1. Digest System Key Numbers

Food ⚷25.

2. A.L.R. Annotations

Liability for injury or death allegedly caused by food product containing object related to, but not intended to be present in, product. 2 ALR5th 189.

Liability for injury or death allegedly caused by spoilage, contamination, or other deleterious condition of food or food product. 2 ALR5th 1.

Liability for injury or death allegedly caused by foreign object in food or food product. 1 ALR5th 1.

Liability for injury or death allegedly caused by foreign substance in beverage. 90 ALR4th 12.

Liability for injury or death allegedly caused by spoilage or contamination of beverage. 87 ALR4th 804.

Products liability: sufficiency of evidence to support product misuse defense in actions concerning food, drugs, and other products intended for ingestion. 58 ALR4th 7.

Products liability: fertilizers, insecticides, pesticides, fungicides, weedkillers, and the like, or articles used in application thereof. 12 ALR4th 462.

Liability of packer, foodstore, or restaurant for causing trichinosis. 96 ALR3d 451.

Master and servant: employer's liability for injury caused by food or drink purchased by employee in plant facilities. 50 ALR3d 505.

Liability for injury caused by spraying or dusting of crops. 37 ALR3d 833.

Right of retailer sued by consumer for breach of implied warranty of wholesomeness or fitness of food or drink, to bring in as a party defendant the wholesaler or manufacturer from whom article was procured. 24 ALR2d 913.

Implied warranty of fitness by one serving food. 7 ALR2d 1027.

Section 8. Liability of Commercial Seller or Distributor of Defective Used Products

1. Digest System Key Numbers

Products Liability ⚷16, 23.1, 25.

2. A.L.R. Annotations

Liability on implied warranties in sale of used motor vehicle. 47 ALR5th 677.

Products liability: application of strict liability doctrine to seller of used product. 9 ALR5th 1.

Validity, construction, and application of odometer requirement provisions of Motor Vehicle Information and Cost Savings Act (15 USCS secs. 1981–1991). 28 ALR Fed 584.

CHAPTER 2. LIABILITY OF COMMERCIAL PRODUCT SELLERS NOT BASED ON PRODUCT DEFECTS AT TIME OF SALE

Section 9. Liability of Commercial Product Seller or Distributor for Harm Caused by Misrepresentation

1. Digest System Key Numbers

Products Liability ⚷7, 23.1, 25.

2. A.L.R. Annotations

Products liability: liability of manufacturer or seller as affected by failure of subsequent party in distribution chain to remedy or warn against defect of which he knew. 45 ALR4th 777.

Actionable nature of advertising impugning quality or worth of merchandise or products. 42 ALR4th 318.

Strict products liability: liability for failure to warn as dependent on defendant's knowledge of danger. 33 ALR4th 368.

Reward for disproving commercial claim. 96 ALR3d 907.

Statements on container that enclosed toy, game, sports equipment, or the like, is safe as affecting manufacturer's liability for injury caused by product sold. 74 ALR3d 1298.

Statements in advertisements as affecting manufacturer's or seller's liability for injury caused by product sold. 75 ALR2d 112.

What constitutes false, misleading, or deceptive advertising or promotional practices subject to action by Federal Trade Commission. 65 ALR2d 225.

Mistake as to chemical or product furnished or misdescription thereof by label or otherwise as basis of liability for personal injury or death resulting from combination with other chemical. 123 ALR 939.

Temporary relief against unfair trade practices under 15 USCS sec. 53. 34 ALR Fed 507.

Section 10. Liability of Commercial Product Seller or Distributor for Harm Caused by Post–Sale Failure to Warn

1. Digest System Key Numbers

Products Liability ⚷14, 23.1, 25.

2. A.L.R. Annotations

Presumption of inference, in products liability action based on failure to warn, that user of product would have heeded an adequate warning had one been given. 38 ALR5th 683.

Products liability: failure to provide product warning or instruction in foreign language or to use universally accepted pictographs or symbols. 27 ALR5th 697.

Products liability: liability of manufacturer or seller as affected by failure of subsequent party in distribution chain to remedy or warn against defect of which he knew. 45 ALR4th 777.

Products liability: admissibility of evidence of postinjury warning measures undertaken by defendant. 38 ALR4th 583.

Strict products liability: liability for failure to warn as dependent on defendant's knowledge of danger. 33 ALR4th 368.

Products liability: admissibility of expert or opinion evidence as to adequacy of warning provided to user of product. 26 ALR4th 377.

Liability of manufacturer or seller for injury or death allegedly caused by failure to warn regarding danger in use of vaccine or prescription drug. 94 ALR3d 748.

Failure to warn as basis of liability under doctrine of strict liability in tort. 53 ALR3d 239.

Discovery, in products liability case, of defendant's knowledge as to injury to or complaints by others than plaintiff, related to product. 20 ALR3d 1430.

Manufacturer's or seller's duty to give warning regarding product as affecting his liability for product-caused injury. 76 ALR2d 9.

Section 11. Liability of Commercial Product Seller or Distributor for Harm Caused by Post–Sale Failure to Recall Product

1. Digest System Key Numbers

Products Liability ⚷23.1, 25.

2. A.L.R. Annotations

Products liability: manufacturer's postsale obligation to modify, repair, or recall product. 47 ALR5th 395.

Validity and construction of "sistership" clause of products liability insurance policy excepting from coverage cost of product recall or withdrawal of product from market. 32 ALR4th 630.

Products liability: Admissibility, against manufacturer, of product recall letter. 84 ALR3d 1220.

Availability and scope of judicial review of National Highway Transportation Safety Administration (NHTSA) denial of consumer petition to conduct "recall" investigation under 15 USCS secs. 1410a et seq .. 95 ALR Fed 782.

CHAPTER 3. LIABILITY OF SUCCESSORS AND APPARENT MANUFACTURERS

Section 12. Liability of Successor for Harm Caused by Defective Products Sold Commercially by Predecessor

1. Digest System Key Numbers

Products Liability ⚷23.1, 25.

2. A.L.R. Annotations

Liability of successor corporation for punitive damages for injury caused by predecessor's product. 55 ALR4th 166.

Successor products liability: form of business organization of successor or predecessor as affecting successor liability. 32 ALR4th 196.

Products liability: liability of successor corporation for injury or damage caused by product issued by predecessor. 66 ALR3d 824.

Comment Note.—Validity and construction of state statute making successor corporation liable for taxes of predecessor. 65 ALR3d 1181.

Similarity of ownership or control as basis for charging corporation acquiring assets of another with liability for former owner's debts. 49 ALR3d 881.

Section 13. Liability of Successor for Harm Caused by Successor's Own Post-Sale Failure to Warn

1. Digest System Key Numbers

Products Liability ⚷14, 23.1, 25.

2. A.L.R. Annotations

Products liability: liability of manufacturer or seller as affected by failure of subsequent party in distribution chain to remedy or warn against defect of which he knew. 45 ALR4th 777.

Strict products liability: liability for failure to warn as dependent on defendant's knowledge of danger. 33 ALR4th 368.

Products liability: liability of successor corporation for injury or damage caused by product issued by predecessor. 66 ALR3d 824.

Failure to warn as basis of liability under doctrine of strict liability in tort. 53 ALR3d 239.

Liability of corporation for torts of subsidiary. 7 ALR3d 1343.

Manufacturer's or seller's duty to give warning regarding product as affecting his liability for product-caused injury. 76 ALR2d 9.

Section 14. Selling or Otherwise Distributing as One's Own a Product Manufactured by Another

1. Digest System Key Numbers

Products Liability ⚷23.1, 25.

2. A.L.R. Annotations

Products liability: seller's right to indemnity from manufacturer. 79 ALR4th 278.

Products liability: liability of manufacturer or seller as affected by failure of subsequent party in distribution chain to remedy or warn against defect of which he knew. 45 ALR4th 777.

"Concert of activity," "alternative liability," "enterprise liability," or similar theory as basis for imposing liability upon one or more manufacturers of defective uniform product, in absence of identification of manufacturer of precise unit or batch causing injury. 22 ALR4th 183.

Products liability: necessity and sufficiency of identification of defendant as manufacturer or seller of product alleged to have caused injury. 51 ALR3d 1344.

Products liability: manufacturer and dealer or distributor as joint or concurrent tortfeasors. 97 ALR2d 811.

TABLE OF CROSS REFERENCES

CHAPTER 4. PROVISIONS OF GENERAL APPLICABILITY

TOPIC 1. CAUSATION

Section 15. General Rule Governing Causal Connection Between Product Defect and Harm

1. Digest System Key Numbers

Products Liability ⚷15.

2. A.L.R. Annotations

Products liability: product misuse defense. 65 ALR4th 263.

Products liability: sufficiency of evidence to support product misuse defense in actions concerning weapons and ammunition. 59 ALR4th 102.

Products liability: sufficiency of evidence to support product misuse defense in actions concerning gas and electric appliances. 58 ALR4th 131.

Products liability: sufficiency of evidence to support product misuse defense in actions concerning paint, cleaners, or other chemicals. 58 ALR4th 76.

Validity and construction of products liability statute precluding or limiting recovery where product has been altered or modified after leaving hands of manufacturer or seller. 41 ALR4th 47.

Liability of one who provides, by sale or otherwise, firearm or ammunition to adult who shoots another. 39 ALR4th 517.

Bystander recovery for emotional distress at witnessing another's injury under strict products liability or breach of warranty. 31 ALR4th 162.

Products liability insurance coverage as extending only to product-caused injury to person or other property, as distinguished from mere product failure. 91 ALR3d 921.

Products liability: proof, under strict tort liability doctrine, that defect was present when product left hands of defendant. 54 ALR3d 1079.

Products liability: contributory negligence or assumption of risk as defense under doctrine of strict liability in tort. 46 ALR3d 240.

Products liability: alteration of product after it leaves hands of manufacturer or seller as affecting liability for product-caused harm. 41 ALR3d 1251.

Privity of contract as essential in action against remote manufacturer or distributor for defects in goods not causing injury to person or to other property. 16 ALR3d 683.

Intervening purchaser's knowledge of defects in or danger of article, or failure to inspect therefor, as affecting liability of manufacturer or dealer for personal injury or property damage to subsequent purchaser or other third person. 164 ALR 371.

Section 16. Increased Harm Due to Product Defect

1. Digest System Key Numbers

Negligence ⚷97–101.

2. A.L.R. Annotations

Products liability: sufficiency of proof of injuries resulting from "second collision". 9 ALR4th 494.

Products liability: vehicular bumpers. 5 ALR4th 483.

Products liability: defective vehicular windows. 3 ALR4th 489.

Products liability: defective vehicular gasoline tanks. 96 ALR3d 265.

Liability of manufacturer, seller, or distributor of motor vehicle for defect which merely enhances injury from accident otherwise caused. 42 ALR3d 560.

TOPIC 2. AFFIRMATIVE DEFENSES

Section 17. Apportionment of Responsibility Between or Among Plaintiff, Sellers and Distributors of Defective Products, and Others

1. Digest System Key Numbers

Negligence ⚷97–101; Products Liability ⚷27.

2. A.L.R. Annotations

Motorcyclist's failure to wear helmet or other protective equipment as affecting recovery for personal injury or death. 85 ALR4th 365.

Products liability: seller's right to indemnity from manufacturer. 79 ALR4th 278.

Products liability: contributory negligence or assumption of risk as defense in action for strict liability or breach of warranty based on failure to provide safety device for product causing injury. 75 ALR4th 538.

Products liability: contributory negligence or assumption of risk as defense in negligence action based on failure to provide safety device for product causing injury. 75 ALR4th 443.

Products liability: injury caused by product as a result of being tampered with. 67 ALR4th 964.

Products liability: product misuse defense. 65 ALR4th 263.

Products liability: sufficiency of evidence to support product misuse defense in actions concerning weapons and ammunition. 59 ALR4th 102.

Products liability: sufficiency of evidence to support product misuse defense in actions concerning gas and electric appliances. 58 ALR4th 131.

Products liability: sufficiency of evidence to support product misuse defense in actions concerning paint, cleaners, or other chemicals. 58 ALR4th 76.

Products liability: sufficiency of evidence to support product misuse defense in actions concerning food, drugs, and other products intended for ingestion. 58 ALR4th 7.

Validity and construction of products liability statute precluding or limiting recovery where product has been altered or modified after leaving hands of manufacturer or seller. 41 ALR4th 47.

Applicability of comparative negligence doctrine to actions based on strict liability in tort. 9 ALR4th 633.

Products liability: contributory negligence or assumption of risk as defense under doctrine of strict liability in tort. 46 ALR3d 240.

Products liability: alteration of product after it leaves hands of manufacturer or seller as affecting liability for product-caused harm. 41 ALR3d 1251.

Products liability: right of manufacturer or seller to contribution or indemnity from user of product causing injury or damage to third person, and vice versa. 28 ALR3d 943.

Purchaser's use or attempted use of articles known to be defective as affecting damages recoverable for breach of warranty. 33 ALR2d 511.

Reliance on dealer's or manufacturer's assurance that article is not dangerous as affecting question of contributory negligence. 55 ALR 1047.

Section 18. Disclaimers, Limitations, Waivers, and Other Contractual Exculpations as Defenses to Products–Liability Claims for Harm to Persons

1. Digest System Key Numbers

Products Liability ⚷26, 27.

2. A.L.R. Annotations

Products liability: admissibility of defendant's evidence of industry custom or practice in strict liability action. 47 ALR4th 621.

Unconscionability, under UCC sec. 2–302 or sec. 2–719(3), of disclaimer of warranties or limitation or exclusion of damages in contract subject to UCC Article 2 (Sales). 38 ALR4th 25.

Construction and effect of new motor vehicle warranty limiting manufacturer's liability to repair or replacement of defective parts. 2 ALR4th 576.

Prospective buyer's release of prospective seller from liability for injuries resulting from trial use or inspection of product for sale. 93 ALR3d 1296.

Construction and effect of UCC sec. 2–316(2) providing that implied warranty disclaimer must be "conspicuous". 73 ALR3d 248.

Validity of disclaimer of warranty clauses in sale of new automobile. 54 ALR3d 1217.

Construction and effect of standard new motor vehicle warranty. 99 ALR2d 1419.

Statements in advertisements as affecting manufacturer's or seller's liability for injury caused by product sold. 75 ALR2d 112.

TOPIC 3. DEFINITIONS

Section 19. Definition of "Product"

1. Digest System Key Numbers

Products Liability ⚷8.

2. A.L.R. Annotations

Products liability: prefabricated buildings. 4 ALR5th 667.

Trademark licensor's liability for injury or death allegedly due to defect in licensed product. 90 ALR4th 981.

Products liability: what is an "unavoidably unsafe" product. 70 ALR4th 16.

Products liability: electricity. 60 ALR4th 732.

Exterminator's tort liability for personal injury or death directly resulting from operations. 29 ALR4th 987.

Recovery, under strict liability in tort, for injury or damage caused by defects in building or land. 25 ALR4th 351.

Liability of blood supplier or donor for injury or death resulting from blood transfusion. 24 ALR4th 508.

Liability of hospital, physician, or other individual medical practitioner for injury or death resulting from blood transfusion. 20 ALR4th 136.

Products liability: transformer and other electrical equipment. 10 ALR4th 854.

Application of rule of strict liability in tort to person or entity rendering medical services. 100 ALR3d 1205.

Applicability of rule of strict liability to injury from electrical current escaping from powerline. 82 ALR3d 218.

Application of rule of strict liability in tort to person rendering services. 29 ALR3d 1425.

What is "consumer product" for purposes of Consumer Product Safety Act (15 USCS secs. 2051 et seq.). 43 ALR Fed 827.

Section 20. Definition of "One Who Sells or Otherwise Distributes"

1. Digest System Key Numbers

Products Liability ⚷40, 42–43.

2. A.L.R. Annotations

Products liability of endorser, trade association, certifier, or similar party who expresses approval of product. 1 ALR5th 431.

Liability of auctioneer under doctrine of strict products liability. 83 ALR4th 1188.

Exterminator's tort liability for personal injury or death directly resulting from operations. 29 ALR4th 987.

Products liability: application of strict liability in tort doctrine to agency merely financing sale or lease-purchase of personal property. 28 ALR4th 326.

Application of rule of strict liability in tort to person or entity rendering medical services. 100 ALR3d 1205.

When is person "engaged in the business" for purposes of doctrine of strict tort liability. 99 ALR3d 671.

Liability of hotel or motel operator for injury or death of guest or privy resulting from condition in plumbing or bathroom of room or suite. 93 ALR3d 253.

Who is "merchant" under UCC sec. 2–314(1) dealing with implied warranties of merchantability. 91 ALR3d 876.

Liability of hospital or medical practitioner under doctrine of strict liability in tort, or breach of warranty, for harm caused by drug, medical instrument, or similar device used in treating patient. 54 ALR3d 258.

Products liability: application of strict liability in tort doctrine to lessor of personal property. 52 ALR3d 121.

Liability of product indorser or certifier for product-caused injury. 39 ALR3d 181.

Application of rule of strict liability in tort to person rendering services. 29 ALR3d 1425.

Liability of bailor for personal injuries or death due to defects in subject of bailment. 131 ALR 845.

Joinder of manufacturer or packer and retailer or other middleman as defendants in action for injury to person or damage to property of purchaser or consumer of defective article. 119 ALR 1356.

Section 21. Definition of "Harm to Persons or Property": Recovery for Economic Loss

1. Digest System Key Numbers

Products Liability ⚷17.1, 18.

2. A.L.R. Annotations

Causes of action governed by limitations period in UCC sec. 2–725. 49 ALR5th 1.

Consequential loss of profits from injury to property as element of damages in products liability. 89 ALR4th 11.

Strict products liability: recovery for damage to product alone. 72 ALR4th 12.

Bystander recovery for emotional distress at witnessing another's injury under strict products liability or breach of warranty. 31 ALR4th 162.

Recovery, under strict liability in tort, for injury or damage caused by defects in building or land. 25 ALR4th 351.

Products liability: what statute of limitations governs actions based on strict liability in tort. 91 ALR3d 455.

Products liability: strict liability in tort where injury results from allergenic (side-effect) reaction to product. 53 ALR3d 298.

Products liability: extension of strict liability in tort to permit recovery by a third person who was neither a purchaser nor user of product. 33 ALR3d 415.

Construction and effect of UCC Art 2, dealing with sales. 17 ALR3d 1010.

Privity of contract as essential in action against remote manufacturer or distributor for defects in goods not causing injury to person or to other property. 16 ALR3d 683.

Statute of limitations: when cause of action arises on action against manufacturer or seller of product causing injury or death. 4 ALR3d 821.

Admiralty products liability: recovery against remote manufacturer or distributor for economic or commercial loss caused by defect in product. 81 ALR Fed 181.

INDEX

References are to Sections, Comments, and Reporters' Notes

A

INDEX

B

INDEX

INDEX

INDEX

E

G

H

I

M

INDEX

INDEX

INDEX

INDEX

S

INDEX

U

X

†